The
ASSASSINATION
of the
ARCHDUKE

✠

Also by Greg King

Wallis: The Uncommon Life of the Duchess of Windsor

*The Resurrection of the Romanovs: Anastasia, Anna Anderson,
and the World's Greatest Royal Mystery*

*Twilight of Splendor: The Court of Queen Victoria
During Her Diamond Jubilee Year*

*The Court of the Last Tsar: Pomp, Power and Pageantry
in the Reign of Nicholas II*

The Fate of the Romanovs

The Mad King: A Biography of Ludwig II of Bavaria

*The Man Who Killed Rasputin: Prince Felix Youssoupov and the Murder
That Helped Bring Down the Russian Empire*

*The Last Empress: The Life and Times of Alexandra Feodorovna,
Tsarina of Russia*

Also by Sue Woolmans

*Twenty-Five Chapters of My Life: The Memoirs of Grand Duchess
Olga Alexandrovna, with Paul Kulikovsky and Karen Roth-Nicholls*

The
ASSASSINATION
of the
ARCHDUKE

*Sarajevo 1914 and the Murder
that Changed the World*

Greg King
and
Sue Woolmans

MACMILLAN

First published 2013 by St. Martin's Press, New York, as
The Assassination of the Archduke: Sarajevo 1914 and the Romance That Changed the World

This edition published in Great Britain 2013 by Macmillan
an imprint of Pan Macmillan, a division of Macmillan Publishers Limited
Pan Macmillan, 20 New Wharf Road, London N1 9RR
Basingstoke and Oxford
Associated companies throughout the world
www.panmacmillan.com

ISBN 978-0-230-75957-2 HB
ISBN 978-1-447-24521-6 TPB

1 3 5 7 9 8 6 4 2

A CIP catalogue record for this book is available from the British Library.

Printed and bound by CPI Group (UK) Ltd, Croydon, CR0 4YY

Visit **www.panmacmillan.com** to read more about all our books
and to buy them. You will also find features, author interviews and
news of any author events, and you can sign up for e-newsletters
so that you're always first to hear about our new releases.

In memory of Sharlene Aadland
– Greg

To the memory of my dear parents
Daphne and Ian Maillot
– Sue

CONTENTS

✥

FOREWORD BY SOPHIE VON HOHENBERG   ix

ACKNOWLEDGEMENTS   xi

AUTHORS' NOTE   xvii

CAST OF CHARACTERS   xxi

INTRODUCTION   xxvii

MAP OF AUSTRO-HUNGARIAN EMPIRE IN 1900   xxxix

HABSBURG FAMILY TREE   xl

HOHENBERG AND CHOTEK FAMILY TREE   xlii

PROLOGUE	*Vienna, January 1889*	1
ONE	*In the Shadow of the Throne*	9
TWO	*Adventure and Illness*	21
THREE	*Romance*	33
FOUR	*'A Triumph of Love'*	47
FIVE	*'Don't Let Her Think She's One of Us!'*	63
SIX	*The Swirl of Gossip*	75
SEVEN	*Attitudes Soften*	85
EIGHT	*'Konopischt Was Home'*	101
NINE	*'Even Death Will Not Part Us!'*	117

Contents

TEN	An Emperor in Training	127
ELEVEN	Diplomacy and Roses	139
TWELVE	'I Consider War to Be Lunacy!'	153
THIRTEEN	The Fatal Invitation	163
FOURTEEN	The Plot	175
FIFTEEN	'I'm Beginning to Fall in Love With Bosnia'	187
SIXTEEN	St Vitus's Day	197
SEVENTEEN	'The Anguish Was Indescribable'	211
EIGHTEEN	United in Death	227
NINETEEN	Headlong Toward Oblivion	239
TWENTY	Ripples from Sarajevo	253

EPILOGUE	275
NOTES	293
BIBLIOGRAPHY	345
INDEX	367

FOREWORD

BY SOPHIE VON HOHENBERG

✛

I vividly remember the first email I received from Sue Woolmans and Greg King. I sat back and thought, Should I answer? Then I remembered an old story.

I believe it was at my sister's wedding. I was standing on the terrace with my grandmother, and we were watching Aunt Sophie, (daughter of Archduke Franz Ferdinand of Austria-Este and Sophie, Duchess of Hohenberg), who was patiently answering the questions of the journalists. I commented to my grandmother, 'How can she stand it?' My grandmother answered that she herself had once, years ago, asked her sister-in-law why she bothered answering all those questions. 'The journalists don't listen, and write what they want anyway, so why bother?' Aunt Sophie had an amazing answer. As if it were the most normal thing in the world she said, 'But I must defend him,' 'him' being her father.

Since then I have read many books about my great-grandfather, and few have done him justice. Sue and Greg's book was different: it was to be a book about my great-grandparents, their private life, and the repercussion of Sarajevo on the Hohenberg children.

The destiny of my grandfather and his siblings is remarkable. They led lives strewn with tragedy and hardship, but they strode through it, their heads held high, with courage, resilience, and faith. They were happy, good-humoured, joyful people, and I admire their stance after all. They were the first orphans of the First World War, and the first victims of the young Czechoslovakian Republic, chased from their home and their country. Their possessions were illegally confiscated without any compensation. The Hohenberg brothers were the first Austrian aristocrats in Dachau concentration camp. They struggled against prejudice, discrimination, and injustice. Their home, Konopischt, was seized almost one hundred years ago, just after the First World War. This larceny was perpetrated by a state before any legal basis existed, right under the nose of the Allies, who did not budge, even when Prince Jaroslav Thun-Hohenstein, the children's legal guardian, tried to protest and started a legal battle. My grandfather Max Hohenberg continued, and I have tried to follow suit after the Iron Curtain fell, picking up where my grandfather had left the battle for our heirloom and for justice, but success still evades me.

I thank Sue Woolmans and Greg King for this book, and for their work in researching this tribute to the people I admire and that are so close to my heart.

Luxembourg, January 2013

ACKNOWLEDGEMENTS

✦

We gratefully acknowledge the permission of Her Majesty Queen Elizabeth II to publish material from the Royal Archives. We would also like to extend our thanks to the registrar of the Royal Archives, Pamela Clark, and her staff for all their help and good-humoured support, and to Lisa Heighway, curator of photographs at the Royal Collection, for patiently answering enquiries.

HSH Georg, Duke of Hohenberg, graciously gave us permission to access the Nachlass Erzherzog Franz Ferdinand, the collected letters and papers of his grandfather Archduke Franz Ferdinand, at the Austrian Haus-, Hof- und Staatsarchiv, Vienna. We are very grateful to him and thank the staff at the Staatsarchiv for their help during our visit. We also thank HSH Prince Albrecht of Hohenberg for sharing family memories with us, and Prince Nikolaus of Hohenberg for his contribution to our research.

HSH Princess Anita of Hohenberg very kindly granted us an interview, provided unrestricted access to the Erzherzog Franz Ferdinand Museum at Artstetten, and allowed us to use material from her archives. We sincerely appreciate her invaluable cooperation on this book. We must also thank Brigitte E. Leidwein of the museum, who has facilitated interviews, patiently answered questions, and searched out obscure archival materials.

Unending support, help, and encouragement have come from HSH Princess Sophie of Hohenberg and her husband, Baron Jean-Louis de Potesta. Princess Sophie has proved an indefatigable supporter, generous with both her time and her family knowledge. We are incredibly grateful to them both, and this book would certainly be the poorer without their generosity and continued interest.

The foremost Austrian scholar on Franz Ferdinand is Professor Dr Wladimir Aichelburg. He has freely shared his knowledge with us and guided us on many points that could have led to mistakes. He has our deepest thanks.

Robby Joachim Götze of the Kustos Kunstsammlung, Museum und Kunstsammlung, Schloss Hinterglauchau in Glauchau, Germany, generously supplied us with the correspondence between the Duchess of Hohenberg and her sister Oktavia, which has been a valuable resource. Miloš Musil, Andrea Leskotová, and Miroslava Janáčková take care of the Chotek property of Velké Březno (Grosspriessen), in the Czech Republic. They warmly welcomed us to the estate and shared much information with us and we thank them for their generous help. We are also indebted to Baron Raimondo Corsi di Turri, who has kindly allowed us to quote from the letters of his grandmother, Lucy Fane Wingfield.

Many people have greatly helped us during the research and writing of this book. Karen Roth has spent hours on translation work for us and been the best friend authors can have, and she has our sincere thanks. Harold Brown of the Victorian B & B in Tunbridge Wells, East Sussex, UK, rummaged around in a drawer to find some important new materials for us for which we are very grateful. Janet Ashton supplied important research materials and offered incisive critical commentary that helped guide us as we wrote. We appreciate all of the thoughts she shared to make this a better book. Penny Wilson read through the manuscript several times and suggested important changes that kept the story on course, especially at times when it could have bogged down in needless detail. Jeannine Evans also read the manuscript and offered helpful corrections and impressions. We must single out Mark Andersen, who has sourced many obscure books we would otherwise not have been able to consult and has helped so much with our picture research. His friendship is truly valued. Milena Currall guided us through the Czech language and so we say 'Děkuji!' to her. Christophe Vachaudez's generous help has been invaluable. We must also acknowledge the generous assistance of H. Mike Pyles in completing this book.

Our agent, Dorie Simmonds, first seized upon the idea for this book with relish and supported us throughout a long and occasionally tangled process. Charles Spicer, our editor at St. Martin's Press, has believed strongly in this book and helped steer us toward completion, as has Georgina Morley, at Pan Macmillan in London. April Osborn, editorial assistant at St. Martin's Press, has guided us in completion of the manuscript and patiently dealt with numerous queries.

A number of people have shared important archival holdings or private materials and patiently answered numerous questions as we wrote this book. We gratefully thank Professor Francis Roy Bridge; Dr Jiri Chramosta; Frances Dimond, formerly of the Royal Archives at Windsor; Dr Susanne Glass, ARD-Korrespondentin für Österreich und Südosteuropa; Bethany Hall; Dr Christoph Hatschek, director of Vienna's Heeresgeschichtliches Museum/Militärhistorisches Institut; Debbie Hopkinson of Manuscripts and Special Collections at the University of Nottingham; Gareth Hughes, collections manager of the Portland Collection; Alastair Hutchinson of Hutchinson Mainprice Solicitors; Baron Viktor Kuchina von Schwanburg; Albert Knoll from the archives at Dachau; Ricardo Mateos Sainz de Medrano; Professor Ilana Miller of Pepperdine University in California; Professor Paul Miller, Marie Curie Fellow at the University of Birmingham; Alberto Penna Rodrigues; Szymon Pozimski of St Peter's College, Oxford; Professor John Röhl; Ian Shapiro; Jiří Smitka, chief of the Department of Family Archives at the State Regional Archives, Prague; Dr Arthur Stögmann, Archiv und

Bibliothek, of the Princely Collections, Liechtenstein; Fürstliche Sammlungen Art Service GmbH & Co OG; Stephen Sullivan, library service adviser, Worksop Library, Nottinghamshire; Bixanne Tam; Richard Thornton, chair, Royal Weekend, Ticehurst, Sussex; and Ulrike Polnitzky and the staff of Bildarchiv und Grafiksammlung, Österreichische Nationalbibliothek.

We acknowledge the helpful assistance and support of the staffs of the Bexleyheath and Welling public libraries, especially Elena Clark and Richard Lord; the staff of the British Library and the newspaper section at Colindale; the staffs of Suzzallo and Allen libraries at the University of Washington in Seattle; and the staff of the Everett Public Library.

A number of people in Sarajevo were unfailingly generous in aiding our research. We must single out Zenaida Ilaria and Sanja Hrelja of the ZPR Agency; Nermina Letic; Avdio Mirsad at Muzejski Sarajctisik; and Dr Ivan Udovicic, director of the Art Gallery of Bosnia and Herzegovina.

To our friends and colleagues, we also extend our most grateful thanks for their support, enthusiasm, and understanding: Bob Achison; Annet Bakker of van Hoogstraten Booksellers, the Netherlands; Diana and Nick de Courcy Ireland; Professor Joe Fuhrmann; Philip Goodman; Coryne Hall; Doris Holloway; Paul Kulikovsky; Joe Little of *Majesty* magazine; Jackie Lees; Frank and Katrina Lennox-Millard; Diana Mandache; Judith Marquiss; Susanne Meslans; Rob Moshein; Carol Mullinder; Robin Olsen; Howard Price; Stella Ramsden; Ted Rosvall, of Rosvall Royal Books; Tony Roth; Brad Swenson, of Buy and Sell Video in Everett, WA; Debra Tate; Marianne Teerink; John Wimbles; Mandy Wong; and Mei Wah Yung.

Sue Woolmans extends her thanks to her work colleagues: Giles Aspen, Sally Braben, Helen Cook, Nigel Dix, Cheryl Gabriel, Gayl Gordon, Colin Grant, Steve Greenwood, Emma Harth, Sarah Hockley, Vic Kent, Jane Lawrence, Helen Lee, Mark Lowen, Jackie Margerum, Bob Nettles, Jo Parsons, Pete Rawlings, Dave Robinson, Mike Sherwood, and Tony Ward.

→ *Acknowledgements* ←

As always, Greg King thanks his parents, Roger and Helena King, for their continued support, belief, and generosity.

Last, but by no means least, Sue Woolmans thanks her long-suffering husband, Mike Woolmans. He's been ignored, starved, and snapped at during the writing process. He was conned into visiting Habsburg palaces on his own honeymoon! Still he has endlessly supported both Greg and myself. He has my love and grateful thanks for all time.

AUTHORS' NOTE

✢

In this book, readers may encounter some curious titles and styles unfamiliar in English. From 1863 to 1875, Franz Ferdinand was known as Archduke Franz Ferdinand of Austria-Hungary; after 1875 he became Archduke Franz Ferdinand of Austria-Este, appending the latter Italian title as part of the inheritance from the Duke of Modena. He was commonly referred to, after 1896, as 'Thronfolger', or 'heir to the throne'. He was never made crown prince (Kronprinz).

A particular note is necessary to explain the numerous changes in Sophie's title and style throughout this book. Born Countess Sophie Chotek, on her 1900 marriage to Franz Ferdinand she was given the title Princess of Hohenberg (Fürstin von Hohenberg in German) with the style of *Fürstliche Gnaden*; this is a non-royal form of 'Highness', roughly equivalent to the English style of 'Your Grace'. This title and style were to be shared by her descendants. On 8 June 1905, Emperor Franz Josef granted Sophie and her children the style of 'Your Serene Highness' (*Ihre Durchlaucht*), which elevated them from mere aristocrats into the lower ranks of the empire's royalty. In 1909, Sophie alone was given a new title and style, raised to the rank of Duchess of Hohenberg

(Herzogin von Hohenberg) with the style 'Your Highness' (*Ihre Hoheit*). In Austria, a duchess ranked higher than a mere princess, and the style of *Ihre Hoheit* singled her out as a more distinguished royal lady, unlike the style of *Fürstliche Gnaden* that Sophie had received on her wedding.

Emperor Karl granted the couple's eldest surviving son, Max, the hereditary title of Duke of Hohenberg (Herzog von Hohenberg), with the titles of prince or princess for his children. He also granted Max the royal style of 'Your Highness' (*Ihre Hoheit*) in 1917. This established the new Ducal House of Hohenberg within the Austrian hereditary peerage. After the revolution of 1918, the new Austrian Republic stripped all aristocrats of their former titles. For the sake of consistency we have used the appropriate titles throughout this book. For example, Franz Ferdinand's eldest surviving grandson is called Georg, Duke of Hohenberg, even though the title is not formally recognized by the Austrian state. Rather than employ curious and convoluted appellations, this seemed the polite thing to do.

We have referred to place names using the German that would have been familiar to Franz Ferdinand and Sophie during their lives. For example, their castle in Bohemia is called Konopischt, and not Konopiště, the modern Czech rendering. Where particularly important we have given the modern renderings of place names in parentheses.

For the sake of consistency, we have rendered all titles in English: Thus we have aide-de-camp instead of *Flügeladjutant*, count instead of *Graf*, duke instead of *Herzog*, and princess, not *Fürstin* or *Prinzessin*. We have also applied this rule to the honorifics accompanying titles. In German, Sophie would be called Herzogin von Hohenberg, or Duchess of Hohenberg. While the use of 'von' would lend a certain literary flair to the story, it would be out of place with titles rendered in English.

Monetary values have been rendered into their rough modern equivalents. Until 1892, Austria-Hungary used gulden; when the country adopted the gold standard, crowns replaced gulden. One gulden was equal to two crowns. Exchange rates for imperial crowns varied in the years covered in this book but in general remained equivalent to £2.55 to £3.82 in 2013 figures. Converting historical values into modern numbers is an inexact business, but we have stuck to the middle ground, rendering one gulden as £6.37 in 2013 figures and one crown as £3.18 in 2013 figures.

CAST OF CHARACTERS

✛

THE HABSBURG FAMILY

ELISABETH (1878–1960) Archduchess of Austria, daughter of Karl Ludwig and Maria Theresa, stepsister of Franz Ferdinand, married Prince Alois of Liechtenstein in 1903.

FERDINAND KARL (1868–1915) Archduke of Austria, third son of Karl Ludwig and Maria Annunciata, youngest brother of Franz Ferdinand, morganatically married to Bertha Czuber.

FRANZ FERDINAND (1863–1914) Archduke of Austria-Este, heir to the Austro-Hungarian throne from 1889, son of Karl Ludwig and Maria Annunciata.

FRANZ JOSEF I (1830–1916) Emperor of Austria from 1848.

FRIEDRICH (1856–1936) Archduke of Austria and Duke of Teschen from 1895, married to Princess Isabella of Croÿ.

ISABELLA (1856–1931) Archduchess of Austria, born a Princess of the mediatized house of Croÿ. Employer of Countess Sophie Chotek.

KARL (1887–1922) Archduke of Austria, nephew of Franz Ferdinand, great-nephew of Franz Josef. Became heir to Austro-Hungarian throne on death of Franz Ferdinand in 1914, and Emperor on the death of Franz Josef in 1916. Married to Zita in 1911.

KARL LUDWIG (1833–1896) Archduke of Austria, father of Franz Ferdinand, brother of Franz Josef.

MARGARETHE (1870–1902) Archduchess of Austria, daughter of Karl Ludwig and Maria Annunciata, sister of Franz Ferdinand, married Duke Albrecht of Württemberg in 1893.

MARIA ANNUNCIATA (1843–1871) Archduchess of Austria, born Princess of Bourbon-Two Sicilies, second wife of Karl Ludwig, mother of Franz Ferdinand.

MARIA ANNUNCIATA (1876–1961) Archduchess of Austria, daughter of Karl Ludwig and Maria Theresa, stepsister of Franz Ferdinand, unmarried.

MARIA CHRISTINA (1879–1962) Archduchess of Austria, daughter of Friedrich and Isabella, married to Prince Manuel of Salm-Salm in 1902. Was expected to marry Franz Ferdinand.

MARIA THERESA (1855–1944) Archduchess of Austria, born an Infanta of Portugal. Third wife of Karl Ludwig and stepmother to Franz Ferdinand.

OTTO (1865–1906) known as 'Handsome Otto', Archduke of Austria, son of Karl Ludwig, younger brother of Franz Ferdinand, married to Marie Josepha of Saxony.

RUDOLF (1858–1889) son of Franz Josef, Crown Prince of Austria-Hungary, married to Stephanie of Belgium in 1881.

STEPHANIE (1864–1945) Crown Princess of Austria, born a Princess of Belgium, she married Rudolf in 1881. Widowed in 1889, she went on to marry Count Elmér Lónyay, a Hungarian aristocrat, in 1900.

ZITA (1892–1989) Archduchess and Empress of Austria, wife of Karl, born a Princess of Bourbon-Parma.

THE CHOTEK AND HOHENBERG FAMILY

ANNA, 'ANITA' (born 1958) Princess of Hohenberg, eldest daughter of Duke Franz and Elisabeth of Luxembourg, great-granddaughter of Franz Ferdinand, owner of Artstetten Castle.

BOHUSLAV (1829–1896) Count Chotek of Chotkow and Wognin, father of Sophie, Duchess of Hohenberg, married to Countess Wilhelmina Kinsky of Wchinitz and Tettau, career diplomat.

ERNST (1904–1954) Prince of Hohenberg, younger son of Franz Ferdinand and the Duchess of Hohenberg, married Marie-Therese Wood, 'Maisie', in 1936.

FRANZ (1927–1977) 2nd Duke of Hohenberg, eldest son of Maximilian, grandson of Franz Ferdinand, married Princess Elisabeth of Luxembourg in 1956.

GEORG (born 1929) 3rd Duke of Hohenberg, second son of Maximilian, grandson of Franz Ferdinand, married Princess Eleonore of Auersperg-Breunner in 1960.

→ *Cast of Characters* ←

HENRIETTE (1880–1964) Countess Chotek of Chotkow and Wognin, youngest sister of Sophie, Duchess of Hohenberg, who took care of Sophie, Max and Ernst after they were orphaned; married her late sister Karolina's husband, Count Leopold of Nostitz-Rieneck.

JAROSLAV (1864–1925) Prince of Thun and Hohenstein, married to Countess Marie Chotek of Chotkow and Wognin, elder sister of Sophie, Duchess of Hohenberg; hunting companion of Franz Ferdinand; guardian to Sophie, Max and Ernst.

MAXIMILIAN (1902–1962) Prince of Hohenberg and 1st Duke of Hohenberg, eldest son of Franz Ferdinand and the Duchess of Hohenberg, married Countess Maria Elisabeth Bona of Waldburg zu Wolfegg and Waldsee in 1926.

OKTAVIA (1872–1946) sister of Sophie, Duchess of Hohenberg; married Joachim, Count of Schönburg-Glauchau and Waldenburg.

SOPHIE (1868–1914) Duchess of Hohenberg, born Countess Chotek of Chotkow and Wognin, married Franz Ferdinand in 1900.

SOPHIE (1901–1990) Princess of Hohenberg, 'Little Sophie', firstborn child to Franz Ferdinand and the Duchess of Hohenberg, married to Count Friedrich of Nostitz-Rieneck in 1920.

SOPHIE (born 1960) Princess of Hohenberg, younger daughter of Duke Franz of Hohenberg and Elisabeth of Luxembourg, great-granddaughter of Franz Ferdinand; currently fighting for the restitution of Konopischt; married in 1983 to Baron Jean-Louis de Potesta.

→ *Cast of Characters* ←

COURTIERS

BARDOLFF, Colonel Karl von (1865–1953) 2nd Head of Franz Ferdinand's Military Chancery.

BECK, Baron Max Vladimir von (1854–1943) tutor and later legal advisor to Franz Ferdinand.

BROSCH, Colonel Alexander von Aarenau (1870–1914) 1st Head of Franz Ferdinand's Military Chancery.

CAVENDISH-BENTINCK, William (1857–1943) 6th Duke of Portland, English landowner and politician who was a hunting friend of Franz Ferdinand.

CONRAD OF HÖTZENDORF, Count Franz (1852–1925) became Chief of Staff of the Austrian Armed Forces; continually promoted war with Serbia and clashed with Franz Ferdinand.

EISENMENGER, Dr Victor (1864–1932) Franz Ferdinand's personal physician.

JANACZEK, Franz (1865–1955) head of Franz Ferdinand's household and his most trusted servant.

MONTENUOVO, Prince Alfred de (1854–1927) *Obersthofmeister* (Lord Chamberlain) of Emperor Franz Josef's court; descended from a morganatic relationship between Archduchess Marie Louise of Austria and Count Neipperg.

POTIOREK, Oskar (1853–1933), Governor of Bosnia-Herzegovina during the visit of Franz Ferdinand and the Duchess of Hohenberg in 1914.

CONSPIRATORS

Čabrinović, Nedeljko (1895–1916) a Bosnian Serb revolutionary and a member of the Young Bosnia movement; threw a bomb at Franz Ferdinand and the Duchess of Hohenberg in Sarajevo.

Cubrilović, Vaso (1897–1990) a Bosnian Serb revolutionary and a member of the Young Bosnia movement.

Dimitrijević, Dragutin, 'Apis' (1877–1917) leader of the Black Hand revolutionary organization; behind the murder of King Alexander and Queen Draga of Serbia and implicated in the murder of Franz Ferdinand.

Grabež, Trifko (1895–1918) a Bosnian Serb revolutionary and a member of the Young Bosnia movement.

Ilić, Danilo (1891–1915) a Bosnian Serb revolutionary and a member of the Young Bosnia movement, main organizer of the assassination in Sarajevo.

Mehmedbašić, Muhamed (1886–1943) a Bosnian Muslim revolutionary; the only member of the group of assassins to escape capture.

Popović, Cvjetko (1896–1980) a Bosnian Serb revolutionary and a member of the Young Bosnia movement.

Princip, Gavrilo (1894–1918) a Bosnian Serb revolutionary and a member of the Young Bosnia movement; seen as the leader of the group, he fired the shots that killed Franz Ferdinand and Sophie.

INTRODUCTION

✛

'Once upon a time,' begins the fairy tale: a dashing young prince, heir to his country's historic throne, meets an impoverished young lady whose grace and beauty steal his heart. Captivated, he pursues her against the wishes of his powerful family, who deem her unsuitable as a future queen. Against all odds, romance blooms and the prince weds his love. Creating an idyllic existence, the couple shies away from a censorious court where wagging tongues condemn their actions, determined to wrest from a cynical world the personal and romantic fulfilment for which they had so nobly fought.

The personal love story of Archduke Franz Ferdinand of Austria-Hungary and Countess Sophie Chotek begins in mystery, exults in marital victory, and plays out against incessant adversity. In many ways, it undeniably mirrors mythic elements of the traditional fairy tale. We have Franz Ferdinand as Prince Charming, born to power and privilege and seeking forbidden love; Countess Sophie Chotek is his Cinderella, beautiful, impoverished, and not at all a proper consort for the future ruler of a great empire. Franz Ferdinand's stepmother, Archduchess Maria Theresa, acts as Fairy Godmother, encouraging the romance in the face of unified Habsburg opposition; the belligerent Archduchess

Isabella serves as the quintessential wicked stepmother, employing Cinderella to labour for hours at humiliating and menial tasks. In Prince Alfred de Montenuovo, Lord High Chamberlain of the imperial court, we find an ogre of epic proportions, inflicting petty insults on the graceful and resolute Sophie. As in every good fairy tale, the heroes even get to attend a glittering ball, where a stunned audience watches in disbelief as the forbidden romance becomes public.

Real life unexpectedly subverted this particular fairy tale in the summer of 1914. Two bullets, fired by nineteen-year-old Serbian nationalist Gavrilo Princip in Sarajevo, abruptly denied Franz Ferdinand and Sophie the happy ending promised in countless romantic stories. JOINED IN MARRIAGE, THEY WERE JOINED BY THE SAME FATE, reads the inscription on their twin white marble sarcophagi. United in death as in life, this most famous Austrian couple passed into history as mustard gas, trench warfare, machine guns, and U-boats subsumed the comfortable world they had known.

A century has passed since that fateful day in Sarajevo. Has any other couple of the last hundred years so inadvertently shaped our modern era? Those two bullets not only ended the lives of Franz Ferdinand and Sophie; they became the catalyst for the First World War and all of the horrors that followed. Without Sarajevo, would there have been a Russian Revolution, a Soviet Union or Nazi Germany, a Second World War, or a Cold War? History reverberates with the effects of this couple's deaths that Sunday in 1914.

Why, then, do Franz Ferdinand and Sophie seem so elusive? Why is it that their private lives and real characters remain shadowed? Perhaps this owes something to the Habsburgs themselves. Franz Ferdinand's was a proud dynasty with an illustrious heritage, but it lacked glamour and scandal when compared to the Romanovs of exotically mysterious Russia. Revolution came to Russia with a bloody vengeance; in Austria, the Habsburgs passed into the obscurity of exile with little notice. Romantic nostalgia envelops the story of Nicholas II, the last Tsar, and his wife, Alexandra. Their Austrian contemporaries, just as devoted, just as in love, and just as tragic in their end, have been overtaken by their notorious assassination.

Archduke Franz Ferdinand, it must be said, was scarcely anyone's idea of a Prince Charming – ill with tuberculosis, armed with a disagreeable temper, and often impetuous. Few people liked him. In his own lifetime he was an enigma. Some younger, less conservative elements and those who personally knew him hailed the archduke as a thoughtful man, with an eager mind and a willingness to listen to opposing voices. Franz Ferdinand had plenty of years to think about the country he would inherit and to ponder possible solutions to its many problems. Rather than cling to unimaginative tradition, as his uncle Emperor Franz Josef did, he was determined to enact sweeping and dramatic reforms. By heritage and by inclination Franz Ferdinand was no liberal, but he was smart enough to embrace ideas of political modernization to save the crumbling empire. If anyone could save the archaic Austro-Hungarian monarchy, his supporters believed, it was the archduke.

Most contemporary opinion was not so generous when it came to the mysterious archduke. Many regarded him as an astonishingly brutal, bad-tempered man; 'narrow in outlook', complained one princess, with a 'suspicious, irritable, and capricious nature', 'overbearing manner', 'bigoted piety', and 'aggressive and fanatical clericalism'.[1] Once on the throne he would oppress religious and ethnic minorities, people whispered, and embark on a grim and backward reign that would be nothing short of tyrannical. This has largely been history's verdict. Franz Ferdinand, it is often said, was a man of autocratic inclinations, a militaristic warmonger, 'a reactionary', a buffoon devoid of personal charm or any semblance of ordinary human emotion.[2]

Everyone was stunned, therefore, when this apparently aloof and stern man showed that he was indeed human by falling in love. Countess Sophie Chotek came from a distinguished Bohemian aristocratic family. She might be pretty and charming, but to an imperial court obsessed with matters of tradition and etiquette, she lacked the titles and noble ancestry necessary for equal marriage to such a rarefied creature as an imperial Habsburg archduke. He would one day become emperor of Austria and king of Hungary; she could never share his throne because, as Franz Ferdinand put it, 'of some trifle in her family tree'.

Princes and kings usually find a way around romantic difficulties. Whether it was the future Tsar Nicholas II insisting on marrying the dangerously unsuitable Alexandra, King Edward VIII and his obsession with American divorcee Wallis Simpson, or even the archduke's uncle Emperor Franz Josef ignoring his mother's warnings to wed his immature and melancholy cousin Elisabeth, passion usually triumphed. Caution goes hand in hand with royal romances; issues of character or controversial temperaments have made many consorts unsuitable. Not so with Sophie. Reasons advanced against Franz Ferdinand's marriage to Sophie Chotek were at once monumental to a Habsburg monarchy steeped in tradition and trivial to many others. There was no flaw in her character, no question about her behaviour; instead, the imperial court deemed her distinguished ancestors, who had loyally served Habsburgs for centuries, not quite distinguished enough. With an egalitarian stance born of necessity as royal ranks dwindled across Europe, the dynasty recognized many aristocratic families as equal when it came to marriage. Not so the Choteks. They might be accomplished, but they weren't good enough to join this illustrious circle.

Unwilling to let this 'trifle' stand in his way, Franz Ferdinand persevered, alternating between mournful pleas and dramatic threats of suicide. When he finally won permission to wed his countess, the victory came at a terrible price. Sophie was forever condemned as morganatic, unequal to her husband. She could never share her husband's titles or his throne; their children would be barred from the imperial succession. She couldn't even be buried next to him, viewed as unfit, even in death, to share eternity with any Habsburg in their crowded Viennese crypt.

Such insults – and there were many over the years – won Sophie sympathy from the less critical segments of society. Others, including members of the imperial family and the Habsburg court, painted her as a scheming, power-hungry, ambitious woman intent on seeing herself one day crowned as empress.[3] The archduke, insisted a courtier, was 'goaded by his domineering wife' on all issues, while famed writer Rebecca West venomously depicted her as a 'small-minded fury' hell-bent on seeing her morganatic sons recognized as heirs to the throne.[4]

The truth was different. If Franz Ferdinand had a brusque public persona and lacked either the desire or ability to charm his future subjects, he was quite a different man in private, and Sophie's only real ambitions seem to have been to make her husband happy and to provide a loving home for their three children, Sophie, Max and Ernst. It's hard to escape comparisons to the more famous Nicholas and Alexandra. Time has slowly revealed the flamboyantly idealized domesticity of the last Romanovs as something of a fiction. The demands of ruling limited the Tsar's interaction with his children, while his wife's morbid character and incessant illnesses increasingly left her an irregular, melancholy presence in their lives. Franz Ferdinand and Sophie, on the other hand, eagerly embraced their love of family life. It was an era of nannies and isolated nurseries, yet Sophie, Max and Ernst were adored and indulged, joining their parents at meals, chatting with the most important and distinguished guests, and enjoying childhoods free from strife and worry. Life was tranquil, and there was never any hint of infidelity or marital unhappiness. Sadly, the halcyon days were not to last.

Today it is easy to look back upon the years before 1914 with a kind of gauzy, romantic nostalgia. It seems a simpler time, when innovation enthralled and peace predominated. The truth, though, was somewhat different. All major powers had fought in at least one war since 1860, usually several, and the modern arms race had begun in earnest; incursion, revolution, revolt and repression were rife. The fifty years preceding that golden summer of 1914 witnessed constant violence. Assassination was common: the sultan of Turkey was killed in 1876; American President James Garfield and Tsar Alexander II of Russia in 1881; President Sadi Carnot of France in 1894; the shah of Persia in 1896; the prime minister of Spain in 1897; the empress of Austria in

1898; King Umberto of Italy in 1900; American President William McKinley in 1901; King Alexander and Queen Draga of Serbia in 1903; Grand Duke Sergei Alexandrovich of Russia in 1905; King Carlos of Portugal and his son Crown Prince Luis Felipe in 1908; Russian prime minister Peter Stolypin in 1911; and King George of Greece in 1913. Royalty and politicians alike fell in precipitous numbers to bombs, bullets and knives in these 'golden' years of peace.

This litany of political assassinations culminated in events at Sarajevo. Perhaps no one anticipated the actual event, but much of Europe harboured a vague uneasiness that the continent was but a mere spark away from total conflagration. Chancellor Otto von Bismarck of Germany had predicted as much, warning that 'some damn foolish thing in the Balkans' would sooner or later plunge all of Europe into a devastating war.[5] His prediction came true that summer of 1914 when the assassination of Franz Ferdinand and Sophie at Sarajevo ushered in an era of unprecedented mass slaughter. 'No other political murder in modern history', wrote Vladimir Dedijer, 'has had such momentous consequences.'[6]

Like every other event that changed the course of human history, that fateful day is still wreathed in ambiguity, subject to nationalist arguments and surrounded by a swarm of historical fallacies. Franz Ferdinand, it is said, only attended the army manoeuvres in Bosnia so that his wife could receive public acclamation. Against all common sense, he insisted on visiting Sarajevo on 28 June. This was St Vitus's Day, the Serb national holiday commemorating the Battle of Kosovo, when in 1389 an unwelcome foreign intruder, in this case the Ottoman Empire, had conquered the land and reduced the Serbs to vassals. It was, said many, as if Franz Ferdinand were seeking to deliberately provoke a recently annexed Bosnia full of anti-Austrian revolutionaries. The archduke, insisted author Rebecca West, 'brought his doom on himself by the tactlessness and aggressiveness of his visit to the Serbian frontier at the time of a Serbian festival'.[7]

None of this was true. As myth surrounds the lives of Franz Ferdinand

and Sophie, so, too, does it swirl – even after a century – around events in Sarajevo. Franz Ferdinand didn't want to make the trip; he repeatedly tried to escape this unwelcome duty, but his uncle Emperor Franz Josef forced him to go. Authorities in Sarajevo compelled the archduke to accept the incendiary date for the visit; officials on the ground in Bosnia certainly lacked all vestiges of common sense when it came to planning the trip. Very real concerns about the couple's safety were received and ignored; threats of potential violence were dismissed, and security was almost non-existent.

Conspiracy theories always enshroud momentous events, from the fate of Grand Duchess Anastasia and the death of President John F. Kennedy to the terrorist attacks of 11 September 2001. It is not surprising, then, that the assassination that sparked the First World War has also led to controversy and speculation. This stretches beyond arguments over the role of the notorious group the Black Hand in organizing the attack or the complicity of the Serbian government. There have long been whispers that something more nefarious was afoot, a plot engineered by officials in Austria-Hungary who wanted the troublesome archduke and his equally troublesome morganatic wife out of the way. Without doubt there were those who trembled when they thought of Franz Ferdinand as emperor. His plans to reorganize the empire threatened conservative notions, and many worried that despite his renunciation, the archduke would find a way to crown his morganatic wife empress and name his eldest son as heir to the throne. Others were certainly looking for an excuse to wage war against the perpetual menace that was Serbia. What better way, it has been suggested, than to provoke some incident in Sarajevo that would justify Austrian aggression against Belgrade?

It is a startling idea, but one that Franz Josef's own daughter-in-law, the former crown princess Stephanie, believed. The assassination in Sarajevo, she insisted, had been nudged along by certain elements in Austria who looked the other way when warnings of danger were raised. Then there are charges that imperial Russia, Serbia's most powerful ally and a country determined to eliminate Austria as an influence in the

Balkans, actively promoted the assassination. According to this theory, Russia feared that when Franz Ferdinand came to the throne he would unite the disparate southern Slavs under the Habsburg flag and thus prevent Romanov expansion in the Balkans. These two ideas form an inexorable part of the Sarajevo story and demand a serious hearing.

Some questions will always remain, but the trauma that quickly followed from that day in Sarajevo is undeniable. By the first week of August 1914, Europe was at war; if Franz Ferdinand and Sophie fell as its first victims, so, too, did their three children become its first orphans. Sophie, Max and Ernst suffered from the chaos unleashed by their parents' assassination, enduring all of the horrors that flowed from that Sunday in 1914. War and revolution, loss of homes and exile, terrified flight from invading armies, and torture at the hands of brutal dictators all became unwanted companions as the twentieth century progressed. Their tragic story echoes the plight of millions, mingling heartbreaking loss with faith and resilient love.

All of these elements – the forbidden romance, the happy family life, the struggles against an oppressive system, assassination, and the ultimate triumph over dark adversity – make the story of Franz Ferdinand, Sophie and their children a modern fairy tale that has, in ways large and small, affected the lives of hundreds of millions of people. Many have previously told the archduke's story, and even more books have dealt with the assassination in Sarajevo. The problem has always been bias, as authors projected onto Franz Ferdinand, Sophie, and the terrorists who killed them their own conceits and nationalistic views. Cutting through a century of popular misinformation is difficult. 'When I arrived in Austria,' says Princess Anita von Hohenberg, Franz Ferdinand and Sophie's great-granddaughter, 'I was a young woman, and the archduke was completely misunderstood. The image is still not perfect, but we're trying to change it.' As for Sophie, Princess Anita comments, 'She was a very down-to-earth person. She was very cheerful, and she was very devoted to her husband and to the children. She was satisfied, very calm, pious, and happy with the way she lived.'[8]

Breaking through old stereotypes is always difficult. There have been a few attempts at accurate portrayals of the couple, notably Gordon Brook-Shepherd's 1984 work *Victims at Sarajevo*. Although focused to a large extent on the archduke's political career, it tried to offer a balanced look at the couple's lives but often ended up repeating erroneous stories. Many others have offered fragmented glimpses of Franz Ferdinand and Sophie in works devoted to their assassination, but the results have been decidedly mixed.

The hundredth anniversary of the Sarajevo assassination calls for a fresh look at Franz Ferdinand and Sophie. Here, we have tried to focus on the personal over the political, to resurrect the couple as they were with each other and with their children. This is the story of the couple's romance and marriage; it is also the story of how the public and the imperial court saw them, how Franz Ferdinand and Sophie came to be viewed during their lives, and how these views often conflicted with reality. Finally, it is the story of their three children and how their lives became, in many ways, emblematic of the trauma unleashed with their parents' deaths.

The task of understanding the couple and bringing them to life is made somewhat more difficult by a rather surprising lack of reliable information. We have drawn on many of the archduke's unpublished letters and papers in the Haus-, Hof- und Staatsarchiv in Vienna, including correspondence within the Habsburg family, but for the most part these reveal only tantalizing glimpses of his private life. Franz Ferdinand was a great letter writer, and his intimate correspondence with Kaiser Wilhelm II would surely provide invaluable insights into his marriage. Sadly, while we possess numerous letters from the kaiser to the archduke, those from the archduke to the kaiser have simply disappeared. Despite extensive searches, no historian has been able to locate them.[9]

Nor is the situation any better when it comes to personal letters between Franz Ferdinand and Sophie. We know that the couple regularly wrote to each other in the years before their romance became public and throughout the lengthy negotiations with the powers that be over their marriage. Surely this correspondence would offer unique personal glimpses into their characters and their love affair. However, their son Max, perhaps hoping to preserve the sanctity of his parents' private thoughts, later destroyed nearly all of it. Their daughter, Sophie, managed to salvage the few scraps that remain, a postcard here or a brief note there, but sadly the confidences, love letters, and intimate exchanges that define the relationship are lost to history.[10]

Most royal and aristocratic personages of the era diligently maintained journals from their youth; it was a way of recording events and, perhaps more important in the Victorian age, demonstrating that time had been usefully occupied. These would be invaluable in establishing dates, particularly of early contacts between Franz Ferdinand and Sophie, and noting their passing feelings on the tumultuous developments they faced. Unfortunately for history, neither Franz Ferdinand nor Sophie kept regular diaries. For the archduke, the only real diary that survives is the one he wrote on his journey around the world in 1892–93. This was later published in a limited edition and revealed very little of his personal thoughts and nothing of his as yet non-existent romance with Sophie. As for Sophie, she never acquired the habit of a daily journal. Although she tried several times to do so, inevitably she abandoned it, and months passed without any entries. One of her diaries for 1891 survives at the couple's former home of Konopischt in the Czech Republic. Unfortunately, it contains only a few isolated lines.[11]

Several of the couple's intimates wrote occasionally observant, occasionally guarded, memoirs; a few isolated letters or passages by friends, relatives and courtiers offer some intriguing glimpses of the archduke's character, marriage and family. Sophie, in particular, remains something of an enigma, at least in terms of her personal feelings, hopes, joys, or frustrations. Few of those close to her ever talked, and those who did viewed her through a prism of grief after she had been effectively canonized by her death at Sarajevo. Even the couple's three children rarely spoke about their parents to their own families.[12] Fortunately, a cache of previously unpublished letters that Sophie wrote to her sister Oktavia finally give her a voice in her story.

In this book we have drawn on archival materials, family anecdotes, memoirs, contemporary press accounts, and other divergent sources to weave a tapestry of Franz Ferdinand and Sophie's life together. At times, owing to a lack of letters and diaries, the picture remains frustratingly vague, but we have attempted to offer insights without indulging in too much speculation. The story stretches from glittering Bohemian castles and gilded Viennese palaces to the unrelenting horrors of Nazi concentration camps, from the Victorian era to the modern age. At its heart, this is the chronicle of a family, who in their triumphs and tragedies not only shaped but also embodied much of the tumultuous twentieth century.

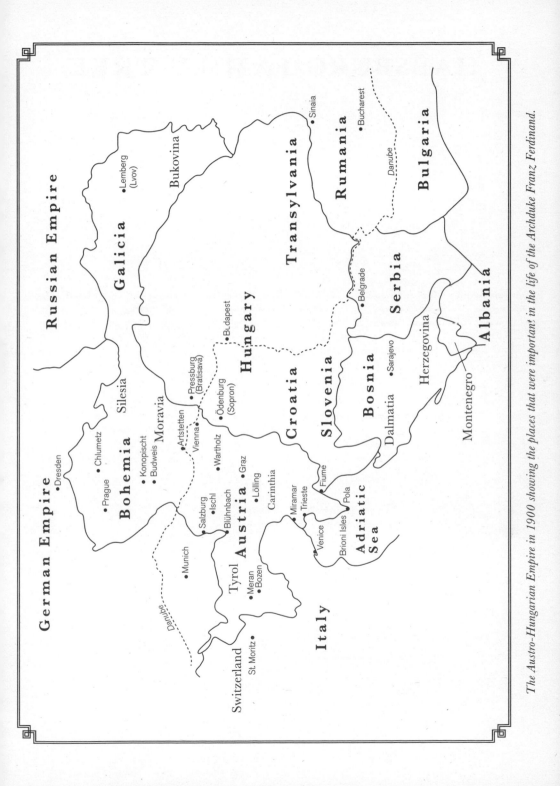

The Austro–Hungarian Empire in 1900 showing the places that were important in the life of the Archduke Franz Ferdinand.

HABSBURG FAMILY TREE

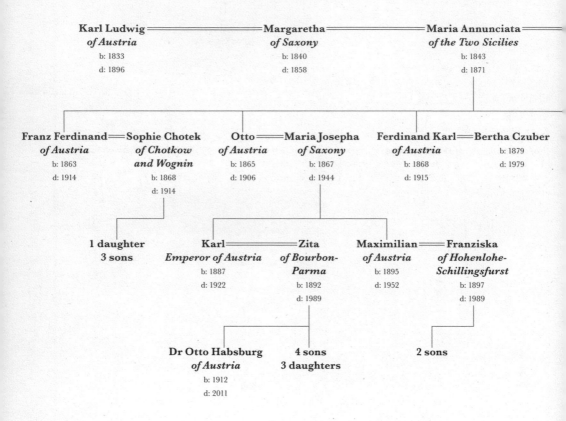

Karl Ludwig ════════════════════ **Margaretha** ════════════════════ **Maria Annunciata** ════
of Austria   *of Saxony*   *of the Two Sicilies*
    b: 1833   b: 1840   b: 1843
    d: 1896   d: 1858   d: 1871

Franz Ferdinand══**Sophie Chotek**   **Otto**══**Maria Josepha**   **Ferdinand Karl**══**Bertha Czuber**
of Austria   *of Chotkow*   *of Austria* *of Saxony*   *of Austria*   b: 1879
 b: 1863   *and Wognin*   b: 1865 b: 1867   b: 1868   d: 1979
 d: 1914   b: 1868   d: 1906 d: 1944   d: 1915
    d: 1914

1 daughter   **Karl**════**Zita**   **Maximilian**════**Franziska**
3 sons   *Emperor of Austria* *of Bourbon-*   *of Austria* *of Hohenlohe-*
    b: 1887   *Parma*   b: 1895 *Schillingsfurst*
    d: 1922   b: 1892   d: 1952 b: 1897
    d: 1989   d: 1989

Dr Otto Habsburg   **4 sons**   **2 sons**
of Austria   **3 daughters**
    b: 1912
    d: 2011

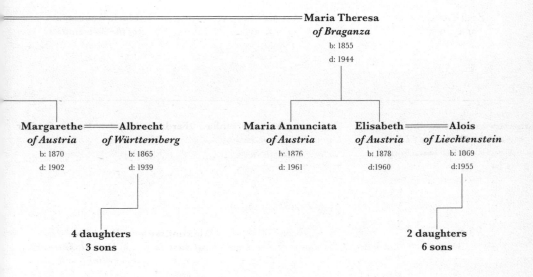

Maria Theresa
of Braganza
b: 1855
d: 1944

Margarethe══════Albrecht
of Austria   *of Württemberg*
b: 1870   b: 1865
d: 1902   d: 1939

Maria Annunciata   Elisabeth══════Alois
of Austria   *of Austria*   *of Liechtenstein*
b: 1876   b: 1878   b: 1869
d: 1961   d:1960   d:1955

4 daughters   2 daughters
3 sons   6 sons

HOHENBERG AND
CHOTEK FAMILY TREE

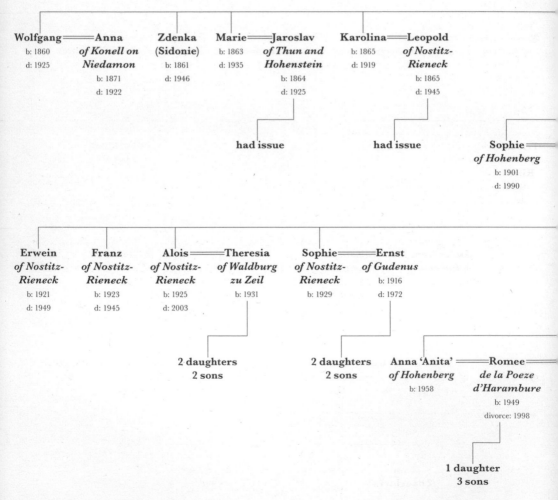

Wolfgang════════Anna
b: 1860   *of Konell on*
d: 1925   *Niedamon*
           b: 1871
           d: 1922

Zdenka
(Sidonie)
b: 1861
d: 1946

Marie════Jaroslav
b: 1863   *of Thun and*
d: 1935   *Hohenstein*
           b: 1864
           d: 1925

had issue

Karolina════Leopold
b: 1865   *of Nostitz-*
d: 1919   *Rieneck*
           b: 1865
           d: 1945

had issue

Sophie════
of Hohenberg
b: 1901
d: 1990

Erwein
of Nostitz-
Rieneck
b: 1921
d: 1949

Franz
of Nostitz-
Rieneck
b: 1923
d: 1945

Alois════════Theresia
of Nostitz-   *of Waldburg*
Rieneck   *zu Zeil*
b: 1925   b: 1931
d: 2003

2 daughters
2 sons

Sophie════════Ernst
of Nostitz-   *of Gudenus*
Rieneck   b: 1916
b: 1929   d: 1972

2 daughters
2 sons

Anna 'Anita'════════Romee════
of Hohenberg   *de la Poeze*
b: 1958   *d'Harambure*
                     b: 1949
                     divorce: 1998

1 daughter
3 sons

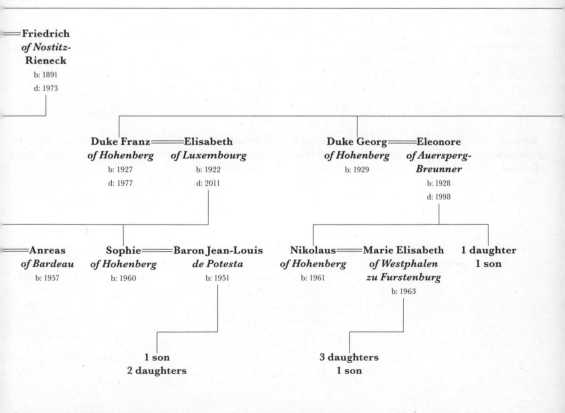

Bohuslav Chotek ══════════════ Wilhelmina Kinsky
of Chotkow and   b: 1835
Wognin   d: 1888
b: 1829
d: 1896

══Friedrich
of Nostitz-
Rieneck
b: 1891
d: 1973

Duke Franz══════Elisabeth   Duke Georg══════Eleonore
of Hohenberg   *of Luxembourg*   *of Hohenberg*   *of Auersperg-*
b: 1927   b: 1922   b: 1929   *Breunner*
d: 1977   d: 2011   b: 1928
                                                             d: 1998

══Anreas   Sophie══════Baron Jean-Louis   Nikolaus══════Marie Elisabeth   1 daughter
of Bardeau   *of Hohenberg*   *de Potesta*   *of Hohenberg*   *of Westphalen*   1 son
b: 1957   b: 1960   b: 1951   b: 1961   *zu Furstenburg*
                                                                    b: 1963

1 son   3 daughters
2 daughters   1 son

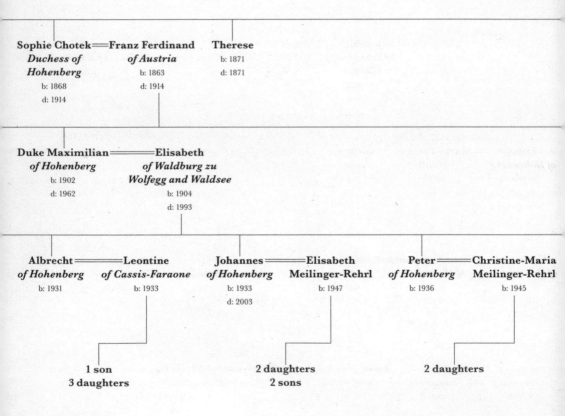

Sophie Chotek══**Franz Ferdinand** **Therese**
Duchess of   *of Austria*   b: 1871
Hohenberg   b: 1863   d: 1871
 b: 1868   d: 1914
 d: 1914

Duke Maximilian══════**Elisabeth**
of Hohenberg   *of Waldburg zu*
 b: 1902   *Wolfegg and Waldsee*
 d: 1962   b: 1904
                      d: 1993

Albrecht══════**Leontine**   **Johannes**══════**Elisabeth**   **Peter**══════**Christine-Maria**
of Hohenberg *of Cassis-Faraone* *of Hohenberg* Meilinger-Rehrl *of Hohenberg* Meilinger-Rehrl
 b: 1931   b: 1933   b: 1933   b: 1947   b: 1936   b: 1945
                                     d: 2003

        1 son   2 daughters   2 daughters
     3 daughters   2 sons

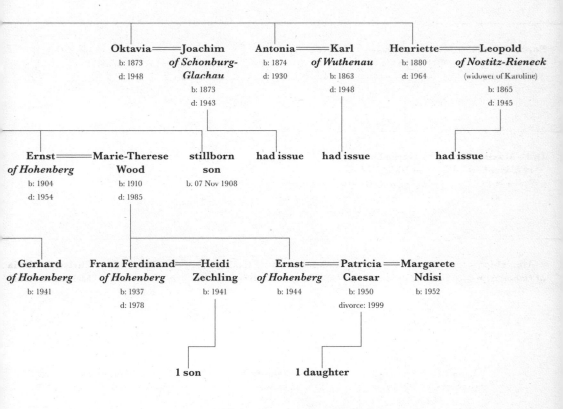

Oktavia══════Joachim
b: 1873   *of Schonburg-*
d: 1948   *Glachau*
             b: 1873
             d: 1943

Antonia══════Karl
b: 1874   *of Wuthenau*
d: 1930   b: 1863
             d: 1948

Henriette══════════Leopold
b: 1880   *of Nostitz-Rieneck*
d: 1964   (widower of Karoline)
             b: 1865
             d: 1945

Ernst══════Marie-Therese
of Hohenberg   Wood
b: 1904   b: 1910
d: 1954   d: 1985

stillborn
son
b. 07 Nov 1908

had issue

had issue

had issue

Gerhard
of Hohenberg
b: 1941

Franz Ferdinand══════Heidi
of Hohenberg   Zechling
b: 1937   b: 1941
d: 1978

Ernst══════Patricia══════Margarete
of Hohenberg Caesar   Ndisi
b: 1944   b: 1950   b: 1952
          divorce: 1999

1 son

1 daughter

The
ASSASSINATION
of the
ARCHDUKE

✦

PROLOGUE

Vienna, January 1889

+

Thick white snow swirled from a night sky, scattering across Vienna's tiled rooftops and shimmering in drifts against the wide boulevards. Slumbering in the Danube Basin against the foothills of the Vienna Woods the city seemed sedate and at peace. A drive between the Ringstrasse's rows of lime trees, made bare by winter, revealed the captivating scene: the neo-Gothic Rathaus, the imposing Court Opera House, immense museums with their marching colonnades, the Parliament building glowering in neoclassical severity, the sprouting spires of St Stephen's Cathedral, and the green-domed Karlskirche. Seemingly suspended between banks of snow and opalescent sky and illuminated by the flickering shadows of ghostly street lamps, Vienna looked impressive, dignified, and magisterial, all that the capital of a great empire should be.

For centuries Vienna had provided the Habsburg dynasty with a theatrical stage set from which to dominate Europe. They ruled from the Alps to the warm waters of the Mediterranean, from the sunshine of Trieste to the dark, mysterious forests of Transylvania, Bohemia, and the edges of imperial Russia. As the pre-eminent Catholic royal house in Europe, Habsburgs had fought, invaded, and married to unite far-flung principalities and provinces beneath their flag, bedecked with a fierce, double-headed eagle. The glories were undeniable. For centuries Habsburgs had been Holy Roman Emperors; they had provided kings to Spain and consorts to Europe. There were illustrious ancestors: the great Emperor Charles V and the influential Empress Maria Theresa ranked among the most distinguished rulers.

Habsburg influence waned when Napoleon swept across Europe and shattered the Holy Roman Empire. A loose confederation of German states fragmented old loyalties and left the dynasty pushing against a rising tide of nationalism and frequent revolt. Only forty years had passed since the Revolution of 1848, when the Habsburgs nearly lost Hungary. Rebellion in Budapest was crushed only with the assistance of Russian soldiers. Twenty years later, Hungarians had sided with an increasingly powerful and militaristic Prussia in the Seven Weeks War; defeat of Habsburg forces at the Battle of Königgrätz marked the end of Austrian domination and inaugurated an uneasy alliance. Budapest blackmailed Vienna into the *Ausgleich* of 1867, which split the realm into two equal halves and established the Dual Monarchy. Maintaining the right to renegotiate the agreement every decade, Budapest continually wrested from a weakened Vienna new concessions that seemed to foreshadow inevitable Hungarian autonomy.[1]

At least Hungary remained a Habsburg domain. By 1889, the dynasty had lost Tuscany, Parma, and the Italian provinces of Lombardy and Venice. Their empire was an anachronistic remnant of a previous age, 'a dynastic fiction', as one wit noted.[2] Some fifty million diverse subjects – Austrian Germans, Magyars, Bohemians, Italians, Rumanians, Moravians, and Poles – were collected beneath the black and yellow Habsburg flag. None were bound together by common ties, languages, or nationalities; lacking allegiance to Vienna, many increasingly yearned to break free of what they deemed Habsburg oppression. Year by year, it seemed, the last vestiges of power were slipping away from the proud Habsburgs. What remained was a ruling family rooted in tradition, its past glories supplanted by a string of failed monarchs, highly incestuous marriages, and a depressing family tendency to weak chins.

At the head of this conflicted nation stood Franz Josef I, Emperor of Austria and Apostolic King of Hungary; King of Bohemia, Dalmatia, Croatia, Slovenia, Galicia, and Jerusalem; Archduke of Austria; Grand Duke of Tuscany, Krakow, and Transylvania; Duke of Lothringia, Salzburg, and Bukovina – a string of titles that went on and on and spoke more of the past than they did of modern realities.[3] Middle age was behind the emperor now; the once dashing and svelte Franz Josef was balding and slightly stooped, with bushy white whiskers and sleepy blue eyes. He was the only ruler most of his subjects had ever known. People spoke of him as 'almighty, a being of a higher order, enthroned in regions beyond human aspiration'.[4] Stung by the constant rebellions and loss of power, Franz Josef retreated to a world of archaic tradition, a universe of perpetual waltzes and sugary confections where he could ignore the unfamiliar and unwelcome modern age. He rode in a motor car only once, and then only at the behest of a visiting King Edward VII; at the age of eighty-four Franz Josef climbed six flights of stairs rather than entrust himself to a suspiciously modern lift.[5]

The idea of change became anathema. Franz Josef preferred to keep to himself, isolated and unchallenged in his opinions. 'A wall of prejudice severs the Emperor from all independent thinking political personalities,' commented one insider. A 'ring of courtiers, military, and medical personnel' shielded Franz Josef from unpleasant views or unwelcome reality. 'The powerfully surging life of our times barely reaches the ear of our Emperor as distant rustling. He is kept from any real participation in this life. He no longer understands the times and the times pass on regardless.'[6] All that mattered was preserving the old order; disagreeable ideas were ignored, left to Franz Josef's successor. The emperor was content to bury himself in petty paperwork, obsessing over bureaucratic details rather than facing contentious problems.[7] His was a universe of absolutes. For Franz Josef, said a courtier, 'only primitive concepts exist. Beautiful, ugly, dead, living, healthy, young, old, clever, stupid – these are all separate notions to him and he is unable to form a bridge leading from one to the other . . . His ideas know no nuances.'[8]

No one ever accused the emperor of being temperamental. Franz Josef was invariably pleasant, guarded and restrained, but his courtly manners concealed a cold, suspicious and intolerant character. He disliked confrontation and did not tolerate contradiction. Everyone feared his displeasure. When the future King George V visited Vienna in 1904, he was surprised that courtiers and members of the imperial family alike all seemed to be 'frightened of the Emperor'.[9] A wrong word, a missed bow, a button undone, a medal out of place – these minor infractions against tradition were enough to send him into paroxysms of inner rage. One night, Franz Josef suffered a choking fit and could not breathe. A doctor, hastily summoned from his sleep, rushed to administer aid only to be met with a glacial look from the gasping emperor, who somehow managed to berate him for not appearing in the customary tailcoat.[10] When it was once proposed that guards on duty at the imperial palaces abandon the practice of presenting arms and saluting Habsburg babies, Franz Josef rejected the idea as an attack on the dignity of the imperial house.[11]

In his private life Franz Josef was a man of dull habits. He lived in regal rooms in a kind of studied Spartan luxury, sleeping on a military cot fitted with the finest mattress and linens. The emperor customarily arose at four each morning to begin his work, took lunch alone, walked in the afternoon, and dined at the unfashionably early hour of half past five.[12] His was a solitary existence, made more lonely by the frequent absence of his wife. More often than not, Empress Elisabeth was away from Vienna. The two first cousins had married when the Bavarian Princess Elisabeth was just sixteen, and much against the wishes of Franz Josef's powerful mother, Archduchess Sophie. The Bavarian royal family was often flamboyant and occasionally eccentric, with a tendency to high-strung temperaments and disconcerting bouts of depression – scarcely promising qualities in a possible empress of Austria. No arguments, however, could stop the passionately enamoured Franz Josef in his quest. It was all breathtaking romance at the beginning, but then the darkness set in.

Elisabeth, known as Sissi, has become a figure of romantic nostalgia, nearly worshipped in modern Vienna, but truth is not as sentimental.

The new empress was a selfish, immature young girl who found life at the imperial court distasteful and confining. Adoring as he was, Franz Josef was never averse to other feminine charms, particularly when his wife evinced horror at the sexual side of married life. Horror soon turned to disgust when the emperor reportedly infected his wife with venereal disease.[13] Ashamed and feeling betrayed, Elisabeth became a virtual stranger at her husband's court, doing everything she could to avoid her loathsome ceremonial duties. Deprived of a happy marriage, the emperor turned to a series of mistresses; there were even illegitimate children, despite his image as a staunchly conservative Catholic.[14] The most famous of his relationships was with actress Katharina Schratt, who became his closest confidante and the sole source of emotional comfort in his later life.

The emperor's contemporary subjects were less forgiving of Elisabeth than her modern admirers. They resented her for the endless, extended sojourns in foreign resorts, as if she despised her adopted homeland. Obsessed with her famed beauty, she starved herself into a state of dangerous anorexia, indulged in self-pity and morbid fantasies, and spent her days composing volumes of questionable poetry.[15]

Perhaps Elisabeth had reason to flee. Life among the Habsburgs was scarcely a pleasant swirl of Strauss waltzes and smiling faces. There was also tragedy. Franz Josef and Elisabeth had lost their first daughter to childhood illness, and misfortune seemed to envelop their family. The emperor's younger brother Maximilian had unwisely accepted the Mexican throne only to be overthrown and executed by firing squad. Thoroughly unhinged by her husband's death, Maximilian's widow, Carlotta, wandered Europe, blaming everyone for his execution until she was finally locked away in a remote castle. Ludwig Viktor, the emperor's youngest brother, had been exiled from Vienna amid rumours of his indiscreet attraction to handsome young men and his penchant for wearing elaborate ball gowns.[16] Even Franz Josef found his family trying. He 'liked only a few of his relations', recalled his valet; 'he quite rightly considered that many of them acted incorrectly'. As a consequence, the emperor 'did not want to see some members of his family at all', and 'others only as seldom as possible'.[17]

Then there was Rudolf, Franz Josef and Elisabeth's only son. His birth in 1858 was a moment for celebration, ensuring the continuation of the Habsburg dynasty, but Rudolf's childhood was anything but joyful. Franz Josef was a stern, aloof and disapproving father; nothing Rudolf did or said ever seemed to please him. He worshipped his mother, but Elisabeth was too self-absorbed, too melancholy, and all too often absent to shape her son's character. In one respect, though, Rudolf was his mother's son: he grew up to become a self-absorbed, melancholy young man, with a predilection for the darker pleasures of sexual liaisons and political misadventure.

His father tried to impose some measure of order onto his son's life by marrying Rudolf off to Princess Stephanie, daughter of King Leopold II of Belgium. A year passed between engagement and wedding, when it was discovered that the fifteen-year-old intended bride had not yet begun to menstruate.[18] Rudolf was glamorous and charming; Stephanie was somewhat less than beautiful and scarcely the kind of woman to keep her husband in marital thrall. It all ended badly shortly after the birth of their daughter, Elisabeth, in 1883, when Stephanie suddenly fell ill. In an ironic twist, Rudolf had infected his wife with venereal disease, just as his father had done with his Elisabeth. Angered and left unable to have any more children, Stéphanie sulked, and Rudolf turned to more convivial company.

Rudolf was the antithesis of his father. Although he fancied himself a gifted political intellectual, he was more of a dilettante. He played in what his father deemed dangerous liberal circles, encouraging dissent and opposing Franz Josef's staunch conservatism. Rudolf's plight was the plight of princes everywhere: he had no real function except to await his father's death. Lacking responsibilities, distrusted by his father, and denied any role that might have kept him usefully occupied, Austria-Hungary's crown prince sank into depression. Morbid and morose, he plunged into a spiral of mistresses and morphine that left him alienated from his family and suffering from gonorrhoea.[19]

The conservative emperor consumed with bureaucratic rule, the reclusive and melancholy empress, and the disturbed and disreputable crown prince – they all formed a triumvirate where impending disaster seemed to simmer just beneath the pleasant surface. The imperial court that January of 1889 somehow seemed to reflect this dichotomy. To the casual observer it was as buoyantly splendid as ever, a universe of eternal waltzes and carefree pleasures. To one visiting sovereign, though, the court, reeking 'of death and decrepitude', was an ossified universe filled with 'archaic countenances, shrivelled intellects, trembling heads, worn out bladders'.[20]

It was a world precariously balanced on tradition and ironclad etiquette. Only those who could boast sixteen quarterings – unbroken descent from eight paternal and eight maternal noble ancestors – were admitted to the highest court functions. The rules were stringently enforced. The wife of Austria's ambassador to Germany could be received at the kaiser's court but not in Vienna if she lacked the necessary string of noble ancestors. On more than one occasion distinguished aristocratic ladies were politely but firmly turned away from palace ballrooms, told that they weren't distinguished enough to join the enchanted circles within. Officers, no matter their rank, were snubbed if they couldn't meet the requirements; the young niece of a prominent English duke once attended an imperial ball over the protests of other guests, who complained that, as she herself had no title, she shouldn't be let through the doors. Husbands were asked to attend without their wives and wives without their husbands if the imperial court decided that they had married beneath their rank.[21]

This undisguised snobbery was yet another dichotomy. The Viennese, said a diplomat, were 'cheery and easy-going', dedicated to 'music and dancing, eating and drinking, laughter and fun. They were quite content to drift lazily down the stream of life, with as much enjoyment and as little trouble as possible.'[22] Pleasantries couldn't disguise the aristocracy's ruthless insistence on its own privilege and the exclusion of those deemed socially unacceptable. 'The present generation of the upper aristocracy', the Viennese newspaper *Neue Freie Presse* commented, 'still wants to dominate the middle class, but they want to dominate the middle class without becoming acquainted with it . . . The aristocracy here is sterile and sequestered.'[23] They passed their days, insisted one visitor, in shallow pursuits, 'discussing the births, marriages and deaths of their acquaintances and friends and the sayings and doings of the Imperial Family. They scarcely ever read; their knowledge of art is exceedingly limited; they have absolutely no general interests; politics remain to them a closed book except when they concern the welfare of the Austrian Empire, and even then occupy them from the arrogant, but not from the instructive point of view.'[24]

That January of 1889, mourning for the empress's father had cancelled the usual round of imperial balls; instead, aristocratic Vienna threw itself into a round of superb and deliberate indulgence. It was fitting that the city of Strauss waltzes seemed consumed with the pleasures of the ballroom. There were merchants' balls, the Housekeepers' Ball, the Coiffeurs' Ball, the Master Bakers' Ball, and the Laundresses' Ball – every conceivable association and organization used the winter social season to celebrate with joyous abandon. This taste for hedonistic excess reached a zenith that month in the Fourth Dimension Ball, where women dressed as witches moved through the crowd, and a rose garden set with twinkling lights bloomed from the ceiling.[25]

All seemed pleasant and pleasurable. Vienna appeared as splendid as ever, the empire secure, the Habsburgs surveying all from a glittering height. However, illusion cloaked reality. Beneath the image of traditional *Sachertortes*, *gemütlich* comforts, and endless Strauss waltzes lay another world, where Vienna led Europe's cities in annual suicides.[26] This was the universe of Freud and Mahler, of sexuality and passion, of intellectuals and artists who haunted smoke-filled coffeehouses with their philosophical worries, of anti-Semitism and impoverished workers crowded into disease-ridden tenements. 'There is a general air of discontent,' one paper had declared as the new year began. A 'breath of melancholy brushes through our society'.[27] Before the month was out, this discontent erupted in unsuspected tragedy that tore the veil of Habsburg complacency forever.

ONE

In the Shadow of the Throne

⊹

Far away from the glamour of a snowbound Vienna, a thin, pale young man with watery blue eyes was enjoying his own pleasures as 1889 began. From his suite of ornate rooms in Prague's Hradschin Castle, he would join the men of his 102nd Bohemian Infantry Regiment at their dinners, the local officials at their fussy receptions, and the obsequious aristocrats in their rococo ballrooms. He hated the fawning attention and the constant scrutiny that came from his position as an Austrian archduke, nephew of Emperor Franz Josef, but there was no escape. Noble birth had trapped Franz Ferdinand in this gilded cage of privilege and duty.

He was twenty-five now, with light brown hair parted neatly down the middle and a dashing, thin little cavalry moustache, yet Franz Ferdinand had never outgrown the aura of fragile delicacy inherited from his late mother. Archduke Karl Ludwig, his father, was strong enough, with the same watery eyes and a robust, determined face cloaked in drooping, mutton-chop whiskers. He was invariably polite; courteous, knowledgeable, and refined, he had, said one lady, 'none of the Habsburg arrogance'.[1] Pleasantries, however, couldn't disguise reality. Karl Ludwig had few interests beyond religion and the arts and sciences. After a brief stint as governor-general of the Tyrol, he stumbled through military and political duties with disinterest until he could retire into private life.

Karl Ludwig's delicate first wife, Princess Margarethe of Saxony, had died in 1858 after two years of marriage. Bride No. 2 came in 1862; this was Princess Maria Annunciata, daughter of the late King Ferdinand II of Naples and the Two Sicilies, a man known as 'La Bomba' after having his rebellious subjects shelled into submission. Nineteen at the time, dark-haired, willowy, she had none of her father's fiery passion and proved to be as delicate as the late Margaretha. Within a year, doctors diagnosed tuberculosis. Her weak lungs forced the couple to Graz, where it was hoped the mountain air would revive her fragile health.

'Graz is pleasant,' the archduke thought; 'it has the benefits of a larger city without the disadvantages.'[2] Here, in the rented Palais Khuen-burg, the couple awaited the birth of their first child. It was a quarter past seven on the morning of 18 December 1863, when the child arrived. The archbishop of Seckau christened the boy that afternoon. Karl Ludwig's mother, Sophie, watched as godfather and great-grandfather Arch-duke Franz Karl announced the names: Franz Ferdinand Karl Ludwig Josef Maria. The first honoured the boy's late Austrian grandfather, Emperor Franz I; the second, his infamous maternal grandfather, King Ferdinand II of Naples and the Two Sicilies.[3]

More children followed: Otto, in 1865; Ferdinand Karl, in 1868; and Margarethe Sophie in 1870. Franz Ferdinand's childhood was unde-manding and comfortable. The family spent winters in a lavish Viennese palace, spring and autumn at some remote hunting lodge, and idyllic summers at Schloss Artstetten, some seventy miles west of Vienna near the famous Benedictine Abbey of Melk in the Danube Valley.[4] One thing was missing, though. Increasingly ill and exhausted, Maria An-nunciata was a mere phantom in her children's lives. Fearing that she would infect her sons and daughter, she forbade them to touch her, kiss her, or even spend time with her. A virtual stranger within her own house, she lived in isolation, growing weaker with the passing years until death finally overtook her in May 1871 at the age of twenty-eight.[5]

Franz Ferdinand was just seven when his mother died. It was not entirely unexpected, but undoubtedly he missed and mourned her; everyone agreed that the young archduke was a curious child, withdrawn, quiet and introspective, though whether this stemmed from his mother's death is a mystery. Luckily for Franz Ferdinand and his siblings, a new and altogether steadier influence soon arrived in the household. Twice widowed and with four children to bring up, Karl Ludwig waited just two years before marrying a third time, in July 1873. His new bride, Maria Theresa, was the daughter of the exiled King Miguel I of Portugal. Where Maria Annunciata had been frail and morose, Maria Theresa was robust, lively and beautiful, with dark hair and sparkling eyes that made her one of the loveliest of European princesses.[6] Not quite eighteen, she was nearly twenty years younger than her husband. Karl Ludwig had been a devoted, patient and loving husband to his first two wives, but with Maria Theresa – at least according to rumour – something changed. Perhaps it was the difference in their ages, or the fact that young officers did not conceal their admiring glances at court, but the archduke allegedly went from sympathetic husband to stern martinet, tormenting his wife and generally making her life miserable.[7]

Whether or not the stories were true, Maria Theresa *did* have a dramatic impact on her new family. She never differentiated between her two daughters with Karl Ludwig, Archduchesses Maria Annunciata, born in 1876, and Elisabeth, born in 1878, and her four stepchildren. Just eight years older than Franz Ferdinand, Maria Theresa gave him and his siblings something that they had never known: a mother. For the first time there was maternal love and affection.[8] To Franz Ferdinand, she was simply 'Mama', and he was her 'Franzi'.

The young Franz Ferdinand needed the attention. From birth he had been delicate and uncertain, and early impressions were not always favourable. 'Franzi was in a bad mood,' noted his uncle Emperor Franz Josef on meeting the three-year-old in 1866, 'but he speaks rather well.'[9] Everyone noticed how introverted he seemed, how distant Franz Ferdinand was even with his own siblings. Ferdinand Karl and his sisters were too young to be true companions, and even though he was younger, Otto overshadowed him. Otto rode better than his older brother, excelled at their fencing lessons, and was vivacious where Franz Ferdinand was reticent. Otto loved noise, while Franz Ferdinand preferred solitary pursuits: long walks, lonely rides in a donkey cart, reading, and afternoons playing alone with his pet rabbits.[10] Hunting became his favourite passion. He spent hours alone in the forest, watching and waiting for a chance to test his skill. At the age of nine he made his first kill, inaugurating what would become a remarkable record of wild trophies. 'I can imagine how pleased you are!' his cousin Crown Prince Rudolf wrote.[11]

Nor did education draw Franz Ferdinand out of his shell. Like many other princes, he was isolated in a castle schoolroom and lectured by tutors, deprived of any chance to meet other boys and subjected to a rigorous regime that lasted from morning until afternoon six days a week with only a few scattered holidays. Count Ferdinand Degenfeld, an unimaginative former army officer, supervised lessons in a curriculum heavy with arithmetic, German, grammar, sciences, geography, history, literature and religion.[12]

It isn't surprising that an archduke in the conservatively Catholic Habsburg family received a reliably conservative education, where reactionary views were advanced and contrary opinions were suppressed. Such concerns shaped Professor Onno Klopp's bigoted and myopic history lectures. Liberal policies, the dangers of modern thought, and dire warnings about a growing Prussian menace threatening the divine mission of the Habsburg monarchy formed the hallmark of these lessons. Klopp was so worried that contrary ideas might influence his pupil that he even literally rewrote the young archduke's history books himself to remove unwanted and pernicious political notions.[13]

Religious instruction reinforced these notions. Gottfried Marschall, a priest attached to Karl Ludwig's household, provided lessons in Catholic history and church dogma. Although often described as a man of liberal inclinations, Marschall was a deeply conservative man whose lectures emphasized the young archduke's future religious duties as a

Catholic Habsburg.[14] Franz Ferdinand made his task easier: even as a young boy he was unusually pious, fascinated by church rituals and standing for hours in the shadows of palace chapels to soak up the atmosphere of intoxicating mysticism.[15] Personal devotion and Marschall's lectures left their mark. For Franz Ferdinand, there was little soul-searching when it came to religion; his Catholic faith settled great issues of philosophical concern, and he saw no reason to question the dogmas and wisdom of the Church. Yet he was also largely free of religious intolerance. Too many people, Franz Ferdinand thought, were insincere in their faith. Those who practised their religion with obvious piety always won his admiration. 'After all, that's what counts,' he once commented. 'Whether they are Christians or Muslims is of much less importance.'[16]

German was the first language for any Habsburg archduke, but there were also lessons in French, English, Czech and Magyar. Most of these efforts failed with Franz Ferdinand. 'His lack of any talent for languages was peculiar,' thought one government minister. He mastered French reasonably well, but English remained elusive and uncertain. At times he seemed proficient only to then stumble and awkwardly search for words. The extremely difficult Magyar language fared worst of all. Franz Ferdinand took lessons in the Hungarian tongue his entire life but never gained any real fluency.[17]

Gymnastics, riding, swimming, fencing and dancing lessons filled the afternoons; at night, Karl Ludwig taught art history and asked inventors, writers, poets, musicians and scientists to offer informative lectures.[18] There were later lessons in military history, naval manoeuvres, architecture and engineering; future Austrian prime minister Max Vladimir Beck taught civil and constitutional law.[19] Nothing had been neglected, but the overall effect was mixed. Education left Franz Ferdinand a well-rounded young man, with a passing knowledge in many topics but a true understanding in few. He despised arithmetic and literature, enjoyed history, and above all adored his brief studies of architecture.[20] Tutors routinely complained that he seemed backward, lacked focus, and spent his days brooding rather than concentrating on his lessons.[21] Perhaps some of the blame lay with the rather unimaginative system itself, but no one would mistake Franz Ferdinand for an academic. His days were so full of competing lectures that 'everything was pell-mell'. As a result, he had 'learned everything and knew nothing'.[22]

Franz Ferdinand's destiny seemed inevitably mapped out from birth: education, a career in the military, and perhaps some ceremonial duties on behalf of the emperor. There was little chance that he would ever come to the throne. After all, his uncle Franz Josef was still alive; his cousin Crown Prince Rudolf was still unmarried and would undoubtedly wed a suitable consort and produce heirs; and his own father, Karl Ludwig, came before him in the imperial succession. Franz Ferdinand's education hadn't even envisioned the possibility. His life would be pleasant, comfortable, and devoted to enhancing the prestige of the Habsburg dynasty, with few opportunities to explore personal interests or carve out any path that diverged too far from tradition.

An unexpected opportunity did come his way when he was twelve. The exiled Duke Franz V of Modena, archduke of Austria-Este, died without heirs. In his five-hundred-page will, the duke left all of his considerable fortune and numerous estates to whichever male Habsburg would couple the Este title to his own and continue the line. Since his son was so far down the line of succession, Karl Ludwig thought that the change of name wouldn't matter and offered up Franz Ferdinand as heir. The young archduke wasn't happy about appending 'Este' to his title, though it seemed a mere inconvenience at the time. It was, after all, an Italian title, and he shared his stepmother's prejudices against the country that had so recently unified at the expense of Habsburg territories. Later, he openly resented the title of Archduke of Austria-Este, feeling that the Italian title somehow singled him out as something of a foreigner among the Habsburgs. Of more immediate concern was another provision: to receive the inheritance, Franz Ferdinand had to gain a working knowledge of Italian within a year. Being a poor linguist, he struggled through the lessons, gathering just enough Italian to satisfy the demands of the will when quizzed by executors.[23]

The young Franz Ferdinand was now, at least in theory, one of the wealthiest archdukes. The Este inheritance included the famous Renaissance Villa d'Este near Rome, the sixteenth-century Castello del Catajo near Padua, the Modena Palais in Vienna, the estate of Chlumetz in Bohemia, and other properties, along with a vast collection of arms, armour and artistic treasures.[24] It seemed promising, but Franz Ferdinand later discovered how provisions in the will tied his hands. There were undeniable assets, but they were outweighed by financial obligations. Nothing could be sold, and annual legacies to Este relatives, pensions for retired servants, and the upkeep of the various estates exceeded any income he received.[25]

The military at least offered a reward at the end of Franz Ferdinand's formal education. In 1878, when the emperor made his nephew an honorary lieutenant in an infantry regiment, Franz Ferdinand was overjoyed. Honorary promotions and army commissions finally brought tangible results in 1883 when he was promoted to lieutenant of the 4th Emperor Ferdinand Dragoon Cavalry Regiment stationed at Enns.[26] 'I am an officer body and soul,' he proudly declared. 'To my mind, that profession is the noblest and highest in the world.' He now set about carving out what was, for an archduke, the only acceptable career.[27]

Entry into the army marked a significant turn for the previously sheltered archduke. Franz Ferdinand was cautious in everything he did. It was a lesson he had been taught since birth: as a prince, he stood apart from others, who would seek his favour and flatter him into indiscreet friendships for their own gain. He must be friendly but not familiar, honest but guarded. Everything he did reflected on the dynasty's dignity; mistakes and minor lapses in judgement permitted to ordinary officers were, for a Habsburg archduke, deemed grievous sins against the emperor.

By temperament and inclination, Franz Ferdinand wasn't the kind of jovial, carefree young man who could quickly win friends and easily slip into unfamiliar social situations. Though he did well in the army, he seemed aloof and intolerant. Fellow officers put his shyness down to conceit, his sense of inadequacy to disdain. Having had few opportunities to interact with others, Franz Ferdinand had never learned to disguise his feelings; bursts of temper that might have been laughed off at home seemed truly frightening to those expecting an agreeable Habsburg. The archduke hated pretence and never tried to win over his comrades. It was to become a common complaint. Franz Ferdinand lacked the one thing most prized in Austria: charm.

The young archduke joined comrades in boisterous dinners and drinking games but couldn't quite abandon his natural reticence. Yet he was not without opportunities for indulgence. Franz Ferdinand wasn't particularly handsome; he was too thin, with prominent ears and heavily lidded eyes that made it seem as if he was on the verge of waking or going to sleep. Young, privileged, and for the first time unencumbered by minders, he faced an unfamiliar world that brimmed with temptations – which his younger brother Otto had proved himself particularly adept at enjoying.

Otto had always been flamboyantly hedonistic. Where Franz Ferdinand was reserved and quiet, Otto was all jocularity, once signing a postcard of a sailor to his brother, 'Oh la la from the sailor!'[28] People called him 'Handsome Otto', and the attention went to his head. He had a wild sadistic streak, and his 'conduct was the town's talk'.[29] There were always stories, perhaps of questionable veracity, about Otto. He supposedly deprived animals of water for days, then allowed them to drink to excess and die in agony, or strapped naked soldiers to hot stoves and watched as their skin blistered. Gossip even held that Otto had once accidentally killed a military cadet by forcing brandy down his throat until he died of alcohol poisoning.[30]

Franz Ferdinand never succumbed to such depravities, though it would have been unusual had he not sown a few wild oats. He danced, drank and hunted with his brother and his fellow officers. Along with public escapades went private encounters of a more intimate nature. Franz Ferdinand once expressed great admiration for the rather dubious physical charms of actress Mizzi Caspar, a woman who had shared his cousin Rudolf's bed, and some discreet singer or dancer probably introduced him to the mysteries of sex.[31]

On 2 July 1885, a woman named Mary Jonke gave birth to a son called Heinrich. She claimed that Franz Ferdinand was the father and in April of the following year tried to sue the archduke in a local district court. After some negotiations, Franz Ferdinand agreed to pay her some 15,000 gulden (approximately £95,500 in 2013) to end all further claims. On 29 August 1889, Marie Hahn, a twenty-one-year-old clerk in a Prague clothing shop, gave birth to a son she named Kurt. Like Jonke, she insisted that Franz Ferdinand was the father. A courtier examined her claim and advised Hahn that if she tried to take her case to court she would lose; Habsburg money bought her silence.[32]

A Habsburg fathering illegitimate children was scarcely scandalous: even Emperor Franz Josef had done so. Neither of the allegations about Franz Ferdinand was ever proved. Perhaps the women did indeed have liaisons with the archduke, but whether the charges were true or not, Franz Ferdinand could not risk the scandal of being sued in court for paternity.[33] Still, rumours of wild escapades reinforced negative stereotypes about him in Vienna. Somewhat surprisingly in light of his own increasingly sordid reputation, Franz Ferdinand's cousin Rudolf now came to the rescue. The crown prince knew only too well how gossip spread through the imperial court and shaped opinion. As out of touch as Franz Josef often was, he always seemed to know the latest family scandals and could, as Rudolf had learned, be blistering in his indictments. Hoping to save his cousin from a similar fate, Rudolf warned Franz Ferdinand against spending too much time away from his regiment and indulging in pleasure. He should 'enjoy [his] health in full, but always in moderation and with intelligence'.[34] The archduke should 'not go riding and hunting too early', which would turn the emperor against him.[35] At times even Franz Ferdinand protested. 'You must admit that Otto and I are treated unfairly,' he complained to Rudolf in 1888. 'If we are seen at some hunts or go to a few lousy dances, there's right off a cry of indignation across Vienna at all Court and army circles over our shirking our duty.'[36]

More warnings came from Archduke Albrecht, the elderly disciplinarian in charge of the empire's army. Albrecht heartily disliked Rudolf and was convinced that nothing good could come of Franz Ferdinand's association with him. Rudolf constantly complained about 'the trouble and unpleasantness that I have to go through with him'; if Franz Ferdinand didn't watch out he, too, would face similar interfering admonitions.[37] Not that Franz Ferdinand had to do anything of note to bring about one of Albrecht's insulting letters. Albrecht complained that Franz Ferdinand was too reserved with some elderly gentlemen; Albrecht complained that Franz Ferdinand was too friendly with young women.[38] It didn't matter what the archduke did, it always seemed to be wrong. Franz Ferdinand tried to ignore it all, content to carry on with his pleasant, ordered routine for the foreseeable future.

That future abruptly changed on the morning of 30 January 1889. Repeated knocks on Crown Prince Rudolf's locked bedroom door at his hunting lodge of Mayerling went unanswered. No one wanted to cause a scene: Rudolf was there with his latest mistress, the young and insipid Baroness Mary Vetsera. At last, after hours of continued silence, a worried servant smashed through the door. Vetsera lay on the mattress, a single red rose clutched in her cold hands and a gaping wound in her head; hanging over the other side of a bed whose white sheets were mottled an ugly crimson sprawled Rudolf, blood trickling from his mouth, and the top of his skull blown away. He had killed her first in a suicide pact, sat with the body for hours, and finally put a bullet through his own brain.[39]

Mayerling was sickly melodrama, a real-life scene from some bad romance novel; most unforgivably, it was exceedingly bourgeois. The suicide of the Catholic Habsburg crown prince sent the imperial court into a panic. Rumours, lies and increasingly wild tales circulated in efforts to conceal an unpleasant truth that Vienna was eventually forced to admit. In death Rudolf had his final revenge against the intransigent father who had denied him any role and never tolerated the slightest hint of change. It was not merely an act of desperation and depression but also an expression of his thwarted ambitions. Before shooting himself, Rudolf had written letters explaining his actions – to his mother, to his wife, to his sister, but not a single line to his distant father.[40]

People were shocked, but perhaps no one was as stunned as was Franz Ferdinand when he tore open the urgent telegram early that afternoon.[41] He left for Vienna and walked through the cold, miserable streets behind his cousin's funeral cortège, aware with each step that his life had forever changed. A few years earlier, Rudolf had pointed to him and joked, 'The man walking towards us will become Emperor of Austria.'[42] It had seemed absurd, but now Rudolf was dead; the late crown prince's daughter Elisabeth only inherited if there were no eligible male Habsburgs. Only his father, Karl Ludwig, stood between Franz Ferdinand and the throne.

For all of his dissolution, Rudolf had been a popular figure, given to lively displays and known for his liberal tendencies. People knew little about Franz Ferdinand. There were unfavourable comparisons not just to Rudolf but also to his popular, if debauched, brother Otto. To most of Vienna, Franz Ferdinand was 'grave, strict, and almost gloomy-looking'; gossip held that he was a narrow-minded conservative and religious bigot, someone whose time on the throne would signal ominous things for all of Austria-Hungary.[43]

The ordeal of meeting the emperor followed the ordeal of the funeral. Grieving the loss of his son, Franz Josef had to face facts and receive the man who, in the wake of tragedy, would take his place. Uncle and nephew had never been close, and they never understood each other. Franz Josef was conservative and traditional. So, too – at least in these years – was Franz Ferdinand, but the uncle suspected otherwise. He believed that his nephew secretly harboured dangerous liberal ideas; it was an irrational fear, based on nothing more than unsavoury rumours and Franz Ferdinand's friendship with the late, unfortunate Rudolf. Never able to overcome his personal prejudices, the emperor simply transferred his disappointment from the deceased Rudolf to the living Franz Ferdinand. Yet, ever the bastion of tradition, Franz Josef bowed to fate. Karl Ludwig was, after all, nearly sixty, and while he might outlive his elder brother by a few years, he would undoubtedly have a short reign. It was inevitable that Franz Ferdinand would one day – perhaps one day soon – come to the throne. There were even rumours that Karl Ludwig tried to extricate himself from the succession only to have the emperor refuse, so doubtful was Franz Josef about his nephew's political inclinations and temperament.[44]

The meeting between uncle and nephew was brief and uncomfortable, and Franz Ferdinand was left with the distinct impression that the emperor somehow blamed him for Rudolf's suicide. 'It's as if this stupidity of Mayerling was my fault,' he supposedly complained after the meeting. 'I have never been treated so coldly before. It seems that the mere sight of me awakens unpleasant memories.' Franz Ferdinand had expected to be made heir presumptive in theory if not in name, but Franz Josef refused to do so. It was as if acknowledging that the nephew now stood in his dead son's place was too great a concession, too painful a wound. 'I shall never know', Franz Ferdinand said, 'whether I'm Heir or not.'[45]

Franz Josef was left unimpressed. Throughout the meeting, he complained, his nephew had 'looked very pale and seemed to be suffering from a chronic cough'. Franz Ferdinand didn't inspire confidence. 'I don't think much of him,' Franz Josef confessed. 'One can't compare him with Rudolf. He is *very* different.'[46] Just how different the two young men were no one could yet say. Time would reveal Franz Ferdinand's strengths and weaknesses, yet more than blood would tie the two cousins together: both of Franz Josef's ill-fated heirs prematurely fell victim to bullets.

TWO

Adventure and Illness

✠

The excesses of Franz Ferdinand's youthful privilege gave way to a more contemplative, responsible character in the wake of Mayerling. He curtailed his hunting, his indulgent escapades, and the wilder pleasures so beloved by his brother Otto. There was still talk of a mistress, a young woman named Mila Kugler supposedly installed in an apartment conveniently close to Franz Ferdinand's Palais Modena in Vienna. The stories brought further warnings from the nosy old Archduke Albrecht. Franz Ferdinand, he insisted, must not follow the example of 'poor Rudolf' but instead live according to his future position.[1]

Albrecht needn't have worried. Franz Ferdinand was back with the army, promoted to colonel and given command of the 9th Hussars Regiment stationed at Ödenburg (now Sopron) in Hungary. The two years he spent there forever coloured his view of Hungarians. German was the official language in the empire's army; the archduke was shocked that Hungarian officers ignored this and issued orders in Magyar. Yet if a Bohemian soldier dared utter a word in his own language, the Hungarians ruthlessly beat him.[2] Budapest, Franz Ferdinand thought, was a disloyal and dangerous hotbed of provocative nationalism calling for revolt against Habsburg rule. 'We are constantly regaled', he complained, 'with the myth of the many loyal and honest elements which may be found in Hungary. I simply will not believe in it any longer.'[3]

Ill health and restlessness rescued Franz Ferdinand from Hungary. In 1892, suffering from weak lungs and looking ahead to his future duties, the archduke hit on the idea of a voyage around the world.[4] This would remove him from the frosty European winter while also broadening his experiences. Franz Josef was not at all convinced about the wisdom of such an adventure. He believed that he had done perfectly well on the throne without benefit of such a far-ranging journey, but Franz Ferdinand appealed to the one person he knew would be sympathetic: his aunt Empress Elisabeth. She, who spent her life roving the Continent, understood her nephew's desire to see something of the world and interceded with her husband, finally winning the emperor's permission.[5]

Royal princes and aristocrats often ended their formal educations with such a journey, but few were as adventurous as Franz Ferdinand. His progress would literally take him around the globe, something no other Austrian archduke had ever attempted. His departure on 15 December 1892, aboard the new armored cruiser *Kaiserin Elisabeth*, proved surprisingly emotional. His entire family saw him off. It would be the first Christmas Franz Ferdinand had spent away from them, and as he watched the coastline recede he was suddenly overcome. 'Deep inside', he confided to the diary he would keep religiously throughout the voyage, 'came the sinking feeling of an infinite longing for the homeland . . . It was homesickness, which I had never known before.'[6] Not that he was alone. A sizeable retinue of chamberlains and minders, servants and cooks, and even a taxidermist, along with his cousin Archduke Leopold Ferdinand, joined him on the cruise. They would keep him comfortable, steer him away from danger, smooth any ruffled diplomatic feathers, and entertain the uncertain young man throughout his adventure.[7]

From Trieste the party cruised down the Dalmatian coast, stopping briefly in Egypt before sailing to India. Hoping to escape unwelcome attention, Franz Ferdinand used the name Count von Hohenberg for much of the trip, though he couldn't evade the embassies and local officials who regularly greeted him with elaborate ceremonial welcomes. His time in British India caused endless worries in London. The future Tsar Nicholas II had visited the exotic country the previous year, and troublesome issues of precedence had caused unintended offence. Only after the personal intervention of the Prince of Wales and a dozen letters between Calcutta and London was the archduke granted a place of honour immediately after the viceroy.[8]

Lack of proficiency in English hampered Franz Ferdinand in this outpost of British colonialism. Officials deemed him 'considerate and amiable', noting his welcome desire 'to be relieved from ceremony as much as possible'.[9] He visited Agra and the famed Taj Mahal, apparently deeply impressed by this monument to love, and generally created good impressions wherever he went. 'He has excellent manners,' reported the Viceroy, 'but is perfectly natural and unaffected, and was very friendly and considerate in his demeanour towards all, whether European or native, with whom he came into contact during his stay.'[10]

Like other aristocratic visitors to the subcontinent, Franz Ferdinand shot tigers, panthers and boars. He liked this much better than the tedious ceremonial dinners he was often forced to endure, though he narrowly escaped disaster in Ceylon when an elephant charged his battue.[11] Hunting continued in the Australian outback, with his prized kangaroos and emus promptly stuffed and shipped back to Austria.[12]

However, hunting could not mask a growing problem aboard ship. The archduke and his cousin Leopold, noted Admiral Miklós Horthy, 'were temperamentally so different' that he had predicted trouble if they travelled together.[13] Leopold freely admitted that he and Franz Ferdinand 'had long detested one another'. Given to melodramatic, highly questionable flights of fancy, Leopold deemed his cousin 'a cad', a man 'utterly lacking in even the remotest glimmer of sensibility or finer feelings'. Each night, he said, Franz Ferdinand drank himself into a stupor, shouting that he was glad Rudolf had killed himself, calling the emperor 'that stupid old boy', and pondering how he could 'get the old man out of the way'. Unwilling to put up with such scenes any longer, Leopold requested a transfer to another vessel.[14]

This was Leopold's version, given long after his cousin's death; the truth was quite different. Claims of drunken quarrels and indiscreet talk disguised problems between the two men that went deeper than mere personality conflicts. Leopold used his position as a Habsburg archduke to belligerent advantage, snobbishly refusing to dine with his fellow officers. Miserable aboard the vessel, he didn't let a day pass without loudly expressing his hope that the ship would sink and relieve him from duty. Even worse was Leopold's supposed infatuation with attractive young sailors. Although he wouldn't associate with the officers, he had no such hesitation when it came to the crew and spent most of his time locked away with one particularly handsome cadet. To avoid further scandal, Franz Ferdinand had Leopold put off the vessel in Sydney.[15]

This tense situation behind him, Franz Ferdinand journeyed to Hong Kong and then Japan, meeting the emperor and posing for photographs wrapped in a kimono and looking distinctly unwell.[16] On 26 August he left Yokohama aboard the gleaming white Canadian Pacific liner *Empress of China* for North America. It was quite a change from the Austrian warship. The archduke mingled with ordinary first class passengers, played tennis on deck with a lady he befriended, and complained that only American girls dared dance with him at night.[17]

The archduke got his first glimpse of North America when the ship docked in Vancouver on 5 September. A young woman, eager to spot so exotic a creature as the heir to a European throne, forced her way onto the vessel, shouting, 'The Prince! The Prince! Where is the Prince!'[18] He travelled south to Washington State, visiting Spokane on 19 September only to find his train surrounded by more anxious young women hoping to meet him. The city, he thought, was oddly intriguing, like some desolate, obscure Asian village, but before he could explore he was bundled aboard a private Pullman carriage for the trip east. A rocky train ride brought him to Yellowstone. The lobby of the Hot Springs Hotel, he complained, was full of curious cowboys spitting tobacco juice. He went off to see the famed Old Faithful but was irritated when rangers prevented him from shooting protected game within the park. Frustrated, Franz Ferdinand picked off a skunk, a porcupine, and several squirrels to add to his collection.[19]

Reporters swamped Franz Ferdinand's train when it arrived in Omaha, jostling, shouting questions, and thrusting outstretched hands at him, an unfamiliar experience that left him thoroughly disgruntled.[20] He arrived in Chicago, reported the local newspaper, having enjoyed a hearty breakfast of 'fruits of all kinds, beef steak, ham and eggs, game and wine, including champagne'.[21] He deemed the city dirty and uninspiring and was annoyed by the constant pushing crowds when he visited the World's Columbian Exposition. Smartly, the archduke concealed his distaste when he met with a group of reporters. Perhaps his fluency had improved during the journey as, according to the *Chicago Tribune*, he spoke in 'excellent English', commenting, 'I was at the fair for only a short time . . . and could see but comparatively little of it. I was much pleased with what I did see and I regret that I could not stay much longer to see more of it.'[22]

After a stop to see Niagara Falls, the archduke was off to New York City. He arrived 'just like any other ordinary, plain, everyday citizen and without the flourish of trumpets,' reported the *New York Herald Tribune*.[23] He dined at the famed Delmonico's Restaurant and attended the theatre, but he found this city even more noisy and discouraging than Chicago. Everywhere he went, it seemed, Americans were preoccupied with 'the Almighty Dollar'. Worse, he was surprised that such a large and prosperous country seemed to have no arrangements for the relief of the poor. 'For the working class', he wrote, 'freedom means freedom to starve.'[24] After ten months and some fifty thousand miles, a French liner finally returned Franz Ferdinand to the familiar shores of Europe, along with thirty-seven cases packed with hunting trophies, weapons from Polynesia, snowshoes from the Rocky Mountains, Native American crafts, ornate dolls from Japan, and intricately carved jade from the Orient.[25]

The tour left Franz Ferdinand convinced of two things. First, Austria, he was certain, needed a stronger navy. Great Britain had conquered much of the globe through her naval power; although he harboured no such aspirations, the archduke thought that a modern fleet would at least help Austria combat any foreign intervention in its remaining coastal provinces. Second, despite his ambiguous feelings about America, Franz

Ferdinand saw in the country and its disparate population a possible model for his own future empire. A union of federal states under centralized authority, he thought, might offer a solution to Austria-Hungary's diverse ethnicities and competing national identities.

Informative and entertaining press accounts had let readers share the archduke's foreign adventures. Franz Ferdinand's future subjects learned even more about him when his lengthy travel diary became a book under the guidance of former tutor Max Vladimir Beck. When the volumes appeared, their sentiments and literary quality seemed so unlike the cold Franz Ferdinand people knew that many wrongly assumed Beck had written them. This infuriated Franz Ferdinand. He hadn't wanted to publish the entries, and to have people question his authorship seemed an outrageous assault. 'People', he bitterly commented, 'simply believe that every Archduke just has to be a nincompoop.'[26]

After the excitement of his world tour, the archduke returned to the military. This time he escaped Hungary, taking up a position as major general in command of the 38th Infantry Brigade at Budweis (now České Budějovice) in Bohemia. Franz Ferdinand was a bit more cynical about life, a bit more irritable, and a bit more pronounced in his dislikes, carefully concealing his surprisingly sentimental side behind a stern facade. Occasional displays of temper and his bristly personality led his comrades to dub him 'the Ogre'.[27] He wasn't quite as bad as the nickname suggests, but he could still be ruthless when it came to incompetence. On learning that the regimental band had ignored a young corporal's funeral in favour of an appearance at a local celebration, he erupted in anger. 'You let the poor corporal go to his last rest without music just to have a few extra bandsmen at a peasants' dance!' he shouted at the commander. 'It's a downright shame!' Soon the chastised officer handed in his resignation.[28]

Time in Bohemia, as in Hungary before it, ultimately fell victim to the archduke's failing health. Pale, dangerously thin, and coughing blood, Franz Ferdinand reluctantly agreed to see a doctor in the summer of 1895. Victor Eisenmenger, a young physician at Vienna's Schrötter Clinic, quickly diagnosed pulmonary tuberculosis, though he carefully kept the grave news from his new patient. It was up to Eisenmenger to save the archduke from the disease that had killed his mother. When Eisenmenger proposed a period of forced rest, Franz Ferdinand's chamberlain, Count Leo Wurmbrand, scoffed, 'This will be very difficult. The Archduke is accustomed to a mode of living that is exactly the opposite of the one that you are proposing to him. Hardly any place will keep him for more than a day. I have not slept in a bed for a fortnight, always on the train.'[29]

It took the emperor's intervention to force the issue. 'I must draw your attention most urgently to the fact that it is your most sacred duty to now only live for your health,' he wrote to his nephew. 'You must go to a quiet place in the mountains as soon as possible and take it very easy there . . . and above all, follow the instructions of your attending doctors right down to the last detail. That is the only way to get your health back, and I hope, just a little for my sake, that you will be a little patient and persevering even though it will be relatively monotonous.'[30]

Franz Ferdinand reluctantly allowed Eisenmenger to usher him to a remote hotel in the Dolomites, where, it was hoped, the mountain air would improve his weak lungs. The archduke found the forced leisure difficult. Always restless, he passed his days shooting the branches off nearby trees or playing with his little fox terrier, Mucki. 'No man can stand this!' he finally complained. 'You are locking me up like a wild animal.' Faced with such a difficult patient, Eisenmenger finally told the archduke the truth about his tuberculosis. A sullen Franz Ferdinand said nothing, but his father, Karl Ludwig, who had come to visit, was not so reticent. 'My son', he sombrely confided to Eisenmenger, 'will not recover.'[31]

Archduchess Maria Theresa urged Eisenmenger to be more vigorous in his orders, offering subtle demonstrations of tender corrections: 'Franzi, it is too cold in the corridor. There, take your shawl.' 'Franzi, it is windy. Put on your overcoat.' 'There is too much smoke in the smoking room.' 'When it is so cold you should not go out at night.'[32] The archduke always obeyed, but Eisenmenger didn't have the same emotional hold over him that Maria Theresa did. Thinking he would have more success in a different environment, he suggested an extended holiday in Egypt, which would offer diversion and the benefit of warm weather.[33]

There was a bit of unpleasantness as soon as Franz Ferdinand arrived in Cairo. 'I need quiet,' he confessed, and asked that there be no receptions or ceremonial welcomes. As soon as he arrived at the Hotel Gezireh, however, he spotted Austria's ambassador, Count Heidler von Egeregg, standing in the lobby, armed with a ceremonial speech and surrounded by a bevy of embassy officials shuffling obsequiously toward him. Franz Ferdinand raced through the lobby and hid in his suite, refusing to come out. 'I purposely behaved so badly,' he admitted, 'to show that no one could force me to do anything!' The count was furious, loudly insisting that the archduke's behaviour proved he was unfit for the throne. He had his revenge a few weeks later during a Sunday mass. Franz Ferdinand asked to be seated with the congregation; the count ignored him and led him to a raised dais at the front of the cathedral, where the archduke would be on public display throughout the service. It was the thing he hated most. 'I cannot endure having people stare at me!' Franz Ferdinand complained.[34]

After visiting museums, the pyramids, and shopping in Cairo's bazaars, the archduke settled into a rented boat for a cruise along the Nile. At first, the very scenery offered diversion: the long, low river, the beggar children crowding the reed-choked banks, the moon rising above ancient monuments. There was even a performance by several belly dancers aboard the vessel, though Franz Ferdinand wasn't amused.[35] He felt imprisoned on the boat. 'What I have suffered alone during this whole month on this nineteenth-century instrument of torture!' he wrote to his stepmother, 'cannot be described, and that also goes for how much I long for you . . . And now I kiss your hands and look madly forward to your arrival, which will save me from going raving mad!'[36]

With his physical state gradually improving, but tired of his illness, the archduke travelled to the Riviera, striking up a friendship with Tsar Nicholas II's tubercular brother, Grand Duke George Alexandrovich. He was astonished that George came and went at will and could do whatever he liked while he himself was under Eisenmenger's control. 'He goes to the casino, to the theatre, and to balls,' he complained to Eisenmenger, 'while I am being locked up in this fashion. I will not submit to it any longer!'[37] Eisenmenger's care actually saved Franz Ferdinand while the Grand Duke eventually died, but all the archduke could see was his continued isolation. A newspaper clipping from Budapest did nothing to improve his mood. The archduke, the article reported, was gravely ill; if he died, true Hungarian patriots would rejoice. 'I think it is positively incomprehensible,' he angrily wrote, 'and possible only in Hungary that one of the most widely read newspapers in a state which up to now is still monarchical is permitted to print such a degrading infamy about a member of the Ruling House.'[38] This only further reinforced his negative attitudes toward his future Magyar subjects.

Medical exile soon gave way to familial expediency in May 1896. While travelling with his family in Palestine after their visit to Franz Ferdinand in Egypt, Karl Ludwig was apparently overcome by religious ecstasy. Ignoring warnings, he drank polluted water from the River Jordan; by the time he had returned to Vienna, typhoid had set in.[39] A cable from his stepmother sent Franz Ferdinand running for the express train, but before he could reach Vienna word came that his father had died. His father's death, coupled with illness and the pressures of being back in Vienna, nearly broke him; fearing a relapse, Eisenmenger quickly swept him away from the capital to continue his cure.[40]

A series of events during his absence from Vienna cemented Franz Ferdinand's dislike of the imperial court in general, and of Prince Alfred de Montenuovo, the emperor's *Obersthofmeister,* or Lord High Chamberlain, in particular. Was it underlying worry over the archduke's unpredictable temperament that caused what happened next? Did people fear that Franz Ferdinand was either a dangerous liberal bent on destroying the old order or a bigoted reactionary who posed a danger to the stability of the throne? Or was it his illness that led some to write him off? The latter, at least, is what the archduke thought, suspecting that his 'enemies at court and in politics' were using his illness 'to isolate him' and 'render him impotent'. Montenuovo, thought Eisenmenger, delighted in 'the most brutal conduct' and already counted the archduke 'among the dead'.[41] He joined with Foreign Minister

Count Agenor Goluchowski in attempting to push Franz Ferdinand aside and promote his younger brother Otto as successor to the throne.[42]

The idea was absurd. By 1896, Otto was widely regarded as the most disreputable of Habsburg archdukes, 'one of the worst men who ever lived,' insisted one aristocrat.[43] Following his loveless marriage to Princess Maria Josepha, daughter of King Georg of Saxony, Otto had been wildly unfaithful and made no attempt to hide the fact, haunting brothels and seducing women across the capital.[44] Franz Josef refused to intercede. He had always favoured Otto over the cold Franz Ferdinand and dismissed his nephew's scandalous behaviour as nothing more than 'youthful folly'.[45]

Franz Ferdinand had a small suite of rooms in the Habsburgs' main Viennese palace, the Hofburg; at Goluchowski's prodding, the emperor gave Otto the immense Augarten Palace, an imposing residence eminently suited to a possible heir to the throne. Franz Ferdinand was ignored, but Otto received a household and personal court of officials. Franz Ferdinand remained hidden, but Otto now carried out public duties in the emperor's name and even received official reports from government ministers. In 1896, when Tsar Nicholas II and his wife paid a state visit to Vienna, Franz Ferdinand was pointedly excluded from the receptions and imperial dinner; the following year, Franz Josef took Otto, not Franz Ferdinand, on his return visit to St Petersburg.[46]

Such public snubs did not go unnoticed in Vienna. Rumour held that Franz Ferdinand would soon be excluded from the succession, and popular newspapers insisted that he was barely clinging to life.[47] All this, he insisted, amounted to an effort to 'bury him alive'.[48] To Countess Marie Thun-Hohenstein, wife of his shooting friend Count Jaroslav and his eventual sister-in-law, the archduke wrote, 'I am deeply wounded and angry at being treated, although I am still alive, as if "past my expiration date". My brother is now established by the court as royal heir.'[49] To Countess Nora Fugger, Franz Ferdinand complained, 'You will understand that in this pathetic and humiliating situation into which I find myself forced, an heir to the throne placed, so to speak, on paid leave of absence, I don't want to show myself in Vienna and have nothing to look for there. It is unbelievable what

Goluchowski, who believes he is some sort of god, and his followers think up just to affront me and alienate me and simply kill me off morally.' He did not blame the weak-willed Otto but instead saved his wrath for the officials behind the situation. 'I am not considered any longer but simply ignored. If they were at least decent enough to ask me whether this bothered me or that could be entrusted to my brother I shouldn't be so upset during my illness. But everything is decreed behind my back and as if I am already dead.'[50]

Contrary to expectations and even hopes, Franz Ferdinand recovered. He emerged from his illness stronger, his frame fuller, and his chest wide and muscular, a far cry from the pale and thin invalid. In fact, noted the Duchess of Edinburgh when the archduke visited London for Queen Victoria's Diamond Jubilee in 1897, he had 'grown into a fat, healthy-looking man'.[51] In March 1898, newspapers in Vienna announced that the archduke would begin to undertake certain duties at the emperor's request and that he had been granted use of the magnificent Belvedere Palace in Vienna, along with a personal household suited to his position.[52]

Despite the changes, Franz Ferdinand never received the title of crown prince. Everyone knew he would inherit the throne, but Franz Josef seemed reluctant to grant his nephew the title Rudolf had once held. When it came to discussions about the future, the emperor always put him off. Franz Josef loathed uncomfortable situations, and with no particular liking for his nephew, he found the idea of a serious meeting about his role an awkward intrusion. 'Like you', he had confided to Franz Ferdinand, 'I have long felt the need to discuss with you all the questions you raise in your letter and much else besides. I have only refrained as you are unwell and doing so might damage your health, for our discussion will be serious and not altogether agreeable; hopefully however it will lead to an understanding and convince you that I only want what is best for you though I must always keep in mind my duty towards the monarchy and the welfare of our family.'[53]

The emperor could have used his nephew's support. The year 1898 not only saw Franz Josef's fiftieth anniversary on the throne but also, as often happened in the last years of Habsburg rule, devastating tragedy.

On 10 September an Italian anarchist stabbed the reclusive Empress Elisabeth to death as she strolled along the shores of Lake Geneva. 'No one', Franz Josef cried in anguish, 'will ever know how much I loved her!'[54] Relations between Franz Ferdinand and his aunt had always been warm, if marred by her frequent absences from Austria, and her support and moderating influence on the emperor would undoubtedly have played a crucial role in the coming, tumultuous years.

Franz Ferdinand was, like his uncle, accustomed to tragedies. Having lost his mother, his father, his favourite cousin, and his understanding aunt, he was now estranged from Otto. During his illness, he learned, his younger brother had belittled his condition and mocked him in public, and the knowledge filled him with 'great bitterness'.[55] At times Franz Ferdinand seemed adrift, and he remained an enigma. Lacking the emperor's courtly manner or his brother's handsome demeanour, he appeared to the public as a serious, strangely aloof man. No one could quite work him out. Winning courtesies alternated with startling displays of emotion, and he could never conceal his contempt for those deemed fools or sycophants. Illness and malicious treatment left him angry. Hurt by the way he had been written off, pushed aside, and plotted against, Franz Ferdinand was forever suspicious.[56] 'You always start out', he explained to one man, 'believing that everyone is an angel, and you'll learn by sad experience. I, on the other hand, regard every man I meet as a scoundrel. In time, he can prove to me that I should have a better opinion.'[57]

Speculation ran wild. Some people suspected that the archduke, like his dead cousin Rudolf, opposed the emperor's conservative policies; just as many were convinced that Franz Ferdinand was a narrow-minded reactionary. This curious archduke seemed to evoke both hope and fear in his future subjects, but he was so mysterious that no one could claim to know the truth. The only thing that seemed certain was that he was a hard man, completely lacking in charm, averse to all ordinary human emotions. This belief was soon shattered when, much to the public's astonishment, they learned that this apparently unsentimental archduke was at the centre of a romance destined to rock the very foundations of the Habsburg monarchy.

THREE

Romance

✣

'Let others make war,' went the empire's unofficial motto; 'you, happy Austria, marry!'[1] Marriage, much to the imperial family's consternation, was just what Franz Ferdinand had pointedly avoided. His sister, Margarethe Sophie, had been married to Albrecht, Duke of Württemberg, for fifteen years; even Otto had a wife and two sons. As 1899 began, the thirty-five-year-old heir presumptive was still single.

'There has always been a certain amount of romance attached to the name of this Archduke,' insisted a turn-of-the-century chronicler, 'in connection with his resistance to all efforts on the part of his relatives and the Austrian government to marry him off to some royal princess.'[2] There were always rumours. Some gossips erroneously insisted that he was in love with Rudolf's widow, Stephanie; talk that he would marry the rather plain Princess Mathilde of Saxony came to nothing.[3] Efforts over the beautiful Princess Hélène of Orléans, daughter of the comte de Paris, were more substantial. 'If he saw Princess Helene of Orleans, her physical and moral qualities might perhaps touch his heart,' a diplomat insisted.[4]

Potential brides were constantly thrown at Franz Ferdinand when he visited London in 1894. 'I felt uncomfortable,' he confided to his future sister-in-law Countess Marie Thun-Hohenstein, 'for the designated fian-cées moved about in a great herd and showed worrisome levels of persis-tence. I sat next to one of these victims on the prowl. The parents, smiles plastered on their faces . . . examined me with rapt attention . . . but as my chosen conversation revolved around the weather, the outlook for favourable harvests, the economy, and similar subjects, I can't have given a very favourable impression.'[5] Another potential bride was deemed 'very amusing, but often had problems with the German lan-guage'. Franz Ferdinand encountered Princess Hélène during a lun-cheon given by the Prince of Wales. Hélène, he wrote with tongue firmly in cheek, 'was seated next to me in so sudden a fashion and in a natural, completely uncalculated way'. He deemed her 'by the far the most jolly and prettiest of the lot, but she has the disadvantage of only speaking French. I had to chitchat in French, and made error after error, which the good lady corrected with undying patience. The Count of Paris, while spying on his "son-in-law", made encouraging signs to his daugh-ter and the parents gave a champagne toast to her health, as if anticipat-ing the joyful celebration to come. During the meal I was dreadfully embarrassed, and felt cold sweat dripping down my forehead.'[6] Yet in the end, Franz Ferdinand was unmoved.

Baron Albert von Margutti, one of the emperor's aides-de-camp, thought that the archduke hoped to marry one of the Prince of Wales's three daughters.[7] Whether he meant Victoria, the middle daughter, or Maud, the youngest, is unknown, nor does the idea seem to have gener-ated any serious discussion.[8] As late as January 1900, the powerful and ambitious Grand Duchess Vladimir of Russia was pondering the idea of marrying off her only daughter, Elena, to the future emperor of Austria-Hungary.[9]

Franz Ferdinand could not simply marry as he wished. As a member of the imperial house, he had to obey the Family Statutes of 1839. His bride must be Catholic and of equal rank; he also had to gain the emperor's permission to marry. Failure to do so meant expulsion from the dynasty and loss of titles and revenues. He could choose from any Catholic royal family, like those in Bavaria, Spain, Belgium, or Portugal, or from any of the numerous German Protestant reigning houses provided the bride converted. He could even select a bride from one of the mediatized houses scattered across Europe, a designation given to certain formerly reigning families recognized as *ebenbürtig*, equal for the purposes of marriage in the 1815 Act of German Confederation or in an 1825 decision by Emperor Franz I of Austria. The traditional rules were strictly enforced. 'If one of my position loves somebody,' Franz Ferdinand once said, 'some trifle in her family tree which makes a marriage impossible is sure to be found. So it comes about that with us man and wife are always related to each other twenty times over. The result is that half of the children are idiots!'[10]

It was not the idea of marriage that scared the archduke. As early as 1888, he wrote to his cousin Rudolf, somewhat tongue in cheek, that he had 'adopted the firm resolve, since it's the only possibility of becoming an eminent member of our family and of leading a pleasant, carefree life', to ask for the hand of some or other princess, 'alias Wax Doll', as he deemed her.[11] 'It would certainly be high time,' he later agreed of all the marital talk, though he seemed reluctant to act.[12] His aunt Empress Elisabeth warned him against accepting any arranged marriage. 'Only marry the woman you love,' she insisted, 'and not one of our blood, or you'll have dreadful children.'[13] To his confidant Countess Nora Fugger, he admitted that he longed 'for peace, for a cozy home, and a family. But I put to you the big question: Whom should I then marry? There is nobody there. You say, Countess, that I should have a wife who is kind, clever, beautiful and good. That's good, but tell me, where can such a woman be found? Sadly, there is nobody to choose from among the marriageable princesses; they are all children, chicks of seventeen or eighteen, one uglier than the other. And I am too old, and have neither the time nor the inclination to educate my own wife. I can readily imagine the ideal woman as I want her to be and with whom I could also be happy: She should not be too young and her character and views should be fully mature. I know of no such princess.'[14]

Perhaps he knew of no such princess, but when he wrote this letter Franz Ferdinand had discovered a woman who fulfilled nearly all of his requirements. She, like Nora Fugger, was aristocratic, a woman of mature age and refined sensibilities, a countess far removed from the petty squabbles and vacuous concerns of the imperial court. Sophie Chotek traced her ancestry back to medieval Bohemian lords with strong ties to the country's history. She even shared his Habsburg descent, albeit from Albert IV, a thirteenth-century count; other marriages tied the family to the Hohenzollern dynasty in Prussia, the Royal House of Baden, and the princes of Liechtenstein. After the Hussite Wars the Choteks, unlike many of their compatriots, remained staunchly Catholic and proved their dedication to the Habsburg throne; in reward, two ancestors had been knights of the prestigious Austrian Order of the Golden Fleece. Choteks had been Bohemian barons since 1556, counts of Bohemia since 1723, and counts of the empire since 1745.[15] As members of the highest Bohemian nobility, the Chotek family occupied a prominent place among the country's elite, having served as provincial governors, ministers to Empress Maria Theresa, and courtiers to Emperor Josef II.[16]

On the surface it was illustrious and promising. Sophie could boast not merely the sixteen noble quarterings needed for admission to the most exclusive court functions but thirty-two uninterrupted generations of aristocratic descent. Distinguished ancestors aside, though, the Choteks lacked the one thing necessary to marry a Habsburg: equal status. Barons, counts, courtiers, and diplomats though they were, the family had never been deemed equal for the purposes of marriage. There was simply no way around the issue. Nevertheless, heart lost and head full of romance, Franz Ferdinand plunged into his own romantic fairy tale with abandon.

Much about Franz Ferdinand's Cinderella was indeed captivating. Charming and beautiful, Sophie Chotek was also cosmopolitan, intelligent and vivacious. Titles and illustrious ancestors, though, had failed to shield her from some of the more unpleasant realities of life. No good fairy tale is complete without youthful hardships and uncertainties, and

Sophie certainly had her share of them. Wealth and privilege had surrounded her grandfather Count Karl Chotek. He had been a diplomat
under Emperor Franz I, serving as district governor of Moravia, governor of the Tyrol, and minister of the police in Bohemia. But on his death
in 1868, his fortune went to his oldest surviving son; Bohuslav received
estates at Grosspriesen (now Velké Březno) and Ciwitz, but little money.
In 1848, at the age of nineteen, he had followed in his father's footsteps,
entering diplomatic service as an attaché at the Austrian Embassy in
Dresden. Within a decade he had a pretty young wife, Countess Wilhelmina Kinsky von Wchinitz, whom he married in 1859. The Kinskys
were one of the most distinguished Bohemian aristocratic families, with
a long history of imperial service and artistic patronage, counting among
their protégés Ludwig van Beethoven.[17] Where Bohuslav was short and
rather unremarkable in appearance, his nineteen-year-old wife, known
as Mintzy, was 'very attractive, extremely intelligent and clever, and she
helped mightily in her husband's career'.[18]

Life as a diplomat was uncertain and demanded constant moves.
There was a respite in 1871, when Count Bohuslav was named provincial governor in Prague. For two months the family lived in the
governor-general's palace at the foot of the immense Hradschin Castle,
but this ended when the government collapsed amid contentious efforts
to equalize Bohemian status within the empire. Diplomatic assign-
ments took Bohuslav from Dresden to Madrid, from St Petersburg to
Brussels, but in the spring of 1868 he was in Stuttgart for his first independent post, serving as Austrian ambassador to the royal court of
Württemberg. Here, on 1 March, Wilhelmina gave birth to a daughter
the couple named Sophie Maria Josephine Albina, Countess Chotek
von Chotkowa und Wognin. Called 'Sopherl', she joined her eight-
year-old brother, Wolfgang, and sisters Zdenka, Marie and Karolina,
ages seven, five and three. Four more children followed: Therese, who
died in infancy in 1871; Oktavia, in 1873; Antonia, in 1874; and Henriette, in 1880.

They were a loving, devoted family, and the children were brought up very simply due to limited finances. Count Bohuslav had no inherited fortune; his Bohemian estate at Ciwitz was a comfortable retreat for happy memories, but it produced no income, and Wilhelmina had brought no great dowry to the marriage. He was completely reliant on his diplomatic salary, but postings as attaché and secretary brought meagre financial rewards. The Austrian government was notoriously thrifty with diplomatic salaries when compared to its European counterparts. His ambassadorial stipend of 23,600 gulden (approximately £150,000 in 2013 figures) was earmarked for official embassy costs and formal entertaining on behalf of the Austro-Hungarian Empire, not to provide for a family's needs. In most cases, this wasn't a problem, as ambassadors usually came from the ranks of wealthy aristocrats, but for Bohuslav, lack of any private fortune meant that his salary of 6,300 gulden (approximately £40,000 in 2013 figures) had to stretch to bring up his eight children. Life as ambassador in Madrid had proved so expensive that after a few months the count had asked for reassignment to the more modest Brussels; even then he had to borrow money from a bank to finance the move. In some ways, Sophie's youth mirrored traditional lore: the beautiful girl of low fortune, awaiting rescue. Bohuslav had no head for money, and he spent lavishly, to the point that his family often had to do without. Luxuries were certainly absent, servants were few, dresses for the girls were plain, and Sophie and her siblings rode public trams to save money.[19]

Hopes for a secure future rested on Bohuslav's diplomatic skills. The count was a popular ambassador in Brussels, and his wife's friendship with King Leopold's consort, Queen Marie Henriette (after whom they named their youngest daughter), seemed to bear fruit when it became known that Crown Prince Rudolf was seeking a bride. Who better, it was suggested, than the king's fifteen-year-old daughter, Stephanie? She was young, not unattractive, and Catholic; with the king's blessing, Bohuslav brought Rudolf to Brussels. Both the count and his wife, with their two eldest daughters, attended the intimate royal breakfast at Laeken Palace as Rudolf studied his proposed bride; Sophie, at thirteen, was deemed too young to attend. Still pliable to his father's wishes, the crown prince agreed to the engagement. Bohuslav envisioned great rewards from negotiating the union – perhaps the rank of prince, a financial settlement, and a more prominent posting. It was not to be; when Rudolf and Stephanie's marriage crumbled, so did all hopes of an improved situation.[20]

Financial difficulties eventually forced the family from Brussels to Dresden. The Saxon court did not demand such extravagant displays, and the city was cheaper for a diplomat of meagre means. Only son Wolfgang entered the civil service; Zdenka obtained a position as a lady-in-waiting to Crown Princess Stephanie in Vienna; Karolina married Count Leopold Nostitz-Rieneck in 1886, and Marie married Count Jaroslav Thun und Hohenstein the following year. However, there were still four young daughters at home, and new responsibilities fell to Sophie when her mother died in June 1888. Rather than return to Austria, Bohuslav remained in Dresden when his diplomatic career ended, as he could stretch his pension further there than in his native land.[21]

Constant scrimping and saving had shaped Sophie's world. She had travelled across Europe to glamorous capitals and watched as her parents mingled with princes and kings, but opportunities for indulgence had been rare. She adored music, played the dulcimer, and was a gifted pianist; although she longed to attend the theatre and opera, lack of money often precluded such extravagance. Social life was extremely difficult. Chotek and Kinsky ancestry opened aristocratic doors, but the customary sweep of elaborate dinners, glittering balls, elegant teas, and refined soirées was simply too expensive for Sophie and her siblings. Because her parents had never been able to entertain on a lavish scale, there were few reciprocal invitations for their children. Vienna, with its rigidly defined social distinctions and wealthy gossips, was not hospitable ground. A courtier recalled how Sophie and her sisters once arrived for some gathering only to be met by brittle Viennese tongues. They were alone, without a maid to tend to their needs, and servants noticed that their shoes had been mended with thread to save money.[22]

By twenty Sophie had grown into a lovely young woman, tall and thin, her dark hair luxuriantly coiled atop her head and a fringe across her brow framing expressive brown eyes. More elegant than pretty, more stately than beautiful, Sophie was graceful, serene and dignified. She was well educated, having acquired not only the usual lessons in history, literature, mathematics, religion and science but also a keen grasp of political affairs from her father. She could converse in German, English and French fluently and stumble through a few words in Czech; she danced elegantly, painted, rode, and played tennis well. Clever and charming, unpretentious and 'very affable', she was both worldly and shy, with an almost childlike optimism and a mischievous sense of humour that endeared her to all of her nieces and nephews.[23]

Yet Sophie's assets could not outweigh reality. She might attract the attention of a minor aristocrat and make a suitable marriage, but her father could not entice potential suitors with an extravagant dowry. Unless and until love came her way, Sophie had only two acceptable choices for an independent life outside of her father's house. Impoverished aristocratic ladies could join convents and become nuns, or they could enter service as a governess or lady-in-waiting. Deeply religious though she was, it was still too early for Sophie to abandon hopes for a rewarding marriage. On the other hand, she perfectly fitted the requirements for a *Hofdame*, or lady-in-waiting. In the Austrian court, the position was filled not by elderly aristocrats but rather by young, unmarried ladies of noble background, educated in social niceties, pleasant to look at, with a gift for languages and, above all, a servile attitude.[24] Enquiries in Vienna revealed that Archduke Friedrich's wife, Isabella, required an additional lady-in-waiting; Sophie passed muster with Countess Simon Wimpffen, who as Isabella's *Obersthofmeisterin*, or mistress of the robes, was in charge of her household, and in short order Isabella deemed the young countess a suitable addition. On 10 August 1888, Sophie joined the archduchess's household as *Hofdame*.[25]

The formidable and rotund Princess Isabella of Croÿ had married Archduke Friedrich in 1878 and produced, much to her consternation, a string of eight daughters; not until 1897 would a son finally arrive. In

Franz Ferdinand and Sophie's fairy tale, Isabella plays the role of wicked stepmother. Ambition and a sense of inferiority clashed in Isabella with disastrous results. She was an unrepentant snob, 'self righteous' and 'not easy to serve', as one of her ladies-in-waiting complained.[26] Even her husband found her erratic and took to extended regimental tours simply to escape her volatile temper, preferring the drill sergeants on the field to the one who ruled his house.[27]

Life with the imperious archduchess, as Sophie soon learned, was not easy. Although immensely wealthy, Isabella was cheap, and to avoid paying maids she used her ladies-in-waiting for menial house-cleaning tasks when she travelled. It was reported that this even included 'certain services of questionable propriety' that a lowly housemaid would ordinarily perform, presumably emptying chamber pots. She made condescending shows of bestowing her cast-off dresses on members of her household, not that the voluminous clothing ever fit the svelte young ladies in Isabella's service. With her abrasive manner, the archduchess demanded much and ignored little. Sophie answered correspondence, accompanied her mistress, partnered house guests in games of tennis, and never voiced a complaint. She might be an aristocrat in her own right, but in Isabella's household she was only an employee, a servant, a distinction Sophie was never allowed to forget.[28]

Isabella's ambition, in fact, unwittingly led to the blossoming and unsuspected romance between Franz Ferdinand and Sophie Chotek. Two of Friedrich's sisters were queens, of Bavaria and of Spain, and in 1895 Friedrich inherited the title Duke of Teschen and the immense fortune that went with it. Armed with money, influence and a string of impressive palaces, Isabella set her sights on the still unmarried Franz Ferdinand. What greater prize was there in the empire? And who better as his future empress than her eldest daughter, Archduchess Maria Christina? Invitations flew fast and furious in the mid-1890s, with the notably single archduke joining Friedrich and Isabella's family at hunting lodges and house parties where, or so Isabella assumed, he could not fail to notice the teenaged Maria Christina's obvious charms and impeccable qualifications.

Frustratingly, exactly when Franz Ferdinand first met Sophie remains a mystery. Their daughter never asked; many years later their eldest son, Max, destroyed nearly all of his parents' private correspondence; and neither the archduke nor the countess kept consistent diaries.[29] They may have encountered each other casually, as the archduke often hunted with her brother-in-law Jaroslav Thun.[30] The first definitive evidence comes from Isabella's own photograph albums. One image shows Franz Ferdinand and Sophie during a shooting party sometime in late 1892; over the years that followed, they posed for the camera at hunts, on the tennis courts, and during the archduke's visits to the Teschen Palace of Feltorony at Pressburg (now Bratislava).[31] With each encounter, attraction grew. To Franz Ferdinand, Sophie offered respite and escape from imperial life. She could speak knowledgeably and maturely on political and world affairs, share jokes, and flatter the archduke with concerned attentions. As for the archduke, in congenial company and away from the rigours of public life, he could be enchanting; still young and vaguely handsome, armed with a glittering inheritance, it was easy for Sophie to cast him as her particular Prince Charming.

Like every good fairy tale, Franz Ferdinand and Sophie's romance features a ball, at which the prince discovers his true love. Legend throws the couple together at an 1894 dance in Prague. Sleek in his uniform, Franz Ferdinand is immediately taken with the beautiful young Sophie, who curtsies low before him and fixes him with a penetrating gaze from her large, velvety eyes. He follows her around the rococo ballroom, the tale goes, dancing every dance with her as the startled guests look on in amazement. Franz Ferdinand disliked ceremonial events, disliked having a thousand eyes turned on him, disliked dancing in public, yet this night he threw caution to the wind. The archduke would not leave the countess's side, providing her with champagne, whispering, even exchanging private jokes – an extraordinary display of emotion from a man popularly thought to be thoroughly resistant to feminine charms. Beneath the light of flickering candles and amid the scent of a thousand roses, romance blossomed.[32]

This is the stuff of legend, engaging and bewitching. It is also, alas for romantics, a bit of imaginative fiction. Buried within the tale is a kernel of the truth, though, for apparently Cinderella did indeed go to a ball and dance with her Prince Charming before anyone knew of the romance. It was April of 1894 when Franz Ferdinand and Sophie both attended a masquerade at the Larisch Palace in Vienna. The archduke later reminded Sophie of 'our dervish ball, which was really so wonderful'.[33] Sharing a dance in a ballroom crowded with Viennese gossips was scarcely the mark of discretion, though thanks to the masks worn, no one present seems to have recognized the evening's real significance. Letters followed. In April, the archduke addressed Sophie with the formal German *Sie*; by summer's end, she had become 'Darling Soph'. He probably confided something of the romance to his brother Otto. Later that year, Otto penned a caricature of Sophie and presented it to her; she sent it on to Franz Ferdinand.[34]

By early 1895, Franz Ferdinand was suffering from tuberculosis and away in Eisenmenger's care. The doctor noticed how his imperial patient spent hours writing mysterious letters and impatiently waited for the post to arrive each morning.[35] 'Even a slight delay excited him and the influence the letters had upon his moods was unmistakable,' said the doctor.[36] Eisenmenger didn't know that the letters were to and from Sophie. They continued when the archduke went to Egypt, and the couple met again in May 1896, though only formally, when Sophie accompanied Isabella to Vienna for Karl Ludwig's funeral.[37]

Several years had passed since Franz Ferdinand met his Bohemian countess. Romance had flourished undetected during apparently innocuous stays with Isabella and Friedrich. Franz Ferdinand was always amiable and social, seemingly happy within the family circle but in reality seizing every chance to be with his countess. The ambitious archduchess was full of advice for 'Dear Franzi', the man she secretly envisioned as her son-in-law. 'It would have pleased me enormously to see the major improvements in your state of health,' she wrote, 'which I had heard about on all sides. The minor visible relapse was hopefully just temporary. Are you now hopefully keeping quite well? It would make me very happy to soon have some news and may I ask you to please telegraph some to me?'[38]

As 1896 ended, Sophie must have seemed even more vulnerable to her adoring archduke. After her father, Count Bohuslav, left the diplomatic service, his health rapidly failed; he died in a private clinic at Görlitz in October 1896, and his body was returned to Bohemia for burial at Waltirsche near the family's estate at Grosspriesen. Her sister Antonia had married Baron Karl von Wuthenau, but Oktavia and Henriette remained at home and were now destitute. Sophie contributed what she could, but their financial care fell to her brother, Wolfgang. Unable to support them on his meagre civil service salary, he appealed to the Imperial Foreign Ministry for a 'favour of mercy' on their behalf; 1,200 crowns (approximately £3,800 in 2013 figures) per year was granted toward their upkeep.[39]

Did Franz Ferdinand view Sophie's situation through fevered fantasy? Sophie made the perfect heroine; orphaned and at the mercy of Isabella, a brittle 'stepmother' if ever there was one, the countess faced an uncertain future. Perhaps through Franz Ferdinand's chivalric lens, Sophie was wistfully fragile, in need of protection. His growing love matched her feelings for this most unlikely Prince Charming. And true love it must have been. In these years, the archduke was still suffering from tuberculosis, yet Sophie risked her entire future on his recovery. She waited and waited, never knowing if one day she would learn that Franz Ferdinand had ultimately succumbed to his illness. Even if he recovered, what chance was there that he would ever be able to marry her? Another eligible young man might come along and seek to wed her, guaranteeing her future, but she seemed prepared to reject him if that happened. Sophie was resolute, daring to hope against hope that somehow, in some way, Fate would smile on her burgeoning romance with the archduke.

Visits to the Teschens continued, but Isabella was no fool. She wanted Franz Ferdinand to marry her daughter, but she also knew that the archduke was attracted to the countess. She was not above dangling Sophie as bait to lure him into the family circle. 'Countess Chotek will be there,' she added to her invitation to join them hunting.[40] Her letters to the archduke dropped the countess's name at every turn, praising her to Franz Ferdinand for her diligent service or thoughtfulness in distributing chocolates to visiting officials.[41] She even took Sophie with her to inspect the archduke's changes to Schloss Konopischt, his principal Bohemian estate.[42]

What did the wily archduchess imagine was happening between her lady-in-waiting and desired son-in-law? She was certainly aware of his feelings for the countess and cynically used her presence for her own benefit. It seems likely, as Franz Ferdinand and Sophie's great-granddaughter Princess Sophie suggests, that Isabella imagined the pair were lovers and that the archduke had taken the countess as his mistress. Tolerating and even indulging what she erroneously believed to be the situation, she may have thought that it was a temporary diversion and that soon the archduke would come to his senses and acknowledge her daughter Maria Christina's suitability as consort. Isabella found nothing extraordinary in her rather cynical approach to her daughter's future happiness; only too late, as Princess Sophie says, 'did she realize it was much more serious'.[43]

Unknown to Isabella, Franz Ferdinand had very different ideas. In 1898, he sent Sophie a postcard of the Belvedere Palace, writing on the back, 'Picture of our home in Vienna.' No one noticed, and Isabella's games continued, at least until a fateful April day in 1899 following one of the archduke's visits to the Teschens at Pressburg. He accidentally left some things behind, among them a pocket watch that a servant handed to Isabella. Thinking that she might find a miniature of her daughter within, Isabella opened it only to discover a portrait of Sophie.[44]

What happened next remains clouded in confusion. According to various versions, a furious Isabella assembled her entire household and proceeded to excoriate Sophie in front of the intimidated and embarrassed audience. At the end of this diatribe she was abruptly dismissed, so quickly that she did not even have time to pack her things.[45] In truth, the situation had been building for some time. The discovery of the watch may simply have been the straw that broke the camel's back and ended the hopeful delusion. No matter the impetus, Sophie did indeed leave the Teschen household. On 23 April 1899, she tendered her resignation as *Hofdame*.[46]

Sophie apparently fled to Vienna to stay with her sister; there are also stories that she went into hiding in a convent, though these seem to be apocryphal.[47] Although she eventually ended up with her sister Maria in Dresden, Sophie may have been so unnerved by the experience that she did indeed seek temporary refuge in a convent. Her great-granddaughter Princess Anita suggests that such a move would have been entirely in character, as the countess sought spiritual guidance and prayed about her situation.[48] That situation, fuelled by Isabella's uncontrollable outrage, was about to need all of the prayers both Franz Ferdinand and Sophie could offer.

FOUR

'A Triumph of Love'

✦

A furious Isabella rushed to Franz Josef complaining of Franz Ferdinand's abominable conduct. He had, she hysterically insisted, made fools out of her family and humiliated her eldest daughter simply to carry on a scandalous affair with her lady-in-waiting.[1] The self-righteous accusations concealed Isabella's own cynical behaviour and knowledge of the situation; the archduke had never given any indication that he was romantically interested in Maria Christina. Yet Isabella was now determined to see Franz Ferdinand punished and Sophie humiliated, and Franz Josef reluctantly agreed to speak to his nephew.[2] It wasn't the sort of confrontation Franz Josef relished, and one suspects he ascribed the entire episode to nothing more momentous than a passing liaison between Franz Ferdinand and the pliable countess he had presumably taken as his mistress.

Experience, though, proved different from expectation. Franz Ferdinand obeyed the summons to see his uncle and listened as the emperor related Isabella's complaints. Such things happened; a few apologies and the passage of time would heal any lingering resentments. He was shocked when Franz Ferdinand revealed the truth: there had been no affair, no intimations about Maria Christina, and therefore no need to apologize. Now that the emperor knew of the countess, though, he might as well know that the archduke was in love with her and that he meant to marry her. 'No,' the emperor supposedly replied in horror, 'such a marriage is impossible! I shall never consent to it!' Franz Ferdinand was adamant, insisting that he had already declared his intention to the countess and would not go back on his promise. Stunned, the emperor gave his nephew a week to reconsider and dismissed him.[3]

'Love makes people lose all sense of dignity,' Franz Josef complained.[4] The week passed, and Franz Ferdinand returned, more determined than ever. Such a marriage, the emperor warned, would harm the country and the throne. The prestige of the dynasty and years of tradition were at stake and not to be discarded over a silly romance. Again Franz Ferdinand was resolute; he refused to give up Sophie. Franz Josef was immune to such sentimental entreaties and now played his trump card: the Choteks were not eligible for marriage to the Habsburgs. Neither the 1815 Act of German Confederation or the Habsburg Family Statutes recognized the Choteks as equal. Any marriage between Franz Ferdinand and Sophie would be a morganatic union that would recognize her unsuitability, ban her from membership of the imperial house, and bar any potential children from the succession.[5]

Morganatic marriages were not unknown. In 1869, King Victor Emmanuel II of Italy married his mistress Rosa Vercellana and created her Countess Mirafiori, Tsar Alexander II wed Princess Catherine Dolgorukaia a month after his wife's death in 1880, and in 1891 the morganatic union between Grand Duke Michael Mikhailovich and Countess Sophie von Merenberg saw him permanently exiled to England. It had even happened with the Habsburgs. In 1829, Archduke Johann had married Anna Plochl, daughter of a postmaster, and when Archduke Heinrich married a singer, Franz Josef had made her a baroness.[6]

However, a morganatic marriage, as one historian noted, 'was regarded as little more than a mortal sin. The plainest of princesses, who in any other station might have considered herself lucky to find a husband, frequently ended up a Queen. To marry outside the golden stockade of royalty was to court disaster.'[7] The very idea was unthinkable for a future emperor. The most Franz Josef conceded was that his nephew should take a year to carefully consider the implications. The message was unspoken but clear. Franz Ferdinand could not contract a morganatic marriage and still remain heir. If he chose Sophie, he would forfeit his place in the imperial house, his title of archduke, his incomes, and his country.

The archduke was not about to give in so easily. He would not abandon Sophie or give up his place as heir presumptive. Inscrutable, divine providence had made him heir; to throw it away was to challenge the very wisdom of God. Therefore he would have both Sophie and the throne. A curious talk with Eisenmenger underscored his determination. Worried about his illness and wanting to ensure both that he was healthy enough to marry and would not pass it on to any children, he cornered the doctor one day and sought assurances. Then, without mentioning Sophie's name, Franz Ferdinand complained, 'I have at last found a woman whom I love and who is suited to me and now they are making the most unheard of difficulties, because of some trifling defect in her family tree. However I shall overcome that.'[8]

A 'trifling defect' – but not to the emperor, and not to Prince Alfred de Montenuovo, the *Obersthofmeister*, or Lord High Chamberlain, of Franz Josef's court. The irony was that Montenuovo was himself the product of a morganatic union. His grandmother Archduchess Marie Louise of Austria had wed Napoleon following his divorce from Empress Josephine; when the former French emperor was exiled to St Helena, Marie Louise remained in Europe in the arms of her chamberlain, Count Adam Neipperg, giving birth to his illegitimate daughter and son while still legally married to Napoleon. After the emperor's death she wed Neipperg in a morganatic union, with her children granted the new princely rank of Montenuovo by Austria's emperor. One of these children, Prince Wilhelm, was Franz Josef's first cousin, and it was his forty-five-year-old son, Alfred, who now ruled the court in Vienna.[9]

A man of hawkish profile, Alfred de Montenuovo never forgot that he was the great-grandson of an Austrian emperor; nor could he forget that his father was the result of an adulterous affair and unequal marriage.

He responded to this inferiority complex by becoming the country's premier snob, a man more exclusive than the Habsburgs in his social circles, and a figure who rigidly insisted on tradition and firm adherence to court etiquette. He took a kind of pride in knowing how universally despised he was. Franz Josef's favourite, Katharina Schratt, loathed him, as did the emperor's youngest daughter, Marie Valerie, along with many other members of the imperial family. Courtiers hated him, servants found him pompous, and society feared him. Montenuovo was such a snob that, despite his marriage to the popular Countess Franziska Kinsky (herself a distant relative of Sophie), his immense wealth, and his fine Viennese palace, he almost never entertained, considering regular Austrian aristocratic society beneath him.[10]

Now, with the emperor's blessing, Montenuovo composed a letter to Sophie. At first he tried to charm her, pouring on the flattery as he outlined how difficult she would make the archduke's life unless she abandoned him. As a loyal subject of the emperor, surely she recognized how a morganatic marriage would harm the prestige of the imperial throne? Such a union would damage the archduke and throw the country into chaos, and all for personal fulfilment. Could she not see the impossibility of the situation? It was far better to end the romance now, to free the archduke of his promise, and to put the good of the country above personal happiness.[11]

This first approach was gentle, but to ensure success Montenuovo also worked behind the scenes. He tried intimidation, warning Sophie's family not to support the proposed marriage; her brother, Wolfgang, might find his career in the Austrian civil service extremely difficult if the romance continued.[12] 'That wasn't fair!' the archduke supposedly erupted on learning of these threats. 'It's all right to test me, but not to tamper with my fiancée!'[13]

When this failed, Montenuovo became truly ugly. Sophie, he insisted, was a mere commoner, an adventuress who had deliberately set out to bewitch the archduke and one day see herself crowned empress of Austria. The prince could barely contain his enthusiasm as he blackened Sophie's name. She was scheming, manipulative, an utterly bourgeois woman unsuited by birth and by temperament for marriage to a Habsburg. Joining forces with Isabella, he spread wild rumours about the Bohemian countess. She was, they whispered, unfit to wed the archduke for she had already shared his bed – and who knew how many other men had also enjoyed her favours?[14] Soon the entire capital buzzed with sordid stories.[15]

Nor was religion out of bounds in this battle. With the emperor's blessing, Franz Ferdinand's old tutor Gottfried Marschall flung himself into the intrigue.[16] Marschall first tried to intercede with his former pupil, arguing that Franz Ferdinand should be forced to choose: either the throne or the countess. It would, he insisted, be the greatest mistake of his reign if the emperor consented to such a union.[17] When this failed, Marschall turned to the countess, using her religion against her and preying on 'her beliefs, her faith, and her loyalty', as her great-granddaughter Princess Sophie recounts.[18] The cleric offered financial and spiritual bribes: If the countess gave up the archduke, the prelate promised, the emperor would reward her family, the pope would be grateful, she would be made an abbess of some convent, and she would thereby fulfil the will of God. If she refused, he said, it was tantamount to questioning the divine providence that had made Franz Ferdinand heir. The tactic worked; a deeply upset Sophie agreed that, despite her love for him, she would end the romance with the archduke.[19]

Franz Ferdinand was furious at this turn of events. He apparently assured Sophie that he meant to marry her and that they should ignore the opposition. Sophie left Vienna to avoid any future confrontations, moving from one sister to the next, hoping to escape attention and remove herself from the centre of the crisis. To maintain contact but not be noticed by the curious eyes of postal officials, she and Franz Ferdinand developed a secret code for their correspondence. The archduke assumed the alias of Count von Hohenberg, the name he used whenever he wished to hide his Habsburg identity, and Sophie asked clerks to immediately deliver any messages from this mysterious aristocrat.[20]

Archduchess Maria Theresa, supportive as always, immediately sided with her stepson on learning of the romance, as did his two half sisters.

Maria Theresa twice took her case to the emperor, pleading for concessions, but the reception was somewhat less than warm. Franz Josef listened to his sister-in-law but was adamant that he would never allow such a marriage. Franz Ferdinand soon learned that the emperor, Isabella, Montenuovo, Marschall, and others had successfully turned his brothers, Otto and Ferdinand Karl, against the romance. Confessing all to Otto, Franz Ferdinand was stunned when his dissolute brother, who now lived quite openly with his latest mistress, hypocritically denounced the very idea. 'Duty for our kind', Otto insisted, 'goes beyond happiness,' adding that it would be an unthinkable blow to the dignity of a Habsburg archduke for his brother to 'marry a Countess'. Franz Ferdinand had no better luck with Ferdinand Karl, who parroted the same opposition.[21]

The rest of the Habsburgs were nearly unanimous in their condemnation. 'I don't fall in love with my lackeys,' a relative commented to Franz Ferdinand.[22] The archduchesses were united in opposition, unable, as one author wrote, to 'forgive Franz Ferdinand for not choosing a wife from among their circle'.[23] Archduchess Isabella, recorded one relative, 'seems to be utterly upset regarding the issue of Countess Chotek'.[24] She joined forces with other like-minded ladies, including Rudolf's daughter, Archduchess Elisabeth, painting Sophie as a scheming adventuress hell-bent on seeing herself crowned empress.[25]

Elderly Archduke Rainer dispatched a prescient letter to Franz Ferdinand, warning against the proposed marriage not because of dynastic considerations but rather because he foresaw inevitable personal difficulties:

> *Try to occupy yourself with serious activities and think carefully on the consequences of the step you propose to take, because I do not believe that this union will bring you lasting happiness. To see a wife you love disadvantaged will cause you pain, and if things should turn out to be different than you expected and the domestic happiness you hoped for is not to be found, everything will be even more difficult to bear. Each man has painful moments to face, some more difficult than others. Thinking on one's duty*

helps overcome these, and the higher one stands, the less one can allow oneself to be deflected away from fulfilling that duty.[26]

The one notable exception to this Habsburg opposition was Crown Princess Stephanie, who brought a personal, sympathetic understanding to the issue. In the spring of 1900 she was fighting to win permission for her own eventual morganatic marriage to court chamberlain Count El-mer Lónyay. Although Franz Josef was horrified, he eventually softened his stance and allowed her to marry on 22 March 1900. She kept her former Austrian titles and was even allowed to appear at court functions, though not with her new morganatic husband.[27]

As the scandal surrounding Franz Ferdinand and Sophie spread, al-lies and enemies aligned. The forbidden romance filtered across Vienna; it was whispered about at court, students chatted about the implications in smoke-filled coffeehouses, and everyone seemed enthralled with the melodrama. Soon reports appeared in European newspapers. 'Rumours abound over a troublesome romance between Archduke Franz Ferdi-nand and Countess Sophie Chotek,' *Le Temps* reported in autumn 1899.[28] One day, it was said, the archduke had 'definitely decided to contract a morganatic marriage'; the next, newspapers insisted that he was intent on the marriage but 'does not want to cede any rights to the crown'.[29] The romance now broke to a captivated world. The arch-duke certainly tried to win opinion over to his side, though stories that Tsar Nicholas II and Kaiser Wilhelm II intervened with the emperor are apocryphal. Archduchess Maria Theresa supposedly wrote to Pope Leo XIII, extolling Sophie's virtues as a pious Catholic and stressing that such a marriage would only help solidify the Church's place in an uncer-tain empire. Whatever happened, something convinced the pope to act, for he now urged that the marriage be allowed, asserting that the contin-ued gossip was only damaging the Habsburg throne.[30] The growing conflict boiled over during a New Year's Day dinner at the Hofburg in 1900. As the imperial family looked on, the emperor raised his glass and pointedly toasted Otto's twelve-year-old son, Karl, while ignoring a pale

Franz Ferdinand. It was, thought Marie Valerie, as if her father were publicly anointing Karl as his preferred heir.[31]

The incident convinced Franz Ferdinand to act. He first turned to Prime Minister Count Franz von Thun and asked his opinion of the proposed marriage. Thun, a distant relative of Sophie, not surprisingly supported the union, arguing that the Choteks could trace their ancestry back centuries and should be considered equal for the purposes of marriage. Such a marriage, he said, would undoubtedly strengthen ties between the crown and Bohemia. However, in September Thun resigned as prime minister; rumour held that Franz Josef had forced him out of office on learning that he was encouraging the romance.[32]

Undaunted, the archduke confided his secret to Max Vladimir Beck, his former legal tutor. 'This fire', he admitted, 'has been blazing in me for five years. It will never burn out.' Franz Ferdinand insisted that, if need be, he would simply wait for the emperor to die and then marry his countess. If this happened, Sophie would become empress: the Habsburg Family Statutes were curiously silent when it came to demanding equal status for the emperor's wife. Whomever the emperor married was automatically deemed equal, and any children they might have could succeed to the throne.[33]

Such talk worried Beck, who now worked with Prime Minister Ernst von Koerber, Thun's replacement, to find some solution. On 9 April Franz Josef handed his prime minister a copy of the Habsburg Family Statutes and asked his opinion on the proposed marriage. Hearing this, Franz Ferdinand tried to force Koerber's hand, insisting that if he could not marry Sophie he would either go mad or kill himself. 'I have reached the end of my physical and moral strength,' the archduke declared, 'and can no longer be responsible for anything!'[34]

With Beck's help, the archduke drafted a letter that could be sent to his uncle:

> *Increasingly weighed down as I am by the agonized situation in which I have for some time found myself, I again turn to Your Majesty's paternal*

heart with the most urgent of pleas to fulfil my deepest and dearest wish, on which depends the whole of my future existence, my happiness, my peace, and my contentment. I can only mention once more that my whim to marry the countess is not a whim but an outflow of deepest affection from years of trial and suffering. Your Majesty's guarantees for my future life lie in my past conduct, in my constant endeavour to act loyally and never, openly or secretly, against Your Majesty's will, as many another might have tried to in my desperate straits . . . I can and will never marry anyone else; for it repels me and I am unable to tie myself to another without love, making her and myself unhappy, while my heart belongs and will always belong to the countess . . . Regarding the belief which Your Majesty deigned to express that my marriage might harm the monarchy, I humbly beg to point out that this very marriage, by turning me back into a happy man who enjoys his work and devotes his full strength to the general welfare will enable me to discharge my duties to the monarchy much better than if I live out my life as an unhappy, lonely man devoured by longings . . . I ask Your Majesty to believe that I am striving only to do my best in a difficult situation; but to this end I must have a chance to feel happy, which is why I beg Your Majesty for the one happiness of my life, for consent to the marriage for which I yearn . . . I shall strive to give Your Majesty firm and faithful support in so far as I am at Your Majesty's command. I shall never do anything against Your Majesty's will, openly or in secret. Yet this makes me the more confident in my appeal to Your Majesty's heart, to grant me my happiness.[35]

The spectre of yet another Habsburg heir killing himself over some troublesome romance finally convinced Franz Josef to act. Throughout May he had met with various officials and legal authorities, exploring his possible options; on 12 June he summoned all senior archdukes to an urgent conference to discuss the situation. While he remained opposed to the marriage, Franz Josef now explained that his nephew was determined to go through with it; that being the case, he would agree to the union and, by doing so, set the terms. If nothing was done, Franz Ferdinand might simply wait, as he had previously threatened, until he came to the throne and then marry Sophie, making her empress. To avoid this possibility it was necessary to amend the Habsburg Family Statutes, for the first time requiring equal status for the emperor's spouse.[36]

With the statute amended, the emperor would allow the morganatic marriage – but this, too, posed a problem. Hungarian law did not recognize the concept of an unequal marriage. Unless something was done, this threatened an untenable situation: Franz Ferdinand one day ruling as emperor with his unequal consort at his side and their children excluded from the imperial house in Austria, but Sophie crowned as queen of Hungary and their descendants laying claim to the throne in Budapest. Such a possibility would forever shatter the dual monarchy, dividing rule between Franz Ferdinand's nearest legitimate male relatives in Austria and his morganatic descendants in Hungary. After much negotiation, Hungarian officials agreed to recognize a morganatic marriage if the archduke acknowledged his wife's unequal status and renounced any succession rights for their children. All of the legal loopholes were now closed.[37]

Franz Ferdinand was oblivious to these machinations. 'I'm raving mad and desperate!' he wrote to Beck.[38] Then, on 23 June, he received a summons from the emperor to discuss the situation. During this meeting Franz Josef presented his nephew with his legal coup: the Family Statutes had been amended, and the Austrian and Hungarian prime ministers had agreed to sanction the union if it was a morganatic marriage. If the archduke married Sophie without agreeing to the emperor's terms he would lose his position as heir; if he waited until he came to the throne to wed her she would still, thanks to the amended statute, be deemed unequal. The only way forward if he wished to immediately make Sophie his wife was a morganatic marriage. Before it could take place, the archduke would be made to swear an oath that he would never elevate her status or grant succession rights to their future children. Franz Ferdinand reluctantly agreed to the terms that would forever condemn his wife and their children to a shadowy world of non-existence as far as the Habsburgs were concerned. It was a future fraught with problems, but in his bliss Franz Ferdinand saw none of them. 'Your Franzi is simply crazy with joy!' he wrote to Sophie. 'Just imagine, Soph: His Majesty sent for me today at two o'clock and kindly gave me permission to marry in Reichstadt on 1 July. Hurrah! Hurrah! Hurrah! This means that I will fall into your arms on the evening of the 29th. And then it will be off to Reichstadt.'[39]

'I hope, nephew,' the emperor supposedly warned, 'that you will never live to regret this.'[40] In private, Franz Josef was both dejected and depressed at this 'utterly unthinkable' and 'monstrous' turn of events. As a courtier noted, he 'considered himself the chosen guardian of the fame and reputation of his House, a House that had claimed and occupied the first place in Europe for more than 600 years'. He resented that the marriage had been forced upon him, and resentment created a gulf between uncle and nephew 'that could no longer be bridged'.[41]

The renunciation came five days later, on the cold, wet morning of 28 June. Franz Ferdinand arrived at the Hofburg in a closed carriage, looking ashen and serious in a white cavalry officer's tunic, and joined a room of wordless archdukes awaiting the emperor; not even Otto and Ferdinand Karl spoke to their brother. A few minutes before noon Franz Josef entered and led the silent procession to the Privy Council Chamber, where courtiers, ministers, diplomats, Members of Parliament, and clerics watched the peculiar ceremony. Standing beneath the purple-canopied dais, Franz Josef declared that:

> *Inspired by the wish to give My Nephew new proof of My special love, I have consented to his marriage with Countess Sophie Chotek. The Countess descends, it is true, from noble lineage; but her family is not one of those that, according to the customs of Our House, we regard as Our equals. As only women from equal Houses can be regarded as equal in birth, this marriage must be regarded in the light of a morganatic marriage, and the children which, with God's blessing, will spring from it cannot be given the rights of Members of the Imperial House. The Archduke will, therefore, to make this certain for all time, today take an oath to the effect that he recognizes all this, that he recognizes his marriage with Countess Chotek to be a morganatic*

one, that the consequences are that the marriage cannot be regarded as one between equals, and that the children springing from it can never be regarded as rightful children, entitled to the rights of members of Our House.[42]

The Foreign Minister, Agenor Goluchkowski, read out the archduke's declaration:

We feel ourselves obligated to declare that our marriage to the Countess Sophie Chotek is not one between equals and not in accord with the statute but is a morganatic union and is to be regarded as such now and for all time. As a consequence neither our wife nor the children which with God's blessing may come from this marriage nor any of their descendants can lay claim to those rights, honours, titles, coats of arms, or privileges that would be accorded to wives of equal rank with their Archducal husbands and the children of such an Archducal union of equality in accord with the statutes . . . With these words we pledge ourselves that this present declaration, of whose meaning and significance we are fully aware, is binding for all time for our wife, our children and the descendants of those children and we further pledge that we will never attempt to retract our present declaration nor to undertake anything which would aim at weakening or dissolving its binding force.[43]

Approaching an altar at the centre of the room, Franz Ferdinand faced Prince Archbishop Cardinal Anton Grüscha of Vienna and Prince Primate of Hungary Cardinal Dr Lorenz Schlauch. Removing his right glove, he placed his hand on copies of his declaration that lay before a crucifix and solemnly pledged that he would obey the provisions of the oath. Crossing himself, he backed away from the altar. It was all over in less than thirty minutes.[44]

Only two days now stood between Franz Ferdinand and Sophie's marriage. The archduke packed a few things in advance of leaving Vienna and with tears of gratitude bid Beck farewell.[45] The evening should have inaugurated a traditional round of festivities surrounding the marriage of the heir to the throne: receptions, banquets, carriage processions through gaily decorated streets lined by cheering crowds, and an elaborate ceremony in St Augustine's Church presided over by the cardinal archbishop of Vienna and attended by the emperor and members of the imperial family.[46]

Tradition, pomp and ceremony – but not for Franz Ferdinand and Sophie Chotek. Their marriage would not even take place in Vienna. Archduchess Maria Theresa offered her summer residence of Schloss Reichstadt (now Zákupy) for the nuptials, a grim fortress in northern Bohemia, most famous as the place where Ferdinand I had lived in retirement after giving up the throne in 1848. She asked local citizens to decorate their houses with flags and bunting on learning that Montenuovo had forbidden any celebratory displays; vindictive as always, he had even instructed that local officials should not offer the customary welcome when the archduke's train pulled into the little station. Even the cardinal archbishop remained in Vienna, unwilling to risk imperial censure by performing the ceremony.[47]

Franz Josef had barely consented to the union. Believing the wedding shamed the dignity of the House of Habsburg, he refused to attend, instead running off to Bad Ischl with his mistress Katharina Schratt. Determined to punish the archduke and make his wedding as humiliating as possible, the emperor let Montenuovo enact another bit of dirty business to keep any conflicted Habsburg family members from the ceremony. Josephine Hohenzollern, a Baden princess distantly related to the ruling German dynasty, had died on 19 June. Although the Austrian court had never before noted her existence, it now decreed twelve days of official mourning, during which members of the imperial family were forbidden to attend any festive celebrations. The period of mourning was timed precisely to end the day after the planned wedding, guaranteeing that no member of the dynasty could attend the ceremony.[48]

Despite this, Franz Ferdinand hoped that his siblings would support him. However, neither Otto nor Ferdinand Karl would attend the wedding; his sister Margarethe, Duchess of Württemberg, also stayed away. 'I felt really sorry for him,' Beck recorded on hearing of this family absence.[49] The only relatives defiantly risking imperial opprobrium by attending the festivities at Reichstadt would be his stepmother, Maria Theresa, and his two half sisters. They were there to greet him on Saturday 30 June when his train pulled into the station. Following orders from Vienna, the provincial governor was absent; only the mayor nervously stepped forward to greet the heir. Although there were no official displays, the people of the town had hung their houses with flags and lined the streets to cheer the archduke on his way to the Schloss. A few hours later Sophie arrived from her cousin Count Karl Maria Chotek's estate at Grosspriesen; a group of schoolchildren serenaded the couple in the castle courtyard before Maria Theresa toasted her stepson and his fiancée at a family dinner, presenting the countess with an elaborate jewel box that had belonged to Franz Ferdinand's late mother.[50]

Seizing on popular sentiments surrounding this modern romantic fairy tale, reporters entertained their readers of this happy dénouement. It was 'A Triumph of Love', with this 'Knight Prince' and his Cinderella.[51] The archduke would 'be joined together in a morganatic marriage with the woman of his heart's choice', an unprecedented union for a Habsburg heir.[52] 'He who fights for his love,' insisted a Czech newspaper, 'who refuses to yield up that which he holds dear despite all opposition – in such a man one can safely place one's trust, for he will defend everything that he prizes with the same energy.'[53] As for Sophie, Vienna's *Neue Freie Presse* commented, 'Countess Chotek will never wear a crown on her head, but she will feel its thorns all the same, as nothing that burdens her husband can remain unknown to her.'[54]

Sunday 1 July 1900 dawned grey and rainy in Reichstadt. At half past ten that morning, accompanied by bells ringing out in celebration from the castle's spires, processions to the chapel began. The archduke, in the dress uniform of a cavalry general whose white tunic sported his Order of the Golden Fleece and the Grand Cross of the Order of St Stephen, escorted his stepmother and two half sisters. Sophie came next. Worried that his career in the Austrian civil service would suffer as a result, her brother, Wolfgang, sheepishly refused to attend; instead, she walked on the arm of her cousin and former guardian Prince Alois Löwenstein-Wertheim-Rosenberg, followed by her cousin Count Karl Maria Chotek as head of the family.[55]

Sophie, declared a newspaper, looked 'delightfully beautiful', even 'girlish'.[56] Her white satin gown, adorned with embroidered silk panels, flounces of chiffon, and bands of lace, was festooned with a garland of myrtle and orange blossoms. Atop her head, among a halo of orange blossoms, was the emperor's wedding present, a diamond tiara, matching the double row of pearls and diamonds around her neck. A veil of antique lace and tulle cascaded to the end of her seven-foot-long brocaded train, and she carried a bouquet of lilies, myrtle, and orange blossoms created in Prague.[57]

Thunderous music from the organ reverberated against the vaulted ceiling and frescoed walls as the procession entered the chapel of St Francis and St Seraphim, watched not by a glittering bevy of Habsburgs but instead by courtiers, town officials, and castle maids. Dean Wilhelm Hikisch, Maria Theresa's confessor, stood framed by the twin columns of the marble altar against a forest of potted palms and wildflowers picked by local schoolchildren as the couple approached. 'The hour has come', the dean declared, 'when the deepest wishes of your hearts will be fulfilled by the conclusion of the indissoluble bond, through which you will be united in an intimate union.' Their voices were loud and clear when Franz Ferdinand and Sophie exchanged vows and made their promises. The dean blessed the rings as 'witnesses for all time to your untroubled marital happiness. That is the warmest wish of many millions of hearts and especially of those who now stand near among us.' Prayers and hymns followed; the entire service, newspapers noted, was devoid of 'court ceremony, with no pomp, no show of luxury', but instead 'of the simplest possible character'.[58]

By noon it was over. Guests posed for a few photographs in a corner room on the castle's first floor, taken by Sophie's cousin Count Karl Maria Chotek, and retreated to the medieval dining room for luncheon. The archduke sat at the middle of a long table, Sophie on his right and his half sister Maria Annunciata on his left, with Maria Theresa opposite the bridal couple. A band from the 94th Infantry Regiment serenaded them as the group dined on salad, roast venison, asparagus, and champagne. At the end, and in the only sign that this was in fact an imperial wedding, the guests rose and sang the national anthem.[59]

Although Franz Josef did not attend, he made his presence felt. He left it to his foreign minister to send a telegram, signed by an aide-de-camp in his name, as if dispatching a personal message smacked entirely too much of approval. Franz Ferdinand would one day sit upon the throne as emperor of the House of Habsburg-Lothringen, but not Sophie. Not only would she never share her husband's position, she now could not even share his name. 'I feel truly honoured to raise the morganatic wife of my nephew,' it announced, 'tax-free, to the ranks of princely hereditary nobility, with the name Hohenberg and the style of Fuerstliche Gnaden' (a lesser, non-royal form of 'Highness', roughly equivalent to the English style 'Your Grace').[60]

The polite language of this impersonal missive failed to disguise the twist of the knife: the reminder of Sophie's morganatic status. In 1245, Anna Hohenberg had left her ancestral castle in southern Germany to marry the head of the Habsburg family and become matriarch of the fledgling dynasty. Hohenberg had been the name Franz Ferdinand used when travelling incognito, the name he used when he had no wish to be identified as a Habsburg. The emperor's meaning was clear: Sophie and any children she might bear would forever be tied to the name her husband had used to escape his illustrious heritage.[61]

It was still raining when, at two that afternoon, the newly married couple climbed into a carriage and set off for the station. Sophie, clad in a gauzy summer dress and black straw hat, bowed as uniformed schoolchildren tossed wildflowers at the passing vehicle.[62] The couple thanked the mayor and then boarded the train to take them to their honeymoon at the archduke's Schloss Konopischt in Bohemia.[63] It had been, Franz Ferdinand confided in a cable to Beck, 'the most beautiful day of our lives'.[64]

FIVE

'Don't Let Her Think She's One of Us!'

✛

For two weeks the newlyweds luxuriated at Konopischt, exulting in their romantic victory. A week after the wedding, Franz Ferdinand wrote to his stepmother:

> We are both unspeakably happy and this we owe above all to you. Where would we be today, if you had not so nobly and touchingly taken us under your wing! We never stop talking of you and our gratitude is boundless. We can offer you nothing but the assurance that you have done such a good work and made your two children happy for the rest of their lives . . . Soph is a treasure and I am indescribably happy! She takes such good care of me; I am in capital shape, healthy, and much less nervous. I feel as though reborn. She adores you and talks of nothing but your love and kindness. I have the complete inner feeling that both of us will be indescribably happy to the end of our days. Dear, good Mama, you were so utterly right to help me! The dear Lord, to whom I pray twice daily with Soph in the chapel, may reward you, my good Mama, for everything you have done for us. I embrace you and my sisters, kiss your hands and am eternally your most faithful and loving son Franzi.[1]

The couple spent their days in the castle garden, strolling along a path named the Ober Kreuzweg, the Upper Stations of the Cross. It had been the name of the street in Dresden where Sophie had taken refuge with her sister amid the furore over the romance, but it also reflected the bitter struggle they had endured to win their union.[2] At the end of two weeks, they left Konopischt for the hunting lodge of Lölling in Carinthia. They tried to be as anonymous as possible, roaming the nearby villages, attending mass, and picnicking in the adjacent forests with unsuspecting couples.[3]

The idyll was not to last. The same Viennese newspapers that had celebrated the romantic union as a triumph of love were now filled with Europe's latest royal scandal. In the midst of Franz Ferdinand and Sophie's honeymoon, King Alexander of Serbia announced his engagement to his mother's lady-in-waiting Draga Masin. She was a commoner with a shady and illicit reputation, a woman deemed utterly unsuitable as a royal consort. Those reporters who had held their pens in check and refrained from condemning Franz Ferdinand's morganatic marriage now let loose all of their venom in drawing unspoken but understood parallels between Sophie and Draga. How, asked the unsympathetic chroniclers, could a king marry beneath his station? In selecting an unsuitable consort Alexander was lowering the very dignity of his throne. He cared more about personal happiness than he did about duty. Franz Ferdinand read the accounts as thinly veiled attacks on his own marriage; he wanted to complain to Franz Josef, but Sophie stopped him, pointing out that this would only make them appear overly sensitive.[4]

In September, Franz Ferdinand and Sophie moved to Vienna, taking up residence for the first time in the Belvedere Palace. One of the city's loveliest baroque buildings, this frothy architectural concoction had begun life as the unlikely summer home of Prince Eugen of Savoy, a professional mercenary of great skill credited with saving Vienna from conquest by the Turks. Beginning in 1717, architect Johann Lukas von Hildebrandt transformed the sloped city plot into a dazzling complex. A single-storey pavilion of severely classical rooms called the Lower Belvedere edged the bottom of the site. Restraint disappeared in the ascending sloped gardens, with their rows of lime trees shading gravelled walks, marble statuary, parterre gardens, and cascades splashing into serene reflecting pools growing ever more grand as they approached the exuberant Upper Belvedere Palace. Dominating the crest of the hill, its windows flanked by carved caryatids and twisted columns and its extremities marked by domed pavilions, the pale stone facade contrasted with a copper roof mellowed a pleasing green with age. It was all so impressive that no one had actually dared live here for centuries. The Habsburgs had last used it in April 1770, when Empress Maria Theresa gave a farewell dinner for her youngest daughter, Marie Antoinette, just before she left to become France's ill-fated queen.[5]

The excesses of the exterior continued within. A magnificent double staircase in white marble ascended between immense cherubs holding ornate black wrought-iron lanterns to the principal floor. At the palace's centre lay the Marmorsaal, its red marble walls adorned with gilded pilasters and its lofty ceiling hung with sparkling crystal chandeliers. Stepping through French doors to a balcony above the gardens revealed a wide panorama of the surrounding city, dotted with church spires that seemed to fuse with the murky green hills of the distant Vienna woods. Strings of elaborate rooms with allegorical stucco reliefs, trompe l'oeil ceilings where mythological gods battled, and floors inlaid with rare and contrasting woods filled the palace's three floors.[6]

Elegant, formal and whispering of an evocative, heroic past, it was all supremely splendid, but as a family home Belvedere Palace was scarcely a model of comfort. Franz Ferdinand spent two years renovating, adding central heating, modern plumbing, electricity and bathrooms before the palace was ready for his new bride in September of 1900. Ceilings in their private apartments overlooking the garden had been lowered to make the rooms less cavernous, and the couple filled the rooms according to the tastes of the day. Neo-rococo sofas and chairs incongruously covered in leather or bright English chintzes sprawled across oriental carpets, potted palms fought for primacy with the heavily patterned damask on the walls, and tables were crowded with framed photo-graphs, fringed lamps, and odd assortments of Victorian bric-a-brac.[7] It was all in the best bourgeois taste, quite comfortable, and utterly out of place amid the baroque rooms.

The emperor came here in early September, to inspect the renova-tions and, more importantly, to meet his nephew's new wife. 'It went fairly well,' Franz Josef wrote. 'She was natural and modest,' he admit-ted, unkindly adding that Sophie 'does not look young any more'.[8] It was the start of a tempestuous and uncertain relationship, where personal cordiality cloaked dynastic disapproval that spilled over into nearly ev-ery aspect of Franz Ferdinand and Sophie's life. In these early days, the emperor still resented the marriage, believing it had been an unwelcome concession forced upon him. He supposedly referred to Sophie as 'that woman at the Belvedere' and even allegedly confided, 'This marriage is blighting my old age. I wish it could be declared invalid.'[9]

Some people, wrote one courtier, looked on Sophie as 'an intruder in the ancient Imperial House'.[10] Franz Ferdinand's two brothers, Otto and Ferdinand Karl, tried to pretend that Sophie simply didn't exist, avoid-ing any occasions at which they might be forced to meet her. The ladies of the imperial family were particularly vicious, insisting that Sophie 'had forced her way into their elite circle where she definitely did not belong'.[11] It was, noted one historian, 'as a lady-in-waiting that Sophie had come to the Court's attention and aroused the wrath of her betters by snaring the Heir to the Throne. It was as a lady-in-waiting that they fought her, as a lady-in-waiting that they humiliated her.'[12] These power-ful women played a spiteful game. When Sophie gave a dinner or a small reception, the archduchesses immediately planned a large event on the same night. By etiquette, this forced Sophie's guests to abandon her invi-tations.[13]

Only former crown princess Stephanie was friendly with the couple. Her daughter, Elisabeth, 'worked herself into a fanatical hatred and deep contempt' spreading 'spiteful rumours and scurrilous tales'.[14] She once complained that she had been forced to acknowledge Sophie when they both attended an aristocratic reception. Elisabeth was pointedly rude and complained, 'Just imagine, *she* leaned across to me!'[15] Nor was Archduchess Isabella, Sophie's former mistress, any more forgiving, regarding her as an unwelcome parvenue and doing all she could to see that she was treated 'rather shabbily'.[16]

Gossip about the newly married couple swept across Vienna, and much of it was gleefully negative. One day, according to a popular tale, police spotted an exotic parrot loose in the city. Cornering it, they listened in horror as the bird launched into a stream of invectives, calling all of the archduchesses 'sluts' and complaining that the emperor 'will live to be a hundred'. It had supposedly escaped from the Belvedere, where Franz Ferdinand and Sophie had allegedly taught the parrot its curious vocabulary.[17]

Such absurd stories formed the backdrop to the official humiliations that rained down on the archduke's new bride. One author referred to these as 'protocol pin pricks', but they were less 'pin pricks' than they were intentional stab wounds, thrust into Franz Ferdinand and Sophie's defenceless bodies by the unpopular Prince Alfred de Montenuovo with the emperor's acquiescence.[18] As *Obersthofmeister* of Franz Josef's court, Montenuovo had strenuously opposed the marriage, and accomplished fact did nothing to change his opinion. In addition to bruiting it about that she had shared the archduke's bed before marriage, Montenuovo also circulated official photographs of the new Princess of Hohenberg, though not before ordering officials in his office to retouch them, adding wrinkles to her face to make her as unattractive as possible.[19]

Montenuovo deployed to advantage the infamous Spanish etiquette of the Habsburg court, a relic of the dynasty's glory days as Europe's supreme ruling family, cloaking humiliations as mere obedience to archaic protocol. When Franz Ferdinand once protested some slight, Montenuovo was brusquely condescending, 'Your Imperial Highness will surely and graciously admit that I never hesitate to comment on all the questions, which I am competent to decide on, and to stand by my convictions . . . Should there be any conflict, then the highest disposition lies with His Majesty . . . I must keep in mind that I am the highest official of a Court elite . . . I only mention this to Your Imperial Highness to explain that such questions are matters of conscience to me and have to be, and ask Your Imperial Highness not to reprimand me.'[20]

This set the tone for the rules Montenuovo laid down governing Sophie's life. As a morganatic spouse, she was excluded from nearly every privilege enjoyed by other Habsburg wives; on the rare occasions when concessions were made, they were done in such a way as to ensure that her unequal position was reinforced. Sophie was not allowed to appear with her husband in public. If he attended a race, opened a museum, toured a factory, or dedicated a school, she had to remain at home or linger in the distant shadows, unacknowledged. If an honour guard saluted Franz Ferdinand, she had to leave, for as a morganatic wife she was not entitled to receive the salutes meant for a Habsburg. If the national anthem greeted the archduke, she had to withdraw, as she was not a member of the imperial family. If officials made a formal welcoming address or presentation, she was not allowed to stand near her husband and give the impression that she in any way warranted official recognition. Franz Ferdinand was forbidden from ever mentioning his wife in any official speech. Sophie could not even accompany Franz Ferdinand to the races, for she was deemed unfit to share his place in the imperial box.[21]

Montenuovo's regulations also barred Sophie from any imperial box at the theatre, opera, ballet, or symphony, essential components of Vienna's winter social season. It was all very splendid when the Habsburgs arrived at the Imperial Opera House, ascending a private staircase of alabaster between immense candelabra of marble and bronze, to take their places in the white and gold imperial box – but not Sophie.[22] With the imperial loge forbidden to her, she had to sit elsewhere. She could not even sit near her husband; the twenty-six boxes of the parquet circle at both institutions were the sole province of the highest society.[23] Franz Ferdinand was not permitted to sit in an ordinary box, which meant that they could never watch any performance together as a couple. Even if she attended an entertainment in a private theatre, she was forbidden to sit with her husband and thus give the impression that she was his equal.[24]

Habsburgs rode in court carriages with gilded spokes, as did foreign diplomats, actors and singers holding imperial contracts, and even tutors to the imperial children. Not Sophie; court carriages were denied to her.[25] She was not even allowed to ride in the same vehicle with her husband in Vienna. Instead, she was restricted to the class of carriages used by ladies-in-waiting at court, an unwelcome reminder of her former position.[26]

Smartly uniformed sentries always guarded Belvedere Palace when Franz Ferdinand was in residence. The minute he left the palace for a meeting, a luncheon, or some other appointment, Montenuovo had the guards pointedly withdrawn. Sophie might remain, but the imperial court deemed her unworthy of its guards.[27]

When her husband gave an official reception or dinner, even in the privacy of the Belvedere, Sophie was forbidden to attend. Diplomats, foreign royalty, or government officials were all considered beyond the narrow scope of suitable associates for her.[28] Not that her absence passed unnoticed. Montenuovo's rules dictated that a place was always laid at the table for her but left conspicuously unoccupied throughout the meal, an open, gaping wound to Franz Ferdinand's pride and love for his wife.[29]

In the autumn of 1900, the shah of Persia visited Vienna, and the attendant ball marked Sophie's first official appearance at court as a married woman. Her obvious exclusion would have been the talk of Vienna, but in Montenuovo's continuing war against the couple, the ballroom became a battleground. 'Don't let her think she's one of us,' one archduchess supposedly warned Montenuovo, not that he was about to let such an opportunity pass.[30]

The old Hofburg Palace blazed with light as the several thousand blessed with coveted invitations ascended crimson-carpeted marble staircases lined with soldiers and crowded into immense, columned halls 'so huge they seemed to have neither walls nor ceilings'. Elaborate cascades of roses and orchids scented the air. The silk of the ladies' fashionable décolleté gowns rustled as they joined officers in rainbow-hued uniforms crossed with gold braid and trimmed with sable and fox. Throats ringed with diamonds and tunics flashing polished medals shone in the soft light of a thousand candles swirling above in a galaxy of crystal chandeliers.[31]

The sudden appearance of the grand master of ceremonies, wrapped in his scarlet uniform and loudly tapping the floor three times with his ivory and silver staff, brought immediate silence.[32] The assembly sank into bows and curtsies as the emperor appeared. Ordinarily he would have led Franz Ferdinand's stepmother, Maria Theresa, as the highest-ranking lady in the land and mother to the heir, but neither she nor her daughters – the only Habsburgs who had supported and attended the wedding – were invited. Instead, he walked with Archduchess Isabella on his arm, a mark of favour many took as a rather unsubtle statement against the marriage.[33] The shah came next, followed by Franz Ferdinand leading the archdukes; the archduchesses; the senior mistress of the robes to the late empress; duchesses, princesses, and widows from equal houses; royal children born into equal houses; and finally Sophie, wearing the diamond tiara given to her by the emperor. She was not allowed to enter with her husband but walked on the arm of a court chamberlain. Archduchesses and ladies recognized as equal in dignity with the imperial house walked on their escorts' right arms; Sophie was made to walk on the left side, to indicate her unequal status.[34] Montenuovo imposed one final humiliation surrounding Sophie's court appearance. The double doors had been opened wide for members of the imperial family as they processed into the room. When Sophie appeared, one of the doors was pointedly and loudly closed, indicating that she was not entitled to the same courtesy and forcing her to turn sideways to fit through the opening.[35]

The unintended consequence of this petty humiliation, as the couple's great-granddaughter Princess Sophie says, only focused all attention on the Princess of Hohenberg and surrounded her with sympathy.[36] Sophie betrayed no sign of discomfort. She moved through the ballroom with such serenity and grace that even her most strident enemies were amazed. Franz Ferdinand watched such scenes in silent rage, clenching and unclenching his fists in impotence.[37]

This dignified performance failed to win Sophie admission to a state banquet held a few days later; to make matters worse, Montenuovo placed Franz Ferdinand between Isabella and Maria Christina. One last ball for the shah remained. Again guests saw one of the great double doors swing shut as Sophie approached; this time she stood in the entrance for a few seconds, an embarrassed blush spreading across her face, before abruptly turning and leaving the palace. Franz Ferdinand was told that she had been unwell. Only on returning to the Belvedere did Sophie confide the truth: on reaching the doorway she found herself alone, with no chamberlain or officer to escort her into the room, and had turned away in shame. The next morning, the couple abruptly left Vienna, but not before a seething Franz Ferdinand fired off an angry letter warning Montenuovo against any such future occurrence and reminding the prince that his own ancestors had been bastards later legitimized in a morganatic union.[38]

Now Montenuovo feigned humiliation. He ran to the emperor, declaring that the heir had insulted him and threatened to resign. It had all been a simple mistake, he insisted. At Franz Josef's request he composed a letter of apology, but the experience left Montenuovo empowered, not chastened. With the emperor on his side, he made no attempt to conceal his dislike of the couple.[39]

Franz Josef may not have composed the list of petty rules, but he usually allowed Montenuovo extraordinary latitude in enforcing them. The emperor, it has often been argued, was simply too old to challenge the restrictive protocol, even had he wished to do so. When some incident occurred and Franz Ferdinand erupted in rage, Sophie tried to calm him with assurances. 'The emperor is old and feeble,' she would supposedly say, attempting to mitigate any animosity.[40] Franz Ferdinand and Sophie's great-granddaughter Princess Sophie sees the emperor's acquiescence as 'narrow-minded, stubborn, scared to a certain extent of making a mistake by changing the rules and regulations, but I don't think it was vindictiveness'.[41]

Perhaps this is true. Yet the emperor could have eased the rules; his later concessions to Sophie show that he was not the impotent prisoner of etiquette as traditionally portrayed. He rarely intervened with Montenuovo; indeed, as more than one courtier noted, Franz Josef personally approved all aspects of ceremony, large and small, at the imperial court. Such questions were always submitted for his approval, and their ultimate disposition lay solely within his discretion.[42]

What of Montenuovo? He seems to have been only too eager to compose and impose his endless restrictions. Some writers have excused him as 'merely a tyrant in the execution of a tyrannical social system' and made light of the 'so-called insults' surrounding Sophie.[43] This is not convincing. The prince's intense personal dislike of Franz Ferdinand, his actions in opposing the marriage, the eagerness with which he spread gossip against Sophie, and the almost gleeful way he used his office against her reveal a man consumed by petty hatred. He persistently and maliciously referred to her in private as 'the lady-in-waiting', as if mere mention of Sophie's name or new title were anathema. Unfortunately for the newly married couple, Montenuovo had the power to affect their lives. Their great-granddaughter Princess Sophie believes that Montenuovo 'was being vicious and doing what he was told in sticking to protocol, because that gave him a certain importance'.[44]

As for Franz Ferdinand, he certainly never imagined that the imperial court would use Sophie's morganatic status to humiliate her. He must have known that certain difficulties lay ahead, but surely the passage of time would ease hostility? Initial opposition to his marriage, he probably imagined, would quickly fade as Sophie proved herself and won the admiration of a sceptical imperial house. Even if not, how much longer, in truth, was his uncle likely to live? A few more years, perhaps, years that might be painful at times but that would ultimately pass.

What did Franz Ferdinand and Sophie want? Not that she be made empress – that much is clear – but it is likely that they envisioned a time when she would be treated with the respect due an archduke's wife. It was a question of simple dignity in accord with Sophie's position as Franz Ferdinand's consort. Too many people erroneously conflated this with some perceived desire to see her morganatic status cast aside. When respect was not forthcoming, Franz Ferdinand's anger took over. He supposedly kept a list of those who had slighted Sophie or refused to associate with her. '*They* will get to know *me*', he commented, 'when I am Emperor!'[45]

Realization that Sophie's situation was not likely to improve in Vienna fell heavily on Franz Ferdinand. As a friend said, he 'suffered most terribly under the conditions resulting from his unequal marriage'.[46] Sophie, on the other hand, balanced his agitation. Although she privately confessed to her sister Oktavia that the situation was 'difficult', what mattered most was that she hated to see her husband so wounded.[47] No matter the turn of events, she was serene and accepted the insulting regulations with a grace few could understand. Her great-granddaughter Princess Anita ascribes this tranquillity to 'her essentially calm personality and deep religious faith. She was never as hurt as he was. Her only goal was to make him happy.'[48]

At the beginning of 1901, Sophie learned that she was pregnant, and the couple retreated to Konopischt for the birth of their first child. Full of nerves, the archduke paced for hours outside the bedroom door that Wednesday 24 July when his wife went into labour. Sophie was thirty-three, and although her sister Antonia, an obstetrician named Lott, and midwife Caroline Woved were in attendance, Franz Ferdinand later confessed that he was 'half-dead from fright' as the ordeal continued. Finally, a baby's cry signalled the end: Sophie had given birth to a daughter. The labour had been difficult, and the new mother was confined to bed for a week; Franz Ferdinand showered her with roses daily. 'Forgive my using a pencil', he explained to Eisenmenger, 'but I am writing on my wife's bed and it's easier. Thank God that everything is happily over, even though the birth was difficult. But Dr Lott did a splendid job, and we're thrilled to bits with our little one, who is delightful and a very strong child.' Archduchess Maria Theresa rushed to Konopischt and stood as godmother to the new infant, who was christened Sophie Maria Franziska Antonia Ignatia Alberta, Princess of Hohenberg. Within the family, she would be known as 'Little Sophie' and 'Pinky'.[49]

The birth of their daughter made Franz Ferdinand even more resentful of the way his wife was treated in Vienna. The capital was an unwelcoming, icy, and brittle place constantly threatening to interrupt their idyll. He now made a fateful decision that only alienated him further from his future subjects. The cobwebbed court held no attractions and promised only unhappiness. From 1901 on, the archduke and his princess would spend as little time as possible at the Belvedere, and then only when official obligations demanded it. Instead, they would find comfort and purpose in family life, in each other, as they stood with determination against a hostile world. 'My Soph', the archduke confessed, 'is everything in the world to me. She is my joy and my future. I simply cannot imagine life without her!'[50]

SIX

The Swirl of Gossip

✛

On 29 September 1902, Sophie gave birth to a second child while staying at the Belvedere. This time it was a son, Maximilian Karl Franz Michael Hubert Anton Ignatius Josef Maria, born Prince of Hohenberg and, like his sister, with the style of Highness. 'The esteemed Lady and her child are in the best of health,' one newspaper assured Vienna. He even had a Habsburg godfather, Franz Ferdinand's uncle Archduke Karl Stephan.[1] During the baptism in the Belvedere's small chapel, Father Laurenz Mayer, priest at the imperial Hofburg, former personal confessor to the emperor, and a man who thus presumably spoke with both religious and official authority, made an offhanded comment that caused Franz Ferdinand and Sophie endless trouble. There was nothing in canon law, Mayer pronounced, that allowed a father to renounce the rights of an unborn child. Since this was exactly what the archduke had done in 1900, Mayer declared that his oath was invalid and that Max could succeed to the throne. Word of this indiscretion swept across Vienna and 'cast suspicion on Franz Ferdinand'.[2]

The gossip revived in 1904, when a second son, Ernst Alfons Franz Ignaz Josef Maria Anton, was born at Konopischt on 17 May. No one knew quite what to think: would these sons one day rule the empire after their father? There was even speculation that the pope might offer a dispensation and thus clear the way for Franz Ferdinand to reject his 1900 agreement.[3] The very idea horrified Franz Josef. 'I cannot help fearing', he allegedly said, 'that when I am dead the renunciation by my nephew of all rights to the succession as regards any children that may be born of this marriage might be disregarded and that would involve the breaking of the legitimate line. I need scarcely say what that would mean. It would mean sowing the seeds of quarrels within My House.'[4]

This worried speculation failed to consider the one person at the storm's centre: Franz Ferdinand. The archduke would never have revoked his word, precisely because he had sworn a religious oath to uphold the renunciation. His 'deeply religious feelings', Eisenmenger insisted, 'did not permit him even to think of violating the oath'.[5] On this point, even his critics agreed; the archduke 'was much too honourable and too good a Catholic to break an oath he had sworn on the Bible'.[6] He gave the same reply whenever the question arose: his sons were meant to be aristocratic landowners, 'able to enjoy life without material cares', but nothing more.[7] 'The Habsburg crown', the archduke once said, 'is a crown of thorns, and no one who is not born to it should desire it. A withdrawal of the renunciation will *never* be considered!'[8]

In the hothouse atmosphere of the Viennese court, however, bland facts never stood in the way of intrigue and malicious gossip. With Franz Ferdinand and Sophie's self-imposed isolation and retreat into private life, rumours thrived. Even Eisenmenger admitted that the archduke 'was one of the most hated men in Austria'.[9] 'From the dark recesses of the imperial palace in the Hofburg', recalled one Viennese aristocrat, 'the gossip spread, by word of mouth and in print, elusive and pervasive, shifting this way and that, fanned by factions, revived by its own victims. It became a consensus; it was accepted as fact; it became history. Attempts to meet it were ruthlessly crushed.'[10]

Much of the Viennese press adopted the imperial court's attitudes toward Franz Ferdinand and Sophie and wove dark, ominous tales of megalomania and even insanity.[11] The couple was so often absent from Vienna, gossip insisted, because the archduke was secretly locked away in some remote asylum. Stories circulated that he spent days playing with his children's toys and mumbling to himself, that he carried a revolver and shot at clocks and furniture, that he once hacked apart the upholstery in his train compartment with a sword in a fit of rage, that he regularly abused his servants and chased them into fearful flight, and that half of those in his household were actually psychiatrists.[12]

Such nonsense thrived in a Viennese court that intrigued against the couple, but the tales were believed precisely because the archduke seemed so remote and uncomfortable in his rare public appearances. He lacked, the writer Stefan Zweig recalled in his autobiography, 'what mattered most for anyone to win true popularity in Austria, an attractive personality, natural charm and a friendly manner. I had often seen him at the theatre. He sat there in his box, a powerful, broad figure with cold, fixed eyes, never casting a single friendly glance at the audience or encouraging the actors by applauding warmly. You never saw him smile, no photographs showed him in a relaxed mood.'[13]

Franz Ferdinand had no talent for playing Prince Charming in public and made no efforts to win popular acclaim. 'He never could bring himself to make any advances to newspapers or other organs that are in the habit of influencing public opinion either favourably or unfavourably,' said Count Ottokar Czernin. 'He was too proud to sue for popularity.'[14] He was content to conceal the devoted husband and father, the man of liberal ideas, or the heir hoping to restructure a crumbling empire. Though he disliked the talk, people could believe whatever they wished. 'Those who know me,' the archduke commented, 'will never believe these things and the others will certainly know me one day.'[15]

Nor did Sophie escape the poisonous gossip. Rumour portrayed her as driven by her 'small minded fury', vain, 'with the rigidity of a drill sergeant' and 'absorbed in snobbish ambitions' that would one day see her crowned as empress.[16] Baron Albert von Margutti, the emperor's aide-de-camp, embraced the court's prejudices surrounding the archduke's 'domineering wife', insisting that Sophie 'had not the slightest intention of accommodating herself to the position of a morganatic wife kept carefully in the background. On the contrary she bent every nerve with a zeal that was not always coupled with the necessary tact.'[17]

Critics seized on the slightest incident and magnified it to monstrous proportion. A few years after the marriage, the emperor was travelling in Bohemia and briefly stopped near Konopischt. Franz Ferdinand came to greet his uncle, bringing Sophie with him unannounced. 'It was obvious', Margutti recorded, 'to any observer that the aged monarch was anything but at his ease when talking to the Princess.' When the imperial train finally pulled away, courtiers stumbled over themselves in 'dismay and apprehension' at Sophie's unexpected appearance, taking it as evidence of her ambition. Count Eduard Paar, the emperor's chief adjutant, even compared her to Countess Mirafiori, the disreputable former mistress and then morganatic wife of King Victor Emmanuel II of Italy. The unflattering remark quickly filtered back to Sophie, who confronted Margutti. 'It's an insult to me!' she declared. 'You can tell Count Paar so. I'm no Countess Mirafiori!' Compared to a scheming royal mistress, Sophie was the offended party, yet the court used the episode against her, insisting it proved that her 'ambition is unbridled and her unusual intelligence will soon show her the way to translate it into fact!'[18]

These false accusations hurled at Sophie played to public perception and, for many, became accepted fact. 'To do Sophie justice,' wrote her acquaintance Daisy, Princess of Pless, 'I must say that I believed she cherished no political or dynastic ambitions.'[19] This was true: Sophie had no grand scheme to gain power for herself or her sons, no desire to thrust herself into the unwelcome limelight, and no ambitions except to make her husband and children happy. As her great-granddaughter Princess Anita says, she 'never attempted to push herself forward' and was always careful in her behaviour, aware that critics were always on the lookout for ammunition against her and her husband.[20]

Nor did Franz Ferdinand allow her to meddle in political decisions. 'Women', he insisted, 'belong in the kitchen, in the cellar, and in the bed.'[21] The archduke's private secretary, Paul Nikitsch-Boulles, insisted that Sophie

> *never had the powerful and disastrous influence over her husband which the public attributed to her. The Archduke was much too self-confident and had a mind of his own to let himself be influenced even in trivial matters by the wills of others – not even by his own dearly beloved wife. And it is assumed that she never made the slightest attempt to achieve anything that lay outside the immediate family life or anything that remotely touched the general public and politics . . . but in private life there were sufficient occasions where she summoned up her whole heart to assert herself with her husband. It seemed like that she was successful, but then the Archduke would insist on the exact opposite, which was in line with his own opinion. But there was never a word of criticism: the decision was taken calmly.*[22]

Franz Ferdinand would occasionally ask his wife's opinions, and Sophie might exert her influence in subtle ways, but nothing suggests that she ever played more than a passing role in her husband's approach to the empire's political problems.

That many of these lies originated at a hostile imperial court simply emphasized the continuing opposition to, and even confusion over, Franz Ferdinand and Sophie's marriage. Uncertainty regulated their lives in Vienna. There were small concessions, grudgingly granted but often humiliatingly executed. In 1902, Sophie was allowed to join the imperial family for their usual New Year's Day dinner, a fact noted in the Viennese press, though her invitations were inconsistent over the next decade.[23] However, apparent favour became an unpleasant ordeal. Sophie's position as a morganatic spouse was made clear. She could not sit near her husband; some accounts speak of her placed awkwardly down the table at the corner rather than along the sides with the other guests.[24] During one such dinner, it was said, she had no sooner taken her place at the table than a chamberlain whispered in her ear: she had mistakenly been seated too prominently and was asked to move to the end of the table as the guests watched.[25] The atmosphere, said Franz Josef's trusted valet Eugen Ketterl, 'was always exceedingly strained'. The emperor resented entertaining his relatives, much less Sophie, and made little effort to make the evenings enjoyable.[26] The emperor was always served first and wolfed down his food; as soon as he finished the table was cleared. Sophie, sitting at the end and always served last, was lucky to get a bite or two before a footman swept in and removed her plate.[27]

To some, Sophie was like a phantom, haunting the court with her unwelcome presence. 'The first time we invited the princess', one ambassador in Vienna recalled, 'we had to solve all kinds of little issues. Would the princess be received at the bottom of the staircase, as would an archduchess? Would she take precedence over the hostess? If she came with her husband, would she walk with him up the stairs, as would an archduchess, or would she walk behind him? All of these details may seem petty and of no consequence, but they were of supreme importance.'[28] Public opinion, however, increasingly sided with her and against Montenuovo. The press reported the slights, detailed her appearances, and even took notice when she sat for a new official photograph.[29] Yet five years of correspondence passed between uncle and nephew before Franz Josef even mentioned her, closing a letter to the archduke with 'I send warm greetings to the Princess.'[30] A few months later, he granted her permission to attend a children's festival being given in the grounds of her own Belvedere Palace, but not until 21 July 1905 did the emperor's seemingly impenetrable reserve show the first signs of a thaw. By imperial order, Sophie and the children were awarded the style of 'Serene Highness' (*Durchlaucht*). This moved them from the empire's aristocracy to the lower ranks of the country's royalty.[31] The new style also brought with it a change in precedence. At court ceremonies, Sophie would still follow the archduchesses, duchesses, princesses, spouses, widows, and noble children deemed of equal birth, but now she could walk in front of the late empress's mistress of the robes and no longer be the last lady to enter a ballroom.[32]

This schizophrenic approach, with apparent favour extended to his wife at one moment only to be followed by an insult the next, took its toll on Franz Ferdinand. He viewed the imperial court, and especially Montenuovo, as 'the root of all evil', perpetual and spiteful thorns in Sophie's side. It was no secret that the archduke planned to make a clean sweep of the court when he came to the throne, firing those he deemed responsible for his wife's humiliations.[33] Montenuovo knew he was a marked man and even kept a letter of resignation in his desk drawer for that future day when Franz Ferdinand came to the throne.[34]

Montenuovo maintained his hold on power only through the emperor's continued favour. A decade earlier he had tried to undermine Franz Ferdinand's position as heir in favour of Archduke Otto, but such options faded after the turn of the century. After a temporary break over his marriage, Franz Ferdinand had reconciled with his sister Margarethe, Duchess of Württemberg, before her death (probably from stomach cancer) in 1902, and now, in 1905, his brother Otto lay dying in Vienna.[35]

A life of debauchery had not been kind to the handsome Otto. His marriage to Maria Josepha produced two sons, but everyone knew it was a farce, and the archduke was quickly back to his drunken nights, mistresses, and fathering illegitimate children with a ballerina.[36] Maria Josepha endured it all, at least until the night her husband led his drunken friends to her bedroom and laughed at how hideously unappealing he really found his wife. Otto was ordered to live elsewhere, though imperial decorum dictated that the couple appear together at court and pretend that nothing was wrong.[37]

Warnings from a disappointed emperor had no effect. Otto had been indulged too long to curtail his wayward habits. Perhaps his syphilis accounted for his increasingly scandalous scenes, as when he appeared one night at the famous and fashionable Sacher Hotel in Vienna, wandering around drunk and naked except for his military cap and a sword sheathed around his waist.[38] No one felt much sympathy for him, including his wife, as syphilis ate away at his once admired face and forced him to wear a leather nose. By the time doctors performed a tracheotomy, Otto had disappeared from public view. He spent his agonized last days hidden away from Vienna, ignored by Maria Josepha and tended to by his saintly stepmother and by Louise Robinson, his latest mistress, who unsuccessfully tried to conceal her questionable past by donning a nun's habit and calling herself Sister Martha.[39]

Otto's deplorable condition posed a moral dilemma for Franz Ferdinand when their stepmother, Maria Theresa, sent word that the end was near. Should Franz Ferdinand go to his brother's side? Despite his own dissolute life, Otto had never forgiven his older brother for marrying Sophie. He had denounced the union, avoided the wedding, and refused to meet the new princess. When Franz Ferdinand refused to go to his brother's deathbed, the act was put down to pure vengeance and, as with so much of the gossip about the couple, ascribed to Sophie's desire to punish her brother-in-law. Yet the truth was not quite as callous. There was, to be sure, an element of bitterness that the decision, but appearing at Otto's bedside presented a moral quandary that went far beyond past feelings of betrayal. The dying archduke's mistress was constantly at his side, and Franz Ferdinand had no desire to meet his brother's adulterous lover or share his grief with her. Even Otto's own wife was unwilling to appear at her husband's deathbed. The very idea of this traumatic and uncomfortable confrontation was unthinkable for the deeply religious Franz Ferdinand. Instead, he led Sophie to the Belvedere's small chapel and the two knelt together, praying for Otto when he finally died on 1 November 1906, at the age of forty-one.[40] 'You can imagine what I went through,' the usually reserved Franz Ferdinand confided to a friend, 'and how I have been feeling, since you know how close we were earlier and how we spent our whole childhood and youth together . . . Poor Otto had suffered terribly during the past year and his death was a true relief for him . . . May God give him eternal rest.'[41]

Ferdinand Karl, the archduke's youngest brother, had also disappeared from public view. A quiet, genial man, devoted to literature, art, and science, he, too, had been estranged from Franz Ferdinand over his marriage and pointedly avoided him until he stumbled into his own romantic misadventure. Soon after snubbing the wedding in Reichstadt, Ferdinand Karl fell in love with Bertha Czuber, daughter of a Viennese professor. She was intelligent, elegant, and beautiful, but Ferdinand Karl's confession that he meant to marry her stunned his older brother. Sophie had been unequal, but at least she had been an aristocrat. He fared no better with the emperor: having allowed the extraordinary union between his heir, Franz Ferdinand, and Sophie, Franz Josef was not about to sanction the morganatic marriage of a minor archduke with no such position to wield in favour of his arguments.[42]

Despite objecting to Franz Ferdinand's marriage as 'beneath the dignity' of the imperial house, Ferdinand Karl now wanted his brother's blessing to marry the woman of his choosing. There were 'violent scenes' between the brothers, and neither would relent.[43] The growing problem was avoided at all costs: in 1904, Ferdinand Karl left the Imperial Army, suffering from tuberculosis, and retreated into private life with Bertha in the Tyrol. There were always rumours about the couple, but when confronted, Ferdinand Karl strenuously denied that he secretly wed the young lady, much less that she was his mistress. The truth finally emerged in 1911, when Ferdinand Karl admitted that he had married Bertha but lied to both the emperor and to his brother to keep the union a secret. 'Through his action Ferdinand has broken the promise he gave me seven years ago not to marry Miss Czuber and entered into this marriage with her without my permission,' the emperor wrote to Franz Ferdinand, adding, 'I urge you to consider the matter as strictly confidential between the two of us.'[44] Franz Ferdinand was shocked, not so much by the actual marriage, which he had already suspected, but by his brother's deliberate deception. Lying to him was one thing; lying to the emperor, he believed, was a sin approaching heresy.[45] He was not the only one who felt betrayed. Franz Josef responded by stripping Ferdinand Karl of his archducal title, his honours and his income, and exiled him permanently from Austria. He would spend the rest of his life as 'Ferdinand Burg', living quietly in the Tyrol with his cherished wife.[46]

Romantic indiscretions within the House of Habsburg had become commonplace. In 1902, Archduke Leopold Ferdinand, who had accompanied Franz Ferdinand on his cruise around the world until he was removed in Australia, renounced his title, took the name Leopold Wölfling, and ran off to Switzerland to marry a postmaster's daughter with a distressing bent for public nudity. At the same time, his sister, Princess Louisa of Tuscany, left her husband, the crown prince of Saxony, with her children's French tutor in tow; she, too, fled to Switzerland. After divorcing her husband, she stunned the continent by marrying an Italian musician the following year.

Such scandals cast a clearer light on Franz Ferdinand and Sophie's marriage. Flaunted mistresses, illegitimate children, deaths by syphilis, and royal divorces made the unequal union between archduke and Bohemian countess seem the model of responsibility and respectability. For all of the erroneous talk depicting Sophie as a scheming adventuress, she had not once put a foot wrong in the archaic imperial court. Initial scepticism over the marriage began to fade. Time might not heal the deliberate wounds; embrace was difficult, but the passing years seemed to promise gradual acceptance of the empire's most unusual and most devoted royal couple.

SEVEN

Attitudes Soften

✛

With Archdukes Otto and Ferdinand Karl dead or dishonoured, Franz Josef was forced to look upon Franz Ferdinand and Sophie's marriage in a more favourable light. Not that he embraced the union. The emperor, insisted his aide-de-camp Count Paar, 'could not forgive' the match, and he 'forever reproached himself in the bitterest terms for having allowed the marriage'.[1] Still, the passing years left Franz Josef increasingly tired, unable or unwilling to fight accomplished fact. Confounding expectations, Sophie had never once caused a scene, put a foot wrong, or goaded her husband into a quarrelsome grab for power. 'Since her arrival in the capital', reported one newspaper, 'she had a very difficult situation, and had to learn to ignore disappointment and humiliation through miracles of perseverance, ingenuity, and tact. Supported by her loving husband, the princess performs these miracles with charm and sweetness; there is nothing sharp to her beautiful qualities. Her charm and intelligence seduce everyone.'[2] Her serenity, the calming effect she had on the archduke's character, and the couple's obvious devotion to one another softened attitudes.

Court appearances by Franz Ferdinand and Sophie were still rare and often left contradictory impressions of imperial favour mingled with humiliations. As Sophie entered a 1909 court ball she found that

Montenuovo had again neglected to provide her with an escort. This time she did not flee from the room in shame; holding her head high, she walked into the room with immense dignity. Taking pity, a young arch-duke apparently ran forward and gave her his arm without thinking of the implications. The next day, Montenuovo was swamped with complaints. It was not merely an irritated Franz Ferdinand protesting but also several archduchesses, who considered that Sophie had no right to walk on the arm of an archduke and that imperial etiquette had been violated.[3]

The princess's first official public function in her own right came six months later, when Sophie christened the new dreadnought *Radetzky* in Trieste. Franz Ferdinand was delighted; it seemed as if the restrictions and animosity against his wife were dissipating. Reality was not as forgiving. August 1909 marked the centennial of Napoleon's expulsion from the Tyrol. Both the emperor and Franz Ferdinand would attend the festivities marking the occasion, but word that the Tyrolean Provincial Committee had also extended an invitation to Sophie sent the imperial court into a panic. The emperor insisted that in asking Sophie the committee was only being polite and that she 'should not attend this official ceremony' as her presence was 'difficult to reconcile with the provisions of ceremonial'. There was a coda, perhaps well meant in theory but insulting in reality. The prin-cess, the emperor assured his nephew, 'belongs in our family circle, and I am delighted to see her at closed, family gatherings'.[4] Intended or not, the message seemed clear: Sophie might be an acceptable companion behind closed doors, but lines had to be drawn in public lest the empire be con-fused about her continued inequality in the eyes of the imperial court.

The complexities of this approach came into sharp focus where foreign royals were concerned. Sovereigns and princes visiting Vienna might pay their respects to Franz Ferdinand and Sophie in private, and she might at-tend any formal events in their honour, but return calls to foreign courts were banned. In January 1902, when Franz Ferdinand travelled to St Petersburg to thank Tsar Nicholas II for appointing him a general of the Imperial Russian Cavalry, Sophie was not allowed to accompany him.[5] Her curious position confused and confounded many. In 1904, when the future George V and his wife, Mary, paid a state visit to Vienna, Sophie was excluded from the official receptions. However, the British royal couple privately called on Franz Ferdinand and Sophie at the Belvedere, most likely at George's insistence, for his wife was less enthusiastic about her Bohemian counterpart. Although she was herself the product of a morganatic marriage, Mary could never forget her own past and the effects of an unsuitable marriage, something later demonstrated when her own son King Edward VIII abdicated the throne to marry American divorcée Wallis Simpson. The call went off successfully, but the difficulties underscored the social tightrope many visiting royals had to walk. Refusing to meet Sophie might please the current emperor but offend his heir. Such private encounters represented something of an uneasy compromise, subtle recognition of Sophie as Franz Ferdinand's wife without risking the ire of Franz Josef. Yet according to both Kaiser Wilhelm II and the gossipy Henry Wickham Steed, George's father, King Edward VII, privately confided that, sooner or later, everyone would have to face the fact that Sophie would, by rights, become empress when Franz Ferdinand came to the throne.[6]

Not many royal courts were as democratic in their thinking. In May 1906, Franz Ferdinand travelled to Madrid for the wedding of King Alfonso to Queen Victoria's granddaughter Princess Victoria Eugenie of Battenberg, herself a morganatic descendant. Sophie was not invited, even though a gala dinner was given at the palace in Madrid in her husband's honour. Not only were there difficulties over protocol, but Alfonso's mother, Queen Christina, was also Archduchess Isabella's sister-in-law. The idea of the formidable Isabella and her former lady-in-waiting sharing such a glittering royal occasion was too fraught with potential dangers. The archduke and his wife travelled on the same train as far as Biarritz, where Sophie stayed in a hotel, using the name Countess of Artstetten, while her husband continued to Madrid.[7]

The situation irritated Franz Ferdinand, and circumstances only combined to make him miserable. It was nearly 110 degrees when his train arrived in the Spanish capital; his lodgings lacked modern plumbing or electricity, but the furniture did come with an infestation of bedbugs.[8] On the day of the wedding, 31 May, he shared a hot, uncomfortable carriage with the future King Albert I of Belgium and the hefty Grand Duke Vladimir of Russia. They were far back enough in the procession to escape injury when a terrorist threw a bomb at the landau carrying the king and his new queen. A blast of heat and smoke, screams, and panic followed. Horses lay dead, footmen who had been walking alongside the landau sat dazed and bleeding, the lifeless eyes of a severed head gazed from the street, and the queen's white wedding dress was covered in blood. The monarchs calmly changed vehicles and continued on through the streets; Franz Ferdinand followed, nervously acknowledging the crowd and having unknowingly come face-to-face with an eerie glimpse of his own future.

The pageantry and peril of such occasions were forbidden to Sophie until 1909, when an unexpected invitation arrived from Rumania. King Carol asked if Franz Ferdinand and his 'consort' would honour him and his queen with a private visit. Never before had a reigning monarch requested Sophie's presence in an official capacity, and the invitation sent the imperial court into a panic. As far as official Vienna was concerned, Sophie was a non-person, in no way entitled to join her husband as 'consort' on such an illustrious occasion. If one European court extended even private recognition to Sophie and treated her equally, surely Franz Ferdinand would use his influence to obtain further invitations. Gradually, and through such encounters, the princess would win the acclaim so strenuously denied to her in Austria-Hungary, making it difficult for the imperial court to continue its exclusionary policies. By protocol, such a foreign visit demanded the emperor's approval, yet Franz Josef now faced an uncomfortable fait accompli. He could allow his nephew to make the journey alone, but to pointedly exclude Sophie when the king had just as pointedly included her in his invitation risked royal unpleasantness and diplomatic scandal, as well as eliciting unwanted sympathy for her unenviable position. With his hand forced, the emperor had little choice but to agree to the invitation. Private though it might be, Sophie was about to visit a royal court and for the first time be received formally as the wife of the heir to the Austro-Hungarian throne.[9]

The trip would avoid the royal court at Bucharest, with its complex questions of etiquette and difficulties over precedence. Instead, Franz Ferdinand and Sophie would visit the king and queen at their summer palace of Peles, in the Carpathian Mountains at Sinaia. For the first time, the archduke's wife travelled with him to a foreign country using her own name, not an alias. King Carol's reply on hearing that the invitation had been accepted eased any lingering worries. He was, he assured Franz Ferdinand, 'more than delighted' by the coming visit. He added assurances that 'my wife and I are looking forward to making the acquaintance of your dear wife, who just like you, dear cousin, will be welcomed by us with open arms'.[10]

On 10 July, the imperial train rattled to a stop at a small Rumanian border town, where the king's nephew and heir, Crown Prince Ferdinand, and his wife, Marie, waited on the platform to welcome Franz Ferdinand and Sophie. The honour guard snapped to attention, a regimental band played the Austro-Hungarian and Rumanian anthems, and for the first time the archduke crossed a red carpet with his wife at his side. The Rumanian prime minister bowed his greetings, and a little girl offered Sophie a bouquet of flowers beneath the sunny sky. King Carol had warned Ferdinand and Marie that they 'must, in all ways, manifest good will' to the visiting couple, and they complied, though not without some reservations.[11] Marie was a granddaughter of both Tsar Alexander II and Queen Victoria; she received Sophie on equal terms, the wife of one heir to the throne greeting another, but later complained 'in no uncertain fashion that there is a vast difference' between a morganatic spouse 'and one of equal birth, especially when the latter can claim direct descent from the reigning houses of Russia and England'.[12]

Nevertheless, the gestures were all pleasant as the crown prince and princess ushered their visitors to a waiting carriage and the two couples set off to Sinaia. Some three hundred Transylvanian Rumanians greeted them with flowers and a choral performance as they paused at the Sinaia Monastery before journeying on to the castle.[13] King Carol and Queen Elisabeth greeted them at Schloss Peles, an immense, medieval-style hunting lodge whose spidery towers rose against the surrounding mountains. The queen stepped forward and caught Sophie in mid-curtsy, sweeping her into her arms and kissing her effusively, to her visitor's visible embarrassment.[14]

Queen Elisabeth was an eccentric figure, with a penchant for poetry and 'a profound sympathy for morganatic marriages'. While the king and the archduke discussed politics over cigars, Elisabeth smothered Sophie with attention. Crown Princess Marie found the somewhat exotic figure of a morganatic consort 'an amiable, decorative lady, very tall and very Viennese looking', whatever that meant, though she insisted that Sophie had 'stereotyped and conventional manners'. At times, Sophie seemed 'quite bewildered' by all the fuss over her, but even Marie admitted that she had 'perfect tact', was 'neither too humble nor too forward', and 'played her part beautifully and to the satisfaction of all sides'.[15] Even the king agreed. Sophie, he wrote, had been 'absolutely charming, and there were no problems about her difficult position'.[16]

Franz Ferdinand was overjoyed when, at a banquet in the castle's Turkish Hall, his wife was seated at the king's right, in the place of honour, not down the table and at the end, as would happen in Vienna. More festive dinners, theatricals, and a comedic opera filled the following evenings. The archduke's mood was ebullient: he reviewed the 3rd Battalion of the Mountain Regiment and happily spent the rest of the trip motoring and walking into the mountains, picnicking with the crown prince and princess, climbing a rope ladder to take tea with the queen in a little pavilion she had built among the branches, and enjoying their time together.[17] Above all, he was delighted that his beloved wife had been treated with such respect and consideration; nearly everyone agreed that she had come through this 'baptism of fire', as the archduke's secretary termed it, admirably.[18]

It was Franz Ferdinand, in fact, who unwittingly provided the only sour note. During the visit, he met with a group of Rumanian exiles from Hungarian-controlled Transylvania, hoping to become King Carol's subjects. Among them was historian Aurel Popovici, whose book suggesting that the Habsburg Empire be divided into a confederation of semi-autonomous states captured the archduke's interest. He listened to complaints about heavy-handed Magyar rule and suppression of ethnic minorities, complaints he knew to be all too valid from his own uncomfortable years in Hungary. Hungarian nationals were furious and demanded that Franz Ferdinand apologize. When he resisted, they had their revenge: as the train carrying the archduke and his wife passed through Transylvania, crowds who came out to cheer the couple were kept away from sidings and railway stations by Hungarian bayonets.[19]

A second, more eventful triumph came four months later, when Kaiser Wilhelm II publicly welcomed Franz Ferdinand and Sophie to Berlin during a trip that was a state visit in all but name. The relationship between Franz Ferdinand and Wilhelm had been uncertain, often tense, and occasionally antagonistic. Although Germany was Austria-Hungary's principal ally, the kaiser had never been a welcome figure in Vienna. A man of complex personality, Wilhelm II suffered from feelings of inferiority. The archduke's feelings stemmed from his wife's treatment, while the kaiser's were more deep-seated. Wilhelm's left arm had been displaced at birth and remained of little use; his mother – Queen Victoria's eldest daughter – treated the deformity as weakness, and a harsh childhood of conflicting influences left the kaiser a bellicose braggart whose abrasive personality concealed a passionate craving for acceptance.

The archduke disliked pageantry, while the kaiser revelled in ceremony; Franz Ferdinand was simple in his tastes, while Wilhelm enjoyed strutting about in a variety of gaudy uniforms. The archduke was reserved and quiet; Wilhelm loved to talk, most often about himself, and loved to be the centre of attention, 'the bride at every wedding and the corpse at every funeral', as one author commented.[20] Yet the two men shared a love of hunting and a dedication to bourgeois domesticity, even if, in the kaiser's case, it was largely a flamboyant show.

The kaiser was an unlikely champion in the archduke's constant battle for Sophie's acceptance. Franz Ferdinand had arrived at a Berlin railway station in 1898 to find the kaiser standing on the platform. Wilhelm watched him alight, fixed him with a stare, and loudly declared, 'Don't imagine that I have come to receive you! I am expecting the Crown Prince of Italy.'[21] Such scenes led the archduke to name the kaiser as '*Europas grösster Mordskerl*' ('Europe's Greatest Joker').[22]

The relationship took a turn in September 1903. Wilhelm arrived in Vienna following a visit with Archduke Friedrich and his wife, Isabella, who filled his head with horror stories about Sophie and allegations about her supposedly scandalous past. He was determined to avoid her, but his chancellor, Prince Bernhard von Bülow, warned the kaiser that he should not offend the archduke. 'If I give in here,' Wilhelm insisted, 'then I will live to see my sons marry ladies-in-waiting and maids!' As the train drew into Vienna, Bülow whispered, 'Your Majesty now has a choice. You can either make the future Emperor of Austria your friend or foe forever more.' Franz Josef and his nephew waited on the platform, and in a few seconds the kaiser made his choice. After greeting the emperor, he turned to Franz Ferdinand and said, 'When can I have the honour of making my obeisance to your wife?'[23] That afternoon, the kaiser took tea with the archduke and his wife at Belvedere Palace, and a friendship was born.[24]

This simple gesture eased Franz Ferdinand's scepticism, and soon he and the kaiser seemed to be the closest of friends. The two regularly hunted together and exchanged effusive letters; to the kaiser, the archduke was always 'Dear Franzi'. Wilhelm, wrote his only daughter, Viktoria Luise, had a 'high regard' for the archduke's 'cleverness, a fact that seemed singularly ignored by his own country'.[25] Now the kaiser had an opportunity to cement the friendship in a very public way; by honouring Sophie, he believed, he would forever win Franz Ferdinand's grateful support.

It was, ironically, 11 November – the date nine years in the future that would mark the end of the great cataclysmic war woven around these two men – when Franz Ferdinand stepped from his train and into the kaiser's welcoming arms at Berlin's Anhalter Station. Bands played along the crimson carpet, Habsburg and Hohenzollern flags fluttered in the rush of wind, and an honour guard from the Kaiser Franz Infantry Regiment snapped to attention and presented arms. When Sophie appeared, the kaiser rushed forward, bowed, kissed her hand, and handed her an enormous bouquet of orchids. The gesture of respect from kaiser to morganatic spouse set the European press aflutter.[26]

Unlike in Rumania, this time Sophie accepted the attention with ease. Moving along the platform at her husband's side in a mauve velvet dress and enormous, ostrich-plumed hat, she 'made a good impression and looked very elegant', said an observer.[27] Yet the impressive pageantry could not fully conceal the subtle reminder of Sophie's morganatic status. The kaiserin, Augusta Viktoria, did not greet her at the station, nor did Crown Princess Cecilie; instead, it was Princess Eitel Friedrich, wife of one of the kaiser's many sons, who did the honours.[28]

Augusta Viktoria did welcome the visiting couple to Potsdam that night. A lavish banquet was arranged in the Neues Palais, though this, too, presented problems. Following precedence would have left Sophie condemned to the distant end of a long table, far away from her husband, the kaiser, his spouse, and his own children at the centre. This, Wilhelm knew, would only upset the archduke. To solve this difficulty, he replaced the traditional long banqueting table with a number of smaller, round tables, declaring that he and his wife would share one with the Austrian visitors. When Sophie appeared, in an orange gown trimmed with fur, the kaiser even took her arm and led her to her seat, to his immediate right, in the place of honour.[29]

Wilhelm and Franz Ferdinand left Berlin for several days of shooting, and in their absence the German imperial family seemed to embrace Sophie. Crown Princess Cecilie gave a dinner in her honour at the Marble Palace, seating Sophie between the kaiserin and Wilhelm's sister Crown Princess Sophie of Greece.[30] Princess Eitel Friedrich escorted her on tours of Berlin and Potsdam, joined her at a reception for a girls' school, and watched as Sophie dedicated a new orphanage. The impressions were highly favourable and the effect almost triumphant.[31] As he left Berlin, Franz Ferdinand was effusive in his thanks, telling the kaiser, 'I'll never forget you and these past few days.'[32]

The prominence of the visit, the kaiser's bow to Sophie and public kiss of her hand, the banquet and the visits – all of these things pleased Franz Ferdinand immensely. However, such triumphs rankled in Vienna, at least in certain quarters. According to one diplomat, when details of the Berlin visit were reported in the Viennese newspapers, a number of archduchesses were furious that Sophie, whom they derisively called 'a maid', was being accorded such honours. The kaiser, they complained, had treated her as if she were a future empress.[33]

Not even embittered gossip could erase the lingering effects of Rumania and Berlin. Sophie had successfully navigated two potential minefields. Nine years of quiet and gracious acceptance of humiliations and snubs had revealed the depth of her character in the face of persistent doubt. No one could deny that the archduke's marriage was a success, and what happened next was so unexpected that it caught both the couple and their critics by surprise.

Perhaps it was reluctant acknowledgment of the inevitable, or perhaps it was a reward – no one would ever be sure. In any event, on 4 October 1909, Franz Josef raised Sophie to the rank of duchess. 'I find myself duly honoured to bestow on your morganatic spouse Sophie', he wrote to his nephew, 'the rank of Duchess of Hohenberg and the style of *"Ihre Hoheit"* [Your Highness]. At My Court I further assign to her the rank of precedence immediately after the youngest Archduchess who has been honoured with the Order of the Star Cross.'[34]

In the Austrian empire, a duchess ranked higher than a mere princess. Now, Sophie went from the aristocratic *Ihre Durchlaucht* (Your Serene Highness) granted in 1905 to the royal *Ihre Hoheit*, which raised her dignity considerably according to the complexities of Austrian titles.[35] With the change Sophie now outranked not only duchesses, princesses, and children deemed equal in the eyes of the imperial house but also the youngest archduchesses not yet of age. Franz Ferdinand's joy knew no bounds. After nine years, the couple's household and staff now had to call their mistress 'Highness'. The archduke declared that anyone guilty of using her old style would have to donate something for charity to one of his children's piggy banks, then promptly forgot his own rule and found himself happily slipping a few coins into the slot.[36]

There were even more welcome changes. The emperor ordered that as of 1 January 1910, military units were to present arms to Sophie and the sentries were to remain in place when she was alone at the Belvedere. She was allowed to become patron of charities and regiments; the musical director of the imperial court, Karl Ziehrer, even composed a special waltz, the 'Söpherl Valz', in her honour, and other composers followed with waltzes, polkas, and tunes bearing her name. For the first time, she was allowed to attend military ceremonies at her husband's side.[37] Hopeful, the couple returned to Vienna and to the Belvedere for the winter social season.

Sophie's first court appearance as Duchess of Hohenberg should have been a moment of personal triumph. 'Recent times', she admitted to her sister Oktavia, 'have been difficult, like at the beginning', and the decision to attend was 'a true dilemma'.[38] Excitement in Vienna ran high: how would the new Duchess of Hohenberg fare at court? Would her precedence change? Would she share the dais where the imperial family sat watching the waltzes? Some four thousand guests, eager to find out, crowded into the Hofburg on the evening of 18 January.[39] Sophie, as usual, had to enter behind the archduchesses. 'What was most awkward for me', she confided to her sister Oktavia, 'was that I could not be part of the procession but as the very last . . . so conspicuous!' She wore a black and white brocade gown, and a veil edged with white ostrich feathers; a sapphire tiara that 'looked really noble,' she confessed, shimmered atop her hair. She could be seen chatting amiably as the night wore on. At one point, Franz Josef stopped and exchanged a few words with her.[40] She walked on the arm of Prince Ludwig of Coburg, and when the imperial family repaired to take supper, for the first time she joined them.[41] Behind closed doors, Montenuovo arranged for her to share a table and seated her, perhaps maliciously, between two of Isabella's daughters.[42] 'You can imagine how happy I was when it was over,' Sophie admitted to her sister.[43]

Yet society remained suspiciously distant. One princess confided to a British diplomat that, although she had formerly been very friendly with Sophie, she no longer felt that she could write or speak to her, or even admit a relationship in public, where censorious eyes were constantly on alert for any whiff of scandal. Most aristocratic women, he reported, followed the same rules, certain that Sophie 'should have refused to marry the Archduke'.[44]

When summer came, the couple briefly returned to Vienna, slowly testing the waters of acceptance. 'It was such a joy that I was able to go to a competitive riding event and the Derby again,' Sophie confided to her sister Oktavia. 'And how different it was! There were so incredibly many people there.' She deemed it all 'great fun', but added that it had been 'melting hot!'[45]

A few months later, when King Edward VII died, Franz Ferdinand hoped that his wife would be allowed to accompany him to the funeral in London. When officials pointed out that spouses did not customarily receive such invitations, and that many foreign royal relatives were not to be invited, the archduke suggested that his wife could travel with him privately, but this, too, raised problems. If George V neglected to invite other foreign royal representatives but received Sophie, unpleasantness might follow. Additionally, if the new Queen Mary received the duchess but neglected to extend such courtesies to other spouses, it would be taken as inexplicable favouritism; if she ignored her presence in London it might be taken as an unintended snub.[46]

The archduke's desire to include his wife was understandable, but in this case, he was seeking not royal acceptance but a blatant exception to established protocol. He was irritable when he set off for London, and the journey did nothing to improve his mood. The archduke shared his train with several other royal mourners, including the recently self-proclaimed Tsar Ferdinand of Bulgaria. The two men loathed each other and waged a kind of running battle across the continent, with Franz Ferdinand successfully arguing that his private compartment should come first in the train and Tsar Ferdinand retaliating by forbidding the archduke passage through his carriage to reach the dining car.[47]

Things scarcely improved in London. 'Hopefully his son will be a better politician,' he commented on the dead monarch to a friend.[48] During the funeral procession, King George V rode after his father's coffin at the side of his cousin Kaiser Wilhelm II, followed by the kings of Greece, Norway, Spain, Denmark, Portugal and Belgium, along with the late king's two grandsons, the future kings Edward VIII (later the Duke of Windsor) and his brother George VI. Franz Ferdinand was forced to walk in the third row, between King Albert I of Belgium and the heir to the Ottoman Empire, and found fault with nearly everything.[49] 'It was extraordinary strenuous and tiring,' the archduke complained. It was hot, and he thought 'it an imposition bordering on the inconsiderate' to have the princes on display in 'the sun baked streets of London' for hours. He deemed the pageantry more akin to 'a coronation or a triumphal procession than a funeral' with 'everything shiny and gold, silver, purple, and scarlet', and the archduke was less than thrilled with many of his fellow guests. He derided Tsar Ferdinand as a 'totally false and unreliable creature who cut a particularly pathetic figure' and looked 'like a pig', insisted that the crown prince of Serbia resembled a 'bad gypsy', and said that American President Theodore Roosevelt lacked manners.[50]

The archduke's erroneous belief that officials had deliberately barred Sophie from the trip to insult her apparently coloured his experiences, and he returned to Austria ever vigilant against any slight. He could not bear to see Sophie subjected to apparent demonstrations of favour at one turn while at the next hounded by vindictive gossip and complaining Habsburgs. The couple very pointedly avoided attending the Imperial Court Ball on 16 January the following year. It was left to the Vienna *Reichspost* to explain their absence. 'We should find it incomprehensible if the position assigned to the consort of the Heir Apparent by the present Court Ceremonial should have been thought unnecessarily painful,' it opined. 'According to this ceremonial, the wife of the Heir Apparent is preceded not only by the married ladies of the Imperial House but even by the youngest princesses . . . As several young archduchesses appeared this year at the court ball for the first time, the rigours of the ceremonial hitherto observed would perhaps have been even more conspicuous. It would be very intelligible if Duchess Sophie of Hohenberg should have wished to avoid a painful situation if only out of regard for her exalted husband.'[51]

Further proof of the court's ambivalence came early that summer. The archduke had been impressed during his world tour with the size of the British navy and its role in controlling and expanding that nation's vast empire. Although Austria had no similar expansionist plans, Franz Ferdinand believed his country should have a competitive naval force. He became an admiral in the Imperial and Royal Navy and supervised and promoted the transformation of the fledgling little fleet into a highly efficient force. The launch of the flagship of this new fleet, the dreadnought *Viribus Unitis*, should have been a moment of personal triumph; instead, it became yet another unwelcome reminder that, for all of the concessions, Sophie was still not deemed worthy to share official recognition. She attended the launch at Trieste along with Franz Ferdinand and his stepsister, Maria Annunciata, but her name was pointedly omitted from the official programme.[52]

Yet the previously unbridgeable gulf between the duchess and the imperial family was slowly narrowing. Her appearances at court would always be contradictory, but the previously icy disdain with which some members of the imperial family had treated her finally began to thaw. Habsburgs, it is true, had previously directed a few words toward her *en passant* in their letters to Franz Ferdinand. In 1907, breaking years of silence, Archduke Friedrich wrote, 'Many thanks indeed to your wife for the friendly greetings, which I most heartily reciprocate.'[53] After Sophie's elevation to duchess, the words were more effusive, stretching to 'hearty greeting to you and Sophie'.[54] Even Archduchess Elisabeth, Rudolf's daughter and the duchess's former enemy, ended a 1911 letter to Franz Ferdinand with 'I kiss Sophie's hand'.[55]

These polite mentions reflected not merely the change in Sophie's status but also a growing realization that with each passing year it was more likely that Franz Ferdinand would soon ascend the throne. It had been easy enough to stand against the marriage a decade earlier, when Franz Josef was still robust and forceful. Now, however, it was a question of hedging bets, of not further alienating the man who might soon become emperor and have control of their destinies. Attitudes may have softened with grudging admiration for Sophie's serene ability to cope with the quarrelsome intrigues and spiteful insults directed against her, but ultimately, for members of the House of Habsburg, the considerations were likely more selfish than humanitarian.

There was, though, one exception: Franz Ferdinand's young nephew Archduke Karl. Following Otto's death, Franz Ferdinand had done his best to act as guardian for his two nephews. 'This task is not being made easy for me,' he confided, 'but I will apply all my capabilities to bring them up to be good Christians, Austrians and Habsburgs.'[56] Karl would, in due course, one day follow Franz Ferdinand to the throne, and the uncle took the nephew into his confidence, insisting that he would not exclude him from political affairs as his own uncle Franz Josef had done with him.

Untainted by years of malicious gossip, young Karl became close to Franz Ferdinand and his wife, spending holidays with the couple while rejecting invitations from Sophie's former mistress, Archduchess Isabella.[57] 'I will continue to be true to you, as I always have been,' Karl assured his uncle in one letter. 'Both you and Aunt have always been so kind to me, so it would only be a sign of gratitude to do everything possible, as best as I can do, in order to follow your wishes.'[58] The young archduke repeatedly expressed his devotion to his 'dear uncle' and seemed equally devoted to Sophie, inevitably ending his letters, 'Kiss Aunt's hand for me.'[59] Appreciating this loyalty, Franz Ferdinand insisted, 'When I am Emperor, I shall have Karl with me in the Hofburg and let him work with me.'[60]

On 21 October 1911, Karl married Princess Zita of Bourbon-Parma at Schloss Schwarzau, with both Franz Ferdinand and Sophie in attendance. The young couple became exceptionally close to Franz Ferdinand and Sophie. After he and Zita spent several weeks with them, Karl wrote, 'Dear Uncle! Dear Aunt! Please excuse me for writing with a pencil while travelling on the train but I really do feel so moved to write this letter. I want to thank you with all my heart for everything you did to please me . . . especially for the very kind welcome which you gave my bride, for your kindness and love. You can't imagine how happy you made me by approving the choice of my heart so much . . . I assure you again that I will do everything possible to come up to your expectations.'[61]

At the time, Zita – like her husband – was delighted to spend time with Franz Ferdinand and Sophie. She later recalled how she had gone up to Sophie during the interval of a play and instinctively kissed her hand. 'Please never do that again in public!' Sophie whispered. 'It's just what people who want to make difficulties are looking for. I've even had threatening letters through the post after things like that.'[62] Yet Zita later painted the relationship between the two couples as more ambiguous. Extremely conservative, territorial about her husband, and staunchly Catholic, Zita viewed the world through a reactionary prism that often led her to distort even the best of intentions. Stories apparently reached her painting Franz Ferdinand as the quintessential 'wicked uncle' who, together with Sophie, had deliberately encouraged Karl to 'pursue a very frivolous life' in an effort to 'ruin him' and thereby eventually place their son Max on the throne.[63]

The tales were nonsense, yet Zita believed them. Somehow, she even blamed Franz Ferdinand for the fact that her husband was not a virgin when they married. 'Guard yourself against women!' the archduke had warned his nephew. Karl's father, Otto, had lived with his mistresses, fathered illegitimate children, and died a horrible death from syphilis; Karl must not follow in his father's footsteps but instead pray for strength. If he could not avoid temptation, Franz Ferdinand insisted, Karl should at least ensure that he was protected against any venereal disease. Zita cast this moral lecture as Franz Ferdinand having prodded her future husband into taking a mistress.[64] The many questionable remarks she later made against Franz Ferdinand must be viewed in the context of Zita's irrational grudge against the archduke.

Franz Ferdinand, it has been alleged, was jealous of Karl. He is said to have caused bitter scenes when, in 1911, the emperor asked the young man, and not Franz Ferdinand, to represent him at the coronation of King George V and Queen Mary and to have complained of press reports that mentioned Karl's name. The idea, though, had been Franz Ferdinand's. 'I would have to ask that His Majesty entrust my nephew Karl with this important representation,' he wrote to Montenuovo. He would be 'most grateful' if Karl, who 'would be sure to carry it out conscientiously', was asked to go in his place.[65] Despite his best efforts, Franz Ferdinand could never escape the sting of erroneous gossip.

EIGHT

'Konopischt Was Home'

✛

Konopischt, Franz Ferdinand and Sophie's daughter fondly recalled many years later, 'was home, the place of our first memories, the cocoon where all our day to day business took place'.[1] Some thirty miles south-east of Prague, nestled atop a wooded hillside, and surveying a forested plain cleaved by a swift river near the small town of Beneschau (now Benešov), Schloss Konopischt was the family's sanctuary. With the passing years, the medieval castle became a place of welcoming familiarity and comfort, a refuge from the embittered gossip of Vienna and the intrigues of the imperial court.

Franz Ferdinand had purchased the twelfth-century structure in 1887 for 12 million crowns (approximately £38,000,000 in 2013 figures); its medieval origins, lofty towers, and commanding situation appealed to his passion for historic, heroic architecture, and he spent a small fortune improving and modernizing the castle. Drawing on the talents of Josef Mocker, his favourite architect and a man who shared the archduke's taste for the Gothic Revival, Franz Ferdinand renovated rooms, installed new water and sewage systems, central steam heating, electricity, a dozen bathrooms with hot and cold running water and a lift, making it the most modern castle in Europe. The archduke relocated the estate village to improve the view, but temporary inconvenience was rewarded with better housing, a modernized brewery, and a new power station to supply the locals with electricity. Additional land was purchased, and a sugar refinery, rock quarries, and forests provided local employment and helped make the estate a self-supporting enterprise.[2]

Life at Konopischt conveyed a kind of relaxed grandeur, unpretentious yet eminently suited to the future emperor. Winter and summer, the first light of day cast dappled shadows over the brooding castle, reflecting off its white walls, immense circular tower, and red-tiled roofs. When the archduke bought the estate, the old castle moat, filled in with earth, had been home to a family of brown bears. Their antics never failed to delight visitors, but the smell eventually became atrocious, and the archduke had the animals transferred to a zoo at Schönbrunn Palace in Vienna.[3]

Dawn saw Konopischt abuzz with activity. Perfection took money and a small army of fifty-five servants. Stewards, footmen, housemaids, cooks, bakers, doctors, clerics, nannies, tutors, scullery maids, gardeners, foresters, carpenters, sentries, coachmen, grooms, chauffeurs and mechanics kept the estate in working order and tended to its owners; there was even a personal photographer who diligently followed the archduke and his family to capture their lives. Some employees came through contacts at the imperial court or had families already established in service. Franz Ferdinand and Sophie also took a more modern approach, relying on the Prague employment firm of Klepetářová to send potential members of their household to Konopischt for interviews.[4]

Very early, Johan Jüptner, the archduke's principal *Kammerdiener*, or valet, would be off along the antler-lined corridors of the family's private rooms on the third floor to wake his master.[5] Franz Ferdinand always rose early, slipping into the bathroom he shared with Sophie and sitting in his dressing gown as Mellich, his personal barber, shaved him. Franz Ferdinand's once thick crown of hair, as Eisenmenger noted, was 'getting ominously thin', and the archduke forever worried that he was going prematurely bald. He sought out every imaginable quack cure, even asking Eisenmenger to report on supposed miracle solutions that cropped up in the American press.[6] Bathed and shaved, the archduke dressed. For all his love of the military, Franz Ferdinand rarely wore uniforms in private, preferring comfortable cotton or wool trousers, linen shirts, and tweed jackets; only for important guests or ceremonial occasions would he don one of the many cumbersome dress uniforms at his disposal.

Prepared for the day, the archduke was usually off to the children's rooms. It was an era when royal and aristocratic children were largely isolated, watched over by nannies and tutors but kept away from their parents except for afternoon tea or formal greetings. Franz Ferdinand and Sophie, though, were different. 'The Little Highnesses', as the children were called in the household, were not cloistered or confined to distant rooms away from their parents.[7] When separated from their children the parents telephoned them every day, or sent letters and telegrams.[8] 'Lots of hugs', 'Papa' might cable to the children; 'Many warm hugs', 'Mama' might telegraph when away.[9] Franz Ferdinand, said Count Ottokar Czernin, 'did everything that a loving father's heart could devise' for his children.[10] His daughter praised him as 'marvellous', noting, 'We were always taken with him on every possible occasion whether travelling or when we were old enough out shooting at home.'[11] As for Sophie, she was, quite simply, 'the heart, the peace-making centre of the family,' her daughter said.[12] She had nursed and bathed the children herself, and she and her husband took the guiding role in their upbringing. The couple doted on them. Within the family, Little Sophie was called Pinky, Max was Maxi, and Ernst was Ernie or Bululu.[13]

The archduke always tried to eat breakfast with his children in their nursery, attacking his customary two boiled eggs, toast and tea as he scanned the day's newspapers. When he lingered with them too long, which often happened, Paul Nikitsch-Boulles, his private secretary, would deliver the morning's mail to the little round table. Inevitably the domestic scene was interrupted when the children, clad in their matching sailor suits, went off to lessons as their father reluctantly retreated to begin his work.[14]

Overlooking the castle's park, Franz Ferdinand's study was a dark, masculine room lined in carved wooden wainscoting and filled with leather chairs, bits of porcelain, tiger skins, oriental carpets, and a hundred souvenirs. A large 1901 painting by Joseph Koppay, depicting Sophie in a white décolleté gown wreathed in ethereal tulle, faced his desk; Little Sophie, her arm draped around her seated father, gazed out from a canvas by Bohemian artist Frantisek Dvorak.[15] The two paintings reflected not only the archduke's love of his family but also his personal taste in art. Franz Ferdinand was a traditionalist who disliked the *Jugendstil*, or art nouveau movement. He preferred old Teutonic works, the crude folk art to be found in Austria's countryside, and the traditional hunting and maritime scenes of Alois Jungwirth, August Ramberg and Alexander Kirchner.[16]

Nikitsch-Boulles, his aide Baron Andreas von Morsey, or Major Alexander Brosch, the archduke's principal aide-de-camp, presented the day's agenda and any important files that had arrived from Vienna. Franz Ferdinand read the reports with careful attention, annotating them in his elegant but cramped hand and quizzing the men over details. He spoke with a noticeable aristocratic clip and, at least with most people, tried to measure his words carefully. If something irritated him he was likely to let loose with his legendary temper. People whispered about the archduke's fits of rage; he recognized this as a personal shortcoming and tried to curtail it, but mistakes and fallacious arguments were likely to be met with 'language little short of harsh'.[17] Yet as Eisenmenger, who knew him well, pointed out, 'exaggeration and generalization were in his mode of speaking', and bursts of temper usually passed quickly and with pleas for forgiveness.[18] He quickly assessed people, often depending on emotion. Those deemed competent were rarely forgiven, but Franz Ferdinand also respected those who spoke the truth or challenged his views. 'There was hardly a topic one could not discuss calmly and openly with him,' said Nikitsch-Boulles. 'He was the first to regret flare-ups of his violent temper and would do everything possible to make up with the person in question . . . He is not only able to cope with the truth himself but also demands it from others, pleasant or not.'[19]

Elise Fiala or Käthe Braunstein, Sophie's lady's maids, attended to her each morning, arranging her hair in a fashionable pompadour with silver-gilt brushes and combs engraved with the duchess's coat of arms.[20] Every inch the dignified and proper Edwardian lady, Sophie habitually wore a corset, whose tight lacing emphasized her petite waist. Not even repeated pregnancies diminished her stately figure; although she filled out with the passing years, Sophie, nearly as tall as her husband, remained surprisingly supple. Marriage and motherhood lent the duchess an air of grandeur exemplifying the Belle Epoque ideal. With her vibrant eyes and graceful manner, she exuded, said a relative, a 'very feminine charm'.[21]

Sophie's elaborate wardrobe added to the regal effect. In the day she favoured simple dresses in soft whites and pastels, adorned with lace panels or coloured gauze. Carefully rolled parasols, large picture hats embellished with feathers, and long white gloves were added for afternoon rides or walks, while evenings saw more elaborate silk or velvet gowns sewn with intricate beading or embroidery and trimmed with fur. Like other fashionable ladies, she patronized the Viennese establishments of Spitzer, Marsch, and Drecol but also purchased more elaborate ensembles from Parisian couturiers like Paquin, Doucet and Worth.[22]

The duchess had always been intensely religious. Despite their sincere wishes, neither Franz Ferdinand nor Sophie ever travelled to Rome to receive a papal blessing in person; instead, they constantly asked others to do so on their behalf.[23] 'Did you talk with the Holy Father?' Sophie quizzed her sister Oktavia when the latter visited Rome in 1910, 'and were you able to mention us?'[24] She sent Oktavia 'the promised Sacred Heart of Jesus Picture', adding, 'it is so lovely and I am convinced that one is so happy to have it'.[25] Each morning, Sophie attended mass in the castle's Chapel of St Hubert, kneeling before the elaborately carved gothic altarpiece from Innsbruck and clutching a crucifix and rosary of lapis lazuli sent to her by the pope.[26] She insisted that her servants and household attend daily prayers and communion as well. Father Lanyi, the couple's personal confessor, complained that Sophie was too zealous in demanding such public signs of devotion; undoubtedly some servants grumbled about the daily services, but no one dared risk the duchess's censure without good cause.[27] Once, a visiting vet had to leave Konopischt early on a Sunday morning; worried that he would miss mass, Sophie had train schedules checked and found that no stops coincided with services. Thinking it better to inconvenience the household at Konopischt than to ignore the man's religious obligations, she asked Lanyi to say a special early mass before the man departed.[28]

Sophie's insistence stemmed from genuine piety. She used her position to quietly undertake charity work, her discretion driven by lack of desire for public acclaim as well as knowledge that she remained a figure of some controversy.[29] Yet she managed, as her great-granddaughter Princess Anita says, 'to support a lot of Christian societies and nunneries, as well as other religious and educational charities, in very important ways. Through her quiet funding, several monasteries and abbeys were opened in Austria.'[30]

Domestic concerns filled Sophie's days. As her husband worked, she dealt with correspondence, consulted with Robert Doré, the chef de cuisine, over meals, and tended to household issues with Baron Rumerskirch, the chamberlain who served as the couple's *Obersthofmeister*, or Lord High Chamberlain.[31] Real power, though, lay with Franz Janaczek, a Bohemian peasant who had worked as a beater at the imperial hunting lodge of Eckartsau before coming into the archduke's service as a valet. Eventually the archduke created him *Haushofmeister* (master of the household) and relied on him for nearly everything. 'Janaczek', he insisted, 'is not content unless he is being driven day and night.'[32]

Whether Janaczek actually enjoyed the demands made of him is conjecture, but such statements gave rise to the popular belief that Franz Ferdinand and Sophie were difficult employers; the archduke was said to be 'exacting and often brutal with his servants'.[33] Even today, guides at Konopischt describe the couple as unreasonably demanding. Life in service, it is true, was not often easy. Wages were low; this was not a mark against Franz Ferdinand and Sophie but common practice in every imperial household, and was compensated for with food and lodging, uniforms, free health care, the promise of a pension on retirement, and regular, generous gifts at Christmas.[34]

Countess Vilma Lanjus von Wellenburg served as Sophie's chief lady-in-waiting. She had nothing but good words for her mistress, calling her a 'noble soul' and adding, 'I was sincerely devoted and loyal to her with all my heart.' Sophie was cautious with money and strictly enforced rules within the household, but there were few complaints.[35] Eugen Ketterl, the emperor's trusted valet and a man in a position to hear all of the rumours, insisted that 'both Franz Ferdinand and his wife showed themselves to be exceedingly kind' to all of their servants, who 'led the most comfortable of lives'.[36] The couple's servants were unusually devoted to them, and most remained with the children after their parents' deaths.[37]

The children passed their mornings at lessons. Their suite at Kono-pischt adjoined their parents' apartments and included a chintz-hung music room for Little Sophie, a playroom crowded with model ships, tin soldiers, dolls, paints, and a large teepee in which to play; and a school-room with desks.[38] The archduke, thought his secretary, envied 'his children their tranquil future. In the entire education that he prepared for them there was nothing that might be construed as a preparation for any eventual succession to the throne. He wanted his boys to enjoy the untrammelled existence of country squires and not the artificial life imposed by court . . . He had similar intentions for his daughter. He believed that she would be a thousand times happier at the side of a socially suitable partner whom she loved than was ever possible with those marriages of convenience, which so often went wrong, entered into by princesses of the imperial house.'[39] They would, he hoped, grow up to become private individuals, 'able to enjoy life without any material cares' but otherwise living lives of anonymity.[40]

On this Little Sophie agreed: 'We were brought up to know that we weren't anything special.'[41] Franz Ferdinand and Sophie wanted their children to be cultured but unspoiled. The archduke, his daughter said, 'was firm with us, but never harsh or unjust'.[42] There was no ceremony in their lives: they were taught to avoid any form of snobbery, to treat the servants with respect, to assist them when possible, and to always thank them. As a result, the trio were said to be the best behaved, best brought up of all Habsburg offspring.[43]

A French governess taught Sophie, while Dr Otto Stankowsky, a Czech clergyman, acted as principal tutor to the young boys. The duchess constantly worried about their influence. 'God grant she is the right one for the souls of the children,' she wrote on hiring a new nanny.[44] They studied arithmetic, history, geography, science, religion and grammar, along with French, Czech, English and Magyar. There were lessons in music, riding, gymnastics and dancing; Sophie inherited her mother's artistic talents and became an accomplished painter and pianist.[45] In time, private instruction, at least for the two boys, gave way to private school. The archduke selected Vienna's exclusive Schottengymnasium, a Benedictine boarding school run along English lines, for his sons. Archduke Karl had graduated from the institution and spoke highly of the curriculum, which included the classics, advanced mathematics and philosophy. It also offered Franz Ferdinand's boys the opportunity to mix with a wide variety of classmates, including the sons of wealthy Jewish merchants and industrialists.[46]

The family nearly always ate luncheon together, and afternoons were generally undemanding. Franz Ferdinand might show guests through the museum he had created on the castle's second floor, where he had installed weaponry, arms, armour, and works of art inherited from the Duke of Modena.[47] More often he went shooting or inspected the park, especially if any visitors shared his interest in gardening.[48] The archduke spent entire afternoons in the park, deciding where trees needed to be planted and, always with reluctance, ordering others felled. He was infuriated to learn that some trees had been lost to carelessness. 'This forest will belong to my children some day,' he said, 'and I do not wish to lessen their inheritance.'[49] The archduke trained his children to love the land, awarding prizes when they could successfully name trees, flowers and shrubs. They were, said an acquaintance, 'introduced to all sectors of economy, forestry, hunting and fishing in a playful way, so that many strangers were amazed at how practically the children were being taught'.[50] The archduke once caught a local farmer stealing some wood and immediately sent for the authorities; yet during the ride back to the castle, he changed his mind. 'Since it's Christmas and I hear that the man's family is really poor,' he said, 'he is not to be punished. Just so he won't be tempted to steal again from my woods, I want you to send him enough firewood for the winter, and to his wife, ten Crowns (£32 in 2013 figures) as a Christmas present from my children.'[51]

This much was true. History has painted Franz Ferdinand and Sophie as unbelievably cheap. The archduke, it is said, 'practically terrorized dealers into giving him articles' at discount prices.[52] One contemporary, while admitting that the archduke was often 'badly swindled' in financial transactions, nonetheless insisted that Franz Ferdinand had a 'reputation for meanness' when it came to money. There were even complaints that Sophie was so cheap that she once had been spotted riding in a one-horse carriage; no proper lady, critics insisted, would ever ride in a carriage pulled by less than two horses.[53] However, Franz Ferdinand worried constantly about his children's future. As an archduke he had no practical experience with money; having learned to haggle over prices when visiting Egypt, he assumed this was how the business world worked. People charged him more, believing that a future emperor had unlimited financial resources, and he was frequently cheated and swindled out of large sums.[54]

Wealthy royals pleading poverty smacks of hypocrisy, but in Franz Ferdinand's case the complaints were somewhat justified. People assumed that the Este inheritance left him immensely rich, but the legacies and upkeep stipulated in the agreement outweighed the income; as late as 1914 the archduke was still handing over most of the proceeds to the Duke of Modena's widow.[55] Additionally, when Franz Ferdinand purchased Konopischt he also agreed to continue numerous pensions for those who had previously worked at the estate. The contract even obliged him to pay salaries to those who did no actual work, like the man whose sole job was to fire the noonday gun from a cannon that had long since been removed from the castle.[56]

With little concept of the value of money, the archduke often spent too freely on his architectural projects, or on gifts for his wife and children, and was then surprised to later find himself in dire financial straits. As a result, Franz Ferdinand had to economize with an eye toward his children's future. The Duke of Modena's will precluded the sale of any of the Este inheritance. It could not pass to the archduke's sons, who were excluded as morganatic descendants, but instead would go to his nephew Karl. Nor did his children, as morganatic descendants, receive any money from the imperial treasury. Their inheritance would come from the archduke's private estates and personal income, a situation that caused their father to be overly cautious when considering that their futures were tied to the very lands surrounding Konopischt.[57]

The park at Konopischt was meant for income, the garden for pleasure. This was the archduke's greatest delight, and one that he had conceived and laid out with the help of two court horticulturalists. The small river below the castle was dammed to create two large ponds where deer and game came to drink; an alpine garden created in 1913 lay hidden in a grove of evergreen and fir trees. Classical statuary from the Este collection dotted the landscape; ornamental fountains splashed against a fringe of trees, and little bridges, one christened the Sophiebrücke in his wife's honour, spanned twisting streams. The most famous of all components, though, was the archduke's Rose Garden. Beginning in 1898, Franz Ferdinand worked with Viennese court gardener Karl Mössner to create elaborate circular parterres below the castle's southern terrace. Thousands of roses bloomed here, over two hundred different varieties collected from around the world and transplanted to Bohemian soil by a delighted archduke. Konopischt was home, but the Rose Garden was Franz Ferdinand's pride and joy.[58]

By late afternoon, the children had usually joined their parents in the park, walking through the forest or driving in a carriage. Little Sophie, Max and Ernst all loved to ride, but not their father; the archduke was a poor horseman and preferred to drive himself in a little trap.[59] What he did like, though, was motor cars. Franz Ferdinand kept a Lohner-Porsche, a Daimler, and a Mercedes for longer excursions and would tear across the countryside at top speeds, scattering terrified animals and farmers alike. In winter they all skated on the park's frozen ponds and sledded down snow-covered mounds; in spring they played tennis, a sport at which both Franz Ferdinand and Sophie excelled, and swam. When they were younger the children had a pet St Bernard; after the overexcited dog suddenly turned on the boys one day, the archduke banished all pets from the castle. Occasional visits to children's concerts, the theatre, or the circus in Prague offered welcome diversions from this pleasant routine.[60]

Washed and scrubbed from their adventures, the children always joined the parents for tea in the Rose Salon. This was Sophie's sanctuary in the old castle, hung with floral fabric, aglow with a shimmering chandelier, warmed by an ornate porcelain stove, and crowded with a profusion of overstuffed neo-rococo sofas and chairs. Fringed lamps, Sophie's favourite yellow roses, potted palms, paintings, and family photographs crowded every inch of space. It was all very Edwardian, very comfortable, and very feminine.[61] After filling themselves with pastries, the children would play on a corner of the carpet beneath their parents' watchful gaze as Franz Ferdinand smoked and read aloud and Sophie did needlework.[62]

Dinners were rarely formal affairs, though the archduke inevitably changed into a uniform or white tie and tails and Sophie would wear an elaborate gown bedecked with jewellery. Franz Ferdinand showered his wife with jewels: ropes of pearls, diamond brooches, pendant earrings, dog collars, sparkling aigrettes, and shimmering necklaces. Sophie had five tiaras, including the one given to her by the emperor, and wore them on formal occasions. Her favourite seems to have been a low bandeau tiara of diamonds and sapphires, which could also be worn as a necklace.[63]

If there were no guests, the family ate in a small dining room adjoining the Rose Salon. The archduke preferred simple food: soups and goulash, roast pork, boiled beef, venison and game, sauerkraut, fried liver, cauliflower, noodles and dumplings appeared on the table with great regularity, washed down with beer. Franz Ferdinand did not enjoy wine or spirits much, though he did like champagne. Coffee was offered only when there were guests, as neither the archduke nor the duchess was particularly fond of it and preferred tea.[64]

A quite different scene unfolded if the couple were entertaining. The children usually joined their parents for dinner, even when guests were present; only on the most formal of occasions did they take their meals separately, though they were always allowed to peer in at the elegant guests and make winning bows and curtsies.[65] Elaborate meals took place in the Lobkowicz Hall, where a mythological feast played out above the heads of diners as liveried footmen served frothy French concoctions smothered in cream sauces. While the family often used rather ordinary china and crystal, adorned with the archduke's monogram, guests were treated to waves of courses served on plates emblazoned with the Habsburg double-headed eagle and gold crowns. The archduke once ordered an extravagant Bohemian crystal service for fifty; when the factory representative pointed out that the ornamentation would add to the cost, Franz Ferdinand dismissed it, saying that cost wasn't an issue. 'Franzi, Franzi!' Sophie had whispered to him. 'One doesn't say that to a Vienna businessman!'[66]

At the end of meals, Sophie withdrew with any ladies, and Franz Ferdinand presided over the table, lingering for port and political discussion.[67] Inevitably, though, everyone ended up in the Rose Salon. From a silver-plated brass box with his initials, the archduke would pull out an Altesse cigar from Vienna and happily puff away.[68] Franz Ferdinand was a chain-smoker, though he abandoned the habit for one day each year, on Good Friday, as a mark of religious respect.[69] Sophie might play the piano, though this was often an exercise in futility; others could appreciate the classical works that tumbled from her fingertips, but not Franz Ferdinand. He shared the emperor's astonishingly bourgeois taste

in music, disliking most classical music and especially loathing Wag-
ner.[70] He liked light operas, Viennese dance music, popular tunes, and
sentimental love songs; he was even known to stop on the streets in
Vienna to listen in contentment to a barrel organ.[71]

Little Sophie, Max and Ernst always joined in these evenings. They
might entertain guests with little theatrical scenes, poetry recitals, and
memorized bits of literature in various languages they were learning.[72]
Occasionally Franz Ferdinand and Sophie joined in, the archduke once
acting the role of Louis XIV and Sophie gaudily dressed as a Gypsy, to
everyone's amusement.[73] 'When I return to my family from my long
daily labours,' the archduke once said, 'and see my wife doing needlework and my children playing about, then I leave my cares at the door
and can hardly grasp the happiness that surrounds me.'[74]

The children, Franz Ferdinand admitted, 'are my whole delight and
pride. I sit with them all day and admire them because I love them so
much. And the evenings at home, when I smoke my cigar and read the
newspapers; Soph knits, and the children roll around and throw everything from the tables, and it is all so incredibly delightful and cosy!'[75]
Imperial decorum often disappeared. The forbidding and enigmatic
archduke known to the public would fill the room with his hearty, roar-
ing laughter, telling jokes and laughing at himself. A favourite anecdote
involved some minor German prince who, unaware of his identity, had
complained to the archduke that he was scheduled to go shooting 'with
that tiresome Franz Ferdinand'.[76] One night, Franz Ferdinand and Sophie led an impromptu conga line through the rooms of their castle to
music from a nearby gramophone. When the archduke entered one of
the female guest's rooms, he found that her maid had washed her under-
wear and hung it from the chandelier to dry; the lady was horrified, but
Franz Ferdinand collapsed in laughter.[77]

Sophie always put the children to bed and said their prayers with
them. This little family was the archduke's entire life, providing 'sanctuary from the excitement and storms of political life' as Eisenmenger recalled.[78] 'Pinky is good enough to eat,' Franz Ferdinand happily confided

to his stepmother. 'Maxi is a clever, delightful boy, and Ernie is so good and will become a beauty.'[79]

Franz Ferdinand and Sophie shared a bedroom, sleeping in twin brass beds pushed against chintz-covered walls hung with religious paintings. It was scarcely a private sanctuary; the archduke often led startled guests through this hidden realm to the adjoining lavatory, whose window, he thought, gave the best view over the garden.[80] The couple might read before retiring. The image of the coldly austere archduke might have suffered had people known that he despised Goethe and Schiller but devoured French literature and the sentimental Austrian novels of Felix Dahn and Peter Rosegger, as well as books on old castles and famous gardens, while Sophie eagerly read the latest works sent to her from London.[81]

Everyone who saw the couple in these private surroundings agreed that theirs was a happy marriage, untroubled by rumours of infidelities, disappointments, or angry scenes. From beginning to end, they remained devoted to each other.[82] On the surface at least, Franz Ferdinand and Sophie seemed like such different personalities. There was his cold public demeanour, his rumoured reactionary views, and, above all, his famous temper. It was always there, people felt, lingering just beneath the surface and waiting to burst forth in a torrent of abuse. The archduke knew this was his worst trait, and outbursts were often followed by genuine apologies. Those who crossed him, particularly those he believed had insulted his beloved wife, might be forever condemned in his eyes, but he was always willing to acknowledge differences of opinion and change his mind when he had been too hasty.[83] Sophie knew how to calm her husband, gently taking hold of his arm and whispering, 'Franzi, Franzi.' They had a personal joke of sorts, a 'delightful' small diamond brooch in the shape of a laughing lamb that the archduke had given to his wife on her birthday in 1910.[84] When one of his famous tempers was brewing, Sophie would pointedly stroke the brooch as a plea for tranquillity.[85]

Sophie never gave any hint that she ever suffered moments of regret, ever strained against the stifled existence, or ever resented the narrow universe in which her life played out. Like her husband, she remains something of an enigma, a woman who went from her own Cinderella background into a real romantic fairy tale replete with a Prince Charming but who rarely uttered a recorded word or voiced any frustration over her life. There must have been times when the pressures were enormous, yet Sophie remained serene, implacable, self-contained, drawing on her religious faith to maintain an optimistic approach to life.[86]

In fact, Sophie became the perfect, aristocratic hausfrau, devoted to the traditional Teutonic virtues of *Küche, Kinder, und Kirche* in an effort to make her husband happy. After 1900, the Church in Austria popularized and promoted an idealized image of women as dutiful, obedient wives and mothers, emphasizing domesticity and self-sacrifice as the highest feminine aspirations.[87] Sophie embraced these ideals and, as Nikitsch-Boulles recalled, 'fulfilled her difficult role to the best of her knowledge and belief. She was not only an affectionate and loving partner, but she understood the manifold characteristics of her husband, often with true self-denial.'[88]

What Nikitsch-Boulles took for self-denial Sophie seems to have embraced as fulfilment. She created a new life for her husband, an alternative universe far away from the difficulties at court and pressures of political inheritance. She was, said an acquaintance, 'admirably intelligent, kind, and good, and ensured a perfectly united household'.[89] His interests, as her great-granddaughter Princess Anita says, became her interests. Whatever Franz Ferdinand wanted to do, Sophie was enthusiastic, finding happiness in their shared pursuits.[90]

For this Franz Ferdinand was truly grateful. 'You don't know how happy I am with my family,' he confided to his stepmother, 'and how I can't thank God enough for all my happiness. After God I have to thank you, Dearest Mama, because it was you who helped me in all respects gain such happiness. The wisest thing I've done in my life is to marry my Soph. She's my everything: wife, adviser, doctor, friend – in a word, my entire happiness . . . We love each other just as much as on our first day of marriage and nothing has marred our happiness for a single second.'[91]

NINE

'Even Death Will Not Part Us!'

⊹

For Franz Ferdinand and Sophie's family, life fell into a pleasant annual routine. They usually spent Christmas at Konopischt. 'Our evening was full of warmth, with true family happiness,' Sophie wrote to her sister Oktavia of the celebrations in 1909. 'Christmas Eve will always be one of the greatest joys in life. I cannot really tell anyone how much I enjoyed it, and the Saviour be thanked!' She was delighted with her 'wonderful' presents: little charms for her bracelets, flower pots, a lamp, and a miniature of her children.[1] 'That I was able to please you with the small Christmas tree makes me very happy,' the archduke wrote to a member of his staff in 1912. 'I just wanted to show you how much we were thinking of you at the time. We are, thank God, very well; we had such a lovely Christmas, the children were blissfully happy, and they give us so much pleasure.'[2]

At the beginning of the year the family usually moved to Vienna, taking up residence at the Belvedere for the social season, though continued difficulties over Sophie's position increasingly led them to seek other diversions. Lovers of winter sports, the family began to pass later winters at the fashionable resort of St Moritz, staying in a large hotel suite nestled against the snow-covered mountains. Clad in overcoat, wool knickerbockers, and a jaunty tam, Franz Ferdinand led his wife and children, bundled in furs and protective hats, in ice-skating on the frozen ponds and skiing on the surrounding slopes.[3]

In the spring, they usually went south, travelling when they received permission aboard the imperial yacht *Lacroma* to the fashionable Adriatic resort of Brioni (now Brijuni). Here, booking into a hotel overlooking the water, they spent their days on the beach, playing and frolicking in the waves.[4] 'Franzi is fine,' Sophie wrote to her sister Oktavia during their 1910 visit, 'he likes it here, and I believe that it is a very good place to recuperate. . . . The good conditions here are as if one were in the depths of India!'[5] If possible, Franz Ferdinand and Sophie celebrated Easter in Trieste, ensconced in the beautiful white Gothic castle built by Franz Josef's ill-fated brother Maximilian that perched at the edge of the Bay of Grignano.[6] Inevitably, this meant grovelling for imperial permission, for Miramar belonged to the crown. Montenuovo had once stopped the archduke from taking his family there, writing that his residence could only be approved by an 'Express All-Highest Command' from the emperor.[7]

On another occasion, Rudolf's daughter, Elisabeth, was at the castle with her children. She had agreed to leave and make way for Franz Ferdinand's family but at the last minute refused, saying that her children were sick and could not be moved. Suspecting she was merely being her usual troublesome self, Franz Ferdinand dispatched Eisenmenger to Trieste to offer a medical opinion. This didn't go over well. 'You've come as a spy!' Elisabeth hissed at the doctor. When he reported that the children were sufficiently recovered to leave, Elisabeth reluctantly agreed but intentionally delayed her departure to cause Franz Ferdinand and Sophie as much inconvenience as possible.[8]

The countryside surrounding Miramar was a beautiful, tropical paradise, and Franz Ferdinand liked to drive his family to some remote spot to picnic. However, the countryside also swarmed with Italian nationalists, potential assassins who would be happy, said the archduke's staff, to toss a bomb or fire a gun at an unwelcome Habsburg. Franz

Ferdinand was philosophical about the dangers. 'I'm sure you have a point,' he said, 'but I will not be put under glass. Our lives are always in danger. We must simply trust in God.'[9]

Late spring might see a brief return to Konopischt, visits to Vienna to attend the races, and stays with aristocratic friends or Sophie's family on country estates for weekend shooting. The archduke had many social acquaintances but few trusted intimates. A Habsburg, he had been taught from birth, had to do without the consolation of friends, who might exploit and betray misplaced confidences. He even once insisted that his only true friends were Eisenmenger and Janaczek. As a result, Franz Ferdinand mainly associated with a small circle of aristocratic friends, with his brother-in-law Albrecht of Württemberg, and with Sophie's brothers-in-law, knowing that he could rely on their discretion.[10]

Early summers at Schloss Artstetten repeated the familiar pattern of Franz Ferdinand's youth. He had inherited the medieval castle, perched high on a green hillside above the Danube village of Pöchlarn, after his father's death, and transformed it into a modern residence. He replaced the sharp roofs of the gleaming white structure's four corner towers with bulbous onion domes, installed bathrooms and central heating, and enhanced the terraced gardens, all with an eye toward the future.[11] Here, the archduke had decided, he and Sophie would eventually be buried.

The decision was born of a tragedy. Wanting a large family, the couple were delighted to find that Sophie was again expecting in 1908.[12] At first everything went well, but Sophie's fourth pregnancy came when she was forty and complications from the flu set in. At 8:00 p.m. on 7 November, she went into premature labour. 'The child, such a nice, strong boy, was born dead,' the archduke wrote to a friend. 'And we had been so happy to have our fourth child!'[13] She was severely weakened, and doctors advised against any future pregnancies.[14] The child had to be buried, but because Franz Ferdinand's wife and children were not Habsburgs, they would be denied the traditional burial given to members of the imperial family in the Capuchin Crypt in Vienna. The archduke could rest there, but not his wife or descendants. In death, as in life,

Franz Ferdinand meant to have Sophie at his side. 'You may tell anyone', he once commented, 'that even death will not part us!'[15]

Konopischt was the couple's favourite home, but it was in Bohemia; Franz Ferdinand wanted to rest in Austria when he died. So he selected Artstetten as a residence for a widowed Sophie and the place where the family would be interred. A new crypt was carved out of the rocky hillside beneath the castle's existing baroque Chapel of St James the Apostle, a vaulted chamber where the body of their premature son could rest without controversy.[16] The archduke put the ever-busy Janaczek in charge and was pleased with the result. 'It is airy and light, as I like it,' he noted. 'Only the entrance is not well designed. It makes too sharp a turn. The pallbearers will knock the coffin in turning the corner, then I'll turn over in my grave!'[17]

As a girl Sophie had often spent summers at the Belgian resort of Blankenberge. It hadn't been particularly fashionable, but its lack of social cachet made it affordable, which was her father's prime consideration. The archduke could have taken his family to elite resorts like Biarritz, Marienbad, Cannes, or Deauville, but they were stuffy and full of pompous aristocrats. Blankenberge in July, he decided, was precisely the sort of ordinary escape his wife and children needed, far removed from the pressures of life under an incessant social microscope. Life here was decidedly informal and relaxed. Staying in a tourist hotel overlooking the surf, the family trekked down to the sandy beach each morning. The archduke usually spent a few hours at a small desk incongruously erected on the shore, reading through official papers and watching as his wife and children romped through the waves and built sandcastles. He always joined them in the afternoon, abandoning his jacket and trousers for a blue wool bathing suit and plunging into the sea with abandon. Sophie's sister Henriette often joined them on these holidays, which usually included visits with the Belgian royal family, the archduke's cousins by marriage, and leisurely strolls through Brussels's museums and art galleries.[18]

The family usually spent a few weeks in late spring and early autumn at Chlumetz, a large neoclassical mansion near Wittingau (now Třeboň) in southern Bohemia. The immense park, traversed by languid rivers and marshy lakes, offered excellent fishing as well as pheasant and woodcock shoots, and the archduke liked to host house parties here for less intimate acquaintances. The estate had come to him as part of the Este inheritance, but this posed a problem. According to the Duke of Modena's will, the property could only pass to a Habsburg. Eventually Franz Ferdinand worked out a solution with his nephew Karl. Karl would append the 'Este' title to his own name and receive the bulk of the Modena inheritance; in exchange, Max and Ernst would receive, respectively, Konopischt and Chlumetz.[19]

Shooting at Chlumetz was limited; from August to October the family usually stayed in some remote lodge so that the archduke could indulge his love of hunting. It was one thing the public knew with certainty about the enigmatic Franz Ferdinand – he loved to hunt. Critics painted it as a pathological obsession. 'Though he could not shoot his enemies,' insisted Rebecca West, 'he found some relief in shooting, it did not matter what . . . He liked to kill and kill and kill, unlike men who shoot to get food or who have kept in touch with the primitive life . . . This capacity for butchery he used to express the hatred which he felt for nearly all the world, which indeed it is safe to say he bore against the whole world.'[20] This unconvincing bit of propaganda became accepted fact: Franz Ferdinand as a ruthless man who delighted in the wholesale slaughter of thousands of defenceless animals to satisfy his bloodlust.

The archduke was widely acknowledged as 'one of the finest shots in the country' and spent hours, armed with his Mannlicher rifle or guns from Nowotny in Prague, roaming the forests and fields, shooting stags, chamois, hare, partridge, pheasant, boar, bears, roebucks, foxes, ducks, geese – anything and everything that moved.[21] That Franz Ferdinand was enthusiastic is beyond dispute: he shot 274,889 animals in his lifetime, although this does not include another thirteen moose he killed in

Sweden.[22] The numbers seem excessive to modern sensibilities, but pursuit was a Habsburg tradition. Franz Josef hunted regularly, though the business of ruling impeded his ability to fully indulge in the sport; with no such constraints on his time, Franz Ferdinand had more opportunities to amass his stunning bag.

A bit of context is in order when looking at the archduke's staggering number of kills. These were the glory days of the Edwardian era, a time of organized mass slaughter enjoyed by royalty and aristocrats alike. No proper country house party in England or on the Continent was without its great shoots. King Edward VII killed some 7,000 pheasants each year at his Sandringham estate alone; one day in 1904, over 1,300 partridges were shot during a royal shoot.[23] The Marquess of Ripon totalled 556,813 animals killed in his shooting career, and many other aristocrats bettered Franz Ferdinand's own records.[24] It was sport, not slaughter, exercise of skilled marksmanship, not massacre, that appealed to the archduke. He enjoyed the recreation. His numbers were inflated to some extent because, owing to his weak lungs, he could not pursue game and instead beaters usually drove the animals toward him.[25] He was obsessed with shooting, in much the same way that he was obsessed with collecting art, obsessed with his gardens and architecture, and obsessed with his family. He was a man of obsessions, with the time and money to indulge them.

Sometimes the archduke took his family to Eckartsau, a Habsburg hunting lodge in the Danube Valley east of Vienna. The woods teemed with deer, but the lodge itself, a little baroque gem built by Empress Maria Theresa, had fallen into disrepair. After Franz Ferdinand restored it, he rarely spent time there. More often, they went to Lölling in Carinthia, staying in a squat lodge at the foot of the Sauer Alps. Franz Ferdinand rented hunting rights in the surrounding forests from Count Henckel-Donnersmark; although the country was rich with chamois and buck, the archduke was never able to negotiate an extended lease nor make the improvements he deemed necessary.[26]

Wanting to acquire his own hunting estate, the archduke purchased

Schloss Blühnbach in 1908. Nestled in a valley at the foot of Hochkönig Mountain near Salzburg, the lodge offered tranquillity, and the surrounding Alpine hills teemed with stag and chamois. Ever anxious to play amateur architect, Franz Ferdinand enlarged the sixteenth-century building, adding a new floor of rooms, bathrooms, and a chapel. The situation, in a small meadow framed by granite mountains fringed with pine, was idyllic, and Blühnbach soon became a favourite annual destination for the family to hunt and picnic in the surrounding forests.[27]

The family loved the informality of Salzburg as well as the Tyrol, where the ambitious archduke restored the medieval Schloss Ambras; he had often spent summers here, and once even considered making it his home.[28] Franz Ferdinand liked to explore isolated villages, chatting unceremoniously with locals and startling innkeepers by sharing a communal bowl of goulash with his staff.[29] He loved to discover county fairs and shops filled with local crafts and antiques to add to his collection. The archduke was an indefatigable collector. 'Few people', said Count Ottokar Czernin, 'have the artistic knowledge possessed in many respects by the Archduke; no dealer could palm off on him any modern article as an antique, and he had just as good taste as understanding.'[30] He bought paintings, stained glass, works of art, sculpture, folk art, furniture, arms and armour, medals, coins, minerals, ceramics, clocks, tombstones, medieval instruments of torture, and old altars from churches – anything and everything that took his fancy, including 3,750 statues of St George, whose struggle to slay the dragon, as his great-granddaughter Princess Sophie points out, reflected his own struggle against tuberculosis.[31]

Along with this passion for collecting went a passion for architectural preservation. Among his more important projects, in addition to Ambras, was the preservation of St Peter's Graveyard in Salzburg and Schloss Taufers. 'A veritable mania of destruction had broken out,' recalled a relative, 'one which was brought to a halt only when a new generation came to realize that irreplaceable cultural treasures had been destroyed and that efforts had now to be made to preserve those which still survived. One of Archduke Franz Ferdinand's many merits is that he vigorously championed the preservation of valuable buildings.'[32] Wanting an Austria with strong and visible ties to its heroic past, he headed preservation committees and often intervened against questionable restorations of the country's abbeys, churches and castles.[33]

Amid this pleasant annual routine, there were occasional visits beyond Austria as well. In 1912, the Royal Horticultural Society held an immense exhibition in London, a display that was the forerunner of the famed Chelsea Flower Shows, and dedicated gardener that he was, Franz Ferdinand was anxious to attend. He obtained permission from the emperor for Sophie to accompany him provided they travel privately and incognito, as Count and Countess Artstetten. With her niece Countess Elisabeth de Baillet-Latour acting as Sophie's lady-in-waiting, the couple arrived in London on 17 May and motored to the Ritz Hotel, where a suite overlooking Green Park awaited them.[34]

Over the next week Franz Ferdinand and Sophie visited the flower show and acted as private tourists, though the city's newspapers prominently reported their every move. One day they visited the famous botanical gardens at Kew and took in Hampton Court Palace on the Thames. They saw the splendours of the Wallace Collection, inspected several country houses outside of the city, and watched Anna Pavlova dance at the newly opened Victoria Palace Theatre.[35] 'I had a great time,' the archduke wrote to a friend, 'and revelled in my favourite passions: art and horticulture.'[36]

Count Albert von Mensdorff, Austria's ambassador, had arranged it all flawlessly, despite the occasional difficulties over protocol and the couple's enforced incognito. Mensdorff even pulled off a spectacular coup: as a relative of the British royal family, he somehow convinced King George V to invite the pair to luncheon, despite Queen Mary's continued misgivings over Sophie's morganatic status. On 23 May, the regal queen welcomed Franz Ferdinand and Sophie to Buckingham Palace. The king's widowed mother, Queen Alexandra, joined them for luncheon, and after the meal Queen Mary played palace tour guide. The king found them 'both charming' and was pleased that, contrary to their public reputations, they 'made themselves very pleasant'.[37] There may have been difficulties communicating; Franz Ferdinand's English was as insufficient as was King George's German, which would have left their wives to translate during the visit. Both the king and queen, George later confessed, greatly enjoyed the afternoon together. Franz Ferdinand had been gracious, and Sophie was 'quite charming'. Even Queen Mary abandoned her preconceptions, admitting that they both 'liked her so much'. Franz Ferdinand told Mensdorff that conversation with the king had been easy as they 'had so many interests and likes and dislikes in common. It was so *gemütlich*. The King and I understand each other so well.'[38]

William Cavendish-Bentinck, the 6th Duke of Portland, was not only president of the Royal Horticultural Society and host of the Chelsea Flower Show but also one of the archduke's hunting circle when on the Continent. Friendly with several of Sophie's relatives as well, he asked the couple to stay with him at Welbeck Abbey, his country estate in Nottinghamshire, for a few days when they left London. Winifred, his amiable and unpretentious duchess, welcomed the visitors to the curious Welbeck, with its underground reception rooms, galleries and tunnels. The stay cemented a friendship between the two couples, and Franz Ferdinand asked them to visit Konopischt. The entire visit had gone exceptionally well, and the archduke left England 'delighted with everything and in the rosiest of humours', as Mensdorff happily recorded.[39] Favourable impressions on all sides paved the way for the following year, when Franz Ferdinand and Sophie would return at the king and queen's invitation for an intimate royal visit that would be nothing short of a triumph.

TEN

An Emperor in Training

⁜

Private life and a happy family offered much to give the archduke a level of fulfilment, but his eventual destiny lay with politics. He was always cautious when it came to political affairs, especially after a debacle in 1901. On April 8, Franz Ferdinand agreed to become patron of the League of Catholic Schools. On the surface this seemed innocuous enough for a Catholic Habsburg, but the move caused an uproar in the press. Critics fumed that in so publicly siding with the Catholic Church, the archduke had openly declared war on liberal voices seeking to weaken Rome's influence on the empire and the traditional ties between pope and Habsburg ruler. The view was not without foundation: Georg von Schönerer, one of the leading voices supporting Austria's break with Rome, was avowedly pro-German, calling for large-scale Protestant conversion and something approaching Austrian unification with Berlin. Franz Ferdinand, like many others, held to the maxim 'Away from Rome means away from Austria'.[1]

In his address of acceptance, the archduke praised the society's 'religious and patriotic work'.[2] The outcry was greatest in Hungary, which had a substantial Protestant population. Franz Josef was furious, writing to his nephew that his actions in taking patronage threatened the domestic tranquillity of the empire. He deemed acceptance of the position 'highly imprudent'. He was so furious that he forbade any member of the imperial family from accepting any position of patronage in the future without his prior consent.[3]

People insisted that Sophie was behind it all, that she had hoped to use the Church to cultivate power and influence for herself.[4] Yet fears that the Catholic Church had in the archduke an impotent pawn were not justified. Franz Ferdinand once insisted, 'I would not shrink from breaking off relations even with the Holy Father if he tried to use his powers in the Church against my own views.'[5]

Franz Ferdinand's most public political alliance also became the most controversial. He greatly admired Karl Lueger, Vienna's popular mayor, whose calls to nationalism and overt anti-Semitism found favour among many in the city, including a young Adolf Hitler. Lueger was contradictory, a man who spewed virulently anti-Jewish rhetoric to attract votes and further his career yet had a number of Jewish friends.[6] Franz Ferdinand, like most turn-of-the-century royal figures, bore certain anti-Semitic attitudes; for him, these stemmed less from religious prejudice, for he actually admired the obvious devotion of Orthodox Jews, than from belief in notions of foreign loyalties and shady conspiracies he assumed were antagonistic to nationalistic, conservative, Catholic rule.[7] Above all, he liked Lueger not because of any shared anti-Semitism but rather because the mayor was notoriously anti-Hungarian in his views and proudly thwarted expressions of Magyar extremism.[8]

Most of Franz Ferdinand's political energies focused on his own secretariat, the famous Militärkanzlerei, or Military Chancery, where policy was developed, argued, and planned for future implementation. Housed in the Lower Belvedere in Vienna, the Military Chancery became a highly efficient institution, designed to provide military and political advice and equip the archduke with a working knowledge of the problems he would face when he came to the throne. In effect, it offered a way for Franz Ferdinand to complete his education and absorb ideas and influences outside official circles. Government ministers, he worried, provided 'only a one-sided and unreliable picture of the real state of affairs'. By amassing divergent views and analysing reports from the best minds in the country, he hoped to prepare for his eventual accession 'independent of the government of Emperor Franz Josef'.[9]

Major Alexander Brosch von Aarenau, an aristocratic scion born in 1870, headed the chancery and acted as the archduke's chief aide-de-camp.[10] He was intelligent, dedicated and tactful, something necessary as the chancery grew and the archduke demanded access to all official documents and papers. Previously the emperor had tried to keep his nephew as isolated as possible and denied him government documents, but Brosch insisted that the chancery receive all reports, not merely the ones Franz Josef thought appropriate for his heir to see. The archduke appreciated Brosch and respected his opinions and advice.[11]

Brosch, in turn, came to know Franz Ferdinand well and left a definitive sketch of his character:

> *The Archduke is open to suggestions and in fact it is easy to convince him of a good thing provided he does not mistrust the speaker in the first place, but one must know the right way to go about it, for the Archduke will on no account tolerate direct contradiction. What he will accept on the other hand more than most people is the unvarnished truth; indeed he demands it. So if one knows how to be frank with him in an acceptable manner that avoids contradiction one can achieve almost anything. Of course that means using a lot of finesse and tact and choosing the right moment; in other words, it's a wearisome business . . . The Archduke is highly gifted; he has a really incredible quickness of perception and a sure eye, especially for military conditions. He is not overburdened by knowledge of military details; he has in particular not extended his knowledge by private study since he has too little stamina and seemingly has never learnt how to study on his own. All the same, the basics, which his tutors gave him, suffice completely for him to form a most correct and quick assessment of tactical and operative situations and to make effective decisions and not spontaneously, which is often only the result of excess book learning . . . The Archduke almost instinctively always*

makes the most appropriate decision . . . He is sharp and often harsh in his judgements and somewhat hasty as well, so that it often happens that he is unjust to people. But once he realizes this he doesn't hesitate to put things right . . . Toward those who work with him the Archduke displays a magical amiability; during the whole six years I never saw an unfriendly gesture or heard a gruff word. Once one has won his confidence, which naturally takes quite some time, then his trust in you endures and knows no limitations.[12]

Brosch left the chancery in 1911 and returned to regular army service, yet the archduke remained in constant communication, asking his advice and assuring him of his continued friendship. After confessing that he had left his post to spend time with his ailing fiancée, Franz Ferdinand wrote to Brosch:

My warmest thanks for your long and detailed letter. Your lines surprised me immensely and I must really scold you for not having long poured out your heart and didn't confide the matters of your heart to me. It saddens me so incredibly much that you kept so much extreme grief and so many worries to yourself all the long time while you were so anxious to serve me in the most devoted manner! The greatest sacrifice that you could well have made was that you didn't say anything and that fills me with the greatest respect as I know how noble your intentions were and what you had to go through! If I only had had a notion of the worries you had at the time of your fiancée's serious illness in the autumn, then I would have certainly given you a holiday, which I now sincerely regret that I didn't as I was unaware of your troubles. That was why I continued to demand your services and summoned you! Dear Brosch, I give you my blessing with all my heart and wish you all the best and much luck . . . Once again, dear Brosch, my warmest wishes for your happiness, which the Duchess and my children are most sincerely part of. Please let me know when your wedding will take place as we would very much like to share that day with you when you find your happiness and contentedness and would like to convey our most cordial wishes to you.[13]

Colonel Karl Bardolff replaced Brosch as head of the chancery and was left to grapple with the growing resentment directed against it by the emperor's own secretariat. The Military Chancery was, in many ways, a kind of shadow government, cultivating officials, military men, and politicians, seeking their views and influence and attempting to formulate policy for the future. Franz Josef, recorded one historian, 'treated the emergence of the Belvedere as an alternative political centre as if it challenged his whole concept of the monarchy. He had no intention of sharing the responsibilities of government.'[14] At times, as happened in 1907 during renegotiation over the terms of the *Ausgleich* with Hungary, Franz Josef ordered officials not to brief his nephew on developments and to deny his chancery access to state papers.[15] Perhaps he simply meant to forestall any unpleasant scenes or undiplomatic outbursts, but the emperor's actions merely confirmed the archduke's worst fears: his uncle was deliberately keeping him in the dark on important issues that one day, perhaps soon, would become his sole responsibility. So intense was the rivalry between uncle and nephew that Franz Ferdinand's secretariat was known as 'the Opposition Cabinet'.[16] Former prime minister Ernst von Koerber knowingly commented, 'We not only have two parliaments, we also have two Emperors!'[17]

The emperor's unsympathetic attitudes prevented Franz Ferdinand from putting his energies and talents to practical use. Franz Josef, said Margutti, found it an 'absolute impossibility' to work with his heir in any productive way. He could not understand his views, and the idea of changing the outdated empire was anathema.[18] There were even rumours that Franz Josef tried to bribe his nephew to renounce his place in the succession to avoid what he predicted would be a catastrophic reign.[19]

Uncle and nephew had never been close, and the archduke's morganatic marriage had simply reinforced all of the emperor's negative opinions. 'You know how strange and unpredictable he is!' he once insisted of the archduke. The emperor thought that Franz Ferdinand was too independent, too liberal, and too open to change; he suspected him of hungering for power and worried that he would destroy the precarious balance that held the empire together. The archduke, for his part, complained that the emperor often treated him like 'the lowest servant' at court.[20] The failure lay with both men: one who could not see beyond tradition and archaic practice, and the other who didn't know how to moderate his views and convincingly make his arguments appeal to the conservative emperor. Neither could understand the other.

The archduke, as Margutti recalled, repeatedly offered his uncle 'many most helpful suggestions. Their value was all the greater as they enlarged the Archduke's outlook while the Emperor only too readily buried himself in details and trivialities and thus not infrequently could not see the wood for the trees. That being the case, Franz Ferdinand's cooperation would have been of great value to the old Emperor, and unsuspected advantages might have flowed from it.'[21] However, it was not to be. Franz Josef was too old and too set in his conservative ways to consider any alternatives. Convinced that he knew best, the emperor was not interested in hearing his nephew's new ideas.

Franz Ferdinand once suggested that the archaic Imperial Appanage Department, which regulated the dynasty's financial welfare, be drastically modernized. In examining the various estates, incomes and investments he discovered corruption, waste and incompetence.[22] When the emperor refused to grant him an audience to discuss the issue, the archduke drafted a ten-page outline of his investigation and proposed changes to eliminate waste and yield more income. Franz Josef received this idea coldly. 'I learned from Prince Montenuovo', the emperor wrote, 'that you would like me to answer your recent exposé concerning the Family Fund. I can now give you that answer . . . I have examined all sides of the question, and conclude that as the guardian responsible for the shared Family Fund, I cannot allow experiments whereby a tried management system that has served Us well for many years is so upset.'[23]

'Franz Josef', says the archduke's great-granddaughter Princess Sophie, 'did the same things with him as he had done with Rudolf: he didn't inform him of things. There was very little communication, so it was very difficult to know what was going on and to advise the emperor.'[24] Franz Ferdinand complained that he 'had to learn everything from the newspapers', that the emperor 'never' listened to him, and that he was 'told less' than the lowest footman.[25] It was immensely frustrating. 'His ardent desires met with cold restraint; his clear vision was condemned to impotent observation,' recalled one official. 'The suppression of his energies was nerve-racking and he was ever plagued by the fear that he would come to the throne too late, when everything would have gone hopelessly wrong.'[26]

Yet Franz Ferdinand was obsequious in his loyalty, respectful, dutiful, and even devout when it came to his uncle. 'You know', he once wrote to Countess Fugger, 'with what love and reverence I am attached to my Emperor, and it is this very love that prompts me to have my own views on politics, at home as well as in foreign affairs, for I hope thereby to be of service to my Emperor and to my country.'[27] He genuinely believed that God had selected Franz Josef to rule (as, indeed, God had presumably selected him to one day rule as well), and his approach was cautious. The archduke loathed the fact that his uncle so often gave in to arguing politicians merely to avoid unpleasant confrontations.[28] Still, he never criticized Franz Josef; he accepted and respected all of the emperor's decisions, holding his uncle in extraordinary esteem. Franz Ferdinand's 'dynastic, religious, monarchic and military sentiments prevented as a matter of course a hostile attitude toward the Emperor,' said Eisenmenger. 'He was not the man to withhold his opinions and yet I have never heard him make the slightest allusion in this direction. On the contrary, he was happy if he was able to tell of the approbation of or a gracious word from the Emperor.'[29] The archduke's grandson Georg, Duke of Hohenberg, adds, 'To undertake any opposition to the Emperor for human or political reasons would never enter his mind . . . To oppose the Emperor, to rebel against his commands, or even to quarrel with him – that was out of the question and unthinkable.'[30]

Aware that he had not been trained for the throne, the archduke educated himself. He read everything – books, newspapers, collected speeches – dealing with politics, scanned through every official paper and memoranda he could obtain, and relied on the Military Chancery to introduce capable men and ideas.[31] 'Some of the leading statesmen in the Dual Monarchy are known to entertain a high opinion of his capacity,' reported a British diplomat, 'while his few intimates speak very favourably of his courtesy and charm of manner. Nevertheless, owing probably to a naturally reserved disposition, and to the difficult circumstances in which an heir-apparent necessarily finds himself placed, the Archduke maintains a carefully guarded attitude, and to the public at large may be described as an almost unknown quantity.'[32] Former prime minister Koerber speculated that, once on the throne, Franz Ferdinand would reveal liberal tendencies, while the minister of war believed that he would 'make more concessions in twenty-four hours than Emperor Franz Josef has made in twenty-four years'.[33] Even Margutti, by no means one of the archduke's admirers, thought that 'with his elastic intellect and his unmistakable capacity for judging political situations and questions without the assistance of endless documents' Franz Ferdinand might well succeed in the nearly impossible task he set for himself of transforming the empire into a modern nation.[34]

Things had to change, of that the archduke was certain. Although essentially conservative in outlook, he feared that competing nationalism and the march of progress would inevitably render the old empire obsolete. The archduke's focus now turned to what might happen, and how he could best preserve Habsburg sovereignty while still making inevitable changes. He viewed Hungary as a perpetual thorn in Austria's side. He never forgot his time there, when Hungarian officers had refused to use German in their commands; how newspapers in Budapest had gleefully reported his illness and approaching death; and how everyone praised the revolutionaries of 1848 and their efforts to break with the Habsburgs.[35] 'The so-called decent Hungarian', he once complained, 'simply doesn't exist and every Hungarian, be he a minister, a prince, a cardinal, a tradesman, a peasant, a stable boy or a servant is a revolutionary and an ass (I exempt the Cardinal from being an ass, but he's a republican).'[36]

Intent on dealing with 'Hungarian traitors' when he came to the throne, the archduke envisioned nothing less than a complete reorganization of the empire.[37] At first he considered breaking apart the old Dual Monarchy by redrawing the map to add a new, third kingdom of southern Slavs, Slovenes, and Croats to the imperial crown. This would reduce Hungarian influence and equalize relations within the empire.[38] Franz Josef, said Margutti, regarded the idea as little short of sacrilege against the existing order.[39]

Eventually the archduke abandoned the notion as impractical. In its place came an idea born of his visit to America: transformation of the empire into a series of loosely federated states with local autonomy under Vienna's authority.[40] 'It is the sole salvation for the monarchy,' he declared in 1912.[41] Rumanian professor Aurel Popovici's 1906 book, *Die Vereinigten Staaten von Gröss-Österrich*, provided the road map: fifteen states, each composed of their own ethnic majorities and predominant languages, linked to Vienna in a reconfigured parliament and reliant on the crown for financial, foreign, and military affairs.[42] Under this plan, the Hungarians would lose their stranglehold over Vienna, while Slavs and other minorities would win equal rights and representation. When Margutti pointed out how difficult a legislative transforming of the Dual Monarchy into the Empire of Federated States would likely be, Franz Ferdinand insisted that it could be done 'by force'.[43]

When it came to the empire's foreign policy, Franz Ferdinand was surprisingly moderate and conciliatory. Since 1882, the Triple Alliance had tied Austria-Hungary, Germany and Italy together in an uneasy bond. Prussia's overt militarism always scared the archduke; several times he expressed fears that Berlin's sabre rattling would one day lead to a European war. Franz Ferdinand deemed Italy no more reliable. He could not forget how it had unified at the expense of Habsburg provinces less than fifty years earlier and how Italy continually threatened to sever their alliance and instead side with France; he even refused to wear the Italian orders inherited with the Este title. Unlike his uncle, though, the archduke accepted Italian unification and loss of Habsburg provinces as accomplished fact. He might vent his frustrations with the country in ill-tempered remarks and make noises about the necessity of building up Austria's fledgling navy to keep the Italians in check, but he never seriously suggested that Austria should seize its lost territories.[44]

The archduke most wanted to revive that which had been lost: an alliance between Austria, Germany and Russia. The three empires had previously been united, first in the Holy Alliance of 1815, and later in the Three Emperors' League (*Dreikaiserbund*) of 1873, but those ties had fallen victim to political and diplomatic machinations. If the alliance could somehow be re-established, Franz Ferdinand felt, the peace of Europe would be assured. The problem was Russia, tied since the 1890s to Republican France. The archduke had been full of enthusiasm for the young Tsar Nicholas II, who came to the throne in 1894, and believed that he could forge a relationship with him to ensure stability. Austria's ambassador in St Petersburg, he urged, should 'work to the end that our relations with Russia become the best imaginable. A complete agreement with Russia, an alliance of the Three Emperors, the maintenance of peace and the strengthening of the monarchic principle – these are my life's ideals for which I shall always be full of enthusiasm and work with all my strength.'[45] Even when the two empires were at odds the archduke never abandoned his dream of an alliance between Habsburgs, Hohenzollerns, and Romanovs.[46] Had he been in a position to actively seek these ties and succeeded in his efforts, twentieth-century history might have been quite different.

Mystery always surrounded the archduke's plans for the throne. People openly questioned whether he would, in fact, abide by the terms of his oath; even today, historians continue to insist that Franz Ferdinand would most likely have abandoned his pledge once on the throne.[47] Hungarians constantly made noise that they might one day revoke their recognition of the morganatic marriage and thus clear the way for Sophie's crowning as queen and Max's eventual accession as king.[48] The Independence Party in Budapest even issued a statement that they did not believe the archduke was bound by his oath: 'Once we crown him, we crown his wife. Hungary cannot be without a queen.'[49]

The issue, of course, was never resolved in Franz Ferdinand's lifetime, but blame for some of the unnecessary continued speculation over the issue can be laid squarely on questionable comments later made by Empress Zita. Although Franz Ferdinand assured his nephew Karl that he would honour his oath, Zita insisted that doubts lingered:

> *Sometimes, it was only a chance remark which rightly or wrongly made me wonder. For example, I remember Uncle Franzi once saying to me when we were talking about a very industrious land agent, 'That man works so hard. I just can't understand anyone doing that unless it is for his own children.' Obviously one could interpret a remark like that to mean that he was thinking of his own case and his own children. My husband quite certainly had this dread. He felt that after succeeding to the throne his uncle might somehow manage it so that his sons could inherit and then an impossible situation would arise. Archduke Karl would continue to be the heir presumptive but due to the Hungarian factor the monarchy could become divided into two camps about its future sovereign.*[50]

Zita interpreted the remark precisely as she wished to do, contrary to all assurances. Never able to abandon the ludicrous notion that Franz Ferdinand's warnings against the perils of temptation had led her husband astray, and extremely jealous of Karl's rights, she nursed a peculiar suspicion against 'Uncle Franzi' that led her to see conspiracies everywhere. She maintained this attitude even in the face of irrefutable evidence to the contrary, for Franz Ferdinand's plans were published in 1926. Composed in various drafts by Brosch and amended by others, the archduke's Accession Manifesto definitively refuted the speculation that he meant to renounce his oath.

Taking the throne as 'Emperor Franz II', the archduke promised 'equal rights of participation in the common affairs of the monarchy' for all of his subjects, as well as extended religious liberties, and envisioned postponing his coronation in Budapest until political inequities could be resolved. Then came the succession and Sophie. Franz Ferdinand invoked his 1900 oath and swore to uphold it, naming Archduke Karl as his heir. There were no claims or succession rights for either Max or Ernst. Sophie, he expressly declared, would be recognized as Her Highness the Duchess of Hohenberg. While she would be accorded the status of first lady in the empire and take precedence as the emperor's consort, she would not be raised to empress or queen.[51]

What might have been: no controversies over the succession, and no crowning of Sophie as empress or queen. What would have become of the empire, had Franz Ferdinand lived to implement his programme of reform and reconstitution of the empire into a federalized system? It is a question without answer, though ironically, Karl and Zita's eldest son believed that he knew. Franz Ferdinand, the late Archduke Otto insisted, 'especially Franz Ferdinand', would have saved the empire and strengthened the monarchy had he lived to realize his plans.[52]

ELEVEN

Diplomacy and Roses

✥

The year 1913 dawned full of promise. It seemed, said one man, 'the golden age of security'.[1] Aristocratic Europe still basked in prosperity, honour and tradition. In Russia the Romanovs celebrated three hundred years on the throne; in Berlin, the kaiser's only daughter married in a lavish ceremony that gathered Europe's extended royal cousins for one last, unsuspected glittering pageant. Yet the tide was slowly turning. The old, carefully ordered world was changing: motor cars and vacuum cleaners, ragtime and art nouveau, Isadora Duncan and daring couples dancing the new tango. Elegantly gowned ladies still waltzed with sleekly uniformed officers, and grand dukes and princes lost fortunes in the gilded casinos of Monte Carlo, but the sinking of the *Titanic* the previous year had rattled complacent attitudes about the privileges of class.

For the man who envisioned a coming reign filled with dramatic reorganization of his empire, the subtle passing of one age to the next seemed ripe with possibilities. Franz Ferdinand was still young; he turned fifty that December. To mark the occasion, he did what was, for him, almost the unthinkable, and in a rare concession to public opinion he authorized a biography of sorts. This took the form of a lengthy, heavily illustrated special edition of the Viennese periodical *Österrichische Rundschau* called *Erzherzog Franz Ferdinand Unser Thronfolger*. Within, a number of essays written by his intimates and approved by the archduke offered the curious public lengthy dissertations on his youth, his military career, his world tour, and his passion for hunting and architecture, as well as photographs of his wife and children at ease in private life.[2]

A long future seemingly spread before the archduke, a future that would finally see him upon the throne and in a position to drastically alter Austria-Hungary's composition. The years had left him robust, his once thin figure now transformed into a barrel-chested mass that seemed powerful, not flabby. He still had bouts of ill health, and years of shooting had left him increasingly hard of hearing.[3] 'For Franzi, it was a relief to have his ears checked,' Sophie wrote to her sister Oktavia. The doctor, 'thank God', had 'only found them a little worse, since he hadn't treated them for three years'.[4] A coughing fit sent him into endless worries that his tuberculosis had returned. Noticing a small lesion on his tongue, he called in Eisenmenger, who quickly assured the archduke that it was nothing but a bump. Only twenty-four hours passed before Franz Ferdinand was in a panic. 'In my hypochondriac condition,' he wrote the doctor, 'it has suddenly occurred to me that perhaps the thing on my tongue is after all cancer! I cannot get rid of this thought now. Please write me two lines quite frankly but do not conceal it from me if you should have any suspicion. I am expecting your letter at once.'[5]

Sophie, too, had changed with age. At forty-five, her figure was fuller, her elegant hair shaded with subtle hints of approaching grey. Four pregnancies and a life of watching her husband suffer over the humiliations she herself serenely ignored had left her health occasionally weakened. She drank red wine to correct an iron deficiency and had prescriptions for migraine tablets, tranquillizers and laxatives. Did Sophie, as some have suggested, suffer from a number of psychosomatic complaints resulting from life with a difficult husband?[6] Given the treatment she endured, it is certainly possible that Sophie lived with anxieties. Who, in her position, would have been free of worries? Although she always appeared serenely accepting of her place in the world according to the Habsburg court, it would have taken a remarkable woman not to occasionally bristle at the insults, even if only because they so hurt her husband. There were undoubtedly times when tranquillizers and migraine tablets would have eased the pressures of life, but her great-granddaughter Princess Anita believes that the majority of medications came in the periods following her difficult pregnancies and onset of menopause. All evidence, she points out, indicates that Sophie was 'a calm person, not prone to hysterics or outbursts'.[7]

The one real health problem was her heart. Both of Sophie's parents had suffered from heart disease, and she was increasingly prone to palpitations and shortness of breath. Doctors prescribed arsenic drops to treat her symptoms; it is not unreasonable to assume that tranquillizers may also have been prescribed during these periods of illness.[8] There was a serious episode in the spring of 1914, when she was laid up for several weeks. Luckily, as Kaiser Wilhelm II noted in a telegram to Franz Ferdinand, the danger soon passed, though he sent his 'most hearty greetings and best wishes for a speedy recovery'.[9]

Little Sophie, Max, and Ernst, too, were getting older. 'I can only report the best about us,' the archduke had written to Brosch the previous year. 'We are, thank God, all well, and the children are growing and thriving marvellously. Max will be starting Gymnasium this year.'[10] They were a handsome family, and there was a public appetite for information about their intimate life. Despite their morganatic status, Sophie and the three children would in due course one day be the emperor's family, if not members of the imperial family themselves. Shops in Vienna regularly sold postcards of the couple and their children, and magazines and newspapers picked up on the interest, regaling readers with glowing descriptions of their happy home life. The archduke found this nearly as difficult to understand as the vile gossip against Sophie. He regarded his family life as a strictly personal matter and resented unwelcome intrusions into this private realm. He was furious when some nosy reporter spotted him giving one of his children a ride on his shoulders, thinking that such scenes were sacrosanct. When one publication described how 'Pinky' brought her father newspapers at their shared breakfast table, Franz Ferdinand dismissed it all as 'treacle'.[11]

Cloistered and out of the public eye, the children were, like their father, enigmas to most Austrians. In 1908, for the sixtieth anniversary of Franz Josef's accession to the throne, they made a rare public appearance, invited to perform in a children's programme along with other offspring of the imperial house. Even then, their morganatic status was reinforced: they were listed last in the programme, behind the youngest member of the imperial family, and the official programme insultingly failed to include their princely titles or styles of 'Serene Highness', as if they were simply the Miss or Masters Hohenberg.

Occasionally unpleasant incidents threatened the secluded safety in which Franz Ferdinand and Sophie raised them. Once, Sophie brought the three children to watch their father at army manoeuvres in Bohemia, and a rumour soon spread that the duchess had ordered the soldiers to repeat a charge so that Little Sophie, Max and Ernst could get a better view. It was nonsense, but sixteen members of the Imperial Parliament actually signed a motion accusing Sophie and the children of disrupting army operations.[12] Under such circumstances, it was simply easier to live in the shadows, away from the harsh scrutiny of gossips always on the lookout for any ammunition, real or perceived, that could be used against Sophie, even if that meant dragging her innocent children into invented scandal.

'We never asked our parents about the problems they were facing,' recalled Little Sophie, 'and I can never remember them sitting down and explaining any of the difficulties to us. The situation was just left unmentioned as though it didn't exist. But of course we knew it did. We were always nervous at being taken along to court because we sensed that we were somehow in a special category. Even at children's parties we were sometimes placed very oddly. There was never any tension at home about it, however, though we noticed certain things even if we didn't talk about them.'[13] Not until 1912 did they actually meet the emperor, and then only by accident. Renovations were underway at the Belvedere, and the family temporarily lodged in a suite of rooms at the Hofburg.[14] One day, the archduke had to inspect the guard in a court-yard, and the children, wanting to watch, crowded into a corridor window to view the scene. Suddenly, they heard a commotion and saw the elderly emperor shuffling down the passage; terrified, they fled back to their rooms. Later that day, however, when after twelve years of marriage Franz Ferdinand dared ask the emperor if he might present his children, Franz Josef surprisingly agreed. As the three shuffled in with bows and curtsies before this mysterious figure, Franz Josef looked at them and wryly said, 'I think we saw each other this morning, didn't we?' It was the only time they would ever see the emperor during their parents' lives.[15]

The difficulties came and went. 'Antagonism', a newspaper reported at the end of 1911, 'has erupted at the Viennese court. Next week, Franz Ferdinand and his wife the Duchess of Hohenberg will leave the capital and retire to Brioni for two months. This is not the trivial matter it may seem. It indicates that the future emperor hears the talk at court balls in Vienna. It is painful for him to see manifested the effects of the oath he so blindly took when he entered into a morganatic marriage.'[16] The archduke confessed to a priest that he 'especially avoided social gatherings in Vienna', as 'the Viennese aristocracy had never forgiven him his union'.[17]

Spring brought renewed difficulty over Sophie's position. When Kaiser Wilhelm II's only daughter married in Berlin in May, both Franz Ferdinand and Sophie were missing. The archduke couldn't understand why they had not received an invitation; certainly there would be problems with etiquette, but he thought the issues could be resolved. Only later did he learn the truth: when the kaiser informed the court in Vienna that the couple would be asked, Franz Josef requested that the invitation be rescinded. Apparently, worries still existed that Sophie might make too favourable an impression on this gathering of royal guests.[18] To atone for this unintended slight, Wilhelm visited the couple at Konopischt that

October and was overly solicitous and charming, shooting with Franz Ferdinand by day and flattering Sophie by night.[19]

The year, though, ended with yet another foreign triumph. After Franz Ferdinand and Sophie's 1912 visit to Great Britain, the Duke of Portland told King George V that he had invited them to shoot at Welbeck Abbey the following autumn. Hearing this, the king decided that he, too, would ask them to visit. The couple was on holiday in Belgium when the invitation arrived. 'With the greatest joy,' the archduke eagerly accepted the 'gracious and friendly invitation', asking the Austrian ambassador to tell the king 'in the warmest possible words' how 'quite exceptionally enchanted' he and Sophie were at the offer.[20]

It was to be a private visit, without the pomp and ceremony surrounding a state visit – not quite the pageant Sophie had experienced at the kaiser's court in 1909, but more intimate. The archduke thought it for the best, declaring:

> *This form of invitation to beautiful England and this form of meeting the King and Queen just suits. And so we can spend* gemütlich *hours together and learn and see more than on official occasions . . . Official occasions (dinners, toasts, receptions, theatre, etc., where I become half sick and rushed to death) are a horror for me and I only undertake them when duty demands. Informal visits like this are much more beneficial for relations between rulers and princes than these frightful standard visits with their nerve- and health- shattering programmes. The King has done just the right thing and I'm especially grateful.*[21]

Franz Ferdinand and Sophie arrived in London on Saturday 15 November, together with the duchess's niece Countess Elisabeth de Baillet-Latour as her lady-in-waiting, and drove to the Ritz, where a curious crowd cheered their entry. After mass the following day, the couple shopped in Bond Street, took in the Wallace Collection, and called on Queen Alexandra and her daughter Princess Victoria at Marlborough House. Ambassador Count Albert von Mensdorff even gave a gala dinner in their honour at the embassy that night, where guests included the formidable Grand Duchess Vladimir of Russia, 'a very sweet and kindly lady,' Franz Ferdinand declared. 'Just think,' the archduke wrote to his son Max, 'Mami and Papi also danced!'[22]

Monday brought the highlight, when a special train took Franz Ferdinand and Sophie from London to Windsor. A frock-coated Franz Ferdinand helped Sophie, in a beige dress and black hat trimmed with pink flowers, onto the station siding, where King George V, his uncle Prince Christian of Schleswig-Holstein, and the mayor greeted them warmly. After inspecting an honour guard, the king led the archduke to a waiting landau and set off for the castle. Sophie, accompanied by her niece and by Count Mensdorff, followed in a second carriage, their progress cheered by a large crowd gathered along High Street before the procession disappeared through the Henry VIII Gate.[23]

Queen Mary received the visitors at Windsor Castle. Sophie 'was very unassuming,' said a witness, 'curtsied low to the King and Queen, and was so simple and nice'.[24] No royal ladies had been asked to join the party. 'It was entirely George's idea not to invite any of our Princesses to stay during the Austrian visit,' Queen Mary wrote. 'It would have been too awkward otherwise.'[25] The decision rested less on social discomfort than it did on ensuring that Sophie was accorded precedence immediately after the queen, so that 'she would not feel her awkward position, as she is made to feel it by the Austrian Court'.[26] Franz Ferdinand and Sophie were given the Tapestry Room Suite in the Lancaster Tower. The rooms, the archduke wrote to his son, were 'beautiful, with lots of gold and damask', but he admitted that he much preferred those at Konopischt or Blühnbach.[27] At half-past eight they joined the king and queen in the State Dining Room for a meal that included consommé, filet of sole, asparagus salad, and soufflé as a band from the Coldstream Guards serenaded them.[28]

Whatever misgivings Queen Mary may once have harboured over the marriage quickly disappeared. 'They are both extremely nice and easy to get on with,' she wrote to her son Prince Albert (the future

King George VI).[29] King and archduke were off to shoot the following morning, but 'a strong wind' hampered the efforts; by the time they had downed a thoroughly English lunch of mulligatawny soup, cottage pie, and apple dumplings, the incessant rain forced the party to abandon shooting altogether.[30] With improved weather the next day, the party of five guns bagged some seventeen hundred pheasants. Another thousand pheasants fell on November 20; with the improved weather the ladies, now joined by the Prince of Wales (later King Edward VIII and then Duke of Windsor), lunched with the group at Virginia Water, though dismal conditions the following day– 'blowing and pouring with rain', as the king complained – made the efforts difficult.[31]

Franz Ferdinand enjoyed the sport, though he was unaccustomed to such high-flying birds. His gun was problematic, but once it was adjusted for the conditions he did quite well, bringing down 281 pheasants and 252 ducks.[32] With practice, said his friend the Duke of Portland, he 'proved himself to be quite first class and certainly the equal of most of my friends. I am convinced that given enough practice in this country he would have been equal to any of our best shots.'[33]

Between shoots there were nightly dinners at the castle. One evening, a balalaika orchestra serenaded them in the Crimson Drawing Room; on another, a madrigal choir performed in the Waterloo Chamber.[34] To her aunt Augusta, the queen wrote:

> *You will be glad to hear that the visit is going off extremely well. The Archduke is most amiable, delighted with everything, and very well appreciative of the beauties of this place, which of course appeals to me. He is making an excellent impression and is enjoying the informality of the visit. The Duchess is very nice, agreeable, and quite easy to get on with, very tactful, which makes the position easier; altogether it is a pleasant visit . . . Last night we took them round the State Rooms after dinner; they looked beautiful all lit up, and were much admired . . . The Archduke was*

delighted at seeing portraits of his two great-grandfathers, Kaiser Franz and
Archduke Karl, and we could scarcely drag him away.[35]

'I think they have enjoyed themselves,' the king wrote when Franz Ferdinand and Sophie departed on the evening of 21 November, 'and their visit has been a great success'.[36] Queen Mary was equally enthusiastic. 'The Archduke', she noted, 'was formerly very anti-English, but that is quite changed now and *her* influence has been and is good, they say, in every way – all the people staying with me who had known *him* before said how much he had changed for the better and that he was most enthusiastic over his visit to us and to England and gratified for the kind way in which he had been received everywhere.'[37] Six months later, recalling the visit, the queen noted that she and her husband had become 'really quite attached to them both' during their stay.[38]

At the end of their Windsor sojourn, Franz Ferdinand and Sophie travelled by train to Nottinghamshire to stay again with the Duke and Duchess of Portland at Welbeck Abbey. The local newspaper reported 'considerable interest' in the visit and even speculated that the archduke's oath 'can be changed and it would be well perhaps if it were changed, for the Duchess has proved herself an admirable wife, has done a great work for the Archduke by bringing him into sympathy with his future subjects, and she might were she Empress do a still greater work for Austria.'[39]

Flags, bunting, and garlands of holly and ivy decorated the local Worksop railway station when the train carrying Franz Ferdinand and Sophie halted on the evening of Saturday 22 November. Crowds cheered them as they drove to Welbeck, and they smiled and bowed in appreciation. Over the next week, the couple toured the countryside, visiting Belvoir Castle, Hardwick Hall, and Chatsworth, which the archduke found enchanting.[40] He spent most of his time shooting. On one outing, a loader tripped and accidentally discharged a gun; the shot blew past Franz Ferdinand's head, just missing him by inches. 'I have often wondered', the Duke of Portland pondered, 'whether the Great War might not have been averted or at least postponed had the Archduke met his death then.'[41] Franz Ferdinand was apparently unperturbed by the incident. When he left, he presented the duke's head steward with a gold case holding a gold watch engraved with his monogram.[42]

The entire visit was deemed a success. Franz Ferdinand and Sophie fondly recalled their 'delightful stay in England' and spoke 'of the innumerable attentions they received from the King and Queen'.[43] The two royal couples, reported Count Mensdorff, were 'all enchanted with one another'.[44] Even the British press was enthusiastic. The *Guardian* noted with satisfaction that the king and queen, 'by inviting the Duchess to visit them with her husband' and 'by receiving her as a royal personage, did something to correct the cruelty of these Austrian marriage rules'.[45]

Franz Ferdinand, Mensdorff insisted, had seemed like a different man during the visit. The archduke was 'very amiable' and 'endlessly friendly to everybody'. His mood lightened on seeing Sophie treated with such thoughtfulness and respect, and he left the country 'in the rosiest mood, delighted with everything and charming to everyone'. If only Franz Ferdinand, said the count, 'could always be like this at home, he would conquer the hearts of the Hungarians and anybody else'.[46]

England armed the couple with yet another foreign triumph, one that seemed to promise a horizon one day free of insults and nagging questions of precedence. Perhaps with these thoughts in mind, Franz Ferdinand and Sophie took up residence at the Belvedere for the 1914 winter social season. They had been inconsistent in doing so over the years, uncertain how Sophie would be treated at court. Despite the gestures toward her, and the imperial family's thaw in their previously icy relations, experience had shown that there were no guarantees. The previous year, thinking that the animosity against his wife was lessening, Franz Ferdinand dared ask if Sophie could accompany him to an ordinary performance at a public theatre. He received a stern rebuke in reply. 'His Imperial and Royal Apostolic Majesty', Montenuovo wrote, 'has determined thus in respect of a most humble request as to whether it would be proper to go to theatres that do not possess royal boxes. In proper company, Highest Gentlemen may visit such theatres, but it is graciously pointed out that this All Highest ruling does not apply to Highest Ladies.'[47] Yet five months after this denial, the emperor had awarded Sophie the Grand Cross of the Elisabeth Order, a mark of personal favour named for his late wife; in addition, she also held the Order of the Star Cross, given to most aristocrats, and had been appointed a dame in the Bavarian Order of St Elisabeth.[48]

With imperial honours and foreign royal visits, it seemed that Sophie was finally moving up in this rarified world, but, for all the marks of favour, the contradictions never disappeared. In February 1914, the couple attended a court ball at Schönbrunn Palace. Maurice de Bunsen, the new British ambassador in Vienna, thought that Sophie 'was looking very well' when she entered the ballroom, but it was obvious that her position was 'still very delicate and difficult'. She spent much of the evening talking with Archduchess Marie Valerie, Franz Josef's youngest daughter; 'some of the others', de Bunsen wrote, 'seemed to avoid her, especially Archduchess Isabella'.[49] As Franz Ferdinand moved through the crowd, Sophie sat at the far end of a raised dais, looking 'far the most intelligent and pleasantest of the lot,' insisted a guest.[50] There was even an unexpected surprise before the evening was out, when Franz Josef sent for Sophie and asked her to sit beside him for a few moments. It was, as one author noted, 'a gesture both trivial and momentous'.[51]

Difficulties came, went, and came again, an incessant ebb and flow that gave with one wave and took away with the next. In the spring of 1914, the tide seemed to be turning in Sophie's favour. Although she did not write to Sophie personally, Marie Valerie tacked on an expression of concern over her health in a letter to the archduke.[52] Then, in the midst of a brief crisis over Franz Josef's health, came the most startling rapprochement of all. 'We are thinking about having a dance in Vienna on 6 and 9 June at our house,' Archduchess Isabella wrote to Franz Ferdinand, 'and would be really pleased if you and Sophie would like to come.'[53] At the time Franz Ferdinand's reign must have seemed imminent. After so many years of opposition, fear of alienating the future emperor's wife seems to have driven the wily archduchess to such a remarkable and cagey concession.

That spring of 1914, the couple abandoned Vienna to welcome the Duke and Duchess of Portland to Konopischt; King George and Queen Mary had even agreed to visit the archduke and duchess at Blühnbach that autumn.[54] The kaiser, too, came to call. On 27 March 1914, when Franz Ferdinand's family was staying at Miramar in Trieste, the kaiser arrived aboard his yacht *Hohenzollern*, and the archduke sailed out to greet him aboard the new Austrian battleship *Viribus Unitis*. For the occasion Franz Ferdinand wore the uniform of a grand admiral in the German navy. He felt that he looked like a fool, but commented that it didn't really matter because Wilhelm II 'is always dressed up himself in the worst possible taste'.[55]

Hints of acceptance led the couple back to Vienna early that summer. The trees were now full, the flowers in bloom, and fashionable society crowded the immense Prater enjoying races and concerts in the warm air. On 2 June, Franz Ferdinand and Sophie took their daughter to the elaborate *Blumenskorso* Flower Parade, looking on at the spectacle and eagerly watched by a curious crowd.[56] Five days later, they attended the Derby in the Prater. In a remarkable concession, Sophie was, for the first time, allowed to join her husband in the imperial box as the stands of frock-coated gentlemen and ladies in summer white looked on in amazement. It was such an unprecedented concession that the Viennese press stumbled over itself to enthral readers with details of Sophie's white dress with its black sash, the black jacket trimmed with white lace, and the black hat with white brim and black ostrich feathers.[57]

Then it was back to Konopischt to welcome Kaiser Wilhelm II. As much as Franz Ferdinand grumbled about him, he appreciated the kaiser's flattering attentions to Sophie. Wilhelm's letters were full of flamboyant assurances of his 'devotion to the duchess', coupled with requests that the archduke kiss her hand on his behalf.[58]

Franz Ferdinand was in such a rush to meet the kaiser's train when it pulled into Beneschau on the morning of 12 June that he forgot his gloves and had to borrow a pair from Baron Andreas Morsey, one of his secretaries.[59] The archduke had donned the uniform of the 10th Prussian Uhlan Regiment, hoping to make just the right impression, but he needn't have worried. Wilhelm stepped from the train clad in a hunting uniform of his own design, with green tunic and breeches and a felt hat adorned with pheasant plumes.[60] He kissed Sophie and greeted the children. Little Sophie, like her mother, wore white, while Max and Ernst sported matching blue sailor suits. Motor cars took them off to the castle. The kaiser had brought his favourite dachshunds, Wadl and Hexl, with him; once set free, they raced into the park, chasing a pet crane before stalking one of the archduke's rare golden pheasants, which they triumphantly brought back and dropped dead at their master's feet. The kaiser was full of horrified apologies, but Franz Ferdinand brushed off the loss of one of the birds he had so carefully raised. Luncheon was delayed until the kaiser's special cutlery, which enabled him to cut meat unaided using only his right hand, was fetched from his train.[61]

Admiral Alfred von Tirpitz, himself a renowned horticulturalist, had come with the kaiser, hoping to see Konopischt's famous rose garden. The archduke's gardeners had spent days nourishing the flowers with warm water to ensure that they were in bloom at just the right moment.[62] Wilhelm found the colourful parterres fascinating, praising the archduke for 'the organizational mastery and the fine colour sense that show through in your landscaping'.[63] There were visits to a local church, an agricultural school, and the surrounding forests before a farewell dinner the following night. Wilhelm led Sophie into the Lobkowicz Hall, where she sat to his right as guests dined on consommé, roast lamb, crayfish, roasted chicken, asparagus in hollandaise sauce, and fresh strawberries and cream while a military band serenaded them with marches and hunting songs.[64]

It had all been innocent; there was, it is true, some talk about Rumania's reliability as an ally if any military conflict broke out. Soon, though, there were rumours of nefarious goings on at Konopischt that summer of 1914 beyond 'the enjoyment of the Archducal rose garden', as the British ambassador in Vienna delicately put it.[65] The First World War, many

Allied governments insisted, had been planned during this visit.[66] James W. Gerard, the American ambassador in Berlin, even insisted that Sophie had been behind it. 'How many in America have heard the name of Sophie Chotek?' he wrote. 'Yet the ambitions of this woman have done much to send to war the splendid youths who from all the ends of the earth gather in France to fight the fight of freedom. The clever German Emperor, playing upon her ambitions, induced the gloomy, hated Franz Ferdinand to consent to the world war.'[67]

Even more persistent was the rumour spread by English journalist Henry Wickham Steed as a piece of Allied propaganda once the First World War began. This became known as 'the Pact of Konopischt'. During the meeting, he insisted, kaiser and archduke had agreed to carve up much of the European continent into spheres of influence between them. According to this story, the end of their planned war would see Franz Ferdinand's son Max crowned as king of an independent Poland, and Ernst crowned as king of Hungary, Bohemia and Serbia.[68]

The subject of Max's future had indeed been raised during the visit, though not in the terms Steed portrayed. The kaiser suggested that Max might become ruling grand duke of an independent Lorraine, which Germany had seized along with Alsace from France as a spoil of the Franco-Prussian War. Franz Ferdinand and Sophie had never planned for their children to be anything but private individuals, at least not before this conversation. Their daughter could one day marry, and their younger son, Ernst, could carve out a career in forestry management on one of the estates he would inherit. However, this proposal about Alsace-Lorraine suddenly seemed immensely appealing. There were Habsburg ties to the province, and Franz Ferdinand and Sophie now apparently approved of this idea that would ensure their eldest son's future.[69]

This was the extent of any discussion: an enticing and unexpected proposal that would one day elevate Max into esteemed royal circles. No one, though, wanted to believe the truth. Rumours about this meeting at Konopischt would one day come back to haunt Max and his siblings.

TWELVE

'I Consider War to Be Lunacy!'

✠

On 6 October 1908, when Austria-Hungary annexed the neighbouring provinces of Bosnia and Herzegovina, it was the culmination of a long and unhappy struggle for European primacy in the Balkans. Things had begun thirty years earlier, when Tsar Alexander II had gone to war with the Ottoman Empire. The Treaty of Berlin that ended the war not only established the neighbouring independent Kingdom of Serbia but also granted semi-autonomy to the Ottoman provinces of Bosnia and Herzegovina. To prevent further Russian incursion into the region, the treaty placed the provinces under Austrian administration. With this move, Austria-Hungary gained some two million new subjects. Just under half were Orthodox, with strong religious and nationalistic ties to the kingdom of Serbia. Belgrade made no secret of the fact that it coveted the provinces and soon hoped to seize them. The other half of the province's populace, roughly divided between Muslims and Catholics, feared Serb expansion and looked to Austria for protection.[1]

Much of Europe viewed the scattered Balkan provinces, states and principalities as something of a perpetual menace. Opinion whispered that they were home to wild savages, brigands and would-be terrorists, always on the brink of some explosive revolution or horrendous outrage.

'Some damn foolish thing in the Balkans', German chancellor Otto von Bismarck predicted, would sooner or later plunge all of Europe into a general war.[2]

Bosnia and Herzegovina, in particular, became a point of contention between Austria and Serbia in the first years of the twentieth century. Initially Belgrade had friendly relations with Vienna, thanks in large part to the pro-Habsburg policies of its ruling Obrenović dynasty, headed first by King Milan and then by his son King Alexander.[3] This changed in the early morning hours of 11 June 1903, when a group of officers, led by Captain Dragutin Dimitrijević, stormed the royal palace in Belgrade. King Alexander was deeply unpopular, and his marriage to his mistress Draga Masin, one of his mother's ladies-in-waiting, led to a swirl of scandalous rumours that discredited the couple. The conspirators swept through the palace, murdering officials as they searched for the king and queen. After several hours of slaughter, they finally found Alexander and Draga, fearfully cowering in a closet. Dragged from the hiding place, the king was shot more than thirty times, and his wife nearly twenty, before the men stripped the corpses and hurled them from the palace balcony into the rain-soaked garden.[4]

Dimitrijević had been in the pay of the Russians at the time of the massacre, and in the new King Peter I, a member of the former ruling Karageorgevich dynasty, St Petersburg now had a monarch friendly to their views in Belgrade. Having been briefed on the plot in advance, the new king showed a curious reluctance to punish those involved in the brutal murders. Indeed, the conspirators were rewarded, publicly hailed as 'saviours of the Fatherland', and Dimitrijević eventually became chief of Serbian intelligence.[5] King Peter was avowedly pro-Russian and anti-Austrian in his policies; he quickly bragged that 'the traditional aspirations of the Serbian people' would soon be met.[6]

This was unsubtle code for the idea of a Greater Serbia, Belgrade's dream to unite Bosnia, Herzegovina, Slovenia, Croatia, Macedonia, and Montenegro under their rule.[7] Such talk worried Austria, but not until the summer of 1908, when the Young Turk Rebellion erupted in

Constantinople, did Vienna decisively act to thwart Serbia's ambitions. Belligerent noises from the Ottoman Empire about reclaiming their lost provinces of Bosnia and Herzegovina threatened the fragile Balkan status quo; if Constantinople didn't act, Belgrade might. To prevent this, Austria would annex the provinces.

The plan horrified Franz Ferdinand. When a group of government and military officials first presented the idea, the archduke argued and argued that seizure of the provinces would likely result in a military conflict. At the very least Serbia would probably fight, and this threatened to bring her ally imperial Russia into the mix. When the men wouldn't listen, he suddenly declared, 'These things can be seen from different points of view. I will fetch my wife.' In a few minutes, he returned with Sophie and asked her to share her opinion on the proposed annexation. The archduke was usually relentless in keeping the political and private sides of his life entirely separate, both from conviction and from worry that involving Sophie would arm her enemies with ammunition to denounce her as an ambitious meddler. Yet he opposed the annexation so strongly that this one time Franz Ferdinand dared to take the risk. Sophie tried a different approach with the men. As a wife and a mother, she explained, she could only look on the idea of military conflict with horror. Many men would be killed, and for what? Was it really so vital to Austria that the provinces be annexed? Several of the men squirmed, clearly uncomfortable with the arguments and at being lectured by the archduke's wife. Seeing this, and perhaps hoping to prevent damage to his master's reputation, Colonel Brosch abruptly cut her off, saying, 'Ladies should not meddle in military decisions.' Sophie rushed from the room. Franz Ferdinand was furious and ordered Brosch to immediately return to Vienna. Thinking his career was over, Brosch wrote a letter of resignation, but Franz Ferdinand quickly forgave him, and the matter was never again mentioned.[8]

It took several more weeks, and additional meetings, before the archduke reluctantly consented to the annexation. 'I would like to be sure that Your Excellency', he wrote to Foreign Minister Alois von Aerenthal, 'is fully aware of my opinion on the matter. If an annexation is considered absolutely necessary then I can only agree to it if the two provinces are declared a land of the empire . . . In general I am completely against all such displays of strength in view of our depressing domestic circumstances.'[9]

Aerenthal met Alexander Izwolsky, his Russian counterpart, in September 1908 at an ornate little villa in Moravia. The two agreed that Austria-Hungary could annex Bosnia-Herzegovina in exchange for recognition of Russian interests in the Bosphorus. Izwolsky even promised that Russia would not back Serbia's inevitable call for military action when the provinces were seized. Austria jumped the gun, however, announcing the annexation before Izwolsky had briefed his own government. Vienna's fait accompli violated the Treaty of Berlin, but Austria justified its action as necessary to prevent Serbian aggression against a disintegrating Ottoman Empire. Germany was furious, Serbia strenuously protested, and Russia threatened to mobilize against the Habsburg Empire. War was avoided only when Vienna blackmailed St Petersburg by threatening to release details of Izwolsky's secret negotiations. Serbia and Russia backed down, but both countries were humiliated and thirsted for revenge against Austria.[10]

The annexation only accelerated the state of perpetual ferment between Austria-Hungary and Serbia. Egged on by imperial Russia, Belgrade became even more determinedly nationalistic. Russian money promoted Slavic secret societies that championed violence as a means of breaking Austria's influence in the Balkans. Funds collected by the Russian Orthodox Church and channelled to Belgrade paid for anti-Austrian propaganda against Habsburg rule in the annexed provinces.[11]

Some of this money went to Narodna Odbrana, or Defense of the People, an organization full of government ministers and the military elite that claimed to be a cultural society but that actually existed to promote violence against Austria. Even Crown Prince Alexander of Serbia contributed to the cause.[12] 'Our people must be told', insisted their propaganda, 'that the freedom of Bosnia is necessary for her, not only out of pity for the brothers suffering there, but also for the sake of trade and the connection with the sea.' The 'necessity of fighting Austria', it proclaimed, was 'a sacred truth' that called for the arming of the populace with 'weapons and bombs' in advance of the 'fight with gun and cannon'.[13]

More money went to a second, more lethal organization. This was the Black Hand, the popular name given to Ujedinjenje ili Smrt (Union or Death). Formed in 1911, the Black Hand included most of those involved in the 1903 murders of King Alexander and Queen Draga, along with lawyers, diplomats, journalists, professors, and government officials – in essence, the elite of Serbian political, educational and military circles. The Black Hand contended that violence was necessary to create a new Greater Serbia. Members went through a preposterously theatrical ritual of swearing in the presence of skulls and on crosses, pistols and daggers to promote violence and to kill themselves if threatened with arrest. The Serbian general staff trained terrorists in shooting and bomb throwing, promoted them to military ranks, and placed them along the Austrian border at frontier crossings. By 1914, the organization's ties to the government of Serbian prime minister Nikola Pašić had cooled considerably, though a network of spies kept him informed of its activities.[14]

This propaganda spilled over into the Serbian press. To mark Franz Josef's eightieth birthday in 1910, a Belgrade newspaper lauded past would-be assassins. Black-bordered newspapers marked the 1910 anniversary of the annexation. 'The day of revenge,' articles assured their readers, was coming. 'We must dismember Austria!' papers declared. It was, the stories ran, the 'sacred obligation' of every Serb to prepare for inevitable war with 'the monster that is called Austria'.[15]

Such sentiments only fed growing perceptions that Serbia was 'a thorough-going nuisance, a nest of violent barbarians whose megalomania would sooner or later meet with the punishment it deserved'.[16] The deteriorating situation stunned many. 'I cannot describe', reported the British ambassador in Vienna in 1913, 'how exasperated people here are by the unending trouble, which that small country, incited by Russia, is fomenting for Austria.'[17] Franz Ferdinand constantly worried about the potential unrest. He complained to Crown Prince Wilhelm of Germany 'very earnestly and very anxiously about the dangerous Serbian propaganda; he foresaw an early European conflict in these intrigues that Russia was fanning.'[18]

The looming threat of a belligerent Serbia now dominated Austrian military policy and presented Franz Ferdinand with unceasing headaches. Ironically, the source of most of his trouble was of his own making. In 1906, he had discovered General Baron Conrad von Hötzendorf, a middle-aged career soldier with a distinguished administrative record, and convinced the emperor to name him *Generalstabschef* (chief of the general staff). Conrad had actually suggested another man, Lieutenant Field Marshal Oskar Potiorek, deputy chief of staff, but the archduke refused to support him and got his way.[19]

The archduke firmly embraced Conrad's ideas for military modernization of an archaic and badly equipped army. He even let himself occasionally be carried away by Conrad's impetuous talk of the need to humiliate Italy and restrain her influence. He was less enthusiastic about the general's perpetual calls for military action. War, Conrad said, was 'the basic principle behind all the events on this Earth'.[20] The general was particularly insistent in continually proposing 'preventative war' against Serbia. At first Franz Ferdinand simply ignored such talk, but Conrad's belligerence eventually made him something of a thorn in the archduke's side.[21]

The archduke's relationship with and promotion of Conrad led many to believe that he shared the general's militaristic views, especially when it came to Serbia. Public opinion portrayed Franz Ferdinand as a half-mad, twitching time bomb, a buffoon relentlessly insistent on waging war against every Balkan nation. One contemporary declared that he 'has undertaken to restore to the Empire its old prestige, and is ready to pay any price to secure Austria-Hungary's place in the Concert of Europe. He has not hesitated, indeed, to play a solo whose discordance could but break up the harmony of that Concert.'[22] The truth was quite different, especially as concerned Serbia and the seemingly endless intrigues in the Balkans.

Talk of a 'preventative' war against Serbia ran high in the wake of the annexation.[23] 'Please restrain Conrad for me,' the archduke wrote to Major Brosch. 'He should stop all this agitating for war. Of course it would be splendid and is very tempting to throw these Serbs and Montenegrins into the frying pan. But what use are such cheap laurels to us if we then face such an escalation through general complications in Europe that we could find ourselves having to fight on two or three fronts, something we could not manage?'[24] To anyone who would listen, Franz Ferdinand repeatedly opposed Conrad's suggested 'policy of brigandage'.[25]

The situation became more perilous when the Balkan Wars erupted. After the Young Turk Rebellion in Constantinople and the annexation of Bosnia and Herzegovina, smaller Balkan countries felt empowered to break away from the Ottoman Empire. In 1912, the newly independent Bulgaria and Montenegro joined Serbia and Greece in forming the Balkan League, and that October they attacked Turkey. Conrad had been forced out the previous year over foreign policy disagreements; now the archduke, fearing a wider war, wanted him back and convinced the emperor to reappoint the general as chief of staff.[26]

It was a mistake. Conrad immediately pounced, suggesting yet another 'preventative war' against Serbia. Franz Ferdinand, fed up with this constant militarism, asked the emperor to relieve Conrad of his command. Franz Josef initially agreed, but as 1913 began, Conrad was fully restored to power and back to singing his constant chorus urging war with Serbia. This, Franz Ferdinand complained just as constantly, would draw Russia into a conflict and result in a general European war.[27] 'What would be the point of fighting Russia?' he once asked. 'Not even Napoleon could succeed. And even if we beat Russia, which to my mind is totally out of the question, a victory like that would still be the greatest tragedy for the Austrian monarchy.'[28]

At a dinner in early February 1913, Franz Ferdinand pointedly celebrated the emperor's reluctance to approve Conrad's incessant plans for war, raising his glass in a toast, 'To peace!' He said, 'What would we have had from a war with Serbia? We'd lose the lives of young men and we'd spend money better used elsewhere. And what, for heaven's sake, would we gain? Some plum trees and goat pastures full of shit, and a bunch of rebellious killers!' To his uncle, he confided fears that a war between Austria and Russia would 'encourage revolution in both countries and thereby cause both Emperor and Tsar to push each other from their thrones. For these reasons, I consider war to be lunacy, and Conrad's constant requests for mobilization as preludes to lunacy.'[29]

Franz Ferdinand's growing animosity against Conrad took a more dramatic turn in the spring of 1913. This time it wasn't merely the general's constant sabre rattling. On 29 May 1913, Viennese papers reported the curious suicide of Colonel Alfred Redl, chief of staff of the 8th Army Corps in Prague and deputy chief of the Austro-Hungarian Counterespionage and Military Secret Service. Redl, it turned out, had been selling military secrets to St Petersburg for a decade after a Russian agent discovered his homosexuality, seduced him, and then threatened him with exposure. On learning of the scandal, Conrad dispatched several officers to confront Redl with evidence of his guilt; after making the general's position quite clear, they placed a loaded revolver on a table and left the room. Redl, not surprisingly, did the 'honourable' thing and blew his brains out.[30]

The archduke was furious. The enforced suicide had taken place before Redl could be properly questioned; he took the secrets of his Russian contacts, and their potentially invaluable information for Austrian espionage, to his grave. That was bad enough, but the piously Catholic archduke was, if anything, even more offended that a man had been made to kill himself. In a rage, he summoned Conrad to the Belvedere and berated him over the episode. Shaken, the general followed the archduke's suggestion that he offer his resignation, but this time the emperor refused to accept it.[31]

The Treaty of London, signed in the spring of 1913, ended the First Balkan War, stripping the Ottoman Empire of most of its European provinces and creating the new principality of Albania as a way to block Serbian access to the Adriatic. Peace wasn't to last: by June, the Second

Balkan War had erupted when Bulgaria, encouraged by Austria, attacked Serbia and Greece, hoping to gain more territory.[32] Conrad again pushed for war against Serbia. 'Don't ever let yourself be influenced by Conrad, ever!' Franz Ferdinand warned Foreign Minister Berchtold. 'Not an iota of support for any of his yappings at the Emperor. Naturally he wants every possible war . . . Let's not play Balkan warriors. Let's not stoop to hooliganism . . . It would be unforgivable, insane, to start a war that would pit us against Russia.'[33]

In September 1913, Serbia planned to invade Albania; Russia refused to intervene and stop her Balkan ally. Reliable as always, Conrad urged war, but Franz Ferdinand turned to Kaiser Wilhelm II, hoping to calm an escalating and dangerous situation. The kaiser agreed, and Serbia backed down in the face of a German ultimatum.[34] 'I was so happy that this war has been avoided,' the archduke wrote. 'I've said that if one approaches the Kaiser with some deftness, avoiding talk of great power and other chicaneries . . . he'll then stand fully with us, and we won't need to resort to a single weapon or any of Conrad's other Big Sticks.'[35]

Persistent calls for war against Serbia and the Redl scandal left the archduke thoroughly disenchanted with Conrad. He appreciated the efforts at modernizing the army, but the general, he was now sure, was a malignant and dangerous force. Anger spilled over into the public arena in October 1913, when the archduke travelled to Leipzig to join the kaiser in unveiling a memorial marking Napoleon's defeat. During a military banquet, Wilhelm asked Conrad to present Austria's senior military officials. The general was on his way across the room to round up the men when Franz Ferdinand caught his sleeve. 'This is for me to do!' he shouted in a voice so loud that the room fell silent. 'Are you the senior army commander here? Isn't it the privilege of the highest-ranking Austrian to present others to His Majesty? I will not allow this! Why have you affronted me?' Conrad could do nothing but stand in silence as the humiliation unfolded, but when he returned to Vienna he was more determined than ever to find some way to wage war on Serbia, and in the process teach the archduke a lesson.[36]

Conrad again tried to get his 'preventative war' in early 1914, suggesting that Austrian troops be mobilized along the Russian border for a display of Habsburg military might.[37] Neither Russia nor its ally France, he insisted in February, was prepared for a general European conflict—'Why are we waiting?'[38] The following month Conrad was back to extolling the virtues of war against Serbia; when the German ambassador in Vienna got wind of this, he quickly warned the general that Franz Ferdinand would undoubtedly oppose the idea, and the kaiser would support him.[39] Not to be put off, Conrad waited a mere ten weeks before trying again. Immediate action to crush Serbia, he suggested to his German counterpart, would offer the chance for a larger European conflict that would forever eliminate Russian influence in the Balkans. The Tsar's soldiers, he insisted, were too unprepared and too weak to fight in any prolonged general war.[40]

Franz Ferdinand had spent the last six years attempting to restrain Conrad. Over and over again, the militaristic general had sought a conflict; between 1 January 1913 and 1 June 1914, Conrad proposed a larger European war against Russia on numerous occasions and a 'preventative war' against Serbia twenty-five times.[41] The archduke had come to loathe the general and continually pushed for his resignation. He even let everyone know that he had already selected General Karl von Tersztyansky, a Hungarian in charge of the Budapest Army Corps, as Conrad's replacement. If Franz Ferdinand had any say in the matter, Conrad's days were numbered.[42]

The archduke was sure that Conrad meant to push Austria into a war with Serbia. He might have worried even more had he known of the general's attitudes the last week of June 1914. On 22 June, Conrad returned to his obsessive theme, warning Austria's foreign minister that enemies surrounded the country. The very survival of the monarchy, Conrad insisted, was at stake. Bold and decisive action, no matter the price, was needed, a 'great sacrifice' that would save the Habsburg throne.[43] All Conrad lacked was a pretext upon which to act.

THIRTEEN

The Fatal Invitation

✣

A collision of wills seemed inevitable between Franz Ferdinand and Conrad, especially after the summer of 1913. On 17 August, the emperor promoted the archduke to inspector general of the empire's armed forces. A delighted Franz Ferdinand decided to rush to Ischl, where the emperor was on holiday, and thank him personally. He tried to bring Sophie, thinking that the emperor would not object to her presence at a private dinner, but he had not counted on Franz Josef's continued ambivalence. On learning of his nephew's plan, the emperor craftily asked Bardolff to dine with him as well. As head of the archduke's Military Chancery, Bardolff's invitation turned a private occasion into an official dinner, and one from which Sophie was thereby excluded.[1]

Three weeks later, in September of 1913, the archduke attended the autumn manoeuvres in Bohemia as inspector general for the first time. Things went badly between him and General Conrad. The archduke berated the general, accusing him of inefficiency, and angrily confronted him over missing church services (Conrad was an atheist). It was, Conrad complained to a friend, 'a scene without parallel'; never before had he been subjected to such brutality.[2] By the time the manoeuvres had ended, Franz Ferdinand was even more determined to replace Conrad.

As for the chief of the general staff, he, too, left Bohemia depressed and disgruntled. On his return to Vienna he again submitted a letter of resignation, but the emperor again refused to accept it.[3] 'As highly as the Archduke formerly praised him to the skies,' said an observer, 'so now he hates him.'[4]

This was the backdrop to the fateful invitation to attend army manoeuvres the following June near the Bosnian capital of Sarajevo. Even after a century the circumstances surrounding the invitation are surprisingly muddy. Conrad gave two contradictory versions. He insisted that he first learned of the visit on 16 September, when the archduke personally told him he planned to attend and to take Sophie with him.[5] Yet Conrad later said he knew nothing of the proposal until 29 September, when General Oskar Potiorek, governor-general of Bosnia, informed him of the archduke's plan.[6] 'On whose initiative the decision to attend the manoeuvres rested,' Conrad wrote, 'I do not know.'[7]

Many historians have assumed that Franz Ferdinand's recent elevation to inspector general of the armed forces demanded his attendance at the Bosnian manoeuvres. This is what his son Max later suggested, saying that his father felt obligated to appear in his role at the head of the Imperial Army.[8] In fact, though, Franz Ferdinand went to Bosnia only as an observer. He did not attend the manoeuvres as inspector general and had no official role in the exercises.[9]

Max suggested that his father was excited about attending the impending manoeuvres in Bosnia.[10] Perhaps this was true, when the proposal merely involved watching the exercises and staying at a nearby resort, but any enthusiasm for the trip quickly waned when it swelled to encompass an unwelcome ceremonial visit to the Bosnian capital of Sarajevo.

Much ink has been spilled pondering why Franz Ferdinand went to Sarajevo. The visit, it has been said, came because the archduke wanted public acclamation; more important, he craved this acclaim for his morganatic wife.[11] Baron Albert von Margutti typically insisted that Sophie was the driving force behind the visit, that she 'eagerly snatched' this 'unexpectedly favourable opportunity for her to present herself to the people as the wife of the heir'.[12] 'Thus for love', insisted one historian, 'did the Archduke go to his death.'[13]

However, the archduke didn't need to seek acclaim under potentially dangerous circumstances – indeed, he disdained such appeals to public opinion. Nor did he need to prove anything where Sophie was concerned. When the initial plan was discussed, it involved only his attendance at the manoeuvres; Sophie would remain at a nearby hotel. There might be a private dinner or two for military officials, but at this stage there was no mention of any visit to Sarajevo; that idea only arose several months later. There would have been no opportunity for Sophie to 'present herself to the people' or to bask in any ceremonial laurels. Indeed, she had already been received at the royal courts of Rumania, Berlin and Great Britain. Even had the first plans called for a visit to Sarajevo, what would the applause of a few thousand Bosnians add to her sense of worth?[14]

Franz Ferdinand had reason to avoid Bosnian crowds. In 1910, a student named Bogdan Žerajić had tried to kill the Austrian governor-general of Bosnia and Herzegovina. All of his five gunshots missed the official; only the sixth, fired by Žerajić into his own brain, hit its mark.[15] Two years later, an assassin with ties to the Black Hand in Serbia killed the Croatian secretary of education, and in August 1913 the governor-general of Croatia was shot and wounded as he left a church. One Croat tried to kill Archduke Leopold Salvator during a spring 1914 visit to Zagreb; another student armed with a revolver was arrested boarding a train to Vienna. His target was Franz Ferdinand, 'the enemy of all South Slavs,' he said, 'and I wished to eliminate this garbage which is hampering our national aspirations'.[16]

Sarajevo itself was hardly friendly territory for a visiting Habsburg. When Oskar Potiorek took up his appointment as Bosnian governor-general in 1911 he found the capital in chaos. Potiorek responded to the constant anti-Austrian, anti-Habsburg sentiments that rippled across the city with repression. Bosnia's parliament was suspended, laws were annulled, Serb nationalist societies and their violent propaganda were banned, the city's press was censored, and Potiorek repeatedly asked for additional troops to keep order.[17]

Yet it was this unstable city that Potiorek now insisted the archduke must visit. The first plans called only for the archduke to attend manoeuvres near Sarajevo on 26–27 June, staying with Sophie at the resort of Ilidže just outside the city.[18] This low-key approach perfectly fitted with Franz Josef's wishes. He let it be known that he did not want the visit to become any kind of triumphal celebration that would eclipse his own previous trip to Sarajevo in 1910.[19]

Potiorek protested that the archduke must visit the city.[20] It was foolish, Bardolff argued, for the archduke to expose himself to such a risk. Potiorek refused to back down. On 17 February 1914, after much negotiation, Franz Ferdinand reluctantly agreed to a short, informal visit to Sarajevo, without any official public appearances. This didn't satisfy Potiorek, who may have thought that a formal visit by the archduke would bolster his own regime and give it the stamp of imperial approval. Five days later, he promised Bardolff that he would 'undertake full responsibility' for security if the visit was a formal one with planned public appearances, but if the archduke insisted on making it a 'more or less sudden unofficial visit', he could not promise adequate protection.[21] So, after much prodding, many promises of safety, and repeated warnings that he could only protect the archduke if the visit was a formal one, Potiorek got his wish. Franz Ferdinand reluctantly agreed to spend a few morning hours in the Bosnian capital. Potiorek tried to fight even this concession; as late as 9 June the governor-general was still attempting, unsuccessfully, to expand the visit into an all-day affair.[22]

Who set the incendiary date for the visit? It is quite true, as one recent historian has declared, that officials in the archduke's Military Chancery selected 28 June.[23] It is also true that this date was forced upon them by Potiorek. Bardolff told the governor-general that they would be in Bosnia for a few days surrounding the manoeuvres; he suggested the archduke and his wife might visit Sarajevo on 29 June. This, Potiorek insisted, was impossible. The visit must be over and Franz Ferdinand and

Sophie gone before the opening of the spa season at Ilidže on 1 July; Potiorek hinted that there would be 'much unpleasantness' if they attempted to lengthen the visit in any way. The manoeuvres would not end until the afternoon of Saturday 27 June; Potiorek's declaration that Franz Ferdinand and Sophie depart by 29 June thus set the date of the visit to Sarajevo for Sunday 28 June. Hearing this news, Potiorek thanked Bardolff profusely.[24]

Potiorek pointedly neglected to mention the significance of this particular date, though he certainly knew what it would mean to the disaffected population in Sarajevo. The 28th of June was St Vitus's Day, or *Vidovdan*, the Serb national holiday marking the 1389 battle of Kosovo, when the Turkish army had reduced Serbia to vassals of the Ottoman Empire. It was a day on which 'every Serb vowed revenge' against unwelcome foreign intruders, when every Serb nationalist would fight for a Greater Serbia.[25] There is no indication that any of the archduke's officials realized the significance of the date, but there is no such excuse for Potiorek, who was, after all, living in Sarajevo and thus must have been aware just how inflammatory an imperial visit on that particular day would be. It was, wrote one historian, tantamount to 'reaffirming the enslavement of the province' to Serb nationalists.[26] Yet Potiorek said nothing.

Was this just monumental stupidity on Potiorek's part? Bosnia, as the governor-general knew from personal experience, was such a hostile environment that he had been forced to maintain his rule through extraordinary measures. The situation was so volatile that Potiorek himself rarely appeared on the streets of Sarajevo, and then only when protected by a sizeable show of force to assure his personal safety.[27] Yet Potiorek now assured the archduke that he would be perfectly safe in the city on the Serbian national holiday.

Rumours of Serb agitation had led to heavy security when Franz Josef visited Sarajevo in May 1910. Nothing was left to chance, and no risk was taken. Before the visit, police swept through Sarajevo. Over two hundred people were arrested merely because they were deemed suspicious, and hundreds more were placed under house arrest for the duration of the visit. All strangers were exiled from the city. When the emperor appeared, an entire garrison lined the streets in a double cordon of soldiers to keep the crowds away from him. The route through the city was planned to avoid large open spots or squares where sizeable crowds could gather. There were, commented one official, 'detectives behind every tree' to protect Franz Josef; more than a thousand special police and detectives had been dispatched from Vienna and from Budapest to guard the emperor.[28] Even Sophie admitted that she had worried. 'Thank God that the Emperor has returned safely from Bosnia,' she wrote to her sister Oktavia.[29]

This established a security precedent that Potiorek promptly ignored. He later insisted that Count Leon von Bilinski, the minister of finance, who had administrative jurisdiction over Bosnia and Herzegovina, had repeatedly interfered in the arrangements.[30] This was not true. Bilinski issued no orders about the visit; he was, in fact, excluded from any involvement in the planning, in contravention to usual custom. Franz Ferdinand disliked Bilinski, but Potiorek loathed him and never briefed him on the trip. He even neglected to send Bilinski copies of the programme for the visit.[31] Bilinski later said that throughout the spring of 1914 he had known only that the archduke was attending manoeuvres outside the city; had he been apprised of the visit to Sarajevo on 28 June he would have strenuously objected.[32]

Potiorek's approach to security was astonishingly negligent. Some twenty-two thousand soldiers would be in the area for manoeuvres, encamped a few miles from the city, yet when Michael von Appel, the commanding general in Sarajevo, asked that they be deployed on the streets he was refused with the excuse that this would offend the local inhabitants. Potiorek even ordered that no soldier be allowed into the city during the visit. 'These instructions had been given by the authorities,' General von Appel wrote, 'and without even consulting us. The city was consequently as good as void of soldiers.'[33]

Security fell to the Sarajevo police. The force numbered 120 men to maintain order in a city of eighty thousand; only half would be on duty that Sunday.[34] When Edmund Gerde, chief of police, learned of the proposal, he objected that the security arrangements were insufficient. Potiorek dismissed this, saying, 'We, the military, have the responsibility for his safety. It is none of your business.'[35]

Gerde was stunned. He suggested that an imperial visit to Sarajevo on St Vitus's Day was inviting trouble. Potiorek ridiculed such concerns, telling Gerde, 'You see phantoms everywhere!'[36] Gerde opposed disclosing the planned route through the city in advance; Potiorek rebuffed him. Gerde asked that the route not be published until the day before the visit to prevent any violent demonstrations; Potiorek rejected the request. Gerde twice offered more warnings that the security arrangements were grossly insufficient only to have them dismissed.[37] The week before the visit, Gerde ordered all secondary pupils not from Sarajevo temporarily sent out of the city; the request was ignored.[38] A mere thirty-five people were arrested on suspicion of possible intrigue. No one was placed under surveillance, even those with police records or who had previously participated in anti-Austrian demonstrations.[39] In frustration, Gerde commented – and not without reason – that the archduke's security while in the city was up to God.[40]

Potiorek ignored actual warnings. Josip Sunarić, vice president of the Bosnian diet, advised that the archduke faced danger in Sarajevo, but the governor brushed him off.[41] Count Collas, head of the political section of the Bosnian provincial administration, told Potiorek that the visit would be dangerous and incite young members of Serb nationalistic societies to violent action; Potiorek dismissed his worries, saying that he was 'afraid of children'. A military intelligence report from Vienna warned of possible danger and stressed that all precautions to ensure the archduke's safety must be taken; Potiorek angrily tore up the document.[42]

The Foreign Office, the Ministry of the Interior, the Austrian Consulate in Belgrade, Austrian military intelligence, and other bodies all reported threats about the visit.[43] A 1913 article from a Serbian émigré newspaper in Chicago came to Vienna's attention.[44] 'The Heir to the Austrian Throne', it declared, 'has announced his visit to Sarajevo next spring. Every Serb should take notice! If the heir wants to go to Bosnia, we will gladly pay his way! Serbs, take up whatever you can: knives, rifles, bombs, or dynamite! Take Holy vengeance! Death to the Habsburg Dynasty!'[45] In the weeks before the visit, pamphlets were distributed in Orthodox churches throughout Serbia describing the archduke as 'the Este dog' and Sophie as 'a monstrous, filthy Bohemian whore' and advocating their murder.[46] At the end of May, Foreign Minister Berchtold sent Bilinski a note warning that Serbian agitators and Serbian propaganda meant to 'show clearly that Bosnia is Serbian land' during the archduke's appearance.[47] Bilinski contacted authorities in Sarajevo, but Potiorek said that Vienna's advice was 'neither desired nor needed'.[48] Potiorek repeatedly insisted that everything was being done to ensure a safe visit.[49]

Yet, in truth, nothing was done. Whether this was intentional or merely one of the most colossal displays of bureaucratic stupidity ever witnessed later became a matter of controversy. Conspiracy theories surrounding possible official Austrian complicity in the events at Sarajevo certainly seem on firm ground when it comes to charges of negligence. This roll call of Potiorek's excessively bad decisions, it has been suggested, stretched the definition of incompetence a bit too thin. The governor-general proved himself incapable of even common-sense measures to protect Sarajevo's illustrious visitors.

What is certain is that, as the visit approached, Franz Ferdinand became increasingly worried. It was not that he lived in fear of his life. Hated as he was, the archduke knew that he made an excellent target for would-be assassins. He often mentioned the fact, frankly and simply, accepting it as part of his life. He was quite calm, for example, when police captured two Turkish anarchists in Switzerland who were bent on killing him. Franz Ferdinand hated the detectives forever shadowing him and worried that people would think he was afraid; he put up with them solely because they were an indispensable part of imperial life and because their presence eased Sophie's worries.[50] When someone once suggested taking extra precautions, he answered, 'Precautions? Safeguards by the Director of the Police? To me, that's all rubbish! We are at all times in God's hands. Everyone is in God's hands . . . Worry and caution paralyse life. To be afraid is always a dangerous business in itself.'[51]

Nevertheless, something about the visit to Sarajevo terrified the archduke. 'The whole trip', recalled his secretary Nikitsch-Boulles, 'appalled him from the beginning.'[52] Eisenmenger, who was certainly close enough to Franz Ferdinand to represent his personal views with some authority, recalled that the archduke deemed the visit 'a rather unpleasant' occasion and confessed that he 'would have much preferred it if the Emperor had entrusted the mission to someone else'.[53]

Early in May 1914, Karl and Zita visited Franz Ferdinand and Sophie at the Belvedere. There was the usual pleasant talk over dinner, but as soon as Sophie left the room to put the children to bed, Franz Ferdinand turned to Karl. 'I don't want your aunt to hear anything of this,' he whispered. 'I know I shall soon be murdered. In this desk are papers that concern you. When that happens, take them, they are for you.'[54]

Did word of the various warnings somehow reach the archduke? That something of the sort must have happened now seems clear, for Franz Ferdinand's growing fears about this particular trip are firmly documented and in stark contrast to his usual casual attitude about possible danger. Reluctant to admit his misgivings, or perhaps even unable to give adequate expression to them, Franz Ferdinand repeatedly sought excuses to get out of the visit. At first he tried to use the emperor's health. On 20 April, the imperial court issued a bulletin alerting the public that Franz Josef was suffering from bronchitis. For several weeks he was seriously ill, and his health seemed to be in decline.[55] Within a month the danger had largely passed, as another bulletin informed the public on 23 May.[56] Yet the archduke seized on the issue, instructing Baron Rumerskirch to contact Montenuovo and seek imperial permission to cancel his attendance at the manoeuvres. He was worried, he said, over the emperor's health, and thought that the local population might be offended by an informal visit. Both were clearly excuses. Montenuovo reported back on 21 May that there was no need to cancel based on the emperor's health 'as the recuperation has progressed so far that in a few days His Majesty will be able to go out, and if everything develops normally, by the end of June will be completely recovered again.' On the other hand, Montenuovo seemed to agree with the second point, that 'with regard to these oriental peoples', it might be best if Franz Ferdinand's first visit to Bosnia were postponed until it could be carried out with the necessary 'great pomp and ceremonies'.[57]

This was Montenuovo's private opinion, but cancellation meant winning permission from the emperor. Early on the morning of 7 June, the archduke met with his uncle at Schönbrunn for forty-five minutes.[58] He asked to be relieved of the trip, saying that he would rather not go. The heat in Bosnia, he hopefully suggested, might prove injurious to his lungs.[59] The emperor refused. 'While leaving the final decision to him', Zita later said, 'the Emperor made it quite clear that he desired the Archduke to go.' This, she said, 'amounted to an order'.[60]

'Do as you wish,' the emperor told his nephew.[61] 'In plain language,' wrote one historian, 'that meant that he saw no reason to cancel a decision that had already been made. Franz Ferdinand had to go. The Emperor's answer was not a carte blanche but had been a command. With that the matter was closed.'[62] The emperor left the archduke with no choice.[63] What consequences might follow if Franz Ferdinand refused? Perhaps there would be no further invitations, no more concessions toward Sophie, perhaps even his removal as inspector general of the army, if he failed to go. Faced with these unknowns, the archduke reluctantly agreed.

Many years later, Franz Ferdinand and Sophie's son Max insisted that the emperor had attempted to talk his father out of attending the manoeuvres but that the archduke had insisted on going.[64] This, though, was clearly wrong. All evidence suggests that he actively sought to escape it. The archduke twice tried to cancel the trip; his last attempt was met with what amounted to an order from the emperor to go. As late as 12

July, Bardolff rang from the Military Chancery to pass on some news about the impending visit. Nikitsch-Boulles gave Franz Ferdinand the details, which included an hour's alteration in the train schedule. The archduke tried to use this minor change to cancel the trip. 'Tell Colonel Bardolff,' he shouted, 'if he keeps on sickening us daily with new aggravations about this Bosnian trip he can hold the manoeuvres by himself! I won't go there at all!' He was so upset that he actually ripped apart the handkerchief in his hand.[65]

Nor was Sophie assured. She was, remembered Eisenmenger, 'in great fear for his life on this trip'.[66] Her son Max recalled that she agreed to go to Bosnia only because she feared for the archduke's safety. 'If there is danger', she told a priest, 'my place is so much more by my husband's side.'[67] To Countess Larisch, she confided, 'It is a dangerous undertaking, and I will not leave the Archduke to face it alone.'[68] Whatever fate held for them, she was determined that they would face it together.

FOURTEEN

The Plot

✢

Word of the impending manoeuvres in Bosnia sent shockwaves through Serbia. Worried officials all whispered the same rumour: the manoeuvres were nothing but a pretext in advance of an Austrian invasion of Serbia. No one worried more than Colonel Dragutin Dimitrijević, chief of Serbian intelligence and head of the Black Hand. Excessively flamboyant, pleasant in demeanour but ruthlessly lethal in reality, Dimitrijević was thirty-seven, balding, and massively built. Even his nickname of 'Apis', the Egyptian word for 'bull', seemed ready-made for his imposing bulk.[1]

Friendship with Dimitrijević, said one man, 'had a dangerous quality, but this made his personality very attractive'.[2] That sense of danger was real enough: Dimitrijević had a burning hatred for Austria and a penchant for violence. In 1903 Dimitrijević had led the coup that assassinated King Alexander and Queen Draga; in 1911 he dispatched a terrorist to Vienna in an unsuccessful attempt to kill Franz Josef; and by 1914 he was plotting another assassination attempt, this one against Tsar Ferdinand of Bulgaria.[3] The intelligence reports he received allowed Dimitrijević to dismiss prevalent rumours that the Bosnian manoeuvres were a smokescreen to conceal a planned Austrian invasion of Serbia. Still, he certainly regarded the archduke as an enemy. He was a

Habsburg, representing an empire that had annexed two of the provinces Belgrade held intrinsic to their dream of a Greater Serbia.[4]

What role did Dimitrijević play in the Sarajevo assassination? He later claimed credit for the plot, insisting that he had ordered and helped facilitate the assassination, though only as chief of Serbian intelligence, not as head of the Black Hand. 'Feeling that Austria was planning a war with us,' Dimitrijević explained, 'I thought that the disappearance of the Austrian Heir Apparent would weaken the power of the military clique he headed, and thus the danger of war would be removed or postponed for a while.' According to his later confession, he 'engaged' Rade Malobabić, the chief Serbian military intelligence operative against Austria-Hungary, 'to organize the assassination on the occasion of the announced arrival of Franz Ferdinand to Sarajevo'.[5]

In January 1914, Dimitrijević almost certainly sent his chief aide, Major Vojislav Tankosić, to a meeting of Bosnian revolutionaries at Toulouse. A veteran of Black Hand operations and participant in the 1903 royal massacre at Belgrade, Tankosić trained *Komitádjis*, would-be terrorists, at the organization's secret academy for violent action. He listened as Muhamed Mehmedbašić, a twenty-eight-year-old Muslim cabinetmaker from Herzegovina, suggested killing Bosnian governor-general Oskar Potiorek. When Mehmedbašić returned to Sarajevo, he recruited Danilo Ilić, a young newspaper editor and, like himself, a member of the Black Hand, into the plot. Ilić played with terrorist ideas, reading the works of Russian anarchist Mikhail Bakunin and wearing a black tie as 'a constant reminder of death'. At some point in the spring of 1914, Ilić seems to have gone to Belgrade and met Dimitrijević, who now suggested Franz Ferdinand as the intended victim. In March, Ilić conveyed this news to Mehmedbašić.[6]

Unknown to Dimitrijević, a second plot against the archduke had arisen that spring of 1914 when a perfect storm of paranoia, ambition and chance collided in Belgrade's coffee shops. Day and night, young, disillusioned students exchanged stories of the recent Balkan Wars, talked of anti-Austrian conspiracies, and boasted of their eagerness to strike a

Archduchess Maria Theresa,
Franz Ferdinand's stepmother.
(Courtesy of Christophe Vachaudez)

Erzherzogin Maria Theresia.

Emperor Franz Josef.
(Courtesy of Christophe Vachaudez)

Franz Josef
Kaiser von Österreich.

Left: Franz Ferdinand in the uniform of a captain in the No. 4 Dragoon Regiment, about 1888. *(Courtesy of Sue Woolmans)*

Above: Countess Sophie Chotek, 1880. *(Courtesy of the Collection of State Castle Velke Brezno, part of the Czech National Heritage Institute, NPU)*

Left: Countess Sophie Chotek and her sisters in 1885, *(left to right)* Zdenka, Sophie, Henriette, Oktavia, Antonie, Marie and Karoline. *(Courtesy of the Collection of State Castle Velke Brezno, part of the Czech National Heritage Institute, NPU)*

The Wedding Day, 1 July 1900.
(Courtesy of Artstetten Castle, Austria)

Prince Alfred de Montenuovo.
(Courtesy of Sue Woolmans)

Above: Franz Ferdinand and Sophie, midsummer 1904, with a hunting companion. *(Courtesy of a Private Collection)*

Left: Franz Ferdinand with his daughter Sophie, about 1906. *(Courtesy of Sue Woolmans)*

A family group, 1906. *(Left to right)*
Max, Franz Ferdinand, Ernst,
Sophie and Little Sophie.
(Courtesy of Sue Woolmans)

Sophie with Little Sophie
and Max, about 1903.
(Courtesy of Sue Woolmans)

Franz Ferdinand and Sophie, with
Sophie's sister Henriette, 1910.
(Courtesy of a Private Collection)

Franz Ferdinand with his
two sons, about 1910.
(Courtesy of Sue Woolmans)

Above: Sophie with her children, about 1910. *(Courtesy of Sue Woolmans)*

Below: The visit of Franz Ferdinand and Sophie to the King and Queen of Rumania, July 1909. *(At the front, left to right)* Crown Prince Ferdinand of Rumania, Sophie, Princesss Marie (daughter of the Crown Prince Ferdinand and Princess), Franz Ferdinand, King Carol of Rumania and Queen Elisabeth of Rumania holding Prince Nicholas. *(Courtesy of Diana Mandache)*

Franz Ferdinand in his study in the Belvedere, 1910, with a painting of Little Sophie displayed behind his desk. *(Courtesy of Sue Woolmans)*

Archduke Karl and his wife Zita.
(Courtesy of Mark Andersen)

Above: Konopiste in 1914 with the Rose Garden in the foreground.
(Courtesy of Sue Woolmans)

Below: Artstetten with the new onion domes added by Franz Ferdinand.
(Courtesy of Sue Woolmans)

Left: Franz Ferdinand and Sophie with their children, about 1912. *(Courtesy of Sue Woolmans)*

Facing page above: Franz Ferdinand and Sophie with Sophie's niece, Countess Elisabeth de Baillet-Latour, aboard *Le Nord* on their way to England, November 1913. *(Courtesy of Sue Woolmans)*

Facing page below: Visit of Kaiser Wilhelm II to Miramare; Franz Ferdinand to his right, Sophie and the children to his left, March 1914. *(Courtesy of a Private Collection)*

Left: Archduke Friedrich, Supreme Commander of the Austrian Army, with General Conrad von Hötzendorf, Chief of the General Staff. *(Courtesy of Sue Woolmans)*

Above: Sophie with her children, 1914. *(Courtesy of a Private Collection)*

Below: Franz Ferdinand and Sophie riding with their daughter in June 1914 at a Flower Festival in Vienna's Prater. *(Courtesy of Sue Woolmans)*

Above: An early twentieth-century view of Sarajevo, showing the Appel Quay and Miljacka River. The Town Hall is the large building on the far right. *(Courtesy of Sue Woolmans)*

Below: Sophie speaking to Governor-General Oskar Potiorek on the steps of the Hotel Bosna at Ilidže, June 25, 1914. *(Courtesy of Sue Woolmans)*

Above: Franz Ferdinand, Sophie, Count Harrach, and General Potiorek in Sarajevo on 28 June 1914. *(Courtesy of a Private Collection)*

Below: The Konak in Sarajevo. *(Courtesy of Sue Woolmans)*

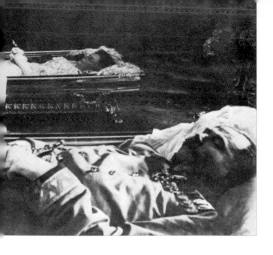

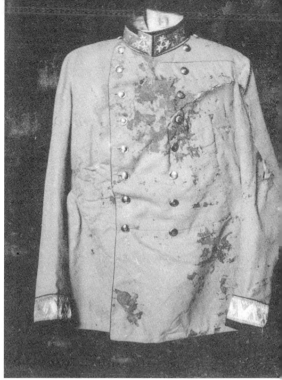

Above: Franz Ferdinand and Sophie lying in state at the Konak, 29 June 1914. *(Courtesy of Greg King)*

Right: Franz Ferdinand's bloodstained uniform. *(Courtesy of Sue Woolmans)*

Below: The tombs of Franz Ferdinand and Sophie at Artstetten Castle. *(Courtesy of Sue Woolmans)*

Above: Duke Maximilian, Princess Sophie, Prince Ernst and his wife Princess Marie-Therese on 28 June 1952. *(Courtesy of Artstetten Castle, Austria)*

Below: Princess Sophie Hohenberg with her husband, Baron Jean-Louis de Potesta. *(Courtesy of Princess Sophie Hohenberg)*

blow against the Habsburgs.[7] Among them were Gavrilo Princip, Nedeljko Čabrinović, and Trifko Grabež.

Princip was the acknowledged leader. Born in July 1894 into an impoverished family of nine children, he grew to hate a system of Austrian rule he deemed oppressive. Princip had attended school in Sarajevo but left for Belgrade after being expelled for participating in violent anti-Austrian demonstrations. During the Balkan Wars he tried to enlist with Serbia's army but was rejected as 'too weak'. Inferiority and desire to prove his worth undoubtedly propelled him toward disaster. Pale, thin and suffering from tuberculosis, Princip idolized Nietzsche and clung to a black view of humanity. In Belgrade, he became an ardent propagandist for the Greater Serbian cause, undergoing training at the Black Hand's secret terrorist academy.[8]

Like Princip, Trifko Grabež was a native of Sarajevo. The son of an Orthodox priest, he left the city after being expelled from school for attacking a teacher. In Belgrade, he shared a dingy room with his friend Princip. Though less of an ideologue than his friend, the consumptive Grabež listened and absorbed his talk of Serb freedom and Austrian repression, drawn to the plot by its mysterious intrigue. Nedeljko Čabrinović was the most carefree member of the group, with an air of nonchalance and an unfortunate habit of speaking too freely. His father owned a cafe on Franz Josef Strasse in Sarajevo; the elder Čabrinović also occasionally worked as an Austrian spy against his fellow citizens, something his son openly resented. Čabrinović was a poor student, 'a very problematic boy', declared one Sarajevo newspaper, who left school at age fourteen. After embarking on a series of unsuccessful careers, he, too, moved to Belgrade. There, he found employment at the Serbian Government Printing Office, publishing anti-Austrian propaganda.[9]

For a century history has often described the Sarajevo assassins in doe-eyed terms: dreamy, naive 'schoolboys', sacrificing themselves for the Serb and South Slav cause, well intentioned if bungling young men playing in a world of Machiavellian politics. 'One can deplore and disagree with the methods of political struggle,' wrote Sarajevo historian

Vladimir Dedijer, who praised them for their 'patriotism, courage, and selflessness', insisting that they belonged in a 'lofty' pantheon of 'primitive rebels'.[10] In truth, Princip and his fellow conspirators were not mere assassins or naive patriots but terrorists, as historian David Fromkin correctly points out.[11] Princip even proudly declared that they hoped to achieve their goals 'by means of terror'.[12] They were willing to kill the archduke, his wife, and any other innocent victims because they believed that the deaths would serve the larger goal of undermining Austria-Hungary as a force in the Balkans.[13]

The trio shared remarkably similar backgrounds and ideas. Born Bosnian Serbs, they had all unwillingly become Austrian citizens after the 1908 annexation. All were nineteen; though born Orthodox, none practised their faith – indeed, Princip was an avowed atheist. They were not members of Dimitrijević's organization but rather identified themselves as part of Mlada Bosna, the Young Bosnia Movement, an offshoot of the Black Hand loosely composed of Serb nationalists and would-be revolutionaries. Burning with a hatred of Austria and its annexation of Bosnia, the young men agreed that they would sacrifice their lives for the cause of unifying southern Slavs.[14]

At some point in the spring of 1914, Princip later insisted, he received several anonymous newspaper clippings detailing Franz Ferdinand's planned visit to Bosnia. Learning of this, he talked to his comrades, and together they decided to kill the archduke in Sarajevo. 'I believe in the unification of all South Slavs,' Princip later said, 'in whatever form of state, and that it be free of Austria.'[15] The idea, the three said, had been theirs alone, and they had acted without assistance from any organization.[16]

This insistence was a lie, designed to conceal the involvement of certain high-ranking officials in Belgrade as the two separate plots fused into a single conspiracy. Dimitrijević brought them together, albeit in an almost accidental way. The three members of Young Bosnia in Belgrade made nuisances of themselves, continually pestering Tankosić, explaining their plan and asking for the Black Hand's assistance. Tankosić, in turn, told Dimitrijević of their plot; it seemed unlikely to succeed, but Dimitrijević casually agreed that the Black Hand could assist the trio. Tankosić handed the young men off to fellow Black Hand member Milan Ciganović for training. Throughout May they practised shooting; Princip proved to have the best aim. On the night of 27 May, the three went through a bizarre, theatrical charade in a darkened basement as hooded members of the Black Hand swore them to secrecy and informed them that they would be working with Mehmedbašić and Ilić in Sarajevo; Princip actually knew Ilić and agreed to cooperate. Ciganović finally handed over the weapons. There were four Belgian automatic revolvers purchased by Dimitrijević, along with six bombs manufactured at the Serbian State Arsenal, small black objects filled with nails and pieces of lead, that could easily be carried in a pocket. There were also vials of cyanide to use if the men were caught.[17]

Historians have needlessly argued about the Black Hand's role in the conspiracy. Dimitrijević's group joined the two separate conspiracies together; trained the assassins; armed them with guns and bombs; and arranged for Princip, Grabež and Čabrinović to be smuggled across the Serbian border into Bosnia by Black Hand agents. With these moves, the Black Hand effectively took control of the operation. Whether Dimitrijević did so as chief of Serbian intelligence or in his position as head of the Black Hand becomes irrelevant. To question the Black Hand's role in the assassination is to play a futile game of semantics.

Princip, Grabež and Čabrinović left Belgrade for Sarajevo the following day. It was, Princip insisted, 'a mystical journey', though many of their hardships were likely exaggerated to paint the assassination as a heroic act by selfless patriots.[18] Black Hand officials planned their route by boat to Šabac, a small Serbian border post facing Austria. There they gave Captain Rada Popović, a frontier official tied to the organization, a note from Ciganović asking that he help them secretly cross into Bosnia. Popović filled out false documents asserting that the three were customs officials entitled to free passage on all Serbian railway lines. By the time they reached the frontier at Loznica, Princip was fed up with Čabrinović. Loquacious and always indiscreet, he wrote letters and postcards to friends heavily hinting that he was involved in some impending major event and that 'something will happen' to the archduke when he visited Sarajevo. As soon as the trio crossed the border into Serbia, Princip cut Čabrinović loose, telling him he could get across the border on his own.[19]

Not until 3 June did the trio reunite in Tuzla, having crossed mountains, rivers and forests by train and on foot. Feeling more assured now, they even bragged about their plan, showing off their revolvers and bombs to the peasants who gave them refuge. Detectives in Tuzla had recognized Čabrinović, and the three left their weapons with Black Hand agent Misko Jovanović, director of the local bank and a member of the Orthodox Episcopal Council, who agreed to temporarily hide them. A confederate would return for them later, bearing a pack of Stephanie brand cigarettes as a sign. A final train journey that night took the young men to Sarajevo.[20]

After being recognized, Čabrinović was sure that the detective in Tuzla would report him to authorities. Having been expelled from Sarajevo for five years, he risked instant arrest by again setting foot in the city. Yet no one reported him, and he boldly returned to his family; Grabež went to his home, and Princip took a room with Ilić's mother. Princip even registered with the Sarajevo police using his real name and address. He had a record for subversive activities, yet Chief of Police Edmund Gerde's orders that all new arrivals be investigated were ignored, and no one was placed under surveillance.[21]

Ilić organized the plot in Sarajevo. Mehmedbašić was already committed; as a member of the Black Hand, he had expressed his willingness to kill the archduke. More cynically, he seems to have been included in the larger conspiracy because he was a Muslim, and his participation would counter the appearance that only Orthodox Serbs had planned the assassination. Ilić brought in two further conspirators. The first was seventeen-year-old Sarajevo high school student Vaso Čubrilović, whose brother Cvjetko was a Black Hand agent who had aided Princip and Grabež across the Bosnian border. Vaso Čubrilović recommended a third man, eighteen-year-old student Cvjetko Popović, who readily joined the plot. Ilić collected the abandoned weapons in Tuzla and brought them to Sarajevo for later distribution.[22]

In Belgrade, Dimitrijević worried that Austria might use an assassination attempt to launch a war against Serbia. What happened next has been the source of endless controversy, for by his own admission he turned to Serbia's traditional protector, imperial Russia, for assurances. There have always been whispers about possible Russian involvement in, or foreknowledge of, the assassinations in Sarajevo.[23] The difficulty is sorting fact from rumour.

By 1914, Russia no longer made a pretence of its aims in the Balkans. Nicholas de Hartwig, the Russian minister in Belgrade, cultivated an atmosphere of intrigue and anti-Austrian sentiment within his embassy. Tsarist agents regularly channelled funds through the ministry to prop up Serb nationalist societies and pay for their propaganda calling for unification of southern Slavs through violence.[24] Hartwig was something less than discreet about his own sympathies. After the Balkan Wars, he insisted, 'Now it is the turn of Austria. Serbia will be our best instrument. The day draws near when . . . Serbia will take back *her* Bosnia and *her* Herzegovina.'[25]

This suggested a Russian willingness to provoke Serbian agitation against Austria, perhaps with the hope that Habsburg influence could be lessened while Romanov influence was strengthened. Given such sentiments, it would have been surprising had Dimitrijević not sought some kind of Russian assurance of support if things went badly. He apparently never told Hartwig of his plans, but admitted that he *had* asked Russian military attaché Colonel Viktor Artamanov how his country would respond if Austria attacked Serbia. Artamanov was actively aiding Black Hand propaganda and could be counted on to maintain his silence and lend support. What precisely was said, though, remains contentious. Did

Dimitrijević merely speak in generalities, as he insisted? Or did he actually confide details of the impending assassination to the attaché? Artamanov later claimed ignorance of the plot, though after interviewing him Luigi Albertini, the foremost scholar on the subject, believed that he was lying. Eventually others contradicted Artamanov, including Captain Alexander Vechkovsky, his own assistant. According to Vechkovsky, Dimitrijević *had* told Artamanov of the planned assassination, and Artamanov *had* consulted with unnamed Russian officials in St Petersburg about the potential consequences.[26]

If Austria attacked Serbia, Artamanov assured Dimitrijević, 'you are not going to be alone'.[27] This is what Dimitrijević said he was told. Was this Russian sanction for the assassination? Or was it merely some vague diplomatic assurance that the Tsarist empire would stand by its Balkan ally? The answer depends on what Artamanov told St Petersburg. A veil of plausible deniability cloaked everyone involved. Official Russian documents concerning the build-up to the First World War were later falsified before publication or disappeared altogether.[28] On balance, it is not unlikely that Dimitrijević told Artamanov of the plot. Nor is it unlikely that Artamanov shared this information with others. However, the murky connections and destruction of official papers makes it impossible to offer any definitive evidence on this critical question.

Perhaps certain Russian circles did indeed know of the planned assassination in advance; there can be no such doubts when it comes to numerous officials in the Serbian government. As with claims that the Black Hand was not the moving force behind the assassination, it is no longer possible to insist on Serbian innocence in the plot. Although the Serbian government did not instigate the conspiracy, it was certainly, as historian Fromkin wrote, 'in large part culpable' for its success.[29]

By his own admission, Dimitrijević – as chief of Serbian intelligence – instituted and promoted the assassination; although this confession came at a time when Dimitrijević was attempting to save his own life, no evidence has emerged to suggest that it was coerced or fabricated. High-ranking Serbian military officials aided the plot, training the assassins and arming them with bombs and revolvers from Serbian arsenals; Serbian state employees falsified papers and smuggled the young terrorists into Bosnia. Colonel Ljubomir Vulović, head of the Serbian Frontiers Service, knew of the plot, having learned of it from Military Chief of Staff Marshal Putnik.[30] Ljuba Jovanović, Serbian minister of education, later said that Prime Minister Nikola Pašić had even discussed the plan during a meeting with several cabinet members. 'Pašić said to us that certain persons were preparing to go to Sarajevo and murder Franz Ferdinand.'[31]

Pašić did indeed know of the plot. A report on the conspirators' progress into Bosnia reached his desk the first week of June. The prime minister knew the names of the three conspirators who had travelled from Belgrade; he knew that they carried bombs and revolvers, that Serbian frontier officials and members of military intelligence had helped them, and that they were on their way to Sarajevo to kill Franz Ferdinand. Pašić even annotated the report in his own hand.[32] This involvement, training, and knowledge left the Serbian government complicit in events in Sarajevo.

Knowledge of the plot presented a problem, however. Pašić was politically weak. Dimitrijević had actually arranged for his dismissal in May of 1914; he was saved only through Russian intervention. Pašić would remain interim prime minister until new elections could be held in August. Dimitrijević and most of the military hated him, and the feeling was mutual. If Pašić exposed the plot, he could eliminate his enemy and deal the Black Hand a fatal blow. Doing so, though, would jeopardize his political career, brand him a traitor to Serbia, and possibly place his life in danger. Yet if he said nothing and Belgrade's foreknowledge was later revealed, Austria would have ample justification to launch a war against Serbia. Either choice seemed personally disastrous.[33]

In the end, Pašić settled on a third option: Vienna would receive a vague warning about possible danger to the archduke in Bosnia. This protected both the conspiracy and the prime minister's political aspirations. If pushed, he could claim he had done his best to avert disaster by warning Austrian authorities. This, at least, was the plan, though apparently Pašić didn't consider the ramifications. Advance warning also meant advance knowledge among the highest circles in Belgrade. When this later became clear, Pašić denied that any warning had been given, but too many Serbian officials confirmed the facts.[34]

Jovan Jovanović, the Serbian minister in Vienna, was charged with the unenviable and delicate task of conveying the most ambiguous warning possible to the Austrian government. On 5 June, he met Finance Minister Count Leon von Bilinski, who had administrative charge of Bosnia and Herzegovina. The archduke's visit, Jovanović warned, 'will cause much discontent among the Serbs, who will consider it a provocative gesture. Manoeuvres held in such circumstances can be dangerous. Some young Serb might slip a live cartridge into his rifle instead of a blank and fire it. That bullet might hit the man who provoked him. Therefore it would be good and reasonable if Archduke Franz Ferdinand were not to go to Sarajevo and if the manoeuvres were not to take place either on St Vitus's Day or in Bosnia.' According to Jovanović, Bilinski seemed unconcerned, shrugging his shoulders and saying, 'Well, let us hope that nothing happens!'[35]

Bilinski did nothing. He did not even report this warning to the Austrian government. How to explain this seemingly incomprehensible decision? For the last three months, Bilinski had waged a futile battle with Governor-General Oskar Potiorek over the visit to Sarajevo. Protests that he was excluded from any decisions and was deliberately kept uninformed of the plans, and his worries about possible danger, had been dismissed. Perhaps it was this sense of frustration that caused Bilinski's inaction.

However, too many people in Belgrade knew of the plot for it to remain a secret. On 14 June, Dimitrijević faced the inevitable and, at a meeting of the Black Hand's Central Executive Committee, finally confirmed the gossip to his comrades. Although no one in the room had any love for the archduke, most of the men were supposedly horrified. The assassination, or even a bungled plot, they insisted, would inevitably give

Austria justification to invade Serbia. Their country was too weak, they said, to fight their Habsburg neighbour. Heated arguments flew back and forth, but it soon became clear that only Dimitrijević and Tankosić fully supported the plot. Faced with almost universal opposition, Dimitrijević allegedly relented and reluctantly said he would call off the assassination.[36]

Whether Dimitrijević actually meant to follow through on this promise remains a mystery. He insisted that he had tried to interrupt the plot but that the would-be assassins had gone ahead anyway. Sometime between 16 June and 18 June, Ilić met with one of Dimitrijević's representatives at Brod. He later said that he had been warned to call off the assassination; when he returned to Sarajevo and informed his fellow conspirators of this, however, they refused. Other evidence suggests that Ilić met with Black Hand operative Rade Malobabić and received final instructions for the assassination in Brod.[37] No matter the arguments, the result was the same: Franz Ferdinand would die.

FIFTEEN

'I'm Beginning to Fall in Love With Bosnia'

✦

For Franz Ferdinand and Sophie, the trip to Bosnia edged ever closer. Two days after Kaiser Wilhelm II's visit, the archduke for the first time opened the park at Konopischt to the public. Thousands of curious visitors poured into the fabled garden, strolling among the roses and inspecting the elegant parterres. In the afternoon, Franz Ferdinand even came out to meet them, asking if the visitors enjoyed the park and seemingly eager for their approval. It was a side of the usually reticent archduke that few ever saw.[1]

With this success behind him, the archduke took his wife to shoot at a nearby aristocratic estate. He seemed depressed when the trip to Bosnia was mentioned, his hostess remembered, and spoke as if disaster were imminent.[2] Then it was off to Chlumetz to spend a few days with their children before leaving for Bosnia; Little Sophie, Max and Ernst would reunite here with their parents when Franz Ferdinand and Sophie returned from Bosnia before continuing on to Blühnbach for the summer. During a drive through the park, Franz Ferdinand pointed out the surrounding forest, oddly commenting that these lands would be Ernst's inheritance.[3]

On Tuesday 23 June, Franz Ferdinand and Sophie left for Bosnia.

They would travel first to Vienna, where they would part ways. The archduke would journey by train to Trieste, board the dreadnought *Viribus Unitis* for the cruise to Metković, and then continue by rail into Bosnia, while Sophie would go directly to Ilidže. Before departing, the archduke pulled the faithful Janaczek aside. He gave him a gold watch, as if thanking him in advance for his service, and handed him keys to his desk at the Belvedere with the request that if anything happened he should pass them on to his nephew Karl. There was a final, odd request: if he didn't return from Bosnia, the archduke said, he expected Janaczek to look after his family. Another peculiar scene took place at the train station. An axle on the couple's private railway carriage burned out, and they had to change into an ordinary first-class compartment.[4] 'That's the way it starts!' Franz Ferdinand spat out as if foretelling the future. 'At first the carriage is running hot, then a murder attempt in Sarajevo and finally, if all that doesn't get anywhere, an explosion aboard the *Viribus*!'[5]

Franz Ferdinand and Sophie arrived in Vienna at seven that night and dined at the Belvedere before the archduke boarded his train to Trieste; Sophie would leave the next day. A worried stationmaster ushered the archduke to his private carriage with apologies, explaining that the electricity was not working. When Nikitsch-Boulles entered a few minutes later, he found Franz Ferdinand glumly seated amid a sea of flickering candles. 'It's like a tomb, isn't it?' the archduke said.[6]

All of this talk, this apparent presentiment about Sarajevo, cannot be put down to later exaggeration. Too many heard the archduke express similar worries over his safety and fears that he would not return from the trip alive. He had tried without success to cancel the journey. Father Edmund Fischer, the archduke's former personal confessor, had once warned, 'Before every journey, on every evening, do accustom yourself to profoundly repent all the miseries of the day and of your whole life, so that you will be prepared to step before God at any moment, even if there isn't a priest at your side. That is a great comfort and gives courage.'[7] Now, facing the prospect of this unwelcome and uncertain trip, it seemed as if Franz Ferdinand were slowly bidding farewell to life.

Sophie arrived in Bosnia first, 'safe and sound', as she cabled her son Max, after a journey that 'went very well'. It was a rainy morning when her train pulled into the station at Ilidže on Thursday 25 June. Motor cars took her and Baron Morsey, Rumerskirch, and her lady-in-waiting Countess Vilma Lanjus von Wallenburg through the little resort town to the Hotel Bosna, where she and Franz Ferdinand would stay. Although she noted the 'very nice reception' at the hotel, there was also a bit of unpleasantness that she let pass without remark.[8] An honour guard stood arrayed along the hotel steps as Sophie's motor car came to a stop. The soldiers remained immobile as she walked past them. Orders had come from Vienna that they were not to acknowledge her or present arms.[9]

Franz Ferdinand arrived later that same afternoon. He found the voyage down the Dalmatian coast aboard the *Viribus Unitis* 'delightful'; the country was 'very interesting', he cabled his daughter, though 'it is very hot'.[10] A small yacht, the *Dalmat*, carried him up the Narenta River to the town of Metković, where a train waited for the journey to Bosnia. There were greetings along the way; at Mostar, the mayor welcomed the archduke to 'our rocky Herzegovina', and the archduke even offered a few words of Croatian in reply.[11]

A fanfare of trumpets greeted the archduke's train as it pulled into Ilidže at three that Thursday afternoon. There were 'deafening cheers' as Franz Ferdinand motored through the town; he was, said a reporter, 'deeply moved with emotion, and saluted the gathered people, smiling and thanking them' as he drove past.[12] Sophie anxiously awaited him; like her husband, she, too, worried about this visit to potentially dangerous Bosnia but was relieved to have 'very good news from him, thank God' as he neared the town.[13] She stood on the hotel steps as his motor car pulled up, embracing Franz Ferdinand as he rushed toward her.[14]

Sprawled on the River Bosna, the fashionable resort of Ilidže centered around a thermal hot springs; acacia trees shaded lush squares where bands entertained elegantly dressed ladies and smartly clad officers enjoying the cafes, tennis courts, flower gardens and mineral baths.[15] At the edge of the park rose the Hotel Bosna, its towering facade adorned with a ponderous arched colonnade along the ground floor. Sarajevo merchant Elias Kabiljo had redecorated the visiting couple's second-floor suite with oriental carpets, inlaid furniture, and old Turkish armour and even fitted out a private chapel for their use; just before they arrived, a local florist had filled the rooms with fragrant roses.[16] 'We have delightful quarters,' the archduke cabled to his daughter. 'The weather is delightful. Good night. I hug you and your siblings very warmly.'[17]

Eight miles away, Sarajevo anxiously awaited the visit coming on Sunday. From its rocky crag, an old Turkish fortress surveyed the city as it nestled along a small valley lush with fruit trees and tall poplars. The slow, shallow waters of the Miljacka River cleaved the city in half, separating the ancient, more exotic quarters from the modern avenues lined with impressive buildings. Even before the annexation the Austrians had not neglected the city, building factories, woollen mills, breweries, a school for Islamic studies, and a power station to provide electricity. The Sarajevo of 1914 was a curious mixture of East and West: streets crowded with officers in uniform, Turks in fezzes, Muslims in turbans, and mysteriously veiled women. All moved at a frenetic pace between narrow alleys lined by red-roofed shops and beneath a forest of church spires and the thin minarets of mosques.[18]

Preparations for Sunday were already under way. Ladders were up nearly everywhere, as men strung floral garlands across streets, bedecked buildings with the Austrian flag, and tacked up innumerable proclamations outlining the route that Franz Ferdinand and Sophie would take through the city. Posters suggested that the people demonstrate their 'great joy' over the couple's appearance 'by decorating our houses, businesses, and shops with flags, flowers, and rugs, particularly along the streets through which His Imperial and Royal Highness will pass'.[19] Sarajevo's newspapers offered their own welcomes. 'Be greeted, our hope!' read the headline on 25 June's Croatian-language paper; 'Hail to you!' announced another above a portrait of the archduke, while the Muslim daily cheered the impending visit of the 'illustrious Prince'. Only Sarajevo's Serbian-language newspaper seemed lukewarm, suggesting that Franz Ferdinand pay heed to 'the justified wishes and needs of the Serb People in our Fatherland'.[20]

Early that Thursday evening the archduke decided to pay an impromptu visit to Sarajevo. With Sophie, he motored into the city to visit the famous bazaar, with its crowded stores featuring furniture, antique weaponry, coins, gold- and silverwork, linens, silks, and carpets.[21] A crowd quickly gathered, watching as they moved through the stalls and shouting the Croatian welcome of 'Zivio!' They sought out the shop run by Elias Kabiljo, which had provided the furnishings and fittings for their suite at the Hotel Bosna, and thanked him for the care he had shown in his decoration. Franz Ferdinand purchased a number of carpets and pieces of porcelain, while Sophie was drawn to some exquisite needlework and jewellery, along with gifts for their children.[22] The 'frenetically cheering' crowd worried Nikitsch-Boulles, who saw no security officers on duty; still, looking around, he noticed 'nothing but gay, cheerful faces'.[23] Among those faces, unknown to Franz Ferdinand and Sophie or any authorities, was a young student, clutching a pistol in his coat pocket. He was close to the couple as they exited the bazaar and nodded to the crowd for a few moments; his fingers instinctively curled around the gun, but a nearby policeman and Sophie's presence apparently convinced him that this was not the moment to assassinate the hated archduke.[24] Seventy-two hours later, Gavrilo Princip would not be so reluctant to open fire on the couple.

A second would-be assassin lurked among the crowds at Ilidže. Word that the archduke and his wife were walking in the hotel park drew another crowd. Franz Ferdinand and Sophie went off to find the young bear cubs that roamed the park as tourist attractions; when he cornered one, the archduke reached out to pet it, thinking they were tame, only to have his finger bitten. The wound was superficial, but he hurried back to the hotel, past the ranks of curious onlookers.[25] There were too many detectives present for Nedeljko Čabrinović to approach Franz Ferdinand

and Sophie. One constable, in fact, saw the young man doing his best to hide behind a tree and gave chase over his suspicious behaviour, but Čabrinović fled into the night. He was well known in Sarajevo, though, and the constable telephoned Sarajevo Chief of Police Gerde with the news that Čabrinović had been shadowing the archduke. Gerde then made a fatal mistake. Thinking that the constable meant Čabrinović's father, who had acted as an Austrian spy, he said, 'Leave him alone.'[26] Like his comrade Princip, three days later Nedeljko Čabrinović would not hesitate to act.

The manoeuvres began on Friday 26 June, and ended the next day. Both mornings, shortly before six, Franz Ferdinand left Ilidže aboard a special train that carried him a short distance to the rocky hillsides where the 15th Army Corps engaged in mock battle with their comrades in the 16th Army Corps under Potiorek's command.[27] In all, some twenty-two thousand soldiers raced up and down the mountains in heavy rain, fog, sleet, and even intermittent snow as the archduke followed their movements through a pair of field glasses. Late Saturday, just before the manoeuvres ended, there was a rustle of bushes and a man suddenly stepped in front of Franz Ferdinand holding a black object in his hands. Detectives pounced, thinking they had cornered an anarchist, but the archduke collapsed in laughter. 'That's the court photographer!' he shouted. 'Let go of him! It's his business! People have to earn a living, you know!'[28]

Sophie visited Sarajevo while her husband was occupied with the manoeuvres. She telephoned her son Max, who had gone to Vienna to take his school examinations, offering some last-minute encouragement, and then set off for the city in an open car. Here, she inspected the Catholic and Orthodox cathedrals, orphanages, convent schools, and a weaving mill, where she purchased a number of carpets. Charity institutions were high on the list: the Great Mosque, the Sarajevo Centre for Youth, the Franciscan Monastery, the Muslim School for Girls, and the Turkish Orphanage, all offered fascinating glimpses of the cosmopolitan city. Throughout, she distributed financial gifts from her private funds and 'took the keenest interest in everything'. Jesuit Father Anton Puntigam, who had once briefly served as Franz Ferdinand's personal confessor, warmly welcomed her to the Augustinian Convent School as students showered Sophie with bouquets of roses and serenaded her with patriotic songs. She moved through their ranks, handing out photographs of her family to the older students and boxes of candy to the younger children.[29] 'Everywhere she went', declared the *Sarajevski List* newspaper, 'people gathered in great numbers, cheering her all the time.'[30] Baron Morsey saw few policemen, however, and those he did spot seemed 'extremely incompetent' and unable to control the eager crowds.[31]

Saturday 27 June, came to a close over Sarajevo and Ilidže. As the last rays of the early summer sun glinted across flags and banners bedecking buildings along the Appel Quay, the conspirators all met one last time to whisper over the planned assassination. To bolster their courage, they gathered at Semiž's Inn, gulping down wine. True to form, Čabrinović had been annoyingly loquacious in the last few days, mingling with friends, drinking, and insisting that 'something will happen' to the archduke during his visit.[32] Princip, by contrast, seemed quiet and preoccupied; he soon slipped away from his friends and up to the city cemetery, where he laid a wreath on the grave of Bogdan Žerajić, the student who in 1910 had tried unsuccessfully to kill the governor-general of Bosnia and Herzegovina. *His* chance would come the following day.[33]

Eight miles away, at Ilidže, Franz Ferdinand and Sophie seemed relaxed, anticipating a celebratory dinner that night at the Hotel Bosna. The archduke had prepared a speech to mark the event, which included the line 'The loyal sentiments which you have expressed on behalf of the provincial government have given my wife and myself much pleasure.' Such a small thing, yet even these two words, 'my wife', Baron Rumerskirch warned, would be bound to cause problems as soon as they were reported back to Vienna. Reluctantly, Franz Ferdinand cut the reference to Sophie from his remarks.[34]

Forty-one guests sat down to the banquet that night in the hotel's dining room, including Bosnia's top military, religious and civil officials.

Franz Ferdinand sat on one side of the long table, between Potiorek and the president of the Bosnian diet, with Sophie opposite him, between the Roman Catholic archbishop of Sarajevo and the Orthodox archbishop of Sarajevo. The French doors had been thrown open, and the flowered gardens perfumed the warm night air as a band from the Sarajevo military garrison entertained with a selection of music by Schumann and Strauss.[35] The menu was lavish: *potage régence* (cream soup with rice and fish), *soufflés délicieux*, and *blaquette de truite en geleé* (local trout), followed by chicken, lamb and beef, asparagus, salad, and ices, and ending with *crème d'ananas en surprise* (pineapple cream with flamed brandy), all washed down with a selection of Madeira, claret, champagne, Hungarian Tokay, and the local wine, Zilavka.[36] The atmosphere was jovial. The guests spoke about the manoeuvres, about Bosnia, and about the recent visit to Konopischt of the kaiser, and news that Max had passed his examinations in Vienna brought a round of toasts from the guests. 'I'm beginning to fall in love with Bosnia,' Franz Ferdinand commented. 'If I still had prejudices, they're gone now.'[37]

When the meal had finished, Dr Josip Sunarić, vice president of the Bosnian diet, chatted with the duchess over coffee. He had repeatedly warned against the visit, suggesting that some rabid pro-Serb nationalist or disgruntled Bosnian might try to assassinate the couple in Sarajevo, but Potiorek had dismissed his concerns. Sophie had heard them, and she now asked Sunarić if he had not exaggerated the danger. 'You were wrong, after all,' she said with a smile. 'Things don't always turn out the way you say they will. Everywhere we have gone here we have been greeted with so much friendliness, and by every last Serb, too, with so much cordiality and spontaneous warmth. We're happy about that.' Sunarić, though, still worried. The visit to Sarajevo the following day, he believed, was fraught with peril. Rather undiplomatically, he looked at Sophie and said ominously, 'I pray to God that when I have the honour tomorrow night of seeing you again, you can repeat those words to me. Then I shall breathe easier, a great deal easier.'[38]

Sunarić was not the only one who was worried. 'Thank God this

Bosnian trip is over!' Franz Ferdinand commented as the night drew toward a close. Attending the manoeuvres had never really been the problem; it was the visit to Sarajevo that had terrified the archduke. It was Rumerskirch who first raised the idea: the archduke had done his duty and fulfilled the emperor's command in attending the manoeuvres; the couple had visited Sarajevo Thursday evening, and Sophie had spent two days touring the city. Everything had been accomplished, and no one could complain that Sarajevo's inhabitants had been deprived of seeing the future emperor. Would it not be better, the baron asked, to abandon the visit planned for the following day? It had never really been a formal part of the trip anyway; an insistent Potiorek had tacked it on, much against the archduke's wishes, in an apparent attempt to demonstrate imperial support for his own regime. The following day's schedule was hardly pressing. The couple would spend less than ten minutes at the city's military barracks before driving through the streets for a half-hour reception at city hall; a short visit to the city's museum would precede luncheon with Potiorek at his official residence. In all, a mere four hours would be spent in the city, and most of that behind closed doors with invited guests. Saving Franz Ferdinand and Sophie from potential danger in Sarajevo, Rumerskirch suggested, far outweighed the risk of irritating Potiorek and a few privileged guests. Nikitsch-Boulles and Morsey agreed, the latter pointing out how inadequate security had seemed when the duchess toured the city.[39]

The archduke had repeatedly tried to get out of the trip; now that he had met the obligations imposed on him by the emperor, he listened to this reasoning with hopeful interest. There had been too many warnings, too many threats, for him to ignore the possible danger that awaited an appearance in Sarajevo. He especially worried that Sophie might be harmed if some Serb nationalist decided to attack him. The more he heard, the more confident he became. There were sure to be complaints if the visit was cancelled, but he could argue, with justification, that he had gone to Bosnia against his wishes and fulfilled his duties. Mind made up, Franz Ferdinand was on the verge of announcing his decision to cancel the visit and return to Vienna that night when Potiorek over-heard the talk and strenuously objected. The very idea, he insisted, was an insult. Such a move, the governor-general declared, would belittle him before the entire province and undermine his authority; the city would feel snubbed, and open rebellion against Habsburg rule might result. Potiorek turned to his adjutant, Lieutenant Erich von Merizzi, to bolster the arguments, and the two men were loud and vehement in their objections, 'pestering' the archduke 'with reasons until he agreed to leave everything as it was'.[40]

One last time, Franz Ferdinand had tried and failed to avoid having to appear in Sarajevo. Now, only twelve hours separated him and Sophie from their Sunday morning visit.

SIXTEEN

St Vitus's Day

✦

The sun rose early on Sarajevo on the morning of Sunday 28 June 1914. As dawn crept across the surrounding mountains, it illuminated a city gently rising from its slumber. Flocks of birds scattered against the sky from poplar trees as church bells tolled and calls to prayer echoed from the spidery minarets. A few early risers straggled along the Appel Quay, down which Franz Ferdinand and Sophie would travel; the street was still in shadow, fringed on one side by the slow waters of the Miljacka River. Deprived of its mountain torrents by summer's approach, the river was shallow, with just a foot of water washing over the rocky bed.

It was fourteen years to the day since Franz Ferdinand's renunciation oath. The action had allowed him to marry Sophie but had condemned her and her children to a twilight existence. 'It will be fourteen years since I married His Imperial and Royal Highness the Archduke,' Sophie had commented shortly before leaving for Bosnia. 'I wish I could relive every single day again.'[1] Franz Ferdinand, pondering the impending visit, confessed similar thoughts. 'I have often found', he had remarked before the trip, 'that there are things in life we would do differently if we had to do them again. But if I had to marry again, I would do what I have done, without change.'[2]

The couple marked the anniversary in prayer, kneeling together in the makeshift chapel at the Hotel Bosna in Ilidže. 'It was such an uplifting sight,' remembered Sophie's lady-in-waiting.[3] Franz Ferdinand dictated a cable to his children at Chlumetz. 'Papa and Mama,' it announced, were well and looking forward to seeing them again. A few minutes before 9:30 a.m., the couple left the hotel for the train station and the ten-minute railway journey into Sarajevo.[4]

A small military band from the 15th Army Corps struck up the national anthem as the train pulled into a Sarajevo station bedecked with flags and bunting. Potiorek waited on a length of crimson carpet to receive the illustrious visitors; at his side stood the city's mayor, Fehim Effendi Čurčić, a black fez atop his head, and a host of local officials. The archduke stepped out first. He wore the uniform of an Austrian cavalry general: black broadcloth trousers with red piping; shining black leather boots; a tight blue serge tunic piped in red, adorned with gold epaulettes, and set with three gold stars along the high collar. An impressive cockade of green peacock feathers sprouted from the top of his helmet. Sophie followed, in a white silk summer dress adorned with panels of lace and ornamented with a small corsage of red and white rosebuds at her waist. A spray of ostrich plumes waved atop her white hat, whose gauzy veil shaded her face; around her shoulders draped an ermine stole, and she carried a tightly rolled white lace parasol.[5]

Their first stop was the Filippović Barracks opposite the station. General Michael von Appel, Sarajevo's military commander in chief, greeted the couple on their arrival a little before ten. Several rows of soldiers waited at attention for the archduke's inspection; normally Sophie would have stood discreetly to the side, but this morning, as if she did not want to be separated from her husband, she walked with him through the ranks. It was all over in just ten minutes, and the archduke and his wife walked to the line of seven motor cars waiting in front of the station.[6]

Special security officers had been detailed to ride in the first car, but as they tried to enter, four local police officers rebuffed them, insisting

that the places belonged to them. Despite loud objections, the special security officers were left behind at the station. Mayor Fehim Čurčić
climbed into the second along with Dr Edmund Gerde, the chief of police. Franz Ferdinand and Sophie were directed to the third and largest of
the vehicles, a dark grey 1910 Viennese Gräf & Stift Bois de Boulogne
open touring car bearing a small black and yellow Habsburg flag mounted
on the left side of the bonnet. The archduke sat on the left of the rear
black leather seat, with Sophie to his right; across from her, on a lower
seat, sat Count Franz Harrach, the car's owner, with Potiorek on a matching seat in front of the archduke. Gustav Schneiberg, one of Franz Ferdinand's hunting staff, and driver Leopold Loyka sat in front. In the fourth
car rode Sophie's lady-in-waiting, Countess Lanjus von Wallenburg;
Baron Rumerskirch; Potiorek's adjutant, Lieutenant Colonel Erich von
Merizzi; and the car's owner, Count Boos-Waldeck. The next two motor
cars carried other members of Franz Ferdinand's entourage, including
Colonel Karl Bardolff, head of the archduke's Military Chancery, and
local officials, while the last vehicle was empty, a reserve car in case of
trouble. There was a bit of a delay: the canvas top on Franz Ferdinand
and Sophie's car was in place, but with the increasing sunshine it was now
folded back so that the crowds could better see them. Sophie abandoned
her ermine wrap as the procession set off for a reception with local dignitaries at the town hall.[7]

The motorcade route took Franz Ferdinand and Sophie down the
Appel Quay along the northern bank of the Miljacka River, lined with
poplar and lime trees. Buildings sported flags and bunting along their
facades; here and there, triumphal arches spanned the broad roadway,
bearing greetings to the couple. Franz Ferdinand looked around with
interest, a reporter saw, and Sophie 'smiled pleasantly at the gathered
people'. The crowds were thick in spots, thin in others; most stood on the
southern side of the street, where the building shadows offered relief
from the sunshine. Here and there, spaced at distant intervals, stood a
few of the Sarajevo police detailed to watch the crowd.[8]

Guns at the old Turkish fortress above the city were firing out a twenty-four-shot salute as the motorcade turned onto the Appel Quay, following its gentle curve along the northern bank of the Miljacka into an avenue lined with would-be assassins. They had met that morning in a back room in Vlasjić's Pastry Shop to receive their weapons and instructions. Working with a map of the route published in the newspaper, Ilić placed his fellow conspirators at strategic intervals along the Miljacka. Mehmedbašić and Čabrinović stood along the river near the Cumurja Bridge. Farther up the quay were Cubrilović and Popović. Princip was near the Lateiner Bridge with Grabež, while Ilić moved about attempting to find the best position from which to shoot.[9]

'The crowd', recalled Popović, 'began to murmur, and everybody pushed to the front lines on the edge of the pavement.'[10] As the car carrying Franz Ferdinand and Sophie appeared, Mehmedbašić froze, unable to act; he later insisted that a policeman had seen him and that if he threw his bomb the plot would be exposed. It was 10:10 a.m. when Čabrinović saw the car approach. That morning he had been in tears, telling his family he was leaving on a long trip and handing them his money, but arrogance soon returned. He jauntily visited a local photographer's studio, sitting for a portrait wearing a dark suit with a high, white starched collar. 'I thought that posterity should have my picture taken on that day,' he said, 'so that a memory would remain behind.'[11]

Unlike Mehmedbašić, Čabrinović did not hesitate. All of the conspirators, he said, were 'determined' to kill only the archduke, 'but if that were not possible, then we would sacrifice her and all the others'.[12] Čabrinović withdrew the bomb from his pocket, struck the detonator cap against a lantern post, and hurled it at the vehicle, aiming at the green feathers atop Franz Ferdinand's helmet. The sound of the percussive cap against the post was so loud that Count Harrach, sitting in the car's front seat, thought that a tyre had blown out; Loyka saw a small black object whizzing through the air toward them and pressed down on the accelerator. The vehicle shot forward with a jolt just as the bomb arced down to earth. The sound also caught Franz Ferdinand's attention; he turned, and on seeing the object he raised his hand in an effort to protect Sophie.

The bomb missed the passengers, hitting the back of the car's rolled-down canvas top and tumbling into the street before detonating in a flash of heat and smoke.[13]

Debris flew, windows shattered, and the crowd erupted in screams at the unexpected explosion; two women fainted, and twenty spectators were injured.[14] The first motor car, holding the mayor and the chief of police, kept going along the route, thinking that the sudden boom was merely a backfire or one of the salutes being fired from the fortress; General Appel, too, a few hundred feet back, at first thought the sound was an artillery salute – at least until he saw people running along the street and heard the screams.[15] Loyka halted the vehicle carrying the archduke and duchess on Franz Ferdinand's orders. Sophie was leaning forward clutching the back of her neck. She thought that an insect had stung her; in fact, a splinter had left a small scratch. More pieces of shrapnel had hit the car's boot, petrol tank, and canvas top.[16]

Harrach jumped out to investigate and soon reported injuries in the fourth car. Shrapnel hit its owner, Count Boos-Waldeck, and Sophie's lady-in-waiting had also been struck. Countess Vilma Lanjus von Wallenburg, though, turned her attention to Merizzi, whose head was bleeding profusely from flying debris. Quick inspection revealed that the adjutant's wound was superficial, and he was taken to the garrison hospital.[17]

After throwing his bomb, Čabrinović jumped over the railing along the Miljacka and plunged some twenty-five feet to the shallow riverbed, swallowing the cyanide in his vial as he did so. Pursuing spectators caught him in the water, hitting and kicking him as the would-be assassin shouted, 'I am a Serbian hero!' The poison failed to act; it was either too old or too weak. Police quickly caught Čabrinović and dragged him away; Princip saw him pass and pondered shooting him to ensure the plot's secrecy, but he waited too long to act.[18]

Chaos filled the Appel Quay. The archduke's worst fears about the visit had been confirmed. Turning to Potiorek, he fixed the governor-general with an icy glare, saying, 'I thought something like this might happen!'[19] After a few seconds, he regained his composure. 'Come on,' he shouted, 'the fellow is insane! Let's go on with our programme!' The car sped the remaining three blocks down the quay to the town hall.[20] Although most of the other conspirators still stood along the quay, none acted, either from fear or from self-preservation. Eventually most of them wandered away, except for Grabež and Princip.[21]

Morning sun dappled the multicoloured walls of the Moorish-style town hall as Loyka pulled to a stop before an immense loggia. Smiling officials lined the red-carpeted front steps: Muslims in fezzes and waist-coats standing on one side, and Christian officials in tailcoats and top hats on the other. The mayor anxiously clutched his welcoming speech; he had arrived only a few minutes earlier, still believing that the loud noise during the procession had been a car backfiring or cannon firing a salute from the fortress. When the archduke and duchess left their car and walked to the bottom of the loggia steps, the mayor launched into his speech. 'Our hearts are full of happiness over the most gracious visit with which Your Highnesses are pleased to honour our capital city of Sarajevo, and I consider myself happy that Your Highnesses can read in our faces the feelings of our love and devotion—'

'What kind of devotion is this?' the archduke angrily interrupted. 'I come to Sarajevo and am greeted with bombs! It is outrageous!' Sophie bent forward and whispered a few words into her husband's ear, touching him gently on the arm. Finally, Franz Ferdinand calmed down, saying, 'All right, now you may speak.'[22]

A flustered Čurčić returned to his prepared remarks. 'All the citizens of the capital city of Sarajevo find that their souls are filled with happiness, and they most enthusiastically greet Your Highnesses' most illustrious visit with the most cordial of welcomes, deeply convinced that this stay in our beloved city of Sarajevo will ever increase Your Highnesses' most gracious interest in our progress and well-being.'[23]

It was Franz Ferdinand's turn to reply. Rumerskirch, who had been sitting next to Merizzi, handed him his speech, the pages now splattered with the lieutenant's blood.[24] With a deep breath, the archduke expressed thanks 'for the resounding ovations with which the population received me and my wife, the more so since I see in them an expression of pleasure over the failure of the assassination attempt. To my sincere satisfaction, I was in the fortunate position of convincing myself personally, during this brief stay in your midst, of the satisfying development of this magnificent region, in the prosperity of which I have always taken the most lively interest.' At the end of these remarks, he added a few sentences in Serbo-Croatian. 'May I ask you to give my cordial greetings to the inhabitants of this beautiful capital city, and assure you of my unchanged regard and favour.' The gathered officials erupted in cheers as the visiting couple climbed the steps and disappeared out of the hot sunshine into the town hall.[25]

The little daughter of the parliamentary leader curtsied to Sophie as she entered, shyly handing her a bouquet of roses; despite the traumatic incident, the duchess smiled, bent down, and stroked the girl's cheek. The couple stood for a moment in the octagonal entrance hall ringed with Moorish arcades that dripped rainbow hues, then parted. Sophie ascended the white marble staircase to the second floor for a private reception with the unveiled wives of local Muslim dignitaries, while Franz Ferdinand drafted a cable to his uncle assuring him that the assassination plot had failed.[26] A witness later recalled:

> *We could not take our eyes off the Archduke but not as you look at the main person in a court spectacle. We could not think of him as royalty at all, he was so incredibly strange. He was striding quite grotesquely, lifting his legs as high as if he were doing the goose step. I suppose he was trying to show that he was not afraid. I tell you, it was not at all like a reception. He was talking with the military governor Potiorek, jeering at him and taunting him with his failure to preserve order. And we were all silent, not because we were impressed by him, for he was not at all our Bosnian idea of a hero. But we all felt awkward because we knew that when he went out he would certainly be killed. It was not a matter of being told. But we knew how the*

people felt about him and the Austrians and we knew that if one man had
thrown a bomb and failed, another man would throw another bomb and
another after that if he should fail.[27]

A telephone call to the garrison hospital brought news that Merizzi's minor wounds were being treated. Franz Ferdinand asked if the man who had thrown the bomb had been arrested; told that he had been, he snapped, 'Just watch it! Instead of rendering the fellow harmless they will be truly Austrian about it all and give him a medal!'[28] Talk turned to the remaining schedule. Driving through the narrow, crowded streets, where another potential assassin might be waiting, worried Franz Ferdinand. 'Do you think more attempts are going to be made against me today?' he asked Potiorek. The provincial governor was full of assurances. 'Go at ease,' he insisted. 'I accept all responsibility.'[29]

This didn't satisfy Rumerskirch and Bardolff, who pressed Potiorek on the issue. 'Do you think Sarajevo is full of assassins?' Potiorek angrily spat back. Yet he reluctantly agreed that the schedule should be changed. The visit to the National Museum could be dropped; doing this, he suggested, would 'punish' Sarajevo's citizens by depriving them of further views of the visiting couple.[30] He insisted that the luncheon at the Konak, his official residence, continue. Franz Ferdinand was unconcerned about such niceties; his first priority, over Potiorek's objections, was to visit Merizzi. 'The man', he shouted, 'is my fellow officer! He is bleeding for me! You'll have the goodness to understand that!'[31]

Rumerskirch asked if it was possible to reach the hospital without passing through the crowded city streets. Potiorek insisted that the safest, most direct route was a drive back along the Appel Quay, though in fact this added to the journey and took in additional streets. The proposal was suicidal: Potiorek's route would take the archduke and his wife straight back into the same crowded street where the bomb had been thrown; if a plot existed, more potential assassins might still be waiting along the route. Wouldn't it be best, Rumerskirch asked, to remain at the town hall until soldiers from the garrison could be positioned along the streets to protect the archduke and his wife? The order would take less than thirty minutes to fulfil and would provide the couple with the necessary security. Potiorek objected; the soldiers, he insisted, did not have proper uniforms to line the streets as an honour guard. This was nonsense – nothing prevented Potiorek from filling the streets with soldiers to ensure the couple's safety. Exasperated, Rumerskirch then suggested that police clear the streets if they could not be lined with troops; again, Potiorek refused.[32]

The archduke could have insisted; instead, he decided to be diplomatic and not press the issue. Bardolff discussed the change of route with Chief of Police Edmund Gerde. He, too, had repeatedly warned Potiorek of danger only to be ridiculed and dismissed. The plan now called for the motorcade to speed straight down the Appel Quay from the town hall to the hospital. Bardolff asked Gerde to repeat the change and to inform the drivers of it. The chief of police recited the plan, mumbling, 'Yes, yes', and then, presumably thoroughly rattled by everything that had happened, promptly neglected to tell the drivers.[33]

Not without reason, Franz Ferdinand continued to worry. 'Maybe we'll get more bombs today,' he remarked grimly.[34] Sophie's safety was his main concern. He asked Morsey to drive her either to the Konak or directly back to Ilidže. When Morsey suggested this, however, she refused. 'As long as the Archduke shows himself in public today,' she said, 'I will not leave him.'[35] When she appeared downstairs, her husband tried again, insisting that she at least ride in a different car. Sophie was adamant, saying, 'No, Franzi, I am going with you.'[36]

It was 10:45 a.m. when Franz Ferdinand and Sophie descended the front steps of the town hall, where the motorcade had drawn up. Count Harrach helped Sophie into the car while Franz Ferdinand entered on the opposite side; as soon as he was seated, Harrach took up a position standing on the running board next to the archduke. If another attempt took place from the quayside, the count thought, he would be able to shield the archduke with his body. With a jolt, the car set off back down the Appel Quay, speeding past Grabež, who did nothing.[37]

A photographer captured the moment, a few seconds later, as the car carrying Franz Ferdinand and Sophie reached the point where the gently arched Lateiner Bridge crossed the Miljacka. The crowd along the quay was sparse, the wheels of the vehicle just beginning their right turn toward Franz Josef Strasse, a gaudy advertisement depicting a twelve-foot-high bottle of wine marking the corner of Moritz Schiller's Delicatessen. Just beyond the lens of the camera stood Gavrilo Princip.

Princip had spent the last half hour wandering the quay before glumly lolling in front of Schiller's Delicatessen. The announced route would take the archduke past this corner and into Franz Josef Strasse toward the National Museum, yet Princip was sure that the schedule would be changed after the bomb attack. He was stunned when the first car turned off the quay and passed directly in front of him; in the second car, Loyka, unaware of the change in plan, simply followed the lead vehicle. Even this error might have passed without incident had not Potiorek intervened. As the car turned, he shouted, 'What is this! This is the wrong way! We're supposed to take the Appel Quay!'[38]

Loyka pulled the exterior handbrakes and brought the vehicle to a sudden halt. A few seconds elapsed before he could throw the car into reverse; Princip, standing only five feet away, swept his eyes over the scene in surprise. 'I recognized the Heir Apparent,' he said. 'But as I saw that a lady was sitting next to him, I reflected for a moment whether I should shoot or not.'[39]

As the car engine loudly rumbled, Princip withdrew his gun, a Belgian-made Browning model 1910 .32 calibre pistol. He later gave contradictory accounts of what happened next, saying that he had deliberately aimed at the archduke only to later insist, 'Where I aimed I do not know.' Nor could he recall how many times he fired; he thought it was twice but added that it was 'perhaps more, because I was so excited'.[40] A local reporter heard three shots, as did Baron Morsey. One, the baron believed, went straight through Franz Ferdinand's plumed helmet, as several of the green feathers were later found torn loose and lying on the car's floorboards.[41] No evidence supports the idea that Princip actually aimed his second shot at Potiorek but that a nearby spectator or member of the police struck his arm and thus caused the bullet to hit Sophie.[42] Nor did Sophie, on hearing the first shot, jump from her seat and inadvertently come between Potiorek and Princip.[43]

A crowd immediately surrounded Princip. Baron Morsey rushed forward, cavalry sabre drawn. Spectators were beating Princip; when Morsey saw that he still held the gun, he turned the hilt of his sword against him, hitting him until the pistol clattered to the pavement. Princip managed to pull the vial of cyanide from his pocket and swallow the contents before it, too, was knocked from his hand. Like that used by Čabrinović, it failed to kill him, apparently having lost its potency.[44]

'So it has happened again!' This is what Potiorek thought he heard the archduke say, almost in a whisper.[45] Harrach saw a small stream of blood trickle from the archduke's mouth. Franz Ferdinand and Sophie both sat upright for a few seconds. Then Sophie turned to her husband; seeing the blood and a stricken look on his face, she screamed, 'For heaven's sake, what has happened to you?' Her face contorted, her eyes closed, and she slumped in her seat, falling across Franz Ferdinand's lap. Both Potiorek and Harrach thought that she had fainted. Potiorek and Harrach heard the archduke speak to her, though only the latter clearly recalled the words: 'Sopherl! Sopherl! Don't die! Stay alive for our children!'[46] Then he slumped forward and his plumed helmet fell from his head to the floor. As Harrach leaned toward him, more blood escaped from the archduke's mouth, spattering the count's cheek. Seeing that Franz Ferdinand was wounded, Potiorek ordered Loyka to drive to the Konak. After a few more agonizing seconds, the car reversed.[47]

Loyka didn't know where the Konak was located, and Potiorek shouted directions. As the vehicle raced across the Lateiner Bridge, Sophie fell forward against the governor-general's arm. For the first time Potiorek saw blood trickle from the archduke's open mouth.[48] The ride was bumpy. Harrach struggled to hold the archduke upright, a handkerchief pressed to his neck where a crimson stain was spreading from an unseen wound. 'Is Your Imperial Highness in great pain?' he asked. 'It is nothing,' Franz Ferdinand said softly. As the car sped toward the Konak, the archduke swooned in and out of consciousness, mumbling over and over, 'It is nothing,' six or seven times until he fell silent.[49] Every detail was burned into Harrach's mind. 'I stood on the wrong side,' he later repeatedly uttered. 'If I had stood on the right-hand side instead of the left, I would have taken the bullets and would have saved their lives.'[50]

Both Franz Ferdinand and Sophie appeared to be unconscious when the car arrived in the shadow of the ugly orange and brown Konak. A young army officer named Ludwig Hesshaimer waited on the steps, armed with a portfolio of his landscapes he hoped to present to the archduke. Instead, he joined several others in lifting Franz Ferdinand from the car, carrying him past the stone lions guarding the staircase and into the building; he later found that his paintings, hastily tucked beneath his arm, were stained with the archduke's blood. Rumerskirch and Bardolff followed with Sophie in their arms, rushing through the foyer and up the main staircase to Potiorek's private suite above.[51]

Bardolff, regimental surgeon Eduard Bayer, Eisenmenger's temporary replacement Dr Ferdinand Fischer, and several others hovered over the archduke. Franz Ferdinand lay on a thickly padded chaise longue in Potiorek's study; his legs hung off one end, his head resting against an upholstered arm, his breathing shallow, his pupils nearly unresponsive, and blood gurgling from his mouth. They struggled to open the clasp of his collar; finally, Baron Morsey slashed the tunic across the chest and cut the rear of the collar. As they removed it and the shirt beneath, they revealed a little gold chain, hung with seven charms, that hung around Franz Ferdinand's neck for good luck.[52] They now saw the wound, a small bullet hole on the right side of Franz Ferdinand's neck just above the collarbone. Morsey cradled the archduke in his left arm; as they tried to raise him up, blood gurgled from Franz Ferdinand's mouth across the baron's face and uniform and spattered the wall. Morsey bent down, grasped Franz Ferdinand's hand in his, and asked in a whisper if he had any message for his children, but there was no reply. 'His Highness's suffering is over,' Bayer announced. Rumerskirch closed his eyes, and

Morsey pulled a small crucifix from his pocket, pressed it to the archduke's silent lips, and placed it and a rosary in his hands.[53]

Sophie had been laid out on an iron bed in an adjoining room. Everyone assumed that she had fainted, but when Dr Karl Wolfgang, senior physician of the garrison hospital, asked Countess Vilma Lanjus von Wallenburg to undress her mistress, they saw the blood seeping along her waist from a small bullet hole in her lower right abdomen. The doctor could find no pulse; Sophie had died in the car during the journey to the Konak. The countess tearfully laid the bouquet of roses presented at the town hall in her hands.[54] 'This so sudden loss', the countess recalled, 'was so horribly awful, because I was to lose my whole joy in life through the death of my beloved mistress . . . I could hardly believe the reality and thought that this was just a bad dream. I wept bitterly; this grief went right down to the deepest marrow of my soul.'[55]

The clock in the study chimed eleven. In a few minutes, two priests arrived, Brother Mihacevii, attired in his Franciscan cowl, and Jesuit Father Anton Puntigam. They said last rites over the bodies. Franz Ferdinand's corpse was carried into the bedroom and placed on the twin iron bed next to his wife. Soon Josef Stadler, the archbishop of Sarajevo, arrived at the Konak to lead the prayers for the dead.[56]

As people knelt, they could hear the rattle and clink from the dining room below. Potiorek had planned a festive luncheon: *consommé en tasse, œufs en gelée, fruits au beurre, bœuf bouilli aux legumes, poulets à la villeroy, riz compôte, bombe à la reine, fromage* and *fruits et dessert*, along with musical accompaniment that had included a waltz called 'No Life Without Love'. Now the china, crystal and silver so carefully arranged down the long table sat unused in the wake of the assassination that had ended two lives distinguished by an extraordinary love.[57]

SEVENTEEN

'The Anguish Was Indescribable'

✛

It was a lazy, early summer day at Chlumetz. Sophie, Max and Ernst had just sat down to luncheon when Otto Stankowsky, the boys' tutor, was suddenly called away from the table.[1] Morsey and Rumerskirch temporarily closed the empire's telephone and telegraph lines until the dead couple's relatives could be told the grim news.[2] Sophie's brother Wolfgang fainted on hearing of her death.[3] Now a stunned Stankowsky learned what had happened in Sarajevo.

The tutor pondered what to do. Learning that Sophie's sister Henriette was on her way to Chlumetz from Prague, Stankowsky decided to wait. It was best to let a relative break the news that the children had lost their parents. When Stankowsky returned to the dining room, Sophie saw that he was 'very pale' and at first assumed he had bad news about his mother, who was ill. Stankowsky refused to say anything. The three children were pondering ideas for a little tableau to act out as a welcome to their parents when their aunt Henriette arrived late that afternoon. 'We ran towards her cheerfully,' Sophie recalled, 'but she had tears in her eyes.' There had, she told them, been an attack on their parents; both were wounded. 'Then we'll visit them in hospital!' Sophie cried. No,

Henriette said, it was better that they all go to church and pray for them. The charade was maintained as day turned to night and the duchess's other siblings arrived at Chlumetz.[4]

Sleep was nearly impossible, but not until the next morning, said Sophie, did they learn 'the dreadful truth'. Stankowsky gently told Max and Ernst of the assassination, while Sophie's brother-in-law Count Karl von Wuthenau, who had spent the night travelling to Chlumetz with his remaining siblings, broke the news to the couple's nearly thirteen-year-old daughter. 'The anguish was indescribable,' Sophie remembered, 'and also the feeling of total bewilderment. All our lives, we had known nothing but love and total security. Now suddenly we simply couldn't imagine what was to become of us.'[5] Ten-year-old Ernst, reported the *Reichspost*, was overcome with grief and 'behaved like a madman'.[6] The following day, Sophie released a brief statement, 'We are very touched by the sympathy and prayers of the public. I ask you to continue to pray for our parents, and for us.'[7]

Sympathetic cables poured in. 'Deeply shaken by the dreadful misfortune that has befallen us,' wrote the children's exiled uncle Ferdinand Karl to Max. 'I am with you and your siblings in thought. God protect you.'[8] Archduke Ludwig Salvator wired, 'With a torn heart, I send you and your siblings my deepest condolences.'[9] From his yacht *Hohenzollern*, Kaiser Wilhelm telegraphed, 'We can hardly find words to tell you children how our hearts bleed, thinking of you and of your indescribable misery! Only two weeks ago we spent such lovely hours with your parents, and now we hear of this terrible grief that you must suffer. May God protect you and give you the strength to bear this blow! The blessing of your parents reaches beyond the grave.'[10]

Franz Josef was at Ischl that Sunday when the telegram arrived from Baron Rumerskirch:

> Stunned and deeply shaken by the incomprehensible, I am broken-hearted to inform you that in the course of a drive through Sarajevo His Imperial Highness and Her Highness were hit by shots from a dastardly assassin's

hand and badly wounded. They were taken at once to the Konak where immediate medical help was present but it was not possible for human help to save them and Their Highnesses passed away after a few minutes without having regained consciousness.[11]

Count Paar, the emperor's adjutant, took the cable to Franz Josef. The old emperor said little. As if overwhelmed at the news, he closed his eyes for a few moments, then spoke – inadvertently, Paar thought – expressing in a moment of weakness a sentiment he never otherwise would have revealed. 'Horrible! The Almighty does not allow Himself to be challenged with impunity. A higher power has restored the old order that I unfortunately was unable to uphold.'[12]

The shocking remarks have been questioned as out of character for the old emperor, yet his subsequent behaviour confirmed his sense of relief. He had always regarded his nephew with suspicion, and his morganatic marriage as an unwelcome, humiliating situation that had dragged the dignity of the imperial Habsburgs through the mud. Certainly no one has questioned the veracity of Franz Josef's daughter Marie Valerie, who rushed to her father on hearing the news although, as she noted in her diary, she knew 'that it would cause him no grief, merely excitement'. She found her father 'amazingly fresh'. He was, she recorded, 'moved, to be sure,' and spoke 'of the poor children with tears in his eyes', but, 'as I knew beforehand, not personally stricken'. In their conversation, he made only a passing reference to the assassination of his heir, telling his daughter coldly, 'For me, it's one great worry less.'[13]

The emperor now acted to tie up loose ends. He ordered Franz Ferdinand's Militärkanzlerei immediately closed. All of the archduke's mail was seized, his files and papers confiscated, and everything sealed in the emperor's archives.[14] Later that Sunday, an adjutant presented the emperor with the proposed text of a public statement on Franz Ferdinand's assassination that included the line 'The death of my Beloved Nephew, a death painful to me . . .' Seeing these words, Franz Josef picked up a pen and crossed through 'a death painful to me'.[15] Colonel

Bardolff confirmed this lack of feeling when he met the emperor a few days later. After delivering an account of events in Sarajevo, Franz Josef quizzed Bardolff. 'And how did the Archduke bear himself?' 'Like a soldier, Your Majesty,' Bardolff replied. 'That was to be expected,' the emperor commented. That was it; not a word of sympathy for the victims before Franz Josef quickly moved on, asking, 'And how did the manoeuvres go?'[16]

Franz Ferdinand's nephew Archduke Karl was spending the summer with his family at Reichenau, southwest of Vienna. He had just sat down on the terrace to eat lunch with Zita when a servant handed over an urgent telegram from Rumerskirch. Karl was puzzled. 'Why him?' he asked. 'He's with Uncle Franzi.' The archduke tore the envelope open and quickly read the news of the tragedy in Sarajevo. He 'went white as a sheet', Zita remembered, and the couple immediately set off for Vienna.[17] Karl was there to greet the emperor when Franz Josef arrived from Ischl on Monday afternoon; in a public sign that Karl was now his heir, he asked the young archduke to sit beside him in the carriage for the drive to Schönbrunn Palace.[18] Fifty years later, Zita insisted that the emperor broke into tears, sobbing, 'I am spared nothing,' though by this time the comment had appeared in dozens of books, attributed variously as Franz Josef's reaction to the death of his son, the death of his wife, or the assassination at Sarajevo.[19]

Yet much of the world believed that the old emperor must be suffering, and sympathies poured in from across the globe. President Woodrow Wilson cabled the sympathy of the United States at 'the atrocious murder' in Sarajevo.[20] 'His Majesty's Government wish also to transmit their most sincere and respectful condolences to His Imperial Majesty,' the British foreign secretary Sir Edward Grey telegraphed to Sir Maurice de Bunsen, the British ambassador in Vienna. Grey added his own 'personal feelings of deep sympathy, as I recall the honour which I had of meeting His Imperial Highness last year and of seeing the pleasure given by his visit to the King and to this country.'[21] To Count Mensdorff, the Austrian ambassador in London, Grey commented, 'We all feel for your

Emperor and for the shock and grief which he must suffer.'[22] King George V noted 'the sad news' in his diary, adding, 'It will be a terrible shock to the dear old Emperor, and is most regrettable and sad.'[23] Queen Mary wrote, 'The horrible tragedy to the poor Archduke and his wife came as a great shock to us . . . Poor Emperor, nothing is he spared . . . I think it is a great blessing that Ferdinand and his wife died together, making the future less complicated with regard to the position of their children.'[24]

In Vienna that Sunday, the sky was 'silken' and blue, the 'air soft and sultry', as people crowded parks and squares, picnicking and listening as military bands played sentimental tunes. Then suddenly the music ceased as word of the assassination spread. Many people, believing the worst about Franz Ferdinand, reacted with relief. 'There was', recalled Stefan Zweig, 'no special shock or dismay to be seen on the faces of the crowd, for the Heir to the Throne had not by any means been popular.'[25] Theatrical performances were cancelled and shops closed to maintain the mood of mourning, but many Austrians almost welcomed the news. 'The town takes it all very quietly,' noted Sir Maurice de Bunsen. 'There is not a sign of emotion anywhere. They must be a very apathetic people.'[26] In the Prater, one man saw 'no mood of mourning' as the round of festivities continued. 'God meant to be kind to Austria,' recorded famed diarist Josef Redlich, 'by saving it from this Emperor.'[27] In many political and official court circles, Eisenmenger said, word of the assassination 'was received with ill-concealed satisfaction. They were relieved to be rid of so powerful and dangerous an opponent.'[28] One courtier greeted the news with the simple 'The ogre is dead.'[29]

This sense of relief spilled beyond Austria. There was no outpouring of grief in Hungary, where Prime Minister István Tisza declared, 'The Lord God has willed it so, and we must be grateful to the Lord God for everything.'[30] King Nicholas of Montenegro professed himself 'delighted' at the assassination; the mood in Paris, Budapest and Italy was almost gleeful.[31] The Russian response was equally cool. The archduke, commented St Petersburg's *Novoe Vremya*, 'had not been amongst Russia's friends'.[32] Another newspaper hoped 'that this new death forces Austria to change her dangerous Balkan policies', while a third warned that Austria should 'not respond to the crime of Sarajevo with any retaliation against our Slav brothers'.[33] Nicholas de Hartwig, the Russian minister in Belgrade, gave a festive bridge party on the night of the assassination; declaring that the archduke's death was a blessing, he refused to lower the embassy flag, and later lied about it when his colleagues called him out.[34] Serbia openly rejoiced at the news. 'This is revenge for the annexation!' crowds shouted in Belgrade.[35] Newspapers hailed Princip as 'a young martyr' and declared that Austrian officials had organized the assassination as a pretext for launching a war against Serbia.[36]

Yet not everyone welcomed the assassination. In Rumania, noted the British ambassador in Bucharest, word of the assassination was greeted

> *with deep regret and indignation. Among the people of this country, to whom he was specially endeared by the sympathy he was believed to have for the Rumanians in Hungary the late Archduke was always popular; and while recently there has been a coolness of public feeling towards the neighbouring Empire, it was recognized that the Heir Apparent himself was strongly in favour of intimate relations with this country.*[37]

To those who had pinned their hopes on his impending reign for needed reforms and a more liberal approach to the empire's problems, Sarajevo was an immense tragedy. The archduke, one Viennese newspaper eulogized, had seemed a cold figure, for he 'disdained the indispensable affability by which the powerful promote their careers ... He was no greeter. He had no winning ways to charm the people ... He radically proved his character by championing the common against the contrived modern ... He wanted to awaken our age from its sickness, so that it would not sleep into its own death.'[38]

Prince Alphonse Clary wrote of his 'most aching heart' and the

tears in my eyes, tears of sorrow, of terrible rage and fury! Oh, the misery of it,
he, our future, our leader, who was to be the strong man, he to whom we all
looked to in the future as our saviour out of all the long-past years of ineptitude:
he is not here any more! . . . How can one bear such felony and must not every
civilized creature on earth stand up and pray for damnation and God's fire of
vengeance on that vile, murderous country, Serbia! They slaughtered their King
and Queen already, but to send their men into our country and kill our leader,
oh, they knew where to set their deadly weapons, they knew the point where
they would hurt Austria most! . . . We are all in such utter misery![39]

Another man was thunderstruck, writing to a friend, 'The end of Austria has now come! I still hold on to this opinion. It wasn't just the Heir to the Throne who was felled to the ground by Princip's bullet, but Austria-Hungary. Even though the decline has been immense during the last years of Franz Josef's reign, however crumbling the monarchy had become, the realization of Franz Ferdinand's plans could have pulled it through.'[40]

To those who had known Franz Ferdinand and Sophie intimately, their assassination was devastating. Colonel Brosch, formerly head of the archduke's Military Chancery, wrote, 'I'm like a wounded animal that only wants to creep into a corner and die there . . . I have completely lost faith in a divine world.'[41] 'It has been, for me, a very great loss,' Archduke Ludwig Salvator confided to a friend, 'and I am quite prostrated from the blow . . . I had just seen him at the railway station three days before, when he was travelling with his wife, and we were to meet later in the summer again. Every year I was spending a couple of days in the intimacy of his family life, living actively for religious love and useful work. The children were charming . . . It is a great loss for our country.'[42]

Countess Elisabeth de Baillet-Latour, Sophie's niece, 'numbed with misery and horror', confessed to Queen Mary:

The loss of my darling beloved aunt, who was the best and noblest woman that ever lived and the dearest friend I had in the world is such intense grief to me that no words can describe it; it is agony that I had never dreamt of before! I belonged to them in a way . . . and knew their every thought almost, and I want her gentle kindness and her love so so dreadfully . . . I hope so much that Aunt Sophy did not realize that she and he were dying, because then thought of leaving the children must have been like the agony of hell to her . . . Aunt Sophy was always haunted by the idea that some day an attempt might be made to take his life, and she never ever left him.[43]

As that fateful Sunday drew to a close, Sarajevo erupted in violence. Crowds of Turks and Croatians 'roamed through the town singing the traditional song and carrying black-ribboned mourning pictures of the Emperor,' reported General Michael von Appel, 'stopped at the houses of the Serbs, broke into them, smashed all the windows, all their furnishings and tore up and ruined everything.' Potiorek ordered hundreds of soldiers into the streets, willing, after the murders, to take the security measures that he had rejected during the visit.[44] By nightfall, said the Vienna *Reichspost*, Sarajevo 'looked like the scene of a pogrom'.[45]

A grim scene unfolded at the Konak. No local pathologist dared undertake an autopsy on a member of the imperial family; finally, after assurances from Vienna, Sarajevo pathologist Pavao Kaunic, assisted by Ferdinand Fischer and Karl Wolfgang, arrived to begin the autopsies. The trio pushed their way past a silent crowd around the Konak's iron railing; the building blazed with candlelight, 'as if a ball was being given,' said Kaunic. 'There was no feeling of death.' Before being led to the bodies, the trio received warnings from Vienna that, even in death, emphasized the differences between Franz Ferdinand and his morganatic wife. Any wounds on the archduke were not to be dissected, but the pathologists could do as they wished with Sophie.[46]

Covered with white sheets, the two corpses lay atop metal tables brought from the garrison hospital. The examinations began a few minutes after ten. A single bullet had struck Franz Ferdinand on the right side of his neck, one centimetre above his collarbone and two centimetres from his larynx; the wound, five millimetres in diameter, bore irregular, jagged edges. The bullet had pierced the jugular vein, passing near the side of the trachea and tearing cartilage before lodging in the cervical vertebrae. Kaunic probed the wound with his fingers but, following instructions from Vienna, made no attempt to retrieve the projectile. The bullet that killed Sophie had passed through the car's rear passenger door; a small piece of horsehair upholstery was found wedged into the wound located four centimetres above her right pelvic bone. This had plugged the wound and prevented a noticeable external loss of blood. The bullet had been tumbling in midair after passing through the door, leaving the entrance wound an elongated oval shape some six centimetres in diameter. Passing through the lower abdomen, the bullet had severed the inferior vena cava – the principal vessel carrying deoxygenated blood from the lower body to the heart – and resulted in massive internal bleeding. The intact 9 mm jacketed bullet was removed during the autopsy.[47]

Sculptor Ludmila Valic and her artist husband, Rudolf, were woken in the middle of the night by a telephone call summoning them to the Konak to make death masks of the couple.[48] When this was done, the bodies were embalmed. The blood vessels were opened, flushed with water, and filled with a mixture of formaldehyde and glycerine. By seven the next morning, the work was finished.[49] The archduke's bloodstained undershirt, along with Sophie's gloves and shoes, were cut apart and distributed as macabre souvenirs of the murdered couple.[50]

A local undertaker delivered the two best coffins from his stock, a gilded bronze one for Franz Ferdinand and a silver one for Sophie. Each was decorated with carved beading, but Sophie's was noticeably smaller than that of her husband.[51] Black crêpe and flowers transformed the Konak's state bedroom into a temporary chapel, its windows shuttered against the morning sun and floral wreaths illuminated in a galaxy of flickering candlelight. Two inclined biers held the coffins, Franz

Ferdinand on the right, Sophie on the left; the archduke's white-gloved hands clutched a crucifix, Sophie's a small bouquet of flowers and a lapis lazuli rosary that her lady-in-waiting had pressed between her fingers.[52]

At six on the evening of 29 June, Archbishop Stadler, accompanied by the cathedral chapter, sang a requiem mass and blessed the bodies. Soldiers carried the coffins to two glass-sided hearses covered with palm fronds, and the sombre cortège began its procession out of the Konak's grounds, around the Emperor's Mosque, and to the railway station.[53] Potiorek filled the streets with soldiers armed with black mourning ribbons. Cavalry and infantry battalions headed the cortège, followed by members of the clergy, a car filled with wreaths that had completely exhausted the city's available supply of flowers, the two hearses, and finally the mourners, led by Morsey, Rumerskirch, Bardolff, Countess Vilma Lanjus von Wellenburg, Potiorek, and Sarajevo's civic officials. A railway carriage, stripped of seats and draped in black, awaited the coffins when they arrived at Bistrik Station. As the archbishop offered a final blessing, 'all present had tears in their eyes', reported the *Sarajevski List*, 'and the deadly silence spoke louder than any words'. Soldiers carried the coffins onto the train. There was a poignant moment when Morsey handed over a thousand crowns (approximately £3,200 in 2013 figures) to the Sarajevo Youth Centre; it had been Sophie's wish, he explained bitterly, a measure of how much she had enjoyed her time in the city. A few minutes past seven, as cannons in the fortress above the city thudded out a 101-gun salute, the train slowly disappeared into the creeping twilight.[54]

The funeral train raced through the night, past stations where honour guards stood at attention, arms were presented, salutes fired, and regimental bands played mourning songs. The sun was setting on the evening of Tuesday 30 June, when the coffins were taken aboard *Viribus Unitis* for the voyage to Trieste. As guns boomed salutes across the water and church bells tolled, naval officers placed the coffins beneath a canopy on the aft deck and formed an honor guard. The ship's honour standard draped the archduke's coffin; a regular naval flag covered Sophie's casket. Franz Ferdinand's personal standard waved above them, flying at half-mast. Churning silvery ribbons of foam and accompanied by a naval escort, the dreadnought slipped away from land, its black pennant fluttering against crimson sunset. It took twenty-four hours to reach Trieste; the coffins, Montenuovo insisted, should not arrive in Vienna until after night had fallen the following evening. So, on Vienna's orders, the bodies rested on deck as the sun set on what would have been Franz Ferdinand and Sophie's fourteenth wedding anniversary. Shortly before eight on the morning of 2 July, a tender brought them to shore as cannons again fired and church bells rang out.[55]

Despite the conflicted feelings that Franz Ferdinand had engendered in life, his assassination and especially the murder of his wife marked a change in public opinion. Where once the archduke had been disdained and feared, death now shrouded him in a mantle of martyrdom that seemed to wash away much of the previous antipathy. Outrage over the assassination spilled into widespread sympathy as ever-increasing numbers gathered to pay their last respects to the murdered couple. It had happened when they left Sarajevo and all along the route to Trieste. Now vast crowds stood beneath the hot sun as the funeral procession moved through Trieste to the Southern Railway Station. The archduke's personal railway carriage had been sent to Trieste for the journey, but, as had happened when the couple left Chlumetz, an axle burned out. Distraught that he had failed his late master in this final duty, Heinrich Stackler, Franz Ferdinand's personal conductor, watched as the coffins were loaded aboard another carriage and finally began their journey to Vienna.[56]

Thus began what one historian termed Montenuovo's 'strategy of massive, administrative pettiness' directed against the dead couple.[57] The funeral, as Baron Albert von Margutti said, 'gave rise to serious difficulties. It was not easy to find a precedent for the burial of the late Archduke's morganatic wife in the unbending regulations of Court Ceremonial.'[58] Although 'they tried to make the best of it,' comments Franz Ferdinand and Sophie's great-granddaughter Princess Sophie, 'it was a rushed affair'.[59] Opinions at the time were not as generous; one Austrian general deemed the ceremonies 'a fanatical attempt to eliminate the dead Archduke as speedily as possible from the sphere of his former activity and, if this could be attained, from the memory of his contemporaries.'[60]

Montenuovo initially made plans only for Franz Ferdinand. The archduke would be given a full state funeral in Vienna in keeping with his position as heir to the throne, and with all of the military ceremonial due to his rank as inspector general of the Imperial Army, before he joined the rest of the Habsburgs in the city's Capuchin Crypt. As far as Montenuovo was concerned, Sophie's family could claim her body and do with it what they wished.[61]

This bit of cold calculation changed when Montenuovo opened Franz Ferdinand's will and read for the first time that he wished to be interred in the crypt at Artstetten. If this was the case, the prince insisted, there was no need to drag out the ceremonies in Vienna. Some service for the archduke would have to take place in the imperial capital, but Sophie's corpse should be sent directly to Artstetten. Under no circumstances could the morganatic Sophie lie in state alongside her husband in the imperial chapel at the Hofburg. When Franz Ferdinand's stepmother, Maria Theresa, and the new heir, Archduke Karl, learned of this plan, both went to Franz Josef and objected strenuously. Reluctantly, the emperor agreed that both Franz Ferdinand and Sophie should share whatever funeral ceremony took place in Vienna.[62]

That funeral, though, would be unlike anything Vienna had ever witnessed. The emperor's role in planning the ceremonies has long been the subject of unnecessary debate. As with the questions of etiquette and the humiliations Montenuovo was allowed to inflict on Sophie in life, Franz Josef was scarcely an impotent hostage to tradition. Throughout his reign he always reviewed proposed ceremonial for important occasions, personally approving the smallest details of every christening, wedding and funeral.[63] Thus it was with the ceremonies for Franz

Ferdinand and Sophie. Montenuovo bore the brunt of contemporary and historical criticism, but the emperor personally approved the plans on the afternoon of 29 June and later publicly confirmed that they had been carried out 'in accordance with my intentions'.[64] The ceremonies that unfolded for Franz Ferdinand and Sophie were as much a result of the old emperor's wishes as they were an expression of Montenuovo's hatred of the despised couple.

Much of official Europe went into mourning. Pope Pius X cancelled all Vatican receptions and issued a statement expressing his 'profound horror' over the assassination. 'We feel', he declared, 'a sharp pain for the loss of such a wise and enlightened prince, and express our deep indignation against the perpetrators of such a despicable attack. We feel only the need to raise our voice with that of all honest people against such an abomination that outrages and shames the honour of civilized humanity.'[65]

Great Britain ordered mourning for a week, Russia for two, Germany for three, and Rumania for a month.[66] Thinking that the death of the heir to the Austro-Hungarian throne meant a state funeral, Europe's royal families began to plan their attendance. King Carol of Rumania, King Victor Emmanuel of Italy, Queen Wilhelmina of the Netherlands, King Ludwig III of Bavaria, King Albert of Belgium, and King Gustav V of Sweden all announced that they would come to Vienna; King George V asked his uncle Arthur, the Duke of Connaught, to attend the funeral; Grand Duke Nicholas Nikolaievich was to represent Tsar Nicholas II.[67] Kaiser Wilhelm went one better than his fellow monarchs, announcing that he and his brother Prince Heinrich would both attend the ceremonies in Vienna.[68]

Then suddenly it was announced that no foreign representatives were invited. The reason officially given was the emperor's health. Montenuovo advised all consulates that, to 'avoid straining His Majesty's delicate health with the demands of protocol', countries and royal houses should be represented only by their respective ambassadors or ministers in

Vienna.[69] Franz Josef, it is true, had been dangerously ill several months earlier with bronchitis, but he had largely recovered by 23 May, as his doctors assured the public and Montenuovo had assured Franz Ferdinand when the latter tried to use his uncle's health as an excuse to avoid the trip to Sarajevo.[70] Six weeks elapsed between that announcement and the funeral; by that time, even British ambassador Maurice de Bunsen reported to London that, 'happily, His Majesty seems to be quite well again'.[71]

There were, de Bunsen noted, widespread complaints 'that the presence of foreign Princes, as announced from many quarters, need not have been declined and the proceedings thus deprived of a visible sign of the sympathy which is everywhere felt for this country in her sorrow.'[72] Things were badly handled. When the king of Rumania tried to make the journey, he was allegedly turned back on orders from Vienna at the Austrian border.[73] Despite this request, the kaiser said he would like to come as a friend of the deceased and assured the emperor that he need not be received. This was not what Vienna wanted to hear; soon, Wilhelm was warned that a 'plot' against him had been uncovered in Vienna and that it would be unwise for him to attend. No such plot existed; even if there had been one, the kaiser insisted, he would have gone to Vienna to pay his respects, but Austrian officials were so forceful in their insistence that he had to abandon the idea. To cover this embarrassment, the kaiser even released a fabricated statement that he had suddenly come down with an attack of lumbago and could not travel.[74]

After objecting to royal participation out of concern for the emperor's health and suggesting non-existent plots to kill distinguished mourners, Vienna offered a third justification. It would have been impossible, they insisted, to invite royal mourners because this might have led to King Peter of Serbia's attendance. With suspicions that his country had been behind the assassinations in Sarajevo, the situation would have been too difficult.[75]

All 'manner of excuses', recalled Prince Ludwig Windischgraetz, were advanced to keep royal mourners away from Vienna.[76] A single, consistent pretext might have passed without comment – after all, everyone was sympathetic to the old emperor and could easily believe that he would find the ceremonies surrounding a large royal gathering tiring – but the shifting excuses merely undermined the case being made. Franz Josef might well have found the funeral ceremonies an unwelcome ordeal, but setting aside personal preference and accepting temporary discomfort came with ruling an empire. By turning mourners away, inventing plots, and bolstering admittedly weak arguments with changing justifications, the court inadvertently revealed its likely real concern: to keep any distinguished visitors away because, as historian Joachim Remak wrote, their presence would accord too much honour to the morganatic Sophie, 'a former lady-in-waiting'.[77]

This vendetta had plagued Sophie in life, subjecting her to scurrilous gossip and her husband to bitter resentment. Now it continued in death, as an amazed Vienna prepared for the most peculiar imperial funeral it had ever witnessed. Reduced pomp was the order from a Montenuovo determined to 'demonstrate that man and wife could not expect to be equal in death' precisely because 'they had never been equal in life'.[78] No one would ever forget the 'startlingly simple' ceremonies about to take place, 'so insulting', an outraged Vienna *Reichspost* declared, 'to the feelings of a grieving people'.[79]

EIGHTEEN

United in Death

✛

The train carrying Franz Ferdinand and Sophie finally reached Vienna's Südbahnhof a little after ten on the night of 2 July. As funeral processions for deceased Habsburgs took place after sunset, the timing of the arrival merely followed custom. Not so the other orders that Montenuovo issued. He had wanted no representative of the imperial family present, but Archduke Karl rebuffed him and stood in silent respect as the train halted.

Although Franz Ferdinand had been inspector general, the elite of the armed forces were conspicuous in their absence. Officers from every regiment in which he had served or had commanded should have walked in the cortège; so, too, should representatives from all branches of the army and the navy. With the emperor's permission, Montenuovo denied these honours; Sophie was not entitled to share in her husband's military honours in life, and the court decided that she could not now share them in death. Members of the 7th Uhlan Life Guards regiment were actually confined to their barracks to prevent their participation; two days later, though, they were summoned to Vienna to march in the funeral of an undistinguished general. Recently nine officers and enlisted men of the empire's fledgling air force had been killed; high-ranking officers had attended their joint funeral. For the dead archduke, only non-commissioned officers who served as valets to senior officers were allowed to participate and carry the coffins to the waiting hearses.[1]

It was a warm night; a dim moon hung in the Vienna sky, illuminating the eerie scene.[2] On the surface, the pageantry seemed impressive as the procession set off through the city streets. Grooms in gold-braided liveries marched at the front of the cortège, holding aloft shimmering lanterns; behind them came a small detachment of non-commissioned officers from the 7th Lancers cavalry regiment, courtiers on horseback, and carriages filled with adjutants and chamberlains. Six black horses, their hooves muffled in felt, pulled the two hearses; that bearing Franz Ferdinand's coffin was larger, more imposing, while Sophie's coffin rested in a smaller hearse. Five non-commissioned officers and twelve extra members of the Life Guards, with drawn sabres or halberds, trotted along the sides of the cortège over the uneven cobblestones. More grooms, more swaying lanterns, and more carriages with courtiers preceded a lancer cavalry division at the rear.[3]

The procession passed the Belvedere and reached the Hofburg just as clock chimes struck eleven. Passing through the ornate Renaissance *Schweizertor*, the cortege halted as non-commissioned officers lifted the two coffins from their hearses and ascended the Ambassadors' Staircase, where they were blessed and incensed by the clergy as the court choir sang Palestrina's *Miserere*. Two members of the Life Guard Archers, two members of the Hungarian Life Guards, and eight pages holding lighted tapers flanked the coffins, followed by extra men from the Life Guards and Cavalry Life Guards. As the choir sang, the coffins were carried through the doors of the Hofkapelle and placed on biers at the front of the chapel.[4]

The chapel's white walls had been draped in black crêpe, its altars covered with black velvet cloths sewn with Franz Ferdinand's coat of arms. A catafalque covered in cloth of gold stretched in front of the main altar; above it, lengths of crêpe draped from a gilded baldachin to the transept's four corners. Tall silver candlesticks, each holding a single lighted white taper, surrounded the biers with a sea of soft, flickering light, illuminating the honour guard: ten members of the Life Guard Archers in red tunics and white breeches, and ten Hungarian Life Guards in scarlet and silver-laced tunics with dolmans draped over their shoulders, heads bowed, gloved hands resting on drawn swords.[5]

Again, it all seemed impressive, but appearances were deceptive. The dead couple's coats of arms, reported a diplomat's daughter, looked 'as though they had been done by a child in rather crude colours'.[6] The bodies remained in the two different closed coffins supplied in Sarajevo. It would have been an easy task to place them in matching coffins when they arrived in Vienna, yet the obvious distinction between the archduke's larger, gilt bronze coffin and Sophie's smaller, less ornate silver casket served as a welcome visual reminder of their unequal status. This was not the only difference: the bier holding Franz Ferdinand's coffin was larger and higher – a full eighteen inches higher – than that on which Sophie's coffin rested, another unsubtle reminder of her morganatic position. An array of red and gold velvet cushions at the foot of Franz Ferdinand's coffin prominently displayed the symbols of his imperial and military ranks: his archducal crown, his admiral's hat, his general's hat, his ceremonial sword, and his medals and awards. Sophie's orders were also present, but for her, a black fan and a pair of white gloves – symbols of a noble lady – were the items most prominently displayed.[7]

The doors to the Hofkapelle opened to the public at eight o'clock on the morning of Friday 3 July. More than fifty thousand people had waited through the night to pay their respects, but such a show of public sympathy was unwanted. Crown Prince Rudolf had lain in state for an entire day, and the viewing period had been extended when the lines proved too long; Archduke Albrecht, who had been inspector general of the Imperial Army, had lain in state in 1895 for two successive mornings and an afternoon.[8] For Franz Ferdinand and Sophie, public viewing was restricted to a mere four hours. In contravention of precedent, Montenuovo declared that only two people could enter the Hofkapelle at a time as masses were sung.[9] One visitor noted 'a priest mumbling away at a very shoddy looking service. I mean, there was nothing – it was very, very shabby.'[10] Although the lines of mourners waiting to pay their respects stretched far back along the Ringstrasse, the doors of the chapel were firmly closed to the public at noon, and tens of thousands were turned away.[11]

Sophie, Max and Ernst came to Vienna with their mother's siblings, staying at the Belvedere with their step-grandmother Maria Theresa and Aunt Henriette. They were not allowed to attend their parents' funeral service in the Hofkapelle; as morganatic descendants of a morganatic marriage, they were deemed unworthy to share the last honours in Vienna with Franz Josef and other members of the imperial house. They were even forbidden to follow the coffins through the streets after the service had ended.[12]

There was, though, a poignant reminder of the absent children throughout the funeral service, a large wreath of white roses standing in front of their parents' coffins with a ribbon inscribed simply 'Sophie, Max, Ernst'.[13] Tributes crowded the chapel: flowers sent by the kaiser; a wreath of white roses laid on behalf of King George and Queen Mary bearing the inscription 'In a token of friendship and affection, from George R and I'; sprays from Europe's royal families and from foreign heads of state, including one on behalf of the American people from President Woodrow Wilson; and even a wreath from the Shoemakers Guild of Lower Austria. Among the Habsburgs, only former crown princess Stephanie had sent a wreath; from the other members of the imperial family, there was nothing.[14]

The funeral took place at four that afternoon. British ambassador Maurice de Bunsen noted that 'much comment has been called forth by the decision to hold the funeral service in the very small Hofburg Chapel, instead of selecting a church capable of holding a much greater number of people.'[15] Many members of the aristocracy were excluded: Even Sophie's brother Wolfgang was denied entrance to the Vienna service.[16] The emperor, wearing the white tunic of an army general and joined by the archdukes and archduchesses, watched from the chapel gallery.[17] Courtiers, government ministers, provincial representatives, the mayors of Vienna and of Budapest, the president of the Austrian parliament, and other senior civic officials filled the chapel, along with members of the diplomatic corps representing their governments. Europeans had been seated in the first pews; the American representative found himself hidden away in the second gallery near the top of the chapel.[18]

Bells tolled as Cardinal Piffl, the archbishop of Vienna, consecrated the coffins with incense and holy water. The choir sang the *Libera*, although there was no accompaniment by an orchestra or even the chapel organ, as was customary.[19] The requiem lasted a mere fifteen minutes, dispensing with a mass, the usual prayers, the traditional hymns, and other religious and ceremonial trappings that had always accompanied other imperial services.[20] Nikitsch-Boulles, Franz Ferdinand's secretary, was seated to the side of the altar and watched the emperor throughout the inexplicably brief requiem. He saw 'not a trace of emotion or sorrow' on his face; instead, Franz Josef looked around 'with complete indifference and the same unmoved facial expressions that he displayed towards his subjects during other occasions. One had the involuntary feeling that Franz Josef was breathing again freely, as if liberated, and doubtless most of his old courtiers shared this feeling.' When it was over, the emperor was the first to rise and abruptly leave the chapel, without 'casting as much as a glance at the two coffins'.[21] As soon as the brief service ended, the doors of the Hofkapelle were closed and locked. For the first time in history, an heir to the Austrian throne had been denied a state funeral.

Six hours passed as the coffins lay in the empty chapel before night fell, interrupted by the arrival of Sophie, Max and Ernst, who were finally allowed to pay their respects when the requiem was over and the official mourners had departed.[22] Escorted by their aunt Henriette, they entered the chapel at half-past seven and, in 'a heart-wrenching scene', cried before their parents' coffins. Before leaving, young Sophie quietly said, 'God wanted Mami and Papi to join Him at the same time. It's best that they died together, because Papi couldn't live without Mami, and

Mami couldn't have gone on without Papi.'[23] At ten that night, noncommissioned officers carried the caskets into the Schweizerhof and loaded them onto the two waiting hearses as members of the court clergy offered a final blessing. More grooms holding swaying lanterns led the cortège through the streets, accompanied by courtiers, a cavalry division, and members of the Life Guards. Once again, no high-ranking military or naval officials escorted the late inspector general.[24] Breaking precedent, Montenuovo had ordered that no tolling bells were to mark the procession and that no stops were to be made at churches along the route for the customary prayers.[25] Montenuovo had also forbidden displays of respect or condolence by the military during the procession, since Sophie was not entitled to such honours.[26] Hearing this, Archduke Karl again interceded with the emperor. Common soldiers from the Vienna garrison, Franz Josef agreed, could line the streets if they wished, but only with the permission of their commanding officers.[27]

To avoid overt displays of pageantry, Montenuovo requested that court chamberlains, privy councillors, high-ranking courtiers, and knights of the Order of the Golden Fleece stay away from the final procession to the train station.[28] This pettiness led to open revolt, 'an unprecedented infringement' on the Lord Chamberlain's 'narrow-minded' protocol. As the hearses left the Hofburg Chapel, a hundred aristocrats – Fuggers and Hohenlohes, Kinskys and Fürstenbergs, Lobkowiczs and Liechtensteins – abruptly joined the cortège on foot, following behind the coffins in a spontaneous tribute that was as much in honor of the dead couple as it was a silent rebuke to Montenuovo.[29] British ambassador de Bunsen noted the general feelings of satisfaction over the unfolding scene, which he took as a clear sign that 'something more must be done to mark the solemnity of the occasion than what took place on the previous night'.[30] As they walked, remembered Margutti, 'many of them passed uncomplimentary remarks, not only about Prince Montenuovo but also, though in veiled form, about the old Emperor'.[31]

Resentment over the abbreviated ceremonies, insisted a recent author, was confined to a handful of the archduke's staff and his 'highly excitable friends'.[32] The newspapers and the public at large, though, were not Franz Ferdinand's 'highly excitable friends'. Too many on all sides of the political spectrum echoed the sentiments. There were widespread complaints. 'Many members of Austria's aristocracy', one correspondent noted, 'feel that the kind of persistent ostracism the duchess faced in life was even more disrespectful in death.'[33] There was, reported another journalist, 'much indignation in Vienna; people openly blame the court and the emperor for the reduced honours given to the august dead'.[34] People, recorded one diplomat, whispered, 'The Imperial Family has no respect, not even for the dead. Their hate pursues its victims beyond the tomb.'[35] 'I was indignant', wrote Prince Ludwig Windischgraetz, 'that every ass should now give the dead lion a kick.'[36] 'There was a general feeling of indignation,' recorded Eisenmenger, 'at the lack of reverence with which the department of the Lord High Steward proceeded with regard to the deceased.'[37] Eugen Ketterl, the emperor's faithful and servile valet, noted that the ceremonies in Vienna justifiably 'caused anger and indignation'.[38] Margutti thought that the emperor had made 'a serious mistake' in reducing 'the pomp of the funeral rites to a minimum'.[39] Even the British ambassador, reporting the 'widespread complaints of the insufficiency of the funeral honours', found it hard to understand.[40] 'It is difficult to believe', he wrote, 'that there could have been any intention to conduct the proceedings in a manner unbefitting the exalted rank of the victims.' Perhaps the ceremonies had been abridged at the request of the emperor, he speculated, to avoid tiring him or interrupting his holiday at Ischl.[41] 'As regards ceremonial,' he reported, someone had assured him that 'the ancient custom has been observed'.[42]

With only six months' tenure in Vienna, de Bunsen might be forgiven his ignorance of how insulting those versed in traditional Habsburg ceremonial found the service and processions. For the death of Viennese mayor Josef Neumayer two years earlier, the imperial court had ordered all shops closed during the funeral; 'for Archduke Franz Ferdinand and the Duchess of Hohenberg', a reporter noted, 'there were no such orders'. The ceremonies in 1914, people complained, 'showed a cold and reckless indifference toward human feeling'.[43] A number of aristocrats threatened to resign their court positions in protest, and just as many demanded that Montenuovo be dismissed from his post.[44] The outcry was so great that Franz Josef took the unprecedented step of publicly defending Montenuovo in the pages of the official *Wiener Zeitung*. The prince, the emperor insisted, enjoyed his 'full confidence'. The funeral arrangements for the archduke, which had been carried out according to the emperor's instructions, demonstrated Montenuovo's 'great and unselfish devotion to My Person and to My House'. They were merely the latest example of his 'excellent and faithful service'.[45] However, no words could erase the painful impressions that lingered in the wake of the Vienna ceremonies.

Montenuovo's pattern of vindictiveness reached beyond the city. 'I'll get the bodies to the railway station for you,' he had callously told Nikitsch-Boulles, 'onto a freight car, and on a train; what you do with them after that is your business.'[46] Montenuovo completely washed his hands of the man he had despised in life and the woman for whom he had had nothing but animosity. He even insisted that it was up to Sophie, Max and Ernst to pay for the cost of returning their parents' bodies to Artstetten. Only after someone complained to the emperor of this meanness did Franz Josef order his Lord Chamberlain to settle the bills.[47]

Left to organize everything, the late archduke's staff turned to Vienna's Municipal Undertakers. Non-commissioned officers carried the coffins through the Westbahnhof as Franz Ferdinand's nephew Karl and the other archdukes looked on. The railway carriage that would take the bodies to Artstetten was an ordinary freight compartment, hastily transformed by Franz Ferdinand's staff with black crêpe into something resembling a mourning carriage, as Montenuovo refused to provide any suitable transport. The carriage was coupled to a train making a milk run along the Danube basin, and, at 10:40 p.m., it set off into the night.[48]

It was nearly one in the morning when the train pulled into the isolated station at Pöchlarn. Local police and fire brigades, clergy, and members of veterans' assemblies had gathered outside the station, but an unexpected torrential downpour made it impossible to conduct a short service in the square as planned. Someone fetched flowers from the train, hastily decorating the station hall before the coffins were brought in and blessed before a small crowd filling the room. 'The scene was startling,' wrote one correspondent. 'The railway lobby was jammed. On one side stood the coffins, surrounded by clergy and mourners; on the other, people lay on benches, trying to sleep while awaiting their trains, or talked so loudly that it was difficult to hear the priests. Everyone was offended and complained about the lack of respect.'[49] When it was over, twelve non-commissioned officers from the 4th Dragoon and the 7th Uhlan Life Guard regiments carried the caskets into the wild night, loading them onto two plain black hearses supplied by the Vienna Municipal Undertakers. Although it was nearly two in the morning, residents of the village still stood along the streets to pay their last respects; high winds whipped the black mourning pennants hanging from building facades and lamps into eerie shapes as lightning flashed across the sky.[50]

Members of Franz Ferdinand and Sophie's household and staff, crowded five to a rented carriage, followed the procession to the edge of the Danube. No bridge existed, and so the cortège swayed and slipped on the rainy decks of a small ferry. The storm was at its height, the turbulent river splashing against the vessel, thunder shaking the sky and lightning illuminating the scene. Terrified at the noise, the horses shied, and one of the hearses slid backward until its rear wheels hung over the deck. Only with great difficulty did the mourners struggle out of their carriages and pull the hearse out of danger. Finally at five, just as the dawn was breaking, the rain-soaked procession climbed the hillside to Artstetten.[51]

Sophie, Max and Ernst had spent the night of their parents' funeral at the Belvedere, restless and sad as the hours ticked by. They left early the next morning by train for Artstetten, never to return to their home in Vienna; the Belvedere was an imperial palace, and as morganatic descendants they were no longer entitled to live in its opulent rooms. Sophie's siblings escorted the children onto the train and rode with them. In a separate compartment rode the more distinguished mourners: Archduchess Maria Theresa and her two daughters; Zita and her mother-in-law, Maria Josepha; Archduke Maximilian; Princess Elisabeth of Liechtenstein; Duke Miguel and Duchess Maria Theresa of Braganza; Duke Albrecht of Württemberg; Prince Alfonso of Bourbon; Infanta Maria Josepha, Duchess of Bavaria; and others. Montenuovo had ordered that the morganatic Hohenberg children were not to share compartments with their father's illustrious relatives. Some seven hundred wreaths, including one from Karl and Zita, filled two additional train carriages.[52] It was a little after eight when the train reached Pöchlarn; Archduke Karl, who had arrived on a separate train two hours earlier, joined them in a convoy of motor cars and hired carriages for the drive up to Artstetten. The storm had left the road a bed of mud; several times, vehicles slid and became stuck, forcing the mourners to get out and wade through the morass before finally reaching the castle.[53]

Montenuovo had refused to assist in the transport of the bodies or the funeral arrangements at Artstetten, but this did not stop him from attempting one last act of revenge against Franz Ferdinand and Sophie. Representatives of the empire's great aristocratic families had been excluded from the previous day's fifteen-minute funeral service in Vienna; now, the Lord Chamberlain, 'determined to exact the rigours of etiquette to the last humiliation', ordered them to attend a longer requiem in the capital.[54] This was scheduled, one suspects not accidentally, to coincide exactly with the funeral at Artstetten, thus ensuring that they would not dignify the proceedings with their presence. At least this seems to have been his hope, but many infuriated aristocrats rebelled at the punitive decree and arrived at Artstetten in open defiance of the court.[55]

Another mourner arrived from Munich. This was Franz Ferdinand's exiled brother Ferdinand Karl, who had been stripped of his rank, titles, and incomes and expelled from the country after contracting a morganatic marriage with Bertha Czuber. At first the emperor refused him permission to attend; only after Maria Theresa personally appealed to him did Franz Josef finally grant his request to pay his last respects to his brother, and then only on the condition that he use the name of his exile, Herr Burg, and that no one address him as 'Imperial Highness'. The mourners, Nikitsch-Boulles noted, quickly ignored this rule.[56]

Franz Ferdinand and Sophie's funeral took place in the Chapel of St James the Apostle at Artstetten at eleven that morning. The crowd of mourners gathered beneath the vaulted roof hung with silver chandeliers, listening as Prelate Dobner von Dobneau from the nearby Maria Tafel Monastery conducted the 'simple but dignified' service as noncommissioned officers from the 4th Dragons and the 7th Uhlan Life Guards Regiment stood guard. At the end of the service, Sophie, Max and Ernst slowly approached the coffins hand in hand. 'They kept their heads down,' a correspondent noted, 'and at times sobs shook their little bodies. Handkerchiefs constantly fluttered near their eyes.'[57]

By noon it was over: the chapel bells tolled as Uhlan guards lifted the archduke's coffin from its bier and carried it outside, followed by huntsmen from Konopischt bearing Sophie's casket. The storm had returned, and the heavens poured down as the sad procession made its way to the new crypt Franz Ferdinand had built just below the chapel. There was a sharp turn as they entered; the archduke had often joked about it, saying that when he died inevitably his bearers would accidentally hit the wall with his coffin. His prediction now came true. As they struggled to manoeuvre around the corner, the men knocked the gilt bronze coffin into the doorway's edge, chipping plaster and barely managing to hold on to their burden before reaching the vaulted alcove.[58] In tears, Max walked forward, hand in hand with his siblings, and placed a small photograph of the three children on their father's coffin before leaving the crypt.[59] Here, in identical white marble tombs engraved with Latin inscriptions reading *Iuncti coniugio Fatis iunguntur eisdem* (*Joined in marriage, they were joined by the same fate*), Franz Ferdinand and Sophie would rest for eternity.

NINETEEN

Headlong Toward Oblivion

✛

Sarajevo, most people agreed, had been a tragedy; few, though, expected serious repercussions as that halcyon summer of 1914 spread out before them. Unrest and localized conflicts broke out all the time, but there had been no major European hostilities since the 1870 Franco-Prussian War, and none was expected now. Given that the conspirators had been Serb nationalists, people expected some Austrian sabre rattling and diplomatic threats against Belgrade but ultimately believed that peace would prevail. So aristocratic thoughts turned to pleasure: the end of the London season, holidays at Marienbad and Deauville, gambling at Monte Carlo, lavish dinners at Maxim's in Paris, and yachting at Kiel or Cowes. No one suspected that the complacent Edwardian age was over, soon to be replaced by a twentieth century christened in Franz Ferdinand and Sophie's blood.

It took thirty days for the old order to hurl itself headlong toward oblivion, as details behind the assassinations slowly emerged. Only Mehmedbašić escaped, fleeing to Montenegro, which, despite an extradition treaty, refused to hand him over to Austria and arranged for his escape. Princip and Čabrinović had been arrested, and Sarajevo judge Leo Pfeffer spent several days questioning them about the crime. Their eventual admissions carefully concealed the role of the Black Hand and Serbian intelligence officials. More details fell into place once Ilić, Grabež, Cubrilović, and Popović were rounded up and interrogated. Within a week of the assassination, Austrian officials knew that high-ranking Serb nationalist officers, including Major Tankosić and Milan Ciganović, had trained Princip and his comrades in Belgrade and armed them with bombs and revolvers from Serbian military arsenals and that Serbian state employees had helped smuggle them into Bosnia.[1] Although changing stories and deliberate lies led Austria to erroneously blame Narodna Odbrana for instigating and aiding the conspiracy, the essentials of the Austrian charge were correct.

Serbia swung wildly between apparent conciliation and open defiance. Two days after the assassination, Belgrade assured Vienna that it would 'do everything to prove that it would not tolerate within its borders the fostering of any agitation . . . calculated to disturb the delicate relationship with Austria-Hungary'.[2] Yet within hours of this message, the Foreign Ministry in Belgrade greeted Austrian requests for cooperation with a curt and dismissive 'Nothing has been done so far, and the matter does not concern the Serbian Government.'[3]

Vienna now believed it had sufficient cause to move against Belgrade. Conrad von Hötzendorf, as might be expected, immediately pushed for action against Serbia, but diplomats were somewhat more cautious; war might be necessary – even desirable – but if it came it needed both public support and the agreement of Austria-Hungary's principal ally, Germany. The first issue soon resolved itself: Franz Ferdinand hadn't been universally beloved, but many *had* looked to him as the empire's future salvation. There was outrage that Sophie had been killed. The assassination in Sarajevo at the hands of terrorists with admitted ties to officials in Serbia hardened attitudes against Belgrade. Worse, open celebration of the assassination by elements of the Serbian press inflamed Austrian opinion. When Vienna protested, Serbian prime minister Pašić insisted that he could not intervene against a free press unless it engaged in 'revolutionary propaganda' or '*lèse-majesté*' against the Serbian throne. This excuse didn't appease Vienna: Pašić would act if Belgrade papers printed something objectionable about the Serbian king, but gleeful articles about the assassination of the heir to Austria-Hungary were deemed acceptable.[4] It all contributed, as British ambassador in Vienna Sir Maurice de Bunsen noted, to increasingly ugly sentiments. There was a growing sense in Austria, he reported, that she 'would lose her position as a Great Power if she stood any further nonsense from Serbia'.[5]

Austria now sounded out possible German reaction if a conflict with Serbia became inevitable. To this end, Franz Josef wrote an impassioned letter to the kaiser decrying 'this horde of criminal agitators in Belgrade . . . The bloody deed was not the work of a single individual but a well organized plot whose threads extend to Belgrade. Although it may be impossible to establish the complicity of the Serbian government, no one can doubt that its policy of uniting all Southern Slavs under the Serbian flag encourages such crimes and that the constitution of this situation is a chronic peril for my House and my territories.' He added, 'It must be the future task of my Government to bring about the isolation and diminution of Serbia.'[6]

Outraged by the murder of his friend and regarding Serbia as a nation of brigands, Wilhelm II agreed, advising Austria to quickly settle accounts with the troublesome Balkan country before any other country could object or interfere. It was, he said, 'purely Austria's affair' and should not involve the German military. The kaiser envisioned not a war but rather an immediate, limited military incursion designed to round up the conspirators and expose the Serbian government's complicity. Russia, he was sure, would not intercede 'because the Tsar would not support' royal assassins. Serbia would bow to Austrian demands and the issue would be settled within a few days.[7]

Austria dragged the situation out. Officials in Vienna spent some two weeks arguing over and drafting the list of formal demands they would present to Serbia. The document was not, as often described, an ultimatum, which suggested a military response. Rather, the Austrian note was a démarche, a formal list of demands to Serbia accompanied by a time limit and a threatened break in diplomatic relations.[8]

Everyone, including officials in Belgrade, knew it was coming. Through diplomatic channels, Serbia hinted that their cooperation would be limited. A week before seeing the note, Belgrade spread word that it would reject any requests for a joint Austrian-Serbian commission of inquiry, refuse to hand over any suspects to Austria, ignore any calls for suppression of inflammatory nationalist societies, and oppose any efforts to censor provocative newspapers that had hailed the assassination, insisting that such measures would 'imply foreign intervention in domestic affairs'.[9] A few days later, Pašić alerted his legations that the country would 'never comply with demands which may be directed against the dignity of Serbia, and which would be unacceptable to any country which respects and maintains its independence.'[10]

At six on the evening of Thursday 23 July, the Austrian minister at Belgrade presented the démarche to Serbia's minister of finance. After outlining evidence that the assassination had been planned in Belgrade and aided by Serbian officials, it laid out ten demands. These included suppression of all publications engaged in anti-Austrian propaganda; dissolution of Serb nationalistic societies that promoted violence against Austria; elimination of anti-Austrian educational propaganda used in Serbian schools; dismissal of all military and civil officials shown to promote anti-Austrian propaganda; suppression of calls for Serbian unification with Bosnia; a joint investigation in Serbia of the assassination and trial of any suspects arrested; immediate arrest of Tankosić and Ciganović; guarantees that Serbia would prevent illegal transport of arms and explosives into Bosnia and punish frontier officials who had smuggled the conspirators across the border; explanation for comments by Serbian officials expressing hostile attitudes toward Austria; and confirmation that the Serbian government meant to act on the listed items. The note appended evidence drawn from the conspirators' confessions and demanded an answer no later than 6:00 p.m. on the evening of Saturday 26 July.[11]

It was, to be sure, an imposing and intimidating list. Sir Edward Grey, the British foreign minister, famously described the démarche as 'the most formidable document I have ever seen addressed by one state to another that was independent'.[12] Yet in retrospect, and aside from the regrettably short time limit placed on any response, Austria's demands were not unwarranted. Serbia *had* harboured terrorist groups and allowed anti-Austrian propaganda in its schools and newspapers. Its military and intelligence elite *had* armed and trained the terrorists; its officials *had* helped the terrorists cross into Bosnia; and members of its government, including the prime minister, *had* known of the plot in advance. Pašić had placed personal considerations of his own re-election and safety ahead of his country's fortunes. Serbia could have prevented the assassination, but it had allowed the conspirators to succeed by giving Vienna only a feeble and deliberately ambiguous warning about possible danger in Sarajevo. 'If a government is powerless to enforce the law within its own domains – if it cannot keep its territory from being used to harm other countries – then it forfeits its right to sovereignty in this respect,' historian David Fromkin noted.[13]

Serbian crown prince Alexander, serving as regent for his father, immediately turned to Russia on reading the démarche. 'The demands contained in the Austro-Hungarian Note', he cabled to Tsar Nicholas II, 'are however unnecessarily humiliating for Serbia and incompatible with her dignity as an independent state.' Adding that the country would only accept a certain number of the points, he appealed to the Tsar's 'noble Slav heart' to come to Serbia's defence 'as soon as possible'.[14] Within a day he had his reply. The crown prince could 'rest assured', the Tsar wrote, 'that Russia will in no case disinterest herself in the fate of Serbia'.[15] Armed with this assurance, Belgrade decided to risk the consequences. Political considerations also played a part: Serbian elections were a month away, and Pašić could not afford to be seen as weak when dealing with Austria.[16]

Delivered to the Austrian Embassy in Belgrade shortly before the 6:00 p.m. deadline on 25 July, the Serbian reply was a masterpiece of equivocation. History has usually portrayed it as a near-capitulation, asserting that Serbia agreed to all but two points. In fact, as Fromkin points out, 'historians no longer believe that'.[17] The Serbian text used deliberately ambiguous language, feigned ignorance about Belgrade's knowledge of the plot, lied about conspirators still in Serbia, granted only partial agreement to some conditions, and rejected other demands. Only two of Austria's ten demands were met with anything approaching compliance; answers to the other eight were rewritten in deliberately ambiguous language or rejected altogether.[18] Seeing this, the Austrian minister in Belgrade declared the Serbian reply unsatisfactory and announced a break in diplomatic relations; at half past six that night, the Austrian Embassy staff left the country on a train bound for Vienna.

Serbia knew its reply was a carefully crafted piece of obfuscation and, armed with Russian assurances, apparently anticipated military action. A day before its delivery, Jovanović confided to the French ambassador in Vienna that Serbia was 'ready for a full resistance'. The Serbian army, he said, was strong, and his country counted on rebellion by Slavs in the Habsburg Empire if Austria attacked his country.[19] Three hours before Serbia delivered its reply, it became the first nation to mobilize an army against Austria.[20] At the same time, and probably not without coincidence, Russia began a secret partial mobilization against Austria that had actually been ordered the previous day, later falsifying documents to conceal the fact.[21]

These belligerent moves intensified the pressure on Franz Josef. Precisely what he envisioned remains unclear. Did he think that Austria could conduct a limited military action against Serbia to finally end their anti-Austrian agitation and terrorist activities? Or did he realize that the system of alliances in place across Europe would inevitably lead to a continental war? He apparently struggled with the decision but finally signed the order for mobilization on the evening of 25 July. In doing so, he feared it was the beginning of the end for Austria. 'If the Monarchy must perish,' he commented bitterly, 'let it at least perish decently.'[22] Within ten days, all of Europe was engaged in a fatal waltz of war.

The young men whose actions had precipitated catastrophe sat in jail cells as the war began, awaiting trial. Bosnian law gave them the gift of life they had taken from Franz Ferdinand and Sophie; it was illegal, according to the country's constitution, to execute anyone under the age of twenty, even those convicted of murder. This knowledge gave Princip and his comrades a certain air of disdain when their trial finally began in October 1914, in a makeshift courtroom at Sarajevo's Filippović Barracks.

A tribunal of three judges would decide guilt or innocence. The conspirators all took the stand but lied about the plot, denying that officials in Belgrade had known of its existence or aided its success. 'I do not feel like a criminal', Princip insisted, 'because I put away the one who was doing evil.'[23] He claimed that Sophie's death had been an accident. This wasn't convincing. Several seconds elapsed before Princip fired his fatal shots; standing less than five feet from the side of the vehicle where Sophie sat, he could not have failed to see her. Indeed, he even admitted that he briefly hesitated on catching sight of the duchess but acted anyway.

Grabež, too, admitted guilt, though the assassination, he insisted, was 'one of the greatest works in history'.[24] Čabrinović tried to emulate these attitudes at first, saying he had participated in the plot because 'we heard it said that Franz Ferdinand was an enemy of the Slavs', but then the facade cracked. 'All of us', he said cautiously, 'nevertheless feel very sorry, because we did not know that the late Franz Ferdinand was the father of a family. We were greatly touched by the last words he uttered to his wife.' Then, in a low voice, he added, 'I humbly submit my apologies to the children of the Heir Apparent and ask them to forgive us.' This was too much for Princip, who jumped from his seat shouting that Čabrinović wasn't speaking for him.[25] 'I have nothing to say in my defence,' Princip declared defiantly.[26]

The tribunal handed down varying sentences. Princip, Čabrinović, and Grabež were to be imprisoned for twenty years. Danilo Ilić, the oldest of the plotters, was sentenced to death by hanging, as was Cubrilović; Popović received thirteen years in prison.[27]

The three young men who had so inadvertently changed the world passed their last years at the Theresienstadt Prison in Bohemia, in harsh conditions that no doubt exacerbated their tubercular conditions. Grabež succumbed to illness in October 1916. Princip lasted longest, despite having unsuccessfully tried to hang himself with a towel. The Great War, he insisted, had nothing to do with the assassination; a visiting doctor recorded that Princip 'cannot feel himself responsible for the catastrophe'.[28] Tuberculosis ravaged Princip in his last years; his left arm was amputated, and his weight was less than ninety pounds when he finally died on 28 April 1918.[29]

Nedeljko Čabrinović had been the first of the trio to die, but not before a remarkable scene took place in his prison cell. Sophie, Max, and Ernst never set foot in the Sarajevo courtroom, but they heard about Čabrinović's apologies. In a gesture of magnanimity that would have put the icy imperial court to shame, Sophie and Max wrote the young assassin a letter; only Ernst refused to sign it.[30] Jesuit Father Anton Puntigam, who had given Franz Ferdinand and Sophie last rites, carried the message to Theresienstadt and handed it over to Čabrinović in his cell. Sophie and Max, their letter read, knew that the young conspirator had expressed his regrets and apologized on the stand. His conscience could be at peace: they completely forgave him his part in the deaths of their parents.[31]

It was 23 January 1916 when Sophie, Max and Ernst got word that Čabrinović had died. Their gesture was as much an expression of their deep religious faith as it was evidence of the optimistic way in which the orphaned trio had been brought up. Life would be difficult for them, their parents had always known. As morganatic descendants of the presumed future emperor of Austria, Sophie, Max and Ernst would inhabit the shadows, caught in a chasm between their father's glittering universe and their mother's tenuous social acceptance. Franz Ferdinand and

Sophie had armed them with pragmatic optimism to survive in a world where they would never be recognized as Habsburgs.

That they were figures of sympathy no one could doubt. Sophie's niece Elisabeth de Baillet-Latour poured out her grief over 'those poor, gentle children' in a letter to Queen Mary. Sophie, Max and Ernst, she declared, had been

> *brought up in continual contact with their parents, and such parents, too!*
> *They have never known anything that hurts: they were overshowered with*
> *the most wonderful love and care and tenderness always, and their home was*
> *such as one reads of in books, but never meets in life. And now they are*
> *standing there, all alone, and their whole lives wrecked, they whose little*
> *lives were built absolutely on one thing only: the love and the tender*
> *watchful care of their father and mother. They don't even know who and*
> *what they are, and nobody will ever understand them, they are the most*
> *sensitive, clinging, tenderhearted little children.*[32]

The two bullets fired that fateful Sunday morning had stripped the nearly thirteen-year-old Sophie, twelve-year-old Max, and ten-year-old Ernst of youthful innocence. They now faced an unfamiliar universe. They had not remained at Artstetten following their parents' funeral but returned to Chlumetz. Later that 4 July in 1914, their passing train stopped in Vienna. For the second and last time in their lives, they met the emperor, in a private and rather formal twenty-minute audience at Schönbrunn.[33] 'Franz Josef', comments Franz Ferdinand's great-granddaughter Princess Sophie, 'wasn't a very warm-hearted person, so it was a bit cool.'[34] After hearing his condolences, the three orphans never saw him again.[35]

The concerns of their new universe soon became apparent. Confounding stories about his alleged miserliness and exaggerated tales of greed, Franz Ferdinand died in debt. He wasn't impoverished – his estate had considerable value – but of actual cash there was almost nothing, and what remained was owed as payment on previous bank loans.

Sophie's personal estate was valued at roughly 2.2 million crowns (approximately £7,000,000 in 2013 figures), and just over 200 pieces of jewellery, along with dresses and furs, bank accounts, and securities, which was divided between her children.[36] By the terms of Franz Ferdinand's 1907 will, the Este inheritance, along with various Modena properties in Vienna and Italy, went to Archduke Karl. Hoping to provide for the children, Franz Ferdinand's lawyer had arranged for the Imperial Collection in Vienna to purchase the archduke's folk art and other artefacts for display in public museums. This brought in 500,000 crowns (approximately £1,500,000 in 2013 figures) that Prince Jaroslav Thun, named executor of his late brother-in-law's estate, promptly invested for the three orphans. Franz Ferdinand named Sophie as his principal beneficiary; as she had died with him, the bulk of the estate, including Konopischt, Artstetten, Lölling, and several properties in Vienna, went to Max. Ernst received Chlumetz, and both he and Sophie were given financial settlements. Still, the lack of cash meant endless worries; keeping up the estates and paying salaries and pensions quickly depleted available funds. Finally, Franz Josef provided them with an annual stipend of 400,000 crowns (approximately £1,300,000 in 2013 figures).[37]

Prince Thun and his wife, Maria, did their best to surround Sophie, Max and Ernst with love and attention; so, too, did their aunt Henriette, who became like a second mother. Sophie commemorated that role in a series of paintings depicting baby chicks that had lost their parents only to be rescued by a new hen, in an obvious reference to her beloved aunt. Henriette, as Max's granddaughter Princess Anita recalls, 'tried to soothe the children through this terrible drama'. Ernst, especially, needed the attention. Depression, loss of appetite, and frequent illness characterized the years immediately after his parents' assassinations. Eventually, though, the resiliency of youth and religious faith buoyed spirits in the protective cocoon created by relatives. Determined that 'they should have a joyous youth' despite their loss, Henriette ensured not merely attention but also comforting familiarity.[38]

Days passed quietly in Vienna and at Artstetten, but the three preferred to spend most of their time at Konopischt, which they regarded as
their real home. Private tutors continued their educations; Max and Ernst
sat for examinations at Vienna's Schottengymnasium. Giving the lie to
notions that Franz Ferdinand and Sophie had been difficult and demanding employers, most members of their household and staff remained
in dedicated service to their children, even when it meant financial hardship. Montenuovo had ruthlessly informed the faithful Janaczek, for example, that as his master was dead, his position as an imperial employee
had ended. Not only would there be no salary from Vienna, but also no
pension. Unbowed by these callous decisions, Janaczek simply followed
Sophie, Max and Ernst to Konopischt.[39]

Konopischt was a bastion of serenity in an increasingly troubled
world. Europe shuddered and shook as young men died in muddy
trenches to the accompanying whirl of artillery shells, but the wooded
Bohemian countryside and fragrant rose garden seemed a million miles
away. The first orphans of the war, though, saw the hospital trains, the
troops crowded aboard transports carrying them away to certain death,
and the rationing that kept forbidden luxuries from their table with the
passing months. Europe was changing as a result of the chaos unleashed
in Sarajevo.

Archduchess Maria Theresa saw it coming. Worried about her stepson's children, she decided that it was time to approach the kaiser. He
and Franz Ferdinand had spent those two days at Konopischt in June
1914, admiring roses and discussing strategic alliances, but also mulling
over Max's future. War always changed borders, and now Wilhelm II's
suggestion that Max might one day become ruling grand duke of an independent Lorraine suddenly seemed more than idle chatter over tea.
So in 1916 she wrote to the kaiser, gently reminding him of his idea that
would ensure the children's security. Stories that Wilhelm didn't even
bother to reply are wrong. In fact, he wrote the archduchess a long letter
on the subject. He still supported the idea, but present circumstances

made it impossible to act in a unilateral manner. Officials would have to sign off on the proposal, and it was unlikely that anything could be settled before the war ended. The dream of a new grand duchy fell victim to political expediency.[40]

On 21 November 1916, after nearly sixty-eight years on the throne, Franz Josef died at the age of eighty-six. In one of the new Emperor Karl's first acts, he dismissed Montenuovo from service. He then attempted to atone for the harm the prince had done. In 1915, Jaroslav Thun had presented a suggested new coat of arms for the Princely House of Hohenberg to the emperor, but Franz Josef refused to grant such a distinction to his late nephew's orphaned children. Karl proved more amenable, approving the new coat of arms and raising Max from the rank of prince to duke and establishing the House of Hohenberg as part of the empire's hereditary peerage.[41] Karl also wanted to ensure the orphaned children's future. After some discussion, he decided to eliminate the annual stipend they had received from the imperial treasury in exchange for a grant of two income-producing estates, the old hunting lodges of Radmer and Eisenerz, and their surrounding forests rich with timber and game.[42] No matter what happened in the future, Karl's actions ensured that Franz Ferdinand and Sophie's children would no longer be dependent on the fortunes of imperial Austria.

Karl's move was almost uncanny in its presentiment, for within six months the Habsburg Empire was on the brink of disaster. Reserved and deeply religious, Karl was an unfortunate emperor, out of his depth, and completely at odds with the war he had inherited. His pacifist tendencies, in fact, proved his undoing. By the spring of 1918, food shortages, strikes and discontent were spreading; the previous year's Russian Revolution had swept away the ruling Romanov dynasty, and America's entry into the war signalled an ominous turn for the Central Powers. Hoping to save his country needless bloodshed and his throne from the fate of the Romanovs, Karl unsuccessfully tried to arrange a separate peace. When word leaked out, he denied it, but publication of his letters exposed the lie, and dissatisfaction with the monarchy grew.[43]

By November it was all coming to an end; the millions of deaths that followed Sarajevo would finally cease. Berlin was in chaos. On 10 November, the day before the Armistice ended the war, Kaiser Wilhelm II abdicated and fled to Holland. Vienna was in an uproar. Government and military officials flooded into Schönbrunn Palace throughout 11 November, all urging that Karl follow the kaiser's example and abdicate. Hearing this, his wife, Zita, was horrified: 'A King never can abdicate!' she insisted. 'He can only be deposed.' So, egged on by his wife, Karl put his name to a document announcing that he was 'relinquishing' his state functions, a declaration that envisioned a return to power one day.[44]

That day never came. Austria proclaimed itself a republic, and the proud Habsburg dynasty, like the Romanovs in Russia and the Hohenzollerns in Germany, fell victim to the tide of history. Sophie, Max and Ernst had survived much: ambiguous lives in the shadow of the throne, the deaths of their parents, and the hardships of war. Now, with their imperial protector gone and the country of their birth banished to oblivion, they could only speculate what the future held.

TWENTY

Ripples from Sarajevo

⊹

The fall of the Habsburg dynasty broke the ancient and familiar thread that had stitched their archaic empire together. Disparate ethnicities and provinces, previously tied to Vienna only by tradition and imperial conquest, now fragmented. Just as few could have imagined an empire without Franz Josef at its head, so, too, was the sudden change from monarchy to republic an unlikely turn of fate. Yet the revolution spared the Habsburgs from the end suffered by their Russian counterparts, condemning them to exile, not execution.

The official order barring any Habsburgs from the country unless they renounced claims to the non-existent throne didn't affect Sophie, Max or Ernst. They had never been Habsburgs, and the new government recognized the validity of Franz Ferdinand's 1900 renunciation, regarding the three as private individuals. When former Habsburg properties and possessions were nationalized, Sophie, Max and Ernst were exempted.

Things were different, though, in Bohemia. On 28 October 1918, the new nation of Czechoslovakia declared its independence from Austria, a move that signalled trouble for the Hohenbergs at Konopischt. The new government initially placed the estate under the 'protective care' of their new administrator, who ominously spent most of his time taking careful inventory of every item in the castle. As Czech nationalism grew, so, too, did feeling against the former ruling Habsburgs, who were now painted as unwelcome occupiers who had for years abused the country and its people. Newspapers in Prague regaled their readers with tales about Franz Ferdinand and Sophie's alleged stinginess and supposed maltreatment of their staff. Nothing was deemed too absurd. One of the most popular themes was British journalist Henry Wickham Steed's infamous 'Pact of Konopischt', asserting that the archduke and Kaiser Wilhelm II had planned the Great War at the castle in June 1914. It was no more believable in 1919 than it had been when first published in 1916, but many Allied propagandists promoted the story as fact in an effort to blame the conflict solely on Austria and Germany. Nor did the new Czech government prove itself a better judge of fact. Officials from Prague came to Konopischt and spent days searching for an alleged secret, sound-proof room in the castle where, they insisted, the archduke and kaiser had plotted the war.[1]

No trace of this fantasy was ever found, but the growing hysteria blaming the country's misfortunes on Franz Ferdinand and his dynasty made the situation at Konopischt increasingly uncomfortable. At first there were petty annoyances at the hands of Prague's administrator, but soon locals invaded the park, wandering through the gardens, waving the new Czech flag beneath the castle windows, and generally making life unpleasant.[2] With newspapers inflaming public opinion against the late archduke and his family, Sophie's sister Henriette – who had come to live at Konopischt with her niece and nephews – worried about their safety. These were uncertain times for former royalty across the Continent; vengeful mobs occasionally turned ugly. Violence had claimed their parents' lives. Would the orphaned children be next?

Prince Jaroslav Thun decided not to tempt fate. After discussing the situation with his sister-in-law Henriette, he suggested that it would be best for everyone to leave Konopischt and come to live with him and his wife, Maria, in Tetschen. He confided the plan to Count Erwein Nostitz-Rieneck, whose brother Leopold was married to Maria and Henriette's sister Karolina; they decided that the count's younger son, Friedrich, should go to Konopischt and escort Sophie, Max, Ernst and Henriette safely back to Tetschen. Everything was to be done quietly so as not to alert the Czech authorities. Count Friedrich arrived at the castle the first week of April 1919, ostensibly to call on his distant cousins. He even wrote his name into the leather-bound visitors book in the castle's hall, unaware that he was to be Konopischt's last private guest.[3]

On 16 April 1919, before Count Friedrich could spirit Henriette and the three children to safety, the Czechoslovakian government acted. At the time, final approval and ratification of the Treaty of Saint-Germain-en-Laye, which dismembered the old Austro-Hungarian Empire and awarded Bohemia to the new Czech nation, was still five months away, but Prague decided to forgo legal niceties and announced the expropriation of all former Habsburg property. The decision wasn't unique; it had happened in Austria as well. What made the announcement so startling was that the Czech government, against all precedent, tradition and evidence, arbitrarily declared that Sophie, Max and Ernst were something they had never been: Habsburgs, and thus Konopischt and Chlumetz were subject to seizure.[4]

Prague asserted that Article 208 of the Treaty of Saint-Germain-en-Laye justified its action. However, the treaty was not in force in April 1919; not until September 10 was it signed and ratified. The Czech government apparently decided it was better to act illegally than to follow the law. Not that waiting until September would have helped their case, for Article 208 was quite specific. Only 'joint property of the Austro-Hungarian Monarchy, as well as all the property of the Crown, and the private property of members of the former ruling house of Austria-Hungary' could legally be seized.[5]

This was precise language. Konopischt and Chlumetz had never belonged to the Habsburg crown. Private funds had paid for Konopischt's purchase, while Chlumetz was not a Habsburg property but rather came to Franz Ferdinand as part of the Este inheritance. In 1916, both estates had legally gone to his heirs, Konopischt to Max and Chlumetz to Ernst.

Both boys were private citizens. Nor was there any legal room to manoeuvre when it came to designating them as Habsburgs. Prague had
always recognized the validity of Franz Ferdinand's renunciation in
1900; it was not, as they now insisted, merely some private family agreement but instead had been a component of Austro-Hungarian law. Even
the empire's parliaments had taken formal notice of the oath and recognized it as legally valid. None of Franz Ferdinand's children belonged to
the imperial family. If they had, Max, not Karl, would have become
emperor when Franz Josef died in 1916.[6]

Prince Thun immediately protested the expropriation, but the
Czechoslovakian government refused to retreat. Appeals to The Hague
also brought no results, and pleas to the Allied signatories of the Treaty
of Saint-Germain-en-Laye were met with indifference. Signatories were
responsible for the treaty's correct implementation, yet no one seemed
to care that the Czechoslovakian government had acted illegally. Victorious Allied governments had endlessly repeated Steed's 'Pact of Konopischt' lie, and there was little sympathy for the defeated powers and
even less for Franz Ferdinand's family. The archduke's friend the Duke
of Portland asked the British foreign minister to personally intervene
with Czech president Tomáš Masaryk. Masaryk assured him that Max
and Ernst would soon be recognized as rightful owners of the two properties; only the acreage of the estates would be reduced by the state.[7]

The promise bought Prague time, though Czech officials did not keep
their word. The validity of Thun's arguments must have worried them,
for, after more than a year of contentious filings, the Czechoslovakian
government acted unilaterally. In 1921, Prime Minister Edvard Beneš
pushed a bill through parliament meant to address the legal holes in his
case. Ignoring the precise language of Article 208 in the Treaty of Saint-
Germain-en-Laye, this new Law 354 for the first time listed the property
of 'Franz Ferdinand and his descendants' regardless of their morganatic
status. It was a bit of retroactive linguistic manipulation that not only ignored the limited provisions of the treaty but also the fact that Max and

Ernst, specified as private individuals, had held title to both Konopischt and Chlumetz since 1916.[8]

Continued protests were too late to make any difference. On 16 April 1919 – the same day on which the Czech government had jumped the gun and expropriated all Habsburg property – Prague had forcibly expelled Sophie, Max and Ernst from Konopischt without warning. The castle manager simply gave the trio a few minutes to gather their things before evicting them from their home. They were each allowed only a single small suitcase in which to take a few items of clothing and their current schoolbooks. When Max tried to retrieve two family photographs hanging on his bedroom wall, he was rudely told that the items were no longer his to take. Childhood toys, most clothing, photograph albums, letters, diaries, Franz Ferdinand's uniforms, and most of Sophie's jewellery – it was all lost, suddenly deemed state property, though this did not stop Masaryk's wife and daughter from descending on the castle to pilfer its contents. Sophie's furs vanished into Charlotte Masaryk's hands, while her daughter took a finely tooled saddle from the stables that had been the archduke and duchess's last present to Sophie. Before they left, the children's luggage was even searched to ensure that they had taken nothing of value to the Czechoslovakian government. The few items hastily crammed into their suitcases would be the only reminders of the estate all three regarded as their true home. They were even forbidden from setting foot in the country – not to visit relatives or attend funerals – without special permission from the government.[9]

Konopischt and Chlumetz had provided most of Sophie, Max and Ernst's income; now it was lost. They were not impoverished by any reasonable standard; rents from a palace on the Reisnerstrasse and an apartment building in Vienna helped supplement the meagre yield from the forests at Radmer. These were assets, though, not ready cash, and the inflation that followed the war occasionally made life difficult.[10] Still, it was the old Bohemian castle that the family had adored. Konopischt had been home, and Sophie, Max and Ernst never ceased to mourn its loss. 'Memories of this maliciously wrecked paradise of his childhood', remembers Max's son Prince Albrecht, 'stirred him up so much.'[11]

Exiled from Konopischt, Sophie, Max, and Ernst divided their time between Tetschen, Vienna and Artstetten. The old castle above the Danube had never really been the family's home. It had been pleasant enough to spend a few weeks there each summer, but Max, as his son Duke Georg says, 'never really liked Artstetten'.[12] Artstetten, the place where their parents were interred in the church crypt, was largely unfamiliar, without the happy memories at Konopischt.

Aunts and uncles tried to create new memories for the trio, and their step-grandmother Archduchess Maria Theresa became as much of a comforting and stable presence in Sophie, Max and Ernst's lives as she had been for their father. 'I very well remember the warm relationship my father had with his step-grandmother and her daughters,' says Prince Albrecht.[13] It was the archduchess who now cemented ties between Hohenbergs and the exiled Habsburgs. Karl had fled Austria in 1918, spending his last years in forced exile until his premature death in Madeira in 1922. Because he had never actually abdicated, Karl remained emperor to royal legitimists; after his death, his young son Archduke Otto inherited the Habsburg mantle. Archduchess Maria Theresa ensured that ties between her Hohenberg grandchildren and the former imperial family remained strong. Sophie, Max and Ernst accepted without question the old imperial dreams; to them, Otto was always the rightful emperor, and they invariably addressed him as 'Your Majesty'.[14]

The children orphaned by Sarajevo were now young adults and began to make their own ways in the world. Sophie was the first to marry. Although they had met through occasional family gatherings, she found something immensely appealing about her distant cousin Count Friedrich Nostitz-Rieneck when he came to Konopischt in the spring of 1919. The dashing young Bohemian aristocrat had been protective and unsuccessfully tried to spirit the trio away before disaster struck. When they left their home for the last time, he went with them, guarding Sophie, Max, Ernst and Henriette from the ugliness of the nationalistic mobs in the park until they had safely reached Prince Thun. Romance quickly blossomed, and on 8 September 1920, Sophie married Friedrich in the Chapel of St George at Prince Thun's castle in Tetschen (now Decin). As the wife of a Czech national, Sophie was now allowed to re-enter the country, quietly settling into private life at her husband's estates of Falkenau and Heinrichsgrün. She gave birth to four children. Erwein, named after her husband's father, was born in 1921; when a second son was born in 1923, he was called Franz after the late archduke. Two more children followed: Alois, in 1925, and Sophie, born in 1929. She now saw less of Max and Ernst; the Czech government still insisted that the brothers could not enter the country without first obtaining official permission.[15]

Shortly after her wedding, the government in Prague let Sophie visit Konopischt. It was a strange experience. The castle had been opened to the public, and she crowded along with tourists inspecting her former home. Taking pity on her, authorities let Sophie retrieve a few personal items from her old rooms, but none of her parents' photograph albums, letters or diaries. The government continued to insist that even with these small tokens, Franz Ferdinand's descendants must pay for his rumoured past crime in planning the Great War.[16]

Unpleasant rumours also swirled about Franz Ferdinand's alleged illegitimate children, and it was left to Max and Ernst to deal with the delicate situation. Kurt Hahn, whose mother had settled her claim several decades earlier in exchange for financial compensation, repeatedly threatened legal action. In 1915, he purchased a Mercedes motor car and sent the bill to the archduke's legal trustees; although he was given more money from the estate after 1917, he refused to renounce his claims. Aware that the Hohenbergs had limited resources, he next turned his attention to the exiled Empress Zita, threatening to write a scandalous set of memoirs unless she paid for his silence. Though this clumsy blackmail only discredited Hahn, Max worried over his continued public announcements and constant threats of legal action. Lacking any way to resolve the claim, and perhaps wondering if it could be true, he tried to do the honourable thing, authorizing a small monthly payment to Hahn.

However, the archduke's putative son was not a man to keep his silence. Hahn again unsuccessfully tried to sue the archduke's estate in 1939 and even changed his name to Franz Ferdinand Hahn before committing suicide in Baden in 1938.[17]

Max had better luck with Heinrich Jonke, who also claimed that Franz Ferdinand was his father. Supporting evidence had always been weak, but the archduke had provided Jonke's mother with substantial payments. Authorities deemed Jonke mentally unbalanced, allowing him to escape serving in the war, but he continually claimed Franz Ferdinand as his father. In 1919 he tried to publish a book about the archduke but found no takers. Even after he married and had a child, Bertha, Jonke refused to slip into obscurity. This time Max refused to make any payments. When Jonke finally took the case to court, a tribunal in Salzburg declared that his claim was unfounded.[18]

Duke Max of Hohenberg could have dealt with the claims himself: after completing his education in Vienna, he had moved to Graz and obtained a doctorate in law. The subject was distasteful, though, and Max abhorred the public spotlight. Essentially quiet and reserved like his mother, he pressed ahead with life, following his career and starting a family. On 16 November 1926, he wed Elisabeth, Countess of Waldburg zu Wolfegg und Waldsee, an old and distinguished family that the Habsburgs had recognized as equal for marriage. Dividing their time between Artstetten and an apartment in Vienna, the couple had six sons: Franz, born in 1927; Georg in 1929; Albrecht in 1931; Johannes in 1933; Peter in 1936; and Gerhard, born in 1941.[19]

Ernst, too, had quietly slipped into private life. After completing his secondary education, he studied forestry, as his father had always wished. With Chlumetz lost, he now concentrated on improving Radmer and Eisenerz. He was the last of the trio to marry; on 25 May 1936 he wed Marie-Therese Wood in Vienna. Known as Maisie, Ernst's wife was actually a distant relative by marriage. Her father, British diplomat Captain George Wood, worked as a courier at the embassy in Vienna, where he had met and married Hungarian countess Rosa von Lónyay de Nagy-Lónya und Vásáros-Namény; her father's family included former crown princess Stephanie's second husband, Count Elmer Lónyay. In March 1937, the couple celebrated the birth of their first child, a son named Franz Ferdinand in honour of his grandfather.[20]

The arrival of a son was to be the last real joy Ernst would know before his world was turned upside down. Both Max and Ernst were open about their monarchist sympathies and desire to restore the Habsburg throne. To this end, Max served as honorary chairman for the Eisenring, or Iron Ring, an organization that promoted a return to the monarchy under the exiled Archduke Otto. On several occasions in 1936 and 1937, Max encouraged public support for the idea, and Otto rewarded him with the prestigious Order of the Golden Fleece. It was his duty as a loyal aristocrat and a loyal Austrian, he believed, to help his cousin's son reclaim the throne, but Max also feared for the country's future. Incessant military rumblings from Adolf Hitler's Berlin terrified him; already there was talk of a coming Anschluss, the unification of Austria with Germany. The best way to guard against this, both Max and Ernst thought, was to strengthen Austria and arm the country with a strong, respected leader like Otto.[21]

The brothers' pro-monarchist, anti-Hitler sympathies did not go unnoticed in Berlin. They both spoke out openly against Germany and its policies: when posters of Hitler went up on Viennese walls, Ernst was caught tearing them down and was forced to apologize under duress.[22] Noble though the actions were, they marked the Hohenbergs out as enemies of the Nazi regime; Ernst, in particular, received numerous death threats. Fearing what might happen, they discreetly brought their families to Vienna in the spring of 1938, staying quietly at the Hotel Imperial as Captain Wood haunted the British Embassy, begging that they be granted asylum. Michael Palairet, the British ambassador, proved less than sympathetic to these pleas, insisting that the Nazis were civilized and would not harm the Hohenbergs. He reluctantly granted Ernst, his wife, and their son temporary asylum within the embassy, but this lasted a mere two days before they were once again left on their own, without any protection.[23]

During this brief asylum, on 12 March 1938, German troops had marched triumphantly into Austria, and Berlin announced the country's annexation as part of the German Reich. Both Max and Ernst tried to hide discreetly at the Hotel Imperial, but with the arrival of the Nazis the manager asked them to leave immediately. They then sought refuge at Captain Wood's apartment, trying to disappear in anonymous shadows, but a mere four days passed before insistent banging on the door interrupted a family dinner. It was the Gestapo, armed with an arrest warrant for Ernst. His anti-Nazi activities made him an enemy of the state, but he was also falsely accused of the deaths, through negligence, of several miners working near the Eisenerz estate; in fact, the mines had not belonged to him, but the Nazis deemed the charge sufficient to brand Ernst as a criminal. His disappearance into the night sent shock waves through the family. A few days later, a friend warned Max that the Gestapo was after him as well for advocating restoration of the Habsburg throne; if he ran, his brother might be killed, and so on 18 March he turned himself over to the occupying German authorities. The two brothers were reunited in a jail cell and subjected to brutal interrogations. There would be no trial. Deemed enemies of the Third Reich, the two brothers were taken from their cell on the night of 25–26 March and pushed into a truck that carried them through the streets to the Westbahnhof and a waiting train that set off into the night.[24]

The destination was Dachau concentration camp, nestled in the suburbs just outside Munich. Max was thirty-six and Ernst just shy of thirty-four. Both were tall, mustachioed, broadly built like their father, and healthy when they entered the hell of Dachau. They always refused to talk about the nightmare of the concentration camps, even with their closest relatives, but silence could not disguise the shattering experiences they were about to endure.[25]

Passing through the Jourhaus Tor, with its infamous motto *Arbeit macht frei*, Max and Ernst were photographed, stripped of their few possessions, and made to stand in silence as their hair was roughly shorn. Pushed naked into communal showers, they were handed thin, striped uniforms: Max was made to wear a green triangle, indicating that he was a political prisoner, while Ernst bore a red one, condemning him as a common criminal.[26] Now that they were his prisoners, Hitler personally ordered that the 'Hohenberg boys' receive no mercy from the state. It was left to Reichsmarschal Hermann Göring to tell SS-Oberführer Hans Loritz, the camp commandant, to single the two brothers out for 'special treatment' under specifically 'harsh conditions'.[27]

Every morning at half past five, Max and Ernst joined the other prisoners as they trudged from their barracks to the immense Appellplatz, where the SS conducted daily roll calls beneath machine guns trained on the miserable group. Tall walls and electrified barbed wire ringed the enclosure. Soldiers marched groups of prisoners to their various work posts, but Max and Ernst were always kept under close guard within the main precincts of the camp. Following Hitler's instructions, they were selected for an especially demeaning assignment. Their days passed on latrine duty. Harnessed to a wooden cart like oxen, Max and Ernst were whipped and beaten through the camp from barrack to barrack. Using spoons, they were forced to clean out the fetid cesspits shared by hundreds of inmates; SS guards taunted them as they worked, hurling rocks into the pools to splash faeces onto the brothers' faces while laughingly calling them 'Imperial Highnesses'. Punches and kicks followed them across the compound, but Max and Ernst dared not respond. At night, stomachs empty from the meagre rations, they retreated to the barracks they shared with hundreds of other inmates, shivering on the wooden shelves that served as beds.[28]

Exhaustion, malnutrition, disease and pneumonia decimated the inmates. Prisoners who did not fall victim to the harsh conditions lived with the constant fear of torture and execution. Beatings, forced marches, grisly shootings, and hangings in front of other inmates marked the days. Yet Max and Ernst remained calm throughout their ordeal. They had endured uncertainty and tragedy before and brought to their time at Dachau an almost ordered surrender born of unwavering religious faith. A fellow prisoner called them 'unflinching, undaunted, and an inspiring example to everyone else. Even in their filthy, ragged prison clothes, they were gentlemen, true nobility. They would lie with us in the dusty roads when we had a few minutes and share lumps of sugar that they had got hold of somewhere. There was not a single person in the entire camp who did not refer to the Hohenbergs without the greatest respect; they were pointed out to new arrivals as examples of how to behave and survive.'[29]

Max and Ernst saved the lives of numerous prisoners. Once Max saw an SS guard chasing a gypsy through the compound; he grabbed and hid the terrified man in a box of sand until the search was finally abandoned. Among those they befriended and rescued was Leopold Figl, who later became chancellor of Austria. Figl remembered his arrival at Dachau and his first encounter with the brothers, who stood silently in the bitter cold as SS guards jeered at them. They shared the little that they had, from cigarettes to scraps of food, earning the unwavering respect of their fellow prisoners. Shivering, dangerously thin, and dressed in rags, these two sons of the former heir to the Austrian throne impressed everyone with their air of 'invisible authority' and 'serene dignity' even as they 'endured the most excruciating humiliations'. Fellow inmates, Figl said, 'would have gone through fire for them'.[30]

Unknown to the brothers, European aristocrats and members of royal families repeatedly tried to win their release. There were pleas from Pope Pius XII, the king of Sweden, Prince Felix of Luxembourg, and Queen Mary; the latter's request that the British Foreign Office objected to the brothers' continued imprisonment attracted attention in Berlin and may have helped soften attitudes.[31] It was Max's wife, Elisabeth, who eventually earned his freedom. Working quietly behind the scenes and using all of her influence as a member of Germany's old nobility, she went to Göring to plead her husband's case. It was an uncomfortable meeting, as Göring insisted that the brothers were rightfully imprisoned for crimes against the German Reich. However, the *Reichs-marschal* was also an immense snob, impressed by titles and royal connections; ignoring Hitler's orders, he secretly agreed to grant Max a conditional release.[32]

It was 24 September 1938, when guards at Dachau pulled Max aside without explanation and ushered him onto a train headed for Vienna. Convinced that he was on his way to a hasty trial and inevitable execution, Max listened in disbelief as officials told him of his release. He was not to promote restoration of the monarchy or engage in anti-Nazi activities and must report weekly to the Gestapo; otherwise, he was free to return home. Shocked, Max went to his old apartment in Vienna but found it empty. He had no money and was desperate to get to his family at Artstetten. Finally, a porter lent him the fare that took Max the last sixty miles to his Danube Valley castle.[33]

There was a tearful reunion with his family before someone asked the obvious question: what of Ernst? Max could only report that he was still alive. Rumour now replaced fact: the following year, papers even erroneously announced Ernst's death at Dachau.[34] The family would not learn until later that in September of 1939, just days after the outbreak of the Second World War, the Gestapo had loaded Ernst onto a train and sent him to Flossenbürg, another concentration camp near the Czechoslovakian border with Bavaria. In truth, Ernst was in a difficult position. Unlike Max, he had been branded not a political prisoner but a criminal, which to the Nazis warranted especially harsh punishment. His marriage to the daughter of an English officer also led to suspicions that he was a potential traitor and spy. Time in Dachau had been marked with humiliations and terrible uncertainty; Flossenbürg was another world entirely, a grim place of starvation and forced labour in the camp's immense granite quarries. Weather, harsh conditions, and illness took their toll on the inmates; temperatures in the wooden barracks dropped below freezing, and pneumonia, dysentery, and typhoid decimated the camp. Already weakened from seventeen months in Dachau, Ernst barely survived the winter.

Dachau and Flossenbürg had failed to break him. Now, on 23 March 1940, the Nazis ordered Ernst sent to Sachsenhausen, a concentration camp some thirty miles north of Berlin. It would have been easy enough to stage some incident and execute him; that he was spared from such a fate was undoubtedly due to the continued, prominent international pressure to release him. But the Nazis resisted. Given prisoner number 17,739 and assigned to Block Five, Ernst was thrown into the forced labour pool and given just enough daily rations to sustain his work. Once a month, authorities permitted him to mail a postcard to his family; this contained no message, only his prisoner number to prove that he was still alive.[35]

These postcards were all that Ernst's family knew of him. The Nazis had seized Radmer, and Marie-Therese took her son Franz to Czechoslovakia, to live with her sister-in-law Sophie as the war continued. On 15 August 1941 the Nazis had appropriated all of the remaining Hohenberg property as the possessions of 'people hostile to the State'. Lölling was gone, as were the apartment building in Vienna, the palace on Vienna's Reisnerstrasse, bank accounts, jewellery and works of art. Hitler took some of it, having already seized the Este collection displayed at Konopischt. Max even lost Artstetten to the Gestapo, though they did not kick him out; the family and their servants, including a retired but still faithful Janaczek, were given a few rooms in which to live, beneath the watchful and ever-vigilant eyes of their Nazi occupiers. They could not even leave the castle without the Gestapo's permission.[36]

The Nazis soon made their ugly presence felt. The Gestapo 'helpfully' suggested that it would be a sign of patriotism for Duchess Elisabeth to purchase and prominently display busts of Hitler and Göring. She dared not refuse, not while her family was at Berlin's mercy, not while Ernst remained their prisoner. Next, authorities decided that Max's six sons should attend the local village school, where they could be exposed to 'proper' influences and trained according to Berlin's dictates. All were ordered to join the Hitler Youth. Knowing how precarious their situation was, they had to agree, though Johannes nearly brought about disaster. Hating the Nazis but unaware of the implications in defying them, he routinely antagonized the officers and skipped compulsory meetings. Only after his father was summoned to a grave lecture and warned of the consequences did Johannes understand how easily his family's freedom might vanish if he disobeyed the Germans.[37]

Ernst's fate remained in doubt. Officials dismissed Marie-Therese's repeated requests for his release with the same litany of excuses: her husband was a criminal and, in any case, her own father was then serving as aide-de-camp to the former King Edward VIII, now Duke of Windsor and governor-general of the Bahamas. Her true allegiance, and that of her husband, they insisted, had to lie with the British. Sophie tried to succeed where her sister-in-law had failed. Her husband, Friedrich, had joined the Nazi Party in an effort to keep his family safe. Surely, she asked, Ernst could be released into her husband's custody, where a trusted party member could watch his movements?[38]

The Nazis, aware that Friedrich Nostitz-Rieneck's loyalties lay with his family and Bohemia, not Berlin, weren't fooled by this deception. By now, Marie-Therese was an impoverished refugee, living with the family of Count Friedrich Schaffgotsch at Schloss Koppitz in Upper Silesia, where she worked at a local nursery planting vegetables. Schaffgotsch had taken her and her young son in out of pity. Through his connections, she began haunting the offices of Ernst Kaltenbrunner, Nazi head of the security service and police, pleading for her husband's release. Kaltenbrunner, in turn, advised her to appeal directly to the odious Heinrich Himmler. Thinking it was a lost cause, she nevertheless wrote out an impassioned plea on behalf of her increasingly ill husband. Expecting nothing but rejection, she was stunned when, in early April 1943, Kaltenbrunner told her that her efforts had succeeded. In a rare display of compassion, Himmler personally agreed to the release; he did so at his own peril, actually concealing the decision from Hitler.[39]

Marie-Therese rushed to Vienna and on 11 April watched in horror as, after five years of separation, her husband stepped off a train. 'I barely recognized him,' she admitted. 'He looked so emaciated and starved.' The release, like that of Max, was conditional. Ernst was required to check in each week at Gestapo headquarters in Vienna, never quite knowing if he would again be arrested for some perceived infraction. Sixty months of incarceration had left Ernst frail and faltering, but the Nazis ordered that he obtain a job. After so many years imprisoned behind barbed wire, he longed for the freedom of nature and suggested that he could return to his career as a forestry manager. He even contacted several aristocratic landowners with large estates; all were willing to give him a position, but the Nazis vetoed the idea. How, they asked, could he, a former prisoner, possibly feel comfortable working for any aristocrat? Ernst had always been the most sensitive of Franz Ferdinand and Sophie's children, and this rejection left him depressed. Increasing air raids over Vienna only added to his worries. After Marie-Therese gave birth to their second child, a son called Ernst, on 1 March 1944, he made an agonizing decision: although he wanted to keep his family together, he sent the children out of danger to stay with relatives. The move came just as the Nazis, desperate for soldiers in the last months of the war, conscripted every available man. Despite his fragile health and increasingly weak heart, Ernst was forced to don a Nazi uniform and begin military training for a final campaign against the Allies.[40]

Luckily, the tide turned before the authorities forced Ernst into deployment, but he now faced the danger of the last, desperate air raids of the war. One night, the couple huddled in a dark shelter as bombs burst above them; when an explosion filled the room with smoke, Ernst managed to pull his wife through a small hole they hastily dug to escape into an adjoining building. Then Soviet troops arrived in Vienna, liberating the city and, as Marie-Therese recalled, looting their apartment of the few belongings left to the couple. Ernst and his wife spent two weeks as refugees, wearing the same clothes and relying on charity, before they were able to return to their apartment. Even then, there was no sense of security: Soviet soldiers soon arrived, demanding food and housing for their troops and holding pistols to the couple's heads until they agreed to let them take a broken gramophone.[41]

At Artstetten, Max, too, faced the conquering Russians. On 8 May

1945, with the end of the war, the Soviet army swept into Artstetten, occupying the castle, tearing through its rooms, and plundering the few remaining valuables. Communists had replaced the Nazis. No one knew what would happen; ruthless and filled with vengeance, the Soviets had a reputation for brutality, raping and killing as they advanced across Europe. Born a prince, son of the future emperor of Austria, Duke Max of Hohenberg would have made some Red Army general a fine prize. When, a few days later, some highly decorated Soviet officers arrived at the castle, Max was sure he was about to be shot. Instead, the men were full of admiration. 'They knew exactly who my father was, and also the full details of his past in the concentration camp,' says his son Duke Georg. After paying their respects, they told a surprised Max that they were appointing him a major in the occupying Soviet army and gave him an armband with the title in Cyrillic to wear; this was meant to avoid any unpleasantness with common Soviet troops. 'My father,' Duke Georg remarks, 'was certainly the only duke in the world whom the Red Army appointed a major.' The new rank went hand in hand with another title when the Soviets appointed Max the mayor of the village of Artstetten.[42]

The war had ended, but Austria was still a place of chaotic uncertainty. Only after considerable difficulty did Max and Ernst finally contact their sister, Sophie, and learn of the tragedies that she, too, had suffered. Hitler's army conscripted Erwein and Franz, her two eldest sons, and sent them off to fight the Allies. In February 1945, word came from Berlin that twenty-two-year-old Franz had been killed fighting in East Prussia. Shortly before the end of the war, she discovered that Erwein had also been dispatched to the Eastern Front, but then there was nothing but silence. Throughout 1945 and into 1946, desperate enquiries went unanswered. Erwein, Sophie told her brothers, had simply disappeared.

In the aftermath of the war, the Czech government under Edvard Beneš expelled all German Bohemians from the country. Official documents again erroneously named Sophie as a Habsburg, and her husband's property and estates were expropriated. It was a recurring nightmare, a repetition of the debacle over Konopischt. Sophie worried what would happen to her family, especially after falsely being declared a member of the former Austrian imperial family. She remembered Konopischt, remembered what had been lost once before; this time, she filled her few bags not with clothing but instead with the few photograph albums and treasured letters she could carry.[43] Together with their two youngest children, Alois and Sophie, she and her husband crowded into the back of a truck and on 2 April 1946 made their way across the border with hundreds of other forced refugees.[44]

There was nowhere else to go but to Artstetten, to once again face an uncertain future in the havoc left by war. Franz Ferdinand and Sophie's children and grandchildren were all safe now and reunited, except for the missing Erwein. Sophie wrote, telephoned, and telegraphed authorities in Berlin and Moscow, begging for information, only to be told that no one knew what had happened to him. Only in 1949 did word finally come that on 1 September he had died. Erwein had been alive all these years, held captive in a Soviet prisoner-of-war camp near Kharkov. Ripples from the bullets fired in Sarajevo had claimed yet another of Franz Ferdinand and Sophie's descendants.

Sophie, Max and Ernst now struggled to rebuild their lives for a third time. Max still had Artstetten, but the Nazis had appropriated both Lölling and Radmer without payment; with Hitler's defeat, the new Austrian government claimed them as former German property in compensation for the war. A lawsuit finally gave Lölling back to Max, but the fight for Radmer was more complicated. Wanting to see what had happened to the estate, Ernst made an arduous journey by train, by truck, and by foot, only to find that the old lodge was empty and mouldering away. The Austrian Federal Forestry Department now occupied the estate and was not at all inclined to hand over what they considered Nazi spoils. It took another lawsuit before Ernst was finally recognized as the rightful owner. Max and Ernst gave the homeless Sophie and her family Schloss Geyeregg at Eisenerz.[45]

Decades of shared tragedies bound the three siblings even more closely together. Having lost so much to assassination, war, imprisonment and revolution, Sophie, Max and Ernst were determined to spend their remaining years not lost in the past but living in an optimistic present. While treasuring his memories, Max, as his son Albrecht recalls, 'told us very little about the short time he spent with his parents. I do not think he liked talking about it'.[46] The trio and their offspring, says Max's granddaughter Princess Sophie, always maintained a 'very, very strong sense of family', with 'a very strong sense of humour', something that helped Sophie, Max and Ernst gradually overcome the horrors of grief and persecution.[47] Family gatherings and holidays were boisterous affairs, as Franz Ferdinand and Sophie's three children reminisced and punctuated happy memories with loud renditions of favourite Viennese folk songs.[48]

But years of brutal incarceration under the Nazis had taken an undeniable toll. On 2 April 1948, Max and Ernst had returned to Dachau for a service commemorating the victims; within, they each carried the unseen emotional scars from their time there as well as the physical effects of those brutal years. Ernst had suffered longer in the camps, and he never quite recovered from the forced labour, starvation and disease. Like his mother, he began suffering from serious heart problems in his forties. There was little doctors could do. Still, when the end came, it was unexpected. On 4 March 1954, he travelled to Graz to discuss conditions at Radmer with local authorities. A maid at the Hotel Steierhof found him in his bed the next morning: Ernst had died of a heart attack in the middle of the night at the age of forty-nine. Max and his son Georg carried the body back to Artstetten for a small, private funeral followed by interment in the family crypt near his parents.[49]

For a while, Max seemed to have escaped the worst effects of his time in Dachau. In 1950, the townspeople in Artstetten elected him mayor, and he held the position for the next decade, living quietly as squire of his father's gleaming white castle above the Danube. By December 1961, however, when the family gathered at Artstetten to celebrate Christmas, he was seriously ill, fatigued, and, like his mother and late brother, suffering from heart trouble. Two weeks later, he collapsed with chest pains; although his son Peter rushed him by car to Vienna for treatment, it was too late. On 8 January 1962, Max died of a heart attack at the age of fifty-nine.[50]

Ernst had passed away with little notice, in keeping with the quietly dignified way he had lived, but in death Duke Max of Hohenberg was lauded and eulogized as the last remaining symbol of a forgotten era, a man whose suffering embodied the evils of war. Sophie, Max and Ernst, declared one newspaper, 'had every reason to turn against the Imperial House. But they refused to pursue the matter. They were always correct citizens of the Republic, yet they reminded us of the lost Habsburgs. Now, we remember this man, who was not permitted to be a Habsburg, but who proved himself to be worth more than any full-blooded Habsburg.'[51]

Max's funeral at Artstetten offered a curious but wholly appropriate tribute. Archduke Otto was forbidden from setting foot in Austria and could not attend; he sent Franz Josef's grandson Archduke Hubert Salvator in his place. There were royal relatives from Liechtenstein and Luxembourg, along with representatives from the old empire's most distinguished aristocratic families. Officials and politicians from Vienna joined the thousands who appeared spontaneously at Artstetten to pay their respects. Among them was a group of former inmates from Nazi concentration camps who marched behind his coffin in silent tribute to their fellow prisoner. The church at Artstetten was so crowded that over a thousand mourners simply stood outside the walls, heads bowed in respect as they listened to the muffled organ music; it was raining, yet no one left. As the congregation sang the old Austrian imperial anthem and the church bells rang, huntsmen from Radmer and the knights of the Order of the Golden Fleece accompanied the coffin out of the church, across the terrace and lawn, and to the crypt, where Max joined his parents and brother.[52]

Only Sophie now remained. Born in an age of empire, she had witnessed the last, golden summer of Europe's great dynasties before tragedy struck. Beginning her childhood in a splendid baroque palace guarded by smartly uniformed officers, she had endured assassination, wars, revolution and loss as imperial families gave way to Hitler and Communism, ocean liners to aeroplanes, gramophones to televisions. Having buried her parents, her two brothers, two children, and her husband in 1973, she lived quietly in Austria, welcoming grandchildren amid rooms adorned with ghostly images of her almost otherworldly youth at the dawn of the century.

Sophie lived to see actors portray her parents in films, and to read the incessant stream of books depicting her father as a brutal reactionary and her mother as a scheming adventuress, yet with unfailing grace and dignity she always found time to speak to any writer. 'I have to defend him,' she would say of her father when relatives protested. 'There's no one left.' In 1981 Sophie took a trip into the nostalgic past, visiting Konopischt for the first time in sixty years. Wandering with her grandchildren through the rooms where she had once lived and played, the elderly woman paused, pointing out objects and smiling as she spoke of how happy her family life had been there.[53] On 27 October 1990, she died at the age of eighty-nine and was laid to rest beside her husband in the family crypt of her son-in-law Baron Ernst Gudenus at Weizberg near Thannhausen. After seventy-six years, death had reunited the family.

EPILOGUE

✛

A hundred years have passed since that fateful Sunday morning in Sarajevo. No newsreels captured those pivotal few seconds in human history, as the motor car halted in front of Moritz Schiller's Delicatessen and a young terrorist opened fire on the city's illustrious visitors, yet the unseen ripples from those moments continue today. The bullets Princip fired did more than kill Franz Ferdinand and Sophie or leave their children orphaned; they inaugurated a century of enormous upheaval and mass slaughter on a scale previously unknown. No other two deaths can have served as the tipping point that led to so much misery and loss.

The memory of that day looms like a shadow over Sarajevo, haunting its narrow streets and quays. Plans for an immense Romanesque church in honour of Franz Ferdinand and Sophie, to be built on the other side of the river from Schiller's Delicatessen, never materialized. With twin spires and a massive bulk, it would have dwarfed everything else in the vicinity.[1] A cross was laid into the roadway at the spot where the assassination took place, and in 1917 a lofty memorial to the slain couple was erected at the corner of the Appel Quay and Lateiner Bridge. It stood a mere two years before being pulled down, an inconvenient reminder of the city's tragic place in history.[2]

After the First World War, Bosnia and Herzegovina became part of a new South Slav state, Yugoslavia, which deemed Princip and his fellow conspirators national heroes. In 1920, their bodies were transferred from Bohemia and interred in a tomb at the First Serbian Orthodox Cemetery. The little stone building, erected in 1939 by the Orthodox Church, was dedicated to Princip's memory with the inscription 'Here Lie the Remains of the Heroes of Vidov-Dan.' Inside rest the bodies of Princip, Čabrinović, Grabež, Cubrilović, and Jovanović, and also that of Žerajić, who had tried unsuccessfully to kill an earlier governor-general of Bosnia.[3]

The Lateiner Bridge was renamed the Princip Bridge, and in 1953 Moritz Schiller's old delicatessen was transformed into the Young Bosnia Museum, dedicated to the memory of the conspirators.[4] Lacking significant artefacts, it was stuffed with anything and everything that had even the slightest link to the conspirators, including such questionable items as a shirt once worn by Princip's uncle.[5] Three years later, two footprints were set into the pavement just outside, marking the spot where Princip had fired his fatal shots. Nearby hung a black marble plaque reading 'On this historic spot, Gavrilo Princip initiated freedom on St Vitus's Day, 28 June 1914.' This monument, wrote Winston Churchill in disgust, 'erected in recent years by his fellow countrymen, records his infamy, and their own'.[6]

Following the break-up of Yugoslavia, Bosnia and Herzegovina declared its independence, and in the early 1990s a bloody civil war began that effectively lasted until 1995. Serb forces surrounded Sarajevo and launched a massive military campaign against the city. The siege that followed lasted nearly four years and left close to twelve thousand inhabitants dead from the relentless Serbian shelling and genocidal massacres, and thousands more traumatized by torture, and systemic rapes, before NATO forces intervened. They made the old Hotel Bosna at Ilidže, where Franz Ferdinand and Sophie had spent their last night, their headquarters and ringed it with razor wire.[7] By the end of the war, close to a hundred thousand Bosnians had been killed, and Sarajevo was left largely in ruins from Serb shelling. Ripples from the bullets fired in Sarajevo had returned to the city of their birth with a vengeance.

With an independent Bosnia and Herzegovina finally established and at peace, the city of Sarajevo struggled to rebuild itself. In the process, it also struggled to come to terms with its most infamous claim to fame. While the Yugoslav monarchy and the Communists that followed had glorified Princip, many Bosnians now view him as a common terrorist. The famous footprints set in cement were destroyed in the siege; the name of the Lateiner Bridge was restored; the plaque on Schiller's Delicatessen hailing Princip's deed was sandblasted from the building, replaced with a simple historical marker making no claim to glory.[8] The Young Bosnia Museum in the delicatessen is gone as well; it has become the 1878–1918 Museum. This includes various displays on the city's history. Ironically the museum promotes many of the improvements brought about by the Austrians during their administration. Waxworks figures of Franz Ferdinand and Sophie stand near a case displaying relics from the assassination, including a reproduction of the sidewalk with Princip's footprints. Avdio Mirsad, the curator, says rather apologetically that the previous government was unconcerned with local history and that many important historical items were lost, sold, or sent back to Vienna.[9]

The Old Town Hall, which became Sarajevo's National Library, was left in a state of near ruin, its walls pocked with damage from the shelling and its contents looted. Shops in Sarajevo today sell souvenir postcards of the couple; a few rather tastelessly include the red silhouette of a shooter aiming at them. There has been recent talk of restoring the monument to Franz Ferdinand and Sophie. The central plaque showing them in profile and the crown from the monument are stored today in the basement of the Art Gallery of Bosnia and Herzegovina.[10]

The Konak still stands, having largely escaped damage in the siege. In March of 2006, Franz Ferdinand's great-nephew the late Archduke Otto visited Sarajevo and was even named an honorary citizen.[11] He stayed at the Konak, walking past the same stone lions guarding the staircase where Franz Ferdinand and Sophie had been carried from their motor car and into Potiorek's old suite of rooms, where only the ornamental plaster ceilings retain a touch of glory.[12] At night, he slept in the state bedroom – the same room where the couple's bodies had lain in state.[13]

Max and Ernst had been loyal to the archduke, working on his behalf for a restoration of the Austrian throne that never came and suffering at the hands of the Nazis for promoting his cause. Throughout their lives they never forgot the old empire, and though their descendants have scattered and withdrawn into private life, most remain dedicated to the same family ideals. Sophie's son, Alois, died in 2003; her daughter, Sophie, remains alive. Ernst's wife, Marie-Therese, died in 1985. Their eldest son, Franz Ferdinand, died in 1978; his youngest son, Prince Ernst, is still alive.

Max's wife, Elisabeth, died in 1993; his eldest son, Franz, who became titular Duke of Hohenberg in 1962 on his father's death, married Princess Elisabeth of Luxembourg, eldest daughter of Grand Duchess Charlotte of Luxembourg, in 1956. They had two daughters: Princess Anna, known as Anita, was born in 1958, and Princess Sophie was born in 1960. Duke Franz died in 1977, and his widow in 2011. With Franz's death in 1977, Max's second son, Georg, became titular 3rd Duke of Hohenberg and head of the family. A career diplomat, he had served as secretary at the Austrian Embassy in Paris and later as Austria's ambassador to the Vatican. His eldest son, Prince Nikolaus, will continue the family name. Of the rest of Max's sons, Albrecht, Peter and Gerhard are still alive; Johannes died in 2003.

Before his death, Duke Franz sold Lölling, but Artstetten passed to his eldest daughter, Princess Anita, who now lives there with her family. In 1982, she opened a portion of the castle as the Archduke Franz Ferdinand Museum, dedicated to the archduke, his wife, and their family, using the other rooms as a private residence and occasionally renting them for corporate events. Among other items displayed here are fragments from the dress Sophie wore when she was killed, a splinter from Čabrinović's bomb, the rosary that Baron Morsey placed in Franz Ferdinand's hands as he lay dying, and the death masks of the couple. The large, whitewashed crypt below is usually open to the public. The tombs of Franz Ferdinand and Sophie sit in a low, vaulted alcove; a niche above holds the remains of their stillborn son, with the tombs holding Max, Ernst and their wives in a modern extension.

Running Artstetten has become a full-time occupation. Some twenty-five thousand to thirty-five thousand visitors come each year to view the Franz Ferdinand Museum there, but the princess receives no public funding. She always has to balance the cost of operation with the expenses of maintaining such a residence. 'We can't afford to do big exhibitions,' she explains, 'though we change things each year and try to show special subjects.' Still, she wonders about the future. 'We'll see how the next ten years are going to be, and if it will be affordable to keep up this house and to open the house to the public.' The alternative, she says, is to merely keep the crypt open, which is what Max wished to do.[14]

The Czechoslovakian government opened Konopischt to the paying public soon after expropriating the estate. In 1941, the Nazis took over, using it as lodging for officers and the park as a training ground for the SS.[15] Hitler had most of the Este collection transferred to Vienna, intending to display it after the war in a new museum in Linz. With the defeat of Nazi Germany, both Max and the government of Austria laid claim to the arms, armour, weaponry, and other items, but despite protests Britain helped return the collection to Konopischt.[16]

Today Konopischt is a major attraction, with three different tours spanning the various rooms and apartments. The items lost to Sophie, Max and Ernst are now proudly displayed here: Franz Ferdinand's uniforms, Sophie's wedding dress, and the bodice of the dress she wore on that day in Sarajevo, along with family paintings and photographs and myriad personal possessions, including the children's toys. 'The first time I went to Konopischt', recalls Princess Sophie, the couple's great-granddaughter, 'they still told the old stories, and it was rather shocking, because the picture they gave of my family was atrocious and so terribly unjust. I was fuming when I left; it was a nasty experience.'[17] Her sister

Princess Anita says she has worked with the director of the castle, requesting changes to the stories asserting that Franz Ferdinand and Sophie were harsh employers and unsympathetic human beings. Through her intervention, gradually the image has softened.[18]

Despite her initial impressions, Princess Sophie made several further visits to Konopischt. On her second trip she attended a shoot with her husband, Baron Jean-Louis de Potesta, and some of his business colleagues in the shadow of the castle. 'I felt so close to my roots,' she says, 'yet so far away.' She had spent her life in Luxembourg but suddenly felt 'very much like I had come home'. The day became 'very emotionally tiring and very tough, and I was often in tears'. At the end, she began to ponder the possibility of seeking legal restoration of the castle to her family. She made a third visit, this time with her children, taking them through the rooms, pointing out objects and explaining their family associations. She raised the idea of lodging a formal legal complaint with the government, asking her children if they agreed. When they did and promised to support her efforts, a legal case began.[19]

Konopischt is a famous tourist attraction. For officials in Prague, the princess says, the decision to pursue a legal claim against the Czech government was 'almost as bad as if I asked for Versailles from the French. For them, Konopischt is something very special. They like it and they don't want to give it back.'[20]

The princess's case is simple: the Czech government illegally seized the estate in April 1919. There was Masaryk's first promise that Max and Ernst would soon be recognized as the legal owners, which was revealed as hollow when the children were forcibly expelled from Konopischt. The government next cited Article 208 of the Treaty of Saint-Germain-en-Laye, which was not even signed and ratified until September of that year, to justify their actions. 'It was an incorrect interpretation of Article 208,' Princess Sophie says, 'and the illegal confiscation, without any compensation, went far beyond anything envisioned by the treaty's signatories. Merely because a government, out of self interest, declares a law valid does not make it right or just.'[21]

Then Prague had falsely insisted that Sophie, Max and Ernst were members of the imperial family and their property subject to expropriation. As they had never been Habsburgs, this was equally flawed. The 1921 law, which retroactively for the first time named Franz Ferdinand's descendants regardless of their morganatic status, was merely a tortured clumsy attempt to legitimize an illegal decision.[22]

In 2000, Princess Sophie filed a lawsuit in the Benešov District Court, based on the claim that the property had been seized illegally and that the rulings made should not apply to Franz Ferdinand and Sophie's children. Dr Jaroslav Brož, the princess's Czech legal counsel, won 'a small victory' when the district court, while rejecting her claim, ruled that the furniture within the castle had rightfully belonged in 1921 not to Franz Ferdinand but to Max.[23]

Dr Brož appealed the decision and launched further claims with the Czech courts, asserting that the expropriation had been a violation of international treaties. The case made its way from district to regional to supreme court and finally to the Constitutional Court of the Czech Republic, which in 2011 rejected the lawsuit, holding firm to their insistence that the children had indeed been Habsburgs. In any case, they insisted, Law 354 was valid. Following this defeat, the princess decided to bring the case before the European Court of Human Rights in Strasbourg, which also ruled against her.[24]

The government's seizure of the estate may yet be overturned, resting, as it does, on shifting excuses and demonstrably false assertions that Sophie, Max and Ernst were Habsburgs. For the rest of their lives the three mourned the loss of this, their true home, but not until the collapse of the Czechoslovakian government did it seem possible to challenge the seizure in a meaningful way. The princess is adamant that, if she ever wins the case, Konopischt will remain open to the public.[25]

Recent Czech history has not been kind to the Hohenbergs or their relatives. The Chotek family is no more. Of Sophie's siblings, Maria died in 1935, surviving her husband, Prince Jaroslav Thun, by nine years. Wolfgang died in 1925, Zdenka in 1946, Oktavia in 1948, and Antonie in 1930. After her sister Karolina died in 1919, Henriette, the youngest sister, married her widowed husband, Count Leopold Nostitz-Rieneck. Henriette died in 1964. The members of the family who remained in Bohemia were evicted after the Second World War; the last of the family who bore the name, Karl, died in Bavaria in 1970.

Other significant players in the lives of Franz Ferdinand and Sophie passed into history. Archduchess Maria Theresa, Franz Ferdinand's devoted stepmother, died in Vienna in 1944 and received a state funeral and burial in the Capuchin Crypt; her two daughters, Maria Annunciata and Elisabeth, died in 1961 and 1960, respectively. Both had served as abbess of the Theresia Convent at Hradschin in Prague, an honorary position always held by Habsburg archduchesses. In 1903, Elisabeth had married Prince Alois of Liechtenstein in another controversial union that some considered unequal; this time, Franz Josef disagreed and attended the wedding to show his support. The present ruling Prince von und zu Liechtenstein is Elisabeth's direct descendant. The archduke's brother Ferdinand Karl died in 1915 of tuberculosis, just a year after Sarajevo.

Colonel Alexander Brosch von Aarenau was killed in action in September 1914.[26] General Conrad von Hötzendorf proved himself an inefficient military commander, losing some 1.5 million men in futile campaigns; he died in 1925. Leopold Loyka, the unfortunate chauffeur on the day of the assassination, later received a financial grant from Emperor Karl that he used to purchase an inn. He died in 1926. Franz Janaczek remained with Franz Ferdinand and Sophie's children until his retirement, always refusing to speak of the archduke or his time with him despite numerous book offers that came his way. He died in 1955 at the age of ninety.[27] Prince Alfred de Montenuovo, the man who inflicted the many humiliations on the archduke's beloved wife, died in 1927.

To avoid his capture, the Serbian government sent Milan Ciganović, who had helped train Princip, Čabrinović, and Grabež in the use of weapons in Belgrade, to America. He returned at the end of the war, was rewarded by the government, and disappeared into obscurity, dying in

1927. Tankosić was killed in action fighting with the Serbian army in the winter of 1915. A year later, perhaps worried that Dragutin Dimitrijević would reveal the Black Hand's previous ties to the Serbian government and wanting to finally break his hold on power, Prime Minister Nikola Pašić and Crown Prince Alexander had him arrested. The charge, that he was plotting to assassinate the crown prince, was known to be false, but both men wanted Dimitrijević out of the way. To ensure this, when he went on trial at Salonika in the spring of 1917, Crown Prince Alexander named Colonel Peter Zivković as head of the presiding military tribunal; as Zivković was not only Dimitrijević's sworn enemy but also an intimate friend of the crown prince, the outcome was predetermined.[28]

Several of Dimitrijević's former colleagues joined him at the Salonika trial, including members of the Black Hand and Sarajevo conspirator Muhamed Mehmedbašić. Mehmedbašić was given fifteen years in prison but was later pardoned for his role in the assassination and returned to Sarajevo. He spent the rest of his life working in the city and died in 1943 during the Second World War. Dimitrijević was not as lucky. On 23 May 1917, he was found guilty of treason; a month later, on the morning of June 26, he was executed by firing squad. As he was driven to his place of execution, Dimitrijević again confirmed his role in events at Sarajevo. 'Now it is clear to me', he said, 'that I am to be killed today by Serbian rifles solely because I organized the Sarajevo outrage.'[29] In 1953, the Yugoslavian Supreme Court granted him a posthumous acquittal.[30]

The assassination at Sarajevo has been commemorated in hundreds of books. Nearly twenty movies and television dramas have played out Franz Ferdinand and Sophie's story and their end. In 1999, the Austrian Mint released a hundred-schilling commemorative coin in their honour; their portraits also grace a 2004 Austrian ten-euro commemorative coin. A plaque has been installed in their memory in the Capuchin Crypt Church in Vienna, traditional resting place of the Habsburgs, commemorating the couple who, in death, could never rest there together.[31]

A few miles from the Capuchin Crypt, the main attraction at the Heeresgeschichtliches Museum, or Military History Museum, is a room devoted to the assassination. Display cases hold the archduke's medals and uniforms; paintings of Franz Ferdinand and Sophie bedeck the crimson walls. At the centre of the room, a case holds the chaise longue on which the archduke died; the uniform he wore that day in Sarajevo, given by his children to the museum, sprawls upon it, the blue tunic slashed diagonally across the chest, the gold collar slit, the left sleeve cut. Bloodstains, barely visible with the passage of time, still cover the area around the throat and spill over the chest.[32]

Several guns are also on display. In 2004, a Jesuit archive in southern Austria handed over a Browning revolver said to have been the one used by Princip. This was supposedly given to Father Anton Puntigam, along with bombs and several souvenirs taken from the dead couple, including petals from Sophie's rose bouquet and the bloodstained pillowcase from the chaise longue in the Konak. Puntigam had offered the relics to the couple's children, who declined to accept them. The gun Princip used supposedly bore serial number 19075, but the gun from Puntigam's collection now on display is marked 19074.[33]

In July 1914, Count Harrach donated his motor car in which the couple had been shot to the emperor, who in turn handed it over to the museum. It dominates the room, like the bloodstained uniform a tangible reminder of that fatal day; a white circle marks the hole in the rear door through which the bullet that struck Sophie passed. When Soviet troops entered Vienna at the end of the Second World War, they commandeered all vehicles, including the infamous car; infuriated that there was no petrol in the tank, they slashed the tyres and fired several shots into its grey sides. Many visitors have noted the car's number plate: A111-118, as if this vehicle, in which the First World War might be said to have begun, also mysteriously heralded the very day, month and year on which it came to an end.[34]

———

Whispers of a conspiracy followed the assassination in Sarajevo. There was talk that the Hungarians or the Jews had been behind it.[35] Hoping to point the finger of blame away from the Black Hand in Belgrade, Princip insisted during his trial that Freemasons had funded the plot and helped the conspirators carry it out, a charge repeated by former German general Erich von Ludendorff.[36] After studying his father's private papers, Max laid the blame on unnamed elements in the German secret police hoping to prevent the archduke's plan to restructure the Habsburg Empire into a collection of federated states. It should be noted, though, that he made these charges in 1937, at a time when he feared the Anschluss was imminent; they may have reflected an attempt to turn Austrian opinion against unification with Germany.[37]

None of these allegations was taken seriously. The assassination has been put down to a series of gross errors and the decisions of stubborn officials; *Schlamperei*, a German term denoting a kind of systematic bureaucratic incompetence, is often used to describe how things went so tragically wrong. Not everyone was as easily persuaded, and speculation about some form of official Austrian complicity gained a persistent life of its own. The question remains: did wilful negligence or deliberation play any part in the events of that fateful Sunday?

The idea, so the theories run, was to get the hated Franz Ferdinand out of the way before he could come to the throne and, at the same time, arm Austria-Hungary with justification to move against Serbia. Newspapers in Vienna openly questioned the competency of government officials who had neglected to keep the assassins 'under observation' before their deed.[38] It was, said one historian, 'strange and startling' that 'the military authorities in Bosnia and the secret police organization made such insufficient preparations for the protection of the Archduke and his wife'.[39]

'The most indescribable state of affairs', declared Hungarian prime minister István Tisza, 'must exist among the police if on the day of the assassination six or seven individuals known to them could take up their positions, armed with bombs and guns, along the route of the late

Successor to the Throne, without the police observing or arresting a single one of them.'[40] Count Julius Andrassy rose in the Hungarian parliament and pointedly asked how those who had planned the visit, aware of Bosnian unrest and pervasive anti-Austrian propaganda, had allowed it to take place on the Serb national holiday of St Vitus's Day. Why, he wondered, had no proper security measures been taken? After the bomb was thrown, why had authorities in Sarajevo allowed the visit to continue? It all smacked, Andrassy thundered, of 'gross negligence' on the part of officials in Vienna and authorities in Sarajevo. He dismissed claims that they had known nothing of the conspiracy as 'incredible'.[41]

Perhaps the Hungarians were always ready to criticize Austria and their charges simply reflected this. Yet many Austrians also believed the worst. After the First World War had ended and Austria became a republic, Leo Pfeffer, the judge who collected evidence in Sarajevo, asserted that certain unnamed, high-ranking Austrian officials had deliberately facilitated the assassination by ignoring warnings and ensuring that security was almost non-existent.[42] Countess Vilma Lanjus von Wallenburg, Sophie's lady-in-waiting, pondered, 'Why was the good Archduke hounded off to the manoeuvres in Bosnia? Perhaps just because he would be murdered there.'[43] Archbishop Stadler of Sarajevo said angrily that he thought Franz Ferdinand and Sophie had been 'purposely sent into a regular avenue of assassins'.[44] Arthur, Count Polzer-Hoditz, who served as an aide-de-camp to Emperor Karl, hinted that Franz Ferdinand's enemies had been responsible for the tragic visit.[45]

It was not merely those in the Habsburg Empire who suspected something nefarious. As early as 1916, the always sensational and often unreliable English journalist Wickham Steed pointed the finger of guilt at Vienna, writing, 'It would certainly not be beyond the power of Austria-Hungary's secret service agents to work up a plot in Belgrade or at Sarajevo were it considered desirable for reasons of imperial policy either to remove obnoxious personages or to provide a pretext for war.'[46] Later, in his memoirs, he was more explicit. 'The possibility of a "removal" of the Heir Presumptive and his consort', he wrote, 'was not thought entirely deplorable from the point of view of the Habsburg family.'[47] Others hoping to divert responsibility from Belgrade seized on these sentiments, and in 1924 the Serbian consul general in Montreal echoed the idea of official Austrian complicity, blaming the Habsburgs themselves.[48]

The most famous of conspiratorial voices belonged to former crown princess Stephanie. 'The secret of Sarajevo', Stephanie declared, 'has been as well guarded as the one of Mayerling. I think the time has come to tell the truth about poor Franz Ferdinand and poor Sophie. They also belonged to the victims . . . Franz Ferdinand and Sophie had dared to defy the Emperor. Bit by bit they paid for their happiness, and finally paid for it with their lives.' Then she added, 'They killed them! Alas! I warned and warned; I knew the methods. Sarajevo was only possible with the ministers' knowledge. The Emperor knew about the dangers that the heir to the throne would be threatened with; he just sat back and watched.'[49]

These were inflammatory words. Was she suggesting deliberate co-operation? Gross negligence? That all of the warnings were purposely cast aside and the couple was deliberately plunged into a dangerous situation in the hope that an assassination attempt might succeed in removing the troublesome archduke?

Some have pointed to General Conrad and Governor-General Oskar Potiorek as likely suspects in any Austrian conspiracy. Both were, it must be admitted, Franz Ferdinand's enemies. Franz Ferdinand had twice blocked important promotions for Potiorek, first as chief of the military staff and then as minister of war. Both men were also eager for an excuse to go to war with Serbia.[50] Under this scenario, it mattered little whether there was an actual assassination or merely some incident that could then be used to justify military action. There have been suggestions that both men lied about the initial invitation to attend the manoeuvres. 'These were not the Archduke's greatest well-wishers', wrote one historian, 'who hastened to fit his alleged desire to see Bosnia into the operations schedule to be approved by His Majesty for 1914.'[51]

Rebecca West expressed these ideas more overtly. 'It must have been quite plain to them both that the assassination of Franz Ferdinand by a Bosnian Serb would be a superb excuse for declaring war on Serbia.'[52]

Potiorek had not been merely negligent in planning the visit; he had been determinedly, arrogantly incompetent. His 'inaction', West wrote, 'would only be credible if one knew that he had received assurances that if anything happened to Franz Ferdinand there would be no investigation afterwards that he need fear.'[53] This, in fact, is precisely what happened. There was no attempt to discover what had gone so grievously wrong in Sarajevo, and no one involved in the planning or execution of the visit was ever held to account. 'If an Archduke should be stung by a fly in some railroad station,' Count von Tchirsky, the German ambassador in Vienna, wrote, 'the station master might well lose his job. But no one is as much as bothered for his share in this slaughter in the streets of Sarajevo.'[54]

'The really remarkable thing', Baron Albert von Margutti said, 'is that at Court no one dared say very much about Sarajevo. Personal considerations counted for too much, a fact that seemed to me highly regrettable, especially in such a case.' He was sure that Potiorek would be fired, if for no other reason than that of what he termed 'Dynastic prestige'.[55] People expected Potiorek to resign, but this never came. Only Franz Josef seemed unmoved. Not only did he order no investigation into what had gone wrong, but he also sought no punishment for officials in Sarajevo who, knowingly or not, had done so much to ensure the success of the conspiracy. The day after the murders, he even asked Bilinski to 'say some highly appreciative words' to Potiorek for his services.[56] Potiorek certainly proved himself as inept a battle commander as he had been provincial governor. Following several serious defeats, he was removed from command. He died in 1933.

Cold calculation and realpolitik are not unknown in military and royal history, and Potiorek's negligence might stretch the limits of coincidence. But conspiracy theories always swirl around momentous events, and suspicions over Sarajevo do not equal proof. 'The imperial house', admits Princess Anita, 'did underestimate the danger', though she finds nothing of a deliberate plot beyond that of Princip and his fellow conspirators.[57] Her sister, Princess Sophie, agrees, calling what happened in Sarajevo '*Schlamperei*, pure *Schlamperei*, Austrian *Schlamperei* . . . It was a mess. People just didn't do their job correctly.'[58]

Perhaps this is true; perhaps allegations of some conspiracy beyond that of Princip and his comrades reflect nothing more than embittered gossip and personal animosities. That some in Austria wanted Franz Ferdinand out of the way is certain, just as it is true that many were actively seeking some excuse for a war against Serbia. What undeniably emerges is that Potiorek made conscious decisions that certainly enabled the conspiracy's success. Franz Ferdinand and Sophie might have lived had the governor-general actually done his job. Whether this was gross incompetence or wilful intent can no longer be proved. Even after a century, it is impossible to fully unravel many lingering questions surrounding the assassination. History is left only with the results of that day.

'Once upon a time . . .' For Franz Ferdinand and Sophie, there was no 'happily ever after' to end their personal fairy tale. Time has left Franz Ferdinand a buffoonish cartoon-like figure, his bristly moustache deemed an accurate representation of the man's dangerous and difficult personality, while Sophie has often been depicted as a scheming adventuress intent on seeing herself crowned empress. Duke Georg of Hohenberg recalls how his grandfather was usually and conflictingly described as both a bigot and a visionary, 'a sinister autocrat', 'a warmonger', and a man of peace all at the same time. The archduke's fight for Sophie, he says, 'turned him into a suspicious observer of human unreliability and vanity'. He persevered until victorious, and together with Sophie endured 'insults, animosity, and intrigues', but one constant remained: the devotion shared by Franz Ferdinand and Sophie to each other and to their children.[59]

Beneath the cool exteriors the couple were 'Franzi' and 'Soph', two people brought together by forbidden romance. Franz Ferdinand raged and roared over the incessant vilification of his wife, but Sophie accepted it as the price to be paid for her personal happiness. Their marriage became a refuge against the cruel court, and they lived quietly, this pair of imperial outcasts, finding pleasure in their family. Surrounding their children with love and attention, they tried to atone for the difficulties they faced as morganatic descendants. To the imperial House of Habsburg, the trio did not exist; to Franz Ferdinand and Sophie, the children became the centre of their increasingly isolated world.

The archduke hunted, patronized the arts, and filled his castles with collected paintings, china and porcelain. His world and interests became Sophie's world and interests. She devoted herself wholeheartedly to her husband and family, to creating peaceful sanctuaries. Even when, as inevitably happened, attitudes softened and signals offered conflicting signs of acceptance mingled with continued hostility, Franz Ferdinand and Sophie carried on with dignified restraint. Public opinion might have turned in his favour had the archduke let his future subjects glimpse the husband and the family man; his image as a reactionary might have been softened, his stern and aloof demeanour viewed not as the sum of the man but rather as merely the public part of a complex personality. Perhaps they might have looked to the archduke – as did so many who actually knew him – not with fear but with hopeful expectation for a reign that would almost certainly have brought important and necessary change to the archaic empire.

Marriage to Sophie won Franz Ferdinand some sympathy; after all, how could a man so determinedly in love, so intent on marrying the lady of his choice in the face of opposition from the imperial court, be truly as cold and heartless as his remote public persona suggested? The few glimpses of the couple's private lives and of their family hinted at the archduke's true passions; perhaps beneath his cool exterior and mercurial moods he could in fact be just as sentimental as any Viennese operetta. He despised appeals to sentiment, though, and failure to play the role of carefree prince cemented his image as a hardened, ruthless man. Princess

Anita recalls a time, not so long ago, when her great-grandfather was 'completely misunderstood. The image is still not perfect. Some people are nasty, calculating how many deer he killed, or what his bag was when hunting, but he worked like mad. He always had his correspondence sent on and spent time sending telegrams. He took very personal care about the forests and collection of bulbs to be planted at Konopischt.'[60]

What would have happened had the archduke come to the throne? We know, despite the suspicions raised by Zita and others, that Franz Ferdinand envisioned no public role for his children, no change to his wife's status. The old Habsburg monarchy would have faced a man who respected tradition but also recognized the need for reform. Would he have been able to enact his plans to transform the empire into a federation of states and save it from disaster? Perhaps the challenge was too great for any single man, yet the fall of the old order was not inevitable. What made it possible, what speeded it toward its death, was Sarajevo.

The late Archduke Otto, Zita's son, said of Franz Ferdinand, 'His was a more serious political tragedy. Sarajevo was really a great crime designed to prevent precisely the evolution Franz Ferdinand wanted. He was murdered because he was a friend of the southern Slavs and neither the Russians nor the Serbs would tolerate this. The Pan-Serbs feared him because they wished to extend their own rule over the people he wished to benefit.'[61]

'If Potiorek, not Franz Ferdinand, had been one of the victims,' wrote historian Samuel Williamson, 'the outcome in July 1914 might have been different.' The archduke, he noted, 'preferred a peaceful policy toward Serbia. He was the person who worried most about the Russian threat. His death also removed a channel of communication with Germany at the dynastic level that might have proved useful in calming tempers in Vienna.' In the end nothing could overcome the forces loosed in Sarajevo. 'Alive,' Williamson noted, 'Franz Ferdinand had acted as brake on the pressures for military action; dead, he became the pretext for war.'[62]

It is a tragic irony that the conflict and chaos unleashed by their parents' deaths in Sarajevo also condemned Sophie, Max and Ernst to lives of suffering. They lost their parents, their home, their country and their possessions. The Second World War brought brutal incarceration in Nazi concentration camps and loss on the battlefield. Yet they remained resilient, infused with the serenity, love and faith they had learned from their parents. 'It's like a clan,' Princess Sophie explains. 'We have our ups and downs, but each generation's parents bred a strong sense of family into their children.'[63]

As blood trickled from his mouth that day in Sarajevo, Franz Ferdinand moaned, 'Sopherl! Sopherl! Don't die! Live for our children!' These words summed up Franz Ferdinand's true passions in life. He would rule, of course, and would implement changes in the Austro-Hungarian Empire, but at heart he most fully embraced his happy family life and the love he had found with Sophie.

Today husband and wife rest within their whitewashed crypt at Artstetten in the peaceful Danube Valley. In 1923, a monument was erected just below the castle, commemorating those who had died in the world war; over the years, other names have been added, among them the two grandsons the archduke and duchess never knew who perished at Soviet hands in the Second World War. It is fitting that Franz Ferdinand and Sophie's names are inscribed at the top of the memorial as the first victims of the First World War.

NOTES

✛

INTRODUCTION

1. Paleologue, 132.
2. See Macartney, 751; Fromkin, 118.
3. Moore, 31; Radziwill, *Sovereigns*, 77.
4. Margutti, 134; West, 345–46.
5. Aronson, 75.
6. Dedijer, 17.
7. West, 365.
8. Information from HSH Princess Anita of Hohenberg to authors.
9. Information from Professor John Röhl to authors.
10. Information from Professor Wladimir Aichelburg to authors; Hohenberg and Scholler, 76.
11. Information from Professor Wladimir Aichelburg to authors; information from HSH Princess Sophie of Hohenberg to authors.
12. Information from HSH Prince Albrecht of Hohenberg to authors.

Notes

PROLOGUE
Vienna, January 1889

1. Crankshaw, 299; Ashley, 177–78.
2. Morton, *Nervous Splendor*, 6.
3. Hamann, *Hitler's Vienna*, 88.
4. Horthy, 40.
5. Aronson, 65; Moore, 20.
6. Cited, Beller, 188.
7. Sosnosky, 'New Light', 59; Margutti, 209.
8. Quoted in Aronson, 67.
9. George V, Diary, in RA/GV/PRIV/GVD/1904, 20 April 1904.
10. Nikitsch-Boulles, 47–48.
11. E. Taylor, *Fall*, 93.
12. Rumbold, 329–31; Horthy, 43; Margutti, 45; Weindel, 243.
13. Marek, 130; Haslip, 141; Palmer, 120–21.
14. Cited, Beller, 138.
15. Crankshaw, 106, 184; Eisenmenger, 120; Larisch, 47–53, 77; Corti, *Elisabeth*, 45.
16. Larisch, 128; Marek, 57, 340; Weindel, 183–84; Radziwill, *Court*, 87–88; Kürenberg, 198.
17. Ketterl, 88.
18. Stephanie, 89–91; Palmer, 221; Crankshaw, 284.
19. Palmer, 249; Morton, *Nervous Splendor*, 117.
20. Aronson, 67.
21. Hamilton, 63; Vivian, 32; Margutti, 174–75; Cantacuzene, 131; Radziwill, *Court*, 137.
22. Hamilton, 49.
23. Cited in Morton, *Nervous Splendor*, 167.
24. Radziwill, *Court*, 131–32.
25. Morton, *Nervous Splendor*, 191–95.
26. Morton, *Nervous Splendor*, 67.
27. Quoted in Morton, *Nervous Splendor*, 184.

ONE

In the Shadow of the Throne

1. Radziwill, *Court*, 57.

2. Praschl-Bichler, *Die Habsburger in Graz*, 95.

3. Aichelburg, *Erzherzog Franz Ferdinand*, 24; *Wiener Zeitung*, December 19, 1863; Weissensteiner, 56; Hohenberg and Scholler, 32; Praschl-Bichler, *Die Habsburger in Graz*, 96–98.

4. Praschl–Bichler, *So lebten*, 113; Aichelburg, *Erzherzog Franz Ferdinand*, 3, 6.

5. Horthy, 72; Hammond, 22–23; Weissensteiner, 58.

6. Cantacuzene, 129; Radziwill, *Court*, 58.

7. Larisch, 129; Radziwill, *Court*, 58–59; Fontenoy, 1:137–38; Radziwill, *Secrets*, 112.

8. Horthy, 72.

9. Franz Josef to Empress Elisabeth, letter of 9 August 1866, in Nostitz-Rieneck, 59.

10. Weissensteiner, 62; Cassels, 8.

11. Weissensteiner, 62.

12. Weissensteiner, 59–60; Cassels, 8; Aichelburg, *Archduke Franz Ferdinand*, 15; Hohenberg and Scholler, 36–38.

13. Brook-Shepherd, *Victims*, 9; Cassels, 9; Kiszling, 11; cited in Dedijer, 90.

14. Eisenmenger, 32; Kiszling, 11.

15. Vivian, 112; Gribble, 302; Moore, 21.

16. Eisenmenger, 210–11.

17. Czernin, 40; Eisenmenger, 210; Aichelburg, *Erzherzog Franz Ferdinand*, 28; Aichelburg, *Archduke Franz Ferdinand*, 15; Brook–Shepherd, *Victims*, 28.

18. Aichelburg, *Erzherzog Franz Ferdinand*, 28, 30; Aichelburg, *Archduke Franz Ferdinand*, 15–16.

19. Brožovsky, *Konopiště*, 8; Kiszling, 11.

20. Eisenmenger, 210.

21. Cassels, 8.

22. Eisenmenger, 210.

23. Brook-Shepherd, *Victims*, 9; Weissensteiner, 64–65; Eisenmenger, 43, 156; Fontenoy, 1:137–38.

24. Mahaffy, 153; Brožovsky, *Konopiště*, 15; Eisenmenger, 132; Hohenberg and Scholler, 44; Meiss, 1.

25. Eisenmenger, 43, 156; Fontenoy, 1:137–38.

26. Aichelburg, *Erzherzog Franz Ferdinand*, 39; Aichelburg, *Archduke Franz Ferdinand*, 17.

27. Eisenmenger, 71.

28. In the Artstetten Archives.

29. Cantacuzene, 100.

30. Larisch, 130; Vivian, 109, 117.

31. Hamann, *Rudolf*, 426.

32. Information from Professor Wladimir Aichelburg to authors; Hammond, 46–47; Meysels, 188.

33. Information from Professor Wladimir Aichelburg to authors; Hammond, 46–47.

34. Rudolf to Franz Ferdinand, letter of 18 December 1883, in Nachlass, box 5.

35. Rudolf to Franz Ferdinand, letter of 21 August 1884, in Nachlass, box 5.

36. Binion, 310, citing Franz Ferdinand to Rudolf, letter of 7 February 1888, in Nachlass, box 5.

37. Rudolf to Franz Ferdinand, letter of 26 November 1884, in Nachlass, box 5.

38. See Albrecht to Franz Ferdinand, letters of 10 February 1886, 3 August 1886, and 13 April 1888, in Nachlass, box 2.

39. Corti, *Elisabeth*, 388–403; Morton, *Nervous Splendor*, 244.

40. Morton, *Nervous Splendor*, 246.

41. Hohenberg and Scholler, 67.

42. Listowel, 92.

43. Ketterl, 120.

44. Pauli, 19.
45. Müller-Guttenbrunn, 17.
46. Kürenberg, 175.

TWO

Adventure and Illness

1. Cassels, 21.
2. Pauli, 24; Brook-Shepherd, *Victims*, 21–22.
3. Franz Ferdinand, letter of November 1895, in Eisenmenger, 174–75.
4. Brook-Shepherd, *Victims*, 23.
5. Horthy, 74; Sosnosky, *Erzherzog*, 9–10; Chlumecky et al., 92; Hohenberg and Scholler, 59.
6. Franz Ferdinand, 1:5.
7. Arco-Zinneberg, *Meine Reise*, 6–7.
8. See, for example, RA/VIC/MAIN/I/88/2, letter of 19 October 1892 from Francis Knollys; RA/VIC/MAIN/I/88/3, letter of 26 October 1892, from Lord Kimberly to Whitehall; Sir Arthur Paget to British Foreign Office, dispatch of 1 November 1892, RA/VIC/MAIN/I/88/5; instructions to Viceroy in Calcutta, 24 November 1892, in RA/VIC/MAIN/N/48/155.
9. Lord Harris to Queen Victoria, 20 January 1893, in RA/VIC/MAIN/N/48/171.
10. Lord Roberts to Queen Victoria, letter of 8 February 1893, in RA VIC/MAIN/N 48/176.
11. Tattersall, 14; Acro-Zinneberg, *Meine Reise*, 12–20; Lord Roberts to Queen Victoria, letter of 6 April 1893, in RA/VIC/MAIN/N/48/184.
12. *Sydney Morning Herald*, 22 May 1893; Brook-Shepherd, *Victims*, 31.
13. Horthy, 75.
14. Wölfling, 78, 80, 82, 90–91.
15. Brook-Shepherd, *Victims*, 31.

16. Arco-Zinneberg, *Meine Reise*, 26.

17. Franz Ferdinand, 2:421, 424; Tattersall, 17; Arco-Zinneberg, *Meine Reise*, 30; Miller, 52; Tate, 145.

18. Sellers, 831; Arco-Zinneberg, *Meine Reise*, 31.

19. May, 337–38; Arco-Zinneberg, *Meine Reise*, 32.

20. May, 338; Sellers, 831.

21. *Chicago Tribune*, 4 October 1893.

22. *Chicago Tribune*, 4 October 1893.

23. *New York Herald Tribune*, 7 October 1893.

24. May, 342.

25. Aichelburg, *Der Thronfolger und die Architektur*, 101.

26. Brook-Shepherd, *Victims*, 34; Pauli, 34.

27. Pauli, 19.

28. Margutti, 113–14.

29. Eisenmenger, 18–20.

30. Franz Josef to Franz Ferdinand, undated letter August 1895, in Hohenberg and Scholler, 74.

31. Eisenmenger, 21–22, 27, 29–32.

32. Eisenmenger, 156.

33. Eisenmenger, 33.

34. Eisenmenger, 51–56, 96.

35. Eisenmenger, 63–66.

36. Franz Ferdinand to Maria Theresa, undated letter, in Hohenberg and Scholler, 80.

37. Eisenmenger, 105–6.

38. Eisenmenger, 174.

39. Nemec, 66; Dedijer, 89.

40. Eisenmenger, 122.

41. Eisenmenger, 143.

42. Remak, 10.

43. Radziwill, *Court*, 66.

44. Vivian, 109, 116–17.

45. Ketterl, 78.

46. Brook-Shepherd, *Victims*, 55; Fontenoy, 2:69–70; Palmer, 284; Cassels, 33.
47. Vivian, 109; cited, Morton, *Thunder at Twilight*, 184–85; Macartney, 750.
48. Czernin, 42.
49. Quoted in Bled, 88.
50. Franz Ferdinand to Countess Nora Fugger, letter of 14 February 1897, in Fugger, 317–20.
51. Grand Duchess Marie Alexandrovna to Crown Princess Marie of Rumania, letter of 21 July 1897, in Mandache, 303.
52. Rumbold, 311; Aichelburg, *Erzherzog Franz Ferdinand*, 40; Eisenmenger, 122; Pauli, 69.
53. Franz Josef to Franz Ferdinand, letter of 7 April 1897, cited in Weissensteiner, 112.
54. Haslip, 411.
55. Vivian, 115–16; Sosnosky, 'New Light', 61; Fontenoy, 2:70.
56. Czernin, 41–42.
57. Conrad, 1:338.

THREE
Romance

1. Jászi, 23.
2. Fontenoy, 2:67.
3. Brook-Shepherd, *Victims*, 39.
4. See RA/VIC/MAIN/I/88/7, letter from the Comte de St Priest to Sir Henry Ponsonby, 10 October 1893; original in French, authors' translation. Mansion-Rigau, letter of 30 November 1894, 41.
5. Quoted in Bled, 94.
6. Franz Ferdinand to Countess Marie Thun-Hohenstein, letter of 27 June 1894, in Rutkowski, 257–59.
7. Margutti, 117.
8. Van der Kiste, 112; Brook-Shepherd, *Victims*, 40–41.

9. Information from Ricardo Mateos Sainz de Medrano to authors.

10. Eisenmenger, 31.

11. Franz Ferdinand to Rudolf, letter of 7 February 1888, cited in Binion, 310.

12. Margutti, 117.

13. Bled, 96.

14. Fugger, 323–34.

15. Brook-Shepherd, *Victims*, 43.

16. Hammond, 18.

17. Hammond, 19–21.

18. *Le Temps*, Paris, 26 November 1913, no. 1913.

19. Pauli, 26; Moore, 27; Radziwill, *Court*, 78; Gribble, 348; Pauli, 25; Hammond, 29–32; Thiériot, 104.

20. Pauli, 26; Hammond, 33–35; Palmer, 220; Stephanie, 88–89.

21. Hammond, 48–49; Pauli, 25.

22. Clary-Aldringen, 155; Pless, *My Private Diary*, 74; information from HSH Princess Sophie of Hohenberg to authors; Ketterl, 124.

23. Fontenoy, 2:68; information from HSH Princess Anita of Hohenberg to authors; Pless, *My Private Diary*, 74; Hammond, 20; Radziwill, *Court*, 78; Gribble, 348; information from HSH Princess Sophie of Hohenberg to authors; information from Professor Wladimir Aichelburg to authors; Radziwill, *Royal Marriage Market*, 7; Clary-Aldringen, 155, 164; Moore, 27.

24. See 'Emperor's New Clothes', http://english.habsburger.net/module -en/des-kaisers-neue-kleider-2013-der-bruch-josephs-ii.-mit-den-tra- ditionen.

25. Hammond, 49–51.

26. Leutrum, 57.

27. Radziwill, *Secrets*, 123; Radziwill, *Court*, 69; Heiszler, Szakács, and Vörös, 12–13; Reid, 8.

28. Pauli, 85; Heiszler, Szakács, and Vörös, 89.

29. Brook-Shepherd, *Victims*, 45; information from Professor Wladimir Aichelburg to authors.

30. Weissensteiner, 122; information from HSH Princess Anita of Hohenberg to authors.

31. Heiszler, Szakács, and Vörös, 17, 68, 72, 89.

32. Information from HSH Princess Sophie of Hohenberg to authors; Hohenberg and Scholler, 77; West, 337; Müller-Guttenbrunn, 16–18; Horthy, 76; Pauli, 17; Brožovsky, *Konopiště*, 8.

33. Franz Ferdinand to Sophie Chotek, letter of 18 August 1894, in Aichelburg, *Der Thronfolger und die Architektur*, 102.

34. Hammond, 72; Aichelburg, *Der Thronfolger und die Architektur*, 102.

35. Hohenberg and Scholler, 76.

36. Eisenmenger, 30.

37. Pauli, 54; Brook-Shepherd, *Victims*, 55.

38. Isabella to Franz Ferdinand, letter of 16 November 1896, in Nachlass, box 3.

39. Hammond, 89–90; Pauli, 105.

40. Brook-Shepherd, *Victims*, 64; Gribble, 304; Hammond, 100.

41. Isabella to Franz Ferdinand, letter of 12 November 1895, in Nachlass, box 3.

42. Isabella to Franz Ferdinand, letter of 23 June 1896, in Nachlass, box 3.

43. Information from HSH Princess Sophie of Hohenberg to authors.

44. Gribble, 305; Radziwill, *Secrets*, 124; Aichelburg, *Erzherzog Franz Ferdinand*, 44; Larisch, 128; Heiszler, Szakács, and Vörös, 14; Pauli, 93; Brook-Shepherd, *Victims*, 63; Nikitsch-Boulles, 21–22; Aichelburg, *Der Thronfolger und die Architektur*, 103; Reid, 11; information from HSH Princess Sophie of Hohenberg to authors; Aichelburg, *Archduke Franz Ferdinand*, 25.

45. Gribble, 306; Radziwill, *Secrets*, 124; Aichelburg, *Erzherzog Franz Ferdinand*, 44; Larisch, 128; Heiszler, Szakács, and Vörös, 14; Pauli, 93; Brook-Shepherd, *Victims*, 63; Nikitsch-Boulles, 21–22; Aichelburg, *Der Thronfolger und die Architektur*, 103; Reid, 11; information from HSH Princess Sophie to authors; Aichelburg, *Archduke Franz Ferdinand*, 25.

46. Hammond, 88.

47. Pauli, 107; Müller-Guttenbrunn, 149–50; Vivian, 122.

48. Information from HSH Princess Anita of Hohenberg to authors.

FOUR
'A Triumph of Love'

1. Pauli, 93–95.

2. Moore, 29.

3. Pauli, 96.

4. E. Taylor, 3.

5. Pauli, 97–102.

6. Brook-Shepherd, *Victims*, 70.

7. Aronson, 7.

8. Eisenmenger, 197.

9. Pauli, 98; Radziwill, *Court*, 89–90; Fontenoy, 2:149–50.

10. West, 338–39; Pauli, 98; Kürenberg, 178; Radziwill, *Court*, 89–90; Margutti, 305; Bourgoing, 372–74; Fontenoy, 2:152; Ketterl, 91–93.

11. Pauli, 98.

12. Brook-Shepherd, *Victims*, 65; Pauli, 105.

13. Pauli, 105.

14. Pauli, 121, 129; Vivian, 122; Morton, *Thunder at Twilight*, 33.

15. Horthy, 77.

16. Bestenreiner, 120.

17. Margutti, 131.

18. Information from HSH Princess Sophie of Hohenberg to authors.

19. Müller-Guttenbrunn, 146–55; Brook-Shepherd, *Victims*, 69; Horthy, 77; Cassels, 42.

20. Brook-Shepherd, *Victims*, 66, 73.

21. Pauli, 115–16, 125; Brook-Shepherd, *Victims*, 67; Radziwill, *Court*, 60, 174–75; Radziwill, *Royal Marriage Market*, 8.

22. Information from HSH Princess Sophie of Hohenberg to authors.

23. Bestenreiner, 119.
24. Letter from Infanta Eulalia to Queen Christina of Spain, 5 June 1900, provided to the authors from the collection of Ricardo Mateos Sainz de Medrano.
25. Pauli, 115; Brook-Shepherd, *Victims*, 67; Radziwill, *Court*, 174–75; Gribble, 297.
26. Rainer to Franz Ferdinand, letter of 2 May 1900, in Nachlass, box 5.
27. Bestenreiner, 123; Gribble, 296; Weindel, 223–25; Pauli, 116–17.
28. *Le Temps*, Paris, 6 November 1899, no. 14031.
29. *Le Matin*, Paris, 6 November 1899, no. 5734; *Le Matin*, 7 November 1899, no. 5735; see also *La Croix*, Paris, 31 October 1899, no. 5075.
30. Information from HSH Princess Anita of Hohenberg to authors; information from HSH Princess Sophie of Hohenberg to authors; Margutti, 264; Crankshaw, 365; Pauli, 126.
31. Corti and Sokol, 252.
32. Pauli, 106–7.
33. Allmayer-Beck, 33–35.
34. Allmayer-Beck, 54; Sieghardt, 63.
35. Franz Ferdinand to Franz Josef, letter of 19 May 1900, quoted in Corti and Sokol, 253–55.
36. Allmayer-Beck, 39–49; Sieghart, 64; Weindel, 227; Steed, *Habsburg Monarchy*, 47–49.
37. Allmayer-Beck, 51–58; Sieghart, 64; Weindel, 227; Steed, *Habsburg Monarchy*, 47–49.
38. Allmayer-Beck, 58.
39. Cited in Bestenreiner, 97.
40. Müller-Guttenbrunn, 154.
41. Margutti, 19, 127–28.
42. Gribble, 307–8; Sosnosky, *Erzherzog*, 35.
43. House Law of the Imperial Family, http://www.heraldica.org/top ics/royalty/hg1839.htm#1900.
44. Pauli, 145–46; Horthy, 78; Sosnosky, *Erzherzog*, 35–36; *Fremdenblatt*, Vienna, 29 June 1900.

45. Allmayer-Beck, 56.

46. Levetus, 166–68.

47. Brook-Shepherd, *Victims*, 80.

48. Pauli, 141–42; Hohenberg and Scholler, 110–11; Kürenberg, 178.

49. Allmayer-Beck, 57.

50. Pauli, 149–50; Bestenreiner, 105.

51. Thiériot, 150–51.

52. *Salonblatt* no. 26, 1 July 1900, cited in Bestenreiner, 105.

53. Cited in Brook-Shepherd, *Victims*, 82.

54. Bestenreiner, 98.

55. Hammond, 133; Pauli, 149; Brook-Shepherd, *Victims*, 80–81.

56. *Neue Freie Presse*, 2 July 1900.

57. Brook-Shepherd, *Victims*, 80–82; Pauli, 149–50; Radziwill, *Secrets*, 116; Bestenreiner, 105–9; Hammond, 134–35; information from HSH Princess Sophie of Hohenberg to authors.

58. Pospišlová, 22; Pauli, 149; Bestenreiner, 105, 110–11; Hohenberg and Scholler, 110–11; Hammond, 133–35; *The Times*, 2 July 1900.

59. Bestenreiner, 111.

60. Aichelburg, *Archduke Franz Ferdinand*, 47; Bestenreiner, 105; information from HSH Princess Sophie of Hohenberg to authors.

61. Pauli, 151–52.

62. Bogle and Bogle, 11.

63. Bestenreiner, 112.

64. Kiszling, 46.

FIVE
'Don't Let Her Think She's One of Us!'

1. Franz Ferdinand to Maria Theresa, letter of 9 July 1900, in Sosnosky, *Erzherzog*, 35–36.

2. Hammond, 139; Morton, *Thunder at Twilight*, 34.

3. Hammond, 138–39.

4. Pauli, 155.

5. Sitwell, 223–29; Husslein-Arco, *Belvedere Palace Chapel*, 38–39.

6. Husslein-Arco, *Belvedere Palace Chapel*, 18, 38–41; Sitwell, 225–26; Praschl-Bichler, *So lebten*, 119–23.

7. Husslein-Arco, *Belvedere Palace Chapel*, 35–40; Aichelburg, *Der Thronfolger und die Architektur*, 102–7; Husslein-Arco and Schoeller, *Das Belvedere*, 165–85.

8. Bestenreiner, 127; Corti and Sokol, 263.

9. Kürenberg, 179.

10. Margutti, 136.

11. Bestenreiner, 119–20.

12. Pauli, 83.

13. Eisenmenger, 239.

14. Eisenmenger, 240; Bestenreiner, 119, 243.

15. Eisenmenger, 239–40; Kürenberg, 179.

16. Eisenmenger, 239–40.

17. Moore, 25–26.

18. Brook-Shepherd, *Victims*, 107.

19. Morton, *Thunder at Twilight*, 33.

20. Montenuovo to Franz Ferdinand, letter of 20 August 1908, in Nachlass, box 3.

21. Morton, *Thunder at Twilight*, 35; Pauli, 157; Bestenreiner, 129; Gribble, 310; Aronson, 69–70; Cassels, 53.

22. Margutti, 178; Levetus, 227–28.

23. Morton, *Thunder at Twilight*, 30.

24. Pauli, 157; Aronson, 69–70; Gribble, 310; Clary-Aldringen, 155; Bestenreiner, 129; Morton, *Thunder at Twilight*, 35; Dedijer, 102.

25. Marek, 22; Palmer, 290.

26. Morton, *Thunder at Twilight*, 35; Pauli, 157; Brook-Shepherd, *Victims*, 110, 113–14; West, 339; Aronson, 69–70; Bestenreiner, 129.

27. Brook-Shepherd, *Victims*, 113–14; Morton, *Thunder at Twilight*, 35.

28. Pauli, 157; Aronson, 69–70; West, 339.

29. Morton, *Thunder at Twilight*, 35; Bestenreiner, 130; Aronson, 69–70; Brook-Shepherd, *Victims,* 111; Eisenmenger, 240.

30. Hammond, 143.

31. Unterreiner, 74–75, 82; Cantacuzene, 130; Vivian, 73–74; Levetus, 385; Hamilton, 62.

32. Ketterl, 228–29; Vivian, 75.

33. Hammond, 143.

34. Bestenreiner, 151; Horthy, 79; Pauli, 157, 162; West, 339; Moore, 31–32.

35. E. Taylor, 4; Aronson, 69–70; Kürenberg, 179.

36. Information from HSH Princess Sophie of Hohenberg to authors.

37. Wölfling, 77–78.

38. Pauli, 163; Hammond, 143; Bestenreiner, 130–31; Wölfling, 78

39. Pauli, 164; Hammond, 144; Bestenreiner, 130.

40. Pauli, 163.

41. Information from HSH Princess Sophie of Hohenberg to authors.

42. Kürenberg, 216; Margutti, 168.

43. Brook-Shepherd, *Victims*, 109, 113.

44. Information from HSH Princess Sophie of Hohenberg to authors.

45. Fugger, 332.

46. Czernin, 51.

47. Sophie to Oktavia, Countess von Glauchau and Waldenburg, letter of 5 January 1910, page 2, in the Schloss Hinterglauchau archives; Cassels, 50.

48. Information from HSH Princess Anita of Hohenberg to authors.

49. Eisenmenger, 201; Pauli, 175; Bestenreiner, 135.

50. Sosnosky, *Erzherzog*, 42.

SIX

The Swirl of Gossip

1. Information from HSH Prince Albrecht of Hohenberg to authors.

2. Bestenreiner, 136–37.

3. Bestenreiner, 136–37; Gribble, 312; Albertini, 2:2–3.

4. Kürenberg, 178.

5. Eisenmenger, 264.

6. Margutti, 132.

7. Czernin, 52; Nikitsch-Boulles, 30–31.

8. Remak, 24.

9. Eisenmenger, 13.

10. Pauli, 12.

11. Moore, 212; Seton-Watson, *Sarajevo*, 90–91; Steed, 'Pact of Konopischt,' 269; West, 346.

12. Morton, *Thunder at Twilight*, 32; Seton-Watson, *Sarajevo*, 90.

13. Zweig, 239.

14. Czernin, 43.

15. Aichelburg, *Erzherzog Franz Ferdinand*, 26.

16. West, 345–46; Moore, 13–15, 31; Radziwill, *Sovereigns*, 77.

17. Margutti, 129, 135.

18. Margutti, 129–32.

19. Pless, *What I Left Unsaid*, 181.

20. Information from HSH Princess Anita of Hohenberg to authors.

21. Eisenmenger, 264.

22. Nikitsch-Boulles, 35.

23. Bestenreiner, 145; Nemec, 155.

24. Morton, *Thunder at Twilight*, 35; Bestenreiner, 130; Aronson, 69–70; Brook-Shepherd, *Victims*, 111.

25. Radziwill, *Court*, 93.

26. Ketterl, 88.

27. Cassels, 12–13; Gainham, 101; Ketterl, 231.

28. *Le Figaro*, Paris, 16 May 1909, no. 136.

29. Bestenreiner, 177.

30. Franz Josef to Franz Ferdinand, letter of 25 March 1905, in Nachlass, box 2.

31. Information from HSH Princess Sophie of Hohenberg to authors.

32. Hammond, 150–51.

33. Eisenmenger, 220, 224.

34. Kiszling, 252–53.

35. Information from Professor Wladimir Aichelburg to authors.

36. Eisenmenger, 252.

37. Radziwill, *Court*, 67; Vivian, 119–20; Gribble, 281; Fontenoy, 2:71–72; Weindel, 145.

38. Larisch, 129–30; Vivian, 118; Gribble, 280; Weindel, 145.

39. Schierbrand, 166; Eisenmenger, 245; Larisch, 130; Gribble, 281; Vivian, 124; Pauli, 216; Bestenreiner, 156.

40. Pauli, 218; Bestenreiner, 156.

41. Bestenreiner, 156.

42. Radziwill, *Secrets*, 117; Radziwill, *Court*, 62–63; Gribble, 287–90; Eisenmenger, 255–56.

43. Eisenmenger, 256; see also Nikitsch-Boulles, 18–19.

44. Franz Josef to Franz Ferdinand, letter of 21 July 1911, in Artstetten Archives, DSCFP 739–42.

45. Information from HSH Princess Sophie of Hohenberg to authors.

46. Radziwill, *Secrets*, 117; Radziwill, *Court*, 62–63; Gribble, 287–90; Eisenmenger, 255.

SEVEN
Attitudes Soften

1. Margutti, 138.

2. *Le Figaro*, Paris, 16 May 1909, no. 136.

3. Brook-Shepherd, *Victims*, 110; Bestenreiner, 186.

4. Pauli, 238; Franz Josef to Franz Ferdinand, letter of 31 July 1909, Nachlass, box 2, cited in Hammond, 157; Kiszling, 167–68.

5. Bestenreiner, 144–45; Pauli, 178.

6. Steed, *Thirty Years*, 1:235–36; Bridge lecture.

7. Information from Ricardo Mateos Sainz de Medrano to authors.

8. Pauli, 104.

9. Pauli, 236; Hammond, 154–55.

10. Höller, 108.

11. Queen Marie of Rumania, 1:513.

12. Margutti, 135.

13. Buhman, 111–13.

14. Czernin, 89; Queen Marie of Rumania, 1:512; Hammond, 154; Nikitsch-Boulles, 130–31; Thiériot, 274–76.

15. Queen Marie of Rumania, 1:512.

16. King Carol of Rumania to the Countess of Flanders, letter of 31 July 1909, provided to the authors from the collection of John Wimbles.

17. Thiériot, 276–77; Buhman, 111–13.

18. Nikitsch-Boulles, 129.

19. Thiériot, 276–77; Pauli, 237.

20. Aronson, 15–16.

21. Röhl, *Wilhelm II*, 1048.

22. Cecil, 2:15; Kann, *Erzherzog Franz Ferdinand*, 120.

23. Bülow, 1:612–14; Kiszling, 147.

24. Pauli, 188.

25. Viktoria Luise, 12.

26. Bestenreiner, 188.

27. Bestenreiner, 189.

28. Thiériot, 277–78.

29. Bestenreiner, 189; Viktoria Luise, 13; Aronson, 70; Gerard, 211.

30. Bestenreiner, 190.

31. Thiériot, 277–78; Brook-Shepherd, *Victims*, 189.

32. Viktoria Luise, 13.

33. Moore, 33.

34. Weissensteiner, 171.

35. Information from HSH Princess Sophie of Hohenberg to authors.

36. Pauli, 238.

37. Thiériot, 274; Bestenreiner, 186, 190.

38. Sophie to Oktavia, Countess von Glauchau and Waldenburg, letter of 13 January 1910, page 4, in the Schloss Hinterglauchau archives.

39. Information from Professor Wladimir Aichelburg to authors.

40. Sophie to Oktavia, Countess von Glauchau and Waldenburg, letter of January 13, 1910, page 2, in the Schloss Hinterglauchau archives.

41. *Le Matin*, 19 January 1910, no. 9458; *La Croix*, 20 January 1910, no. 8228.

42. Brook-Shepherd, *Victims*, 110–11; Bestenreiner, 191.

43. Sophie to Oktavia, Countess von Glauchau and Waldenburg, letter of 13 January 1910, page 2, in the Schloss Hinterglauchau archives.

44. Sir Maurice de Bunsen to British Foreign Office, dispatch of 23 February 1914, in PS/PSO/GV/C/P609/4.

45. Sophie to Oktavia, Countess von Glauchau and Waldenburg, letter of 8 June 1910, page 2, in the Schloss Hinterglauchau archives.

46. Bestenreiner, 190; Brook-Shepherd, *Victims*, 201; Bridge lecture.

47. Aronson, 7.

48. Franz Ferdinand, letter of 13 May 1910, in private collection.

49. Aronson, 1.

50. Bridge lecture; Franz Ferdinand, report on King Edward VII's funeral, 22 May 1910, in Nachlass, box 2.

51. *Reichspost*, 17 January 1911.

52. Tattersall, item no. 102, page 25.

53. Friedrich to Franz Ferdinand, letter of 3 February 1907, in Nachlass, box 3.

54. Friedrich to Franz Ferdinand, letter of 14 November 1910, in Nachlass, box 3.

55. Elisabeth to Franz Ferdinand, letter of 10 June 1911, in Nachlass, box 3.

56. Franz Ferdinand to Thun, letter of 11 November 1906, quoted in Kann, *Erzherzog Franz Ferdinand*, 141.

57. Pauli, 232.

58. Karl to Franz Ferdinand, letter of 7 August 1911, in Nachlass, box 3.

59. Karl to Franz Ferdinand, letter of 13 December 1905, in Nachlass, box 3; Karl to Franz Ferdinand, letter of 22 March 1907, in Nachlass, box 3.

60. Polzer-Hoditz, 56.

61. Karl to Franz Ferdinand, letter of 13 August 1911, in Nachlass, box 3.

62. Brook-Shepherd, *Victims*, 109–10.

63. Moore, 182.

64. Brizi (website).

65. Franz Ferdinand, undated letter to Montenuovo, cited in Nidda, 221–22.

EIGHT
'Konopischt Was Home'

1. Thiériot, 255.

2. Aichelburg, *Erzherzog Franz Ferdinand*, 47; Aichelburg, *Der Thronfolger und Architektur*, 23–24; Brožovsky, *Konopištĕ*, 2–7, 12–14; Brožovsky, *Konopištĕ Château*, 8, 11–15, 18–21; Thiériot, 256; Mihola, 43, 51–52.

3. Eisenmenger, 129; Brožovsky, *Konopištĕ Château*, 19.

4. Mihola, 63, 87.

5. Aichelburg, *Attentat*, 62.

6. Eisenmenger, 194.

7. Bestenreiner, 138.

8. Pauli, 193.

9. Franz Ferdinand to Little Sophie, telegram of 24 June 1914, in Aichelburg, *Attentat*, 18; Sophie to Max, telegram of 25 June 1914, in Aichelburg, *Attentat*, 25.

10. Czernin, 51.

11. Brook-Shepherd, *Victims*, 98.

12. Weissensteiner, 146.

13. Franz Ferdinand to his children, telegram of 24 June 1914, in Aichelburg, *Attentat*, 18.

14. Nikitsch-Boulles, 30; Thiériot, 252.

15. Brožovsky, *Konopištĕ Château*, 47.

16. Eisenmenger, 207; Aichelburg, *Archduke Franz Ferdinand*, 29.
17. Margutti, 111.
18. Eisenmenger, 176–77.
19. Nikitsch-Boulles, 67.
20. Tattersall, item nos. 59 and 61, page 20; information from Professor Wladimir Aichelburg to authors.
21. Brook-Shepherd, *Victims*, 86.
22. Moore, 295.
23. Musil and Hladiková, 6.
24. Sophie to Oktavia, Countess von Glauchau and Waldenburg, letter of 3 May 1910, page 4, in the Schloss Hinterglauchau archives.
25. Sophie to Oktavia, Countess von Glauchau and Waldenburg, letter of 8 June 1910, page 2, in the Schloss Hinterglauchau archives.
26. Bestenreiner, 252; Brožovsky, *Konopiště*, 14; Brožovsky, *Konopiště Château*, 6.
27. Eisenmenger, 211.
28. *La Croix*, 1 July 1914, no. 9600.
29. Information from HSH Princess Sophie of Hohenberg to authors.
30. Information from HSH Princess Anita of Hohenberg to authors.
31. Thiériot, 260.
32. Eisenmenger, 132; Thiériot, 88–89.
33. Schierbrand, 180.
34. Information from HSH Princess Sophie of Hohenberg to authors.
35. Bestenreiner, 251–53.
36. Ketterl, 125–26.
37. Information from HSH Princess Anita of Hohenberg to authors.
38. Brožovsky, *Konopiště*, 28.
39. Nikitsch-Boulles, 30–31.
40. Czernin, 52.
41. Weissensteiner, 146.
42. Brook-Shepherd, *Victims*, 98.
43. Bestenreiner, 138.

44. Sophie to Oktavia, Countess von Glauchau and Waldenburg, letter of 13 January 1910, page 2, in the Schloss Hinterglauchau archives.
45. Information from HSH Princess Sophie of Hohenberg to authors.
46. Franz Ferdinand to Brosch, letter of 15 June 1912, in Chlumecky, *Erzherzog*, 47; de Waal, 183–84.
47. Eisenmenger, 134–35; Brožovsky, *Konopiště*, 18, 21; Aichelburg, *Erzherzog Franz Ferdinand*, 48.
48. Clary-Aldringen, 157.
49. Eisenmenger, 129–30.
50. P. E. Fischer, *Ein Erinnerungsblatt*, 18.
51. Pauli, 232.
52. Macartney, 750.
53. Moore, 24, 35–36; Paget, 222.
54. Eisenmenger, 244–45.
55. Eisenmenger, 243–44; Radziwill, *Court*, 76.
56. Mihola, 63.
57. Eisenmenger, 243–44; Aichelburg, *Attentat*, 91; Bestenreiner, 280–81; Aichelburg, *Erzherzog Franz Ferdinand*, 48.
58. Brožovsky, *Konopiště*, 12–15, 23–24; Zerzan, 4–5; Mihola, 31–32.
59. Margutti, 111.
60. Hohenberg and Scholler, 138; Pauli, 210; Cassels, 48.
61. Brožovsky, *Konopiště Château*, 31.
62. Cassels, 48.
63. Information from HSH Princess Sophie of Hohenberg to authors.
64. Bestenreiner, 139, citing *Neues Wiener Tagblatt*, 2 July 1931; Thiériot, 279.
65. Cassels, 48.
66. Tattersall, item no. 20, page 41.
67. Clary-Aldringen, 156.
68. Tattersall, item nos. 76 and 77, page 22.
69. Musil and Hladiková, 9.
70. Czernin, 40.
71. Eisenmenger, 130.
72. Brook-Shepherd, *Victims*, 98.

73. Mihola, 75.
74. Pauli, 268.
75. Sosnosky, *Erzherzog*, 37–38.
76. Czernin, 40, 47.
77. Cassels, 49.
78. Eisenmenger, 263.
79. Sosnosky, *Erzherzog*, 37–38.
80. Eisenmenger, 129.
81. Czernin, 40; Eisenmenger, 129, 209; Zeepvat, 322; Thiériot, 266.
82. Funder, 189; Sosnosky, *Erzherzog*, 37; Clary-Aldringen, 157; Pless, *What I Left Unsaid*, 145.
83. Czernin, 45.
84. Sophie to Oktavia, Countess von Glauchau and Waldenburg, letter of 13 March 1910, page 4, in the Schloss Hinterglauchau archives.
85. Brook-Shepherd, *Victims*, 86.
86. Levetus, 188; Rumbold, 309; Seton-Watson, 'Archduke Franz Ferdinand,' 290.
87. Hamann, *Hitler's Vienna*, 369.
88. Nikitsch-Boulles, 35.
89. *L'Ouest-Éclair*, Rennes, France, 30 June 1914, no. 5670.
90. Information from HSH Princess Anita of Hohenberg to authors.
91. Sosnosky, *Erzherzog*, 37–38.

NINE
'Even Death Will Not Part Us!'

1. Sophie to Oktavia, Countess von Glauchau and Waldenburg, letter of 25 December 1909, pages 1–2, in the Schloss Hinterglauchau archives.
2. Franz Ferdinand to Brosch, letter of 1 January 1912, in Chlumecky, *Erzherzog*, 37–38.
3. Information from HSH Princess Sophie of Hohenberg to authors; Brook-Shepherd, *Victims*, 93; Pauli, 233–34.

4. Aichelburg, *Der Thronfolger und das Meer*, 38–39; Brook-Shepherd, *Victims*, 93; Bestenreiner, 193.

5. Sophie to Oktavia, Countess von Glauchau and Waldenburg, letter of 13 March 1910, pages 2–3, in the Schloss Hinterglauchau archives.

6. Fabiani, 10–11; Praschl-Bichler, *So lebten*, 97–98.

7. Kiszling, 273.

8. Eisenmenger, 241–43.

9. Pauli, 267; Bardolff, 131.

10. Horthy, 74; Eisenmenger, 143; Czernin, 45.

11. Aichelburg, *Erzherzog Franz Ferdinand*, 3, 6; Aichelburg, *Archduke Franz Ferdinand*, 14.

12. See *Le Figaro*, 8 September 1908, no. 252.

13. Franz Ferdinand to Baron Biegeleben, letter of 6 January 1909, provided to the authors by Professor Wladimir Aichelburg.

14. Bestenreiner, 137; Aichelburg, *Attentat*, 87.

15. Pauli, 189.

16. Information from HSH Princess Sophie of Hohenberg to authors; information from HSH Princess Anita of Hohenberg to authors; Aichelburg, *Erzherzog Franz Ferdinand*, 6–8.

17. Eisenmenger, 202–3.

18. Pauli, 259: Aichelburg, *Der Thronfolger und das Meer*, 65–67; Clary-Aldringen, 157.

19. Brook-Shepherd, *Victims*, 87–88; Nikitsch-Boulles, 36–38; Aichelburg, *Erzherzog Franz Ferdinand*, 48; Aichelburg, *Der Thronfolger und die Architektur*, 109–11.

20. West, 334.

21. Rumbold, 309; Brook-Shepherd, *Victims*, 96; Czernin, 40; Tattersall, 13; Chlumecky et al., 99–102.

22. Information from Professor Wladimir Aichelburg to authors; Aichelburg, *Erzherzog Franz Ferdinand*, 33.

23. Watson, 21–23.

24. Ruffer, 44–47, 135.

25. Ketterl, 113.

26. Eisenmenger, 141–45, 192–93; Hohenberg and Scholler, 83.

27. Crankshaw, 350; Eisenmenger, 200; Chlumecky et al., 101–2; Praschl-Bichler, *Die Habsburger in Salzburg*, 112–15; Praschl-Bichler, *So lebten*, 120–21; Aichelburg, *Der Thronfolger und die Architektur*, 115–16.

28. Praschl-Bichler, *So lebten*, 103; Aichelburg, *Archduke Franz Ferdinand*, 28; Chlumecky et al., 55–57.

29. Ketterl, 126.

30. Czernin, 40.

31. Information from HSH Princess Sophie of Hohenberg to authors; Ketterl, 126; Eisenmenger, 134–35; Brožovsky, *Konopiště*, 18, 21; Aichelburg, *Erzherzog Franz Ferdinand*, 48.

32. Clary-Aldringen, 58–59.

33. Franz Ferdinand to Brosch, letter of 20 January 1909, in Nachlass, box 5.

34. Bestenreiner, 192.

35. *The Times*, May 29, 1912; Bridge lecture.

36. Franz Ferdinand to Brosch, letter of 15 June 1912, in Chlumecky, *Erzherzog*, 39.

37. King George V, diary, 23 May 1912, in RA/GV/PRIV/GVD/1912.

38. Bridge lecture.

39. Bridge lecture.

TEN

An Emperor in Training

1. Pauli, 172–73; Hamann, *Hitler's Vienna*, 249.

2. *Wiener Zeitung*, 9 April 1901.

3. Brook-Shepherd, *Victims*, 137; Franz Josef to Franz Ferdinand, letter of 18 April 1901, and letter of 20 April 1901, in Nachlass, box 1; Dedijer, 107–9.

4. Pauli, 174; Weindel, 285–86.

5. Margutti, 124.

6. Hamann, *Hitler's Vienna*, 289–91; Gainham, 90.

7. Cited in Dedijer, 106.

8. Steed, *Habsburg Monarchy*, xxix; Marek, 353–54; Johnston, 202.

9. Polzer-Hoditz, 50.

10. On Brosch, see Chlumecky, *Erzherzog*, 370–71.

11. Margutti, 133.

12. Chlumecky, *Erzherzog*, 355–60.

13. Franz Ferdinand to Brosch, letter of 12 January 1912, in Chlumecky, *Erzherzog*, 38–39.

14. Palmer, 296–97.

15. Kiszling, 104.

16. Aichelburg, *Erzherzog Franz Ferdinand*, 40.

17. Williamson, 'Influence', 418.

18. Margutti, 123.

19. Moore, 211.

20. Conrad, 3:503.

21. Margutti, 134.

22. Eisenmenger, 220–21.

23. Nikitsch-Boulles, 52–55.

24. Information from HSH Princess Sophie of Hohenberg to authors.

25. Cited in Dedijer, 115.

26. Sosnosky, 'New Light,' 62.

27. Fugger, 225.

28. Margutti, 115.

29. Eisenmenger, 219.

30. Georg, 3rd Duke of Hohenberg, 293.

31. Margutti, 115.

32. Rumbold, 309.

33. Kiszling, 315.

34. Margutti, 263.

35. Eisenmenger, 174–75.

36. Franz Ferdinand to Beck, letter of 28 August 1905, in Kiszling, 83.

37. Conrad, 1:564–45.

38. Margutti, 123; Gribble, 344–45; Schierbrand, 101–2; Albertini, 2:13–22; Horthy, 81; Fay, 2:6–27; Bardolff, 136–79; Kiszling, 87–90; Macartney, 805; Valiani, 9–10.
39. Margutti, 209.
40. Czernin, 57.
41. Albertini, 2:14.
42. Albertini, 2:12–14; Chlumecky, *Erzherzog*, 5.
43. Margutti, 118–19, 125.
44. Margutti, 116–21; Crankshaw, 327.
45. Franz Ferdinand to Prince Franz Liechtenstein, letter of 14 November 1897, in Eisenmenger, 171.
46. Czernin, 58.
47. See Fromkin, 115.
48. Weindel, 229; Chlumecky, *Erzherzog*, 217–18.
49. Pauli, 154.
50. Brook-Shepherd, *Victims*, 116.
51. See Vienna *Reichspost*, 28 March 1926; Sosnosky, *Franz Ferdinand*, 79–99.
52. Sulzberger, 380.

ELEVEN
Diplomacy and Roses

1. Zweig, 1.
2. Dedijer, 467, fn. 1; see also Chlumecky et al.
3. Nidda, 111.
4. Sophie to Oktavia, Countess von Glauchau and Waldenburg, letter of 29 June 1910, page 2, in the Schloss Hinterglauchau archives.
5. Eisenmenger, 260.
6. Sosnosky, *Erzherzog*, 113; Bestenreiner, 149.
7. Information from HSH Princess Anita of Hohenberg to authors.
8. Bestenreiner, 253.

9. Kaiser Wilhelm II to Franz Ferdinand, telegram of 31 May 1914, in Nachlass, box 5.

10. Franz Ferdinand to Brosch, letter of 15 June 1912, in Chlumecky, *Erzherzog*, 39.

11. Eisenmenger, 283.

12. Dedijer, 103.

13. Brook-Shepherd, *Victims*, 113–14.

14. Aichelburg, *Der Thronfolger und die Architektur*, 104.

15. Information from HSH Princess Sophie of Hohenberg to authors.

16. *La Croix*, 30 December 1911, no. 8829.

17. *L'Ouest-Éclair*, Rennes, France, 30 June 1914, no. 5670.

18. Kiszling, 204–5.

19. Brožovsky, *Konopiště*, 24; Pauli, 261.

20. Franz Ferdinand to Mendsdorff, letter of 23 July 1913, cited in Brook-Shepherd, *Victims*, 205.

21. Quoted in Bridge lecture.

22. Franz Ferdinand to Max, undated letter of November 1913, provided to authors by Professor Wladimir Aichelburg.

23. Nikitsch, 165–66; *The Times*, 18 November 1913.

24. Dugdale, 276.

25. Queen Mary to Augusta, Grand Duchess of Mecklenberg-Strelitz, letter of November 27, 1913, in RA/QM/PRIV/CC26/72.

26. Dugdale, 276.

27. Franz Ferdinand to Max, undated letter of November 1913, provided to authors by Professor Wladimir Aichelburg.

28. King George V, diary, 17 November 1913, in RA/GV/PRIV/ GVD/; royal menus, 17 November 1913, in RA/MRH/MRHF/ MENUS/MAIN/WC.

29. Queen Mary to Prince Albert, letter of 20 November 1913, in RA/ GV/PRIV/RF/11/162.

30. King George V, diary, 18 November 1913, in RA/GV/PRIV/ GVD; royal menus, 18 November 1913, in RA/MRH/MRHF/ MENUS/MAIN/WC.

31. King George V, diary, 19 November 1913, in RA/GV/PRIV/GVD/; King George V, diary, 20 November 1913, in RA/GV/PRIV/GVD/; King George V, diary, 21 November 1913, in RA/GV/PRIV/GVD/1913.

32. Nikitsch-Boulles, 166–67; Information from Professor Wladimir Aichelburg to authors.

33. Portland, 246–47.

34. King George V, diary, 18 November 1913, in RA/GV/PRIV/GVD/; royal menus in RA/MRH/MRHF/MENUS/MAIN/WC; *The Times*, 22 November 1913.

35. Queen Mary to Augusta, Grand Duchess of Mecklenberg-Strelitz, letter of 20 November 1913, in RA/QM/PRIV/CC26/71.

36. King George V, diary, 21 November 1913, in RA/GV/PRIV/GVD/.

37. Queen Mary to Augusta, Grand Duchess of Mecklenberg-Strelitz, letter of 27 November 1913, in RA/QM/PRIV/CC26/72.

38. Queen Mary to Augusta, Grand Duchess of Mecklenberg-Strelitz, letter of 5 July 1914, in RA/QM/PRIV/CC26/92.

39. *Worksop Guardian*, 21 November 1913.

40. Bridge lecture.

41. Portland, 246–47.

42. *Worksop Guardian*, 28 November 1913.

43. Sir Maurice de Bunsen to Lord Stamfordham, 23 February 1914, in RA/PS/PSO/GV/C/P/609/4.

44. Mensdorff, diary, 24 November 1913, cited in Brook-Shepherd, *Victims*, 208.

45. *The Guardian*, 29 June 1914.

46. Bridge lecture.

47. Cited in Brook-Shepherd, *Victims*, 190.

48. Information from Professor Wladimir Aichelburg to authors.

49. Sir Maurice de Bunsen to British Foreign Office, 23 February 1914, in RA/PS/PSO/GV/C/P/609/4.

50. Undated letter from Lucy Fane Wingfield, 1914, in Artstetten Archive.

51. Brook-Shepherd, *Victims*, 211.

52. Marie Valerie to Franz Ferdinand, letter of 29 April 1914, in Nachlass, box 3.

53. Isabella to Franz Ferdinand, letter of 25 May 1914, in Nachlass, box 3.

54. Portland, 331.

55. Kiszling, 273–74; Albertini, 2:508; cited in Brook-Shepherd, *Victims*, 212.

56. Tattersall, 23.

57. *Neue Freie Presse*, 8 June 1914.

58. Kaiser Wilhelm II to Franz Ferdinand, telegram of 27 November 1913, in Nachlass, box 6; Kaiser Wilhelm II to Franz Ferdinand, telegram of 24 May 1913, in Nachlass, box 6.

59. Kiszling, 277.

60. E. Taylor, *Fall*, 147.

61. Aichelburg, *Attentat*, 107; Brook-Shepherd, *Victims*, 230.

62. Aichelburg, *Attentat*, 107.

63. Kaiser Wilhelm II to Franz Ferdinand, telegram of 14 June 1914, in Nachlass, box 6.

64. Kiszling, 279; Morsey, 486.

65. Sir Maurice de Bunsen to Sir Edward Grey, 19 June 1914, 28011, document no. 1 in Gooch.

66. Mijatović, 247; Steed, 'Pact of Konopischt', 256–71; Kautsky, 53–55; Fay, 2:37–41; Aichelburg, *Attentat*, 108–9; Albertini, 1:533–34; Sosnosky, *Erzherzog*, 43–44; Morsey, 486.

67. Gerard, 210.

68. Steed, 'Pact of Konopischt', 270–71.

69. See Brook-Shepherd, *Victims*, 231–32; Sosnosky, *Erzherzog*, 43–44.

TWELVE

'I Consider War to Be Lunacy!'

1. Crankshaw, 308; Remak, 32–35; MacKenzie, *Apis*, 9–10.

2. Aronson, 75.

3. Ludwig, 67.

4. MacKenzie, *Apis*, 41–47; MacKenzie, '*Black Hand*', 258–58; West, 11–12; Gedye, 196–97; Cassels, 68; Dedijer, 85–86; Remak, 51.

5. West, 12; Chirol, 8; Sulzberger, 202; Aronson, 81; Remak, 52; Dedijer, 25.

6. Aronson, 81.

7. Remak, 34.

8. Funder, 304.

9. Chlumecky, *Erzherzog*, 98–99.

10. Albertini, 1:201–7, 1:281–86.

11. Sulzberger, 203; Williamson, *Austria-Hungary*, 126–42.

12. Asprey, 184; Remak, 43; Fay, 2:76–85.

13. See Appendix 2, *Austro-Hungarian Red Book*.

14. Remak, 44–49; E. Taylor, *Fall*, 196; Albertini, 2:82–86; Aronson, 94; MacKenzie, '*Black Hand*', 44.

15. See various Belgrade papers in Appendix 1, *Austro-Hungarian Red Book*.

16. Crankshaw, 377.

17. Würthle, 96.

18. Crown Prince Wilhelm of Germany, 123.

19. Conrad, 1:33–36.

20. Strachan, 69.

21. Conrad, 1:142.

22. Weindel, 292.

23. Conrad, 1:142.

24. Chlumecky, *Erzherzog*, 96.

25. Margutti, 116.

26. Williamson, 'Influence,' 423.

27. Kiszling, 192–93.

28. Margutti, 70.

29. Kiszling, 193–97.

30. Asprey, 260–81; Clary-Aldringen, 161–64; Conrad, 3:338–80; E. Taylor, *Fall*, 175–76; Marek, 416–19.

31. Asprey, 260–81; Conrad 3:338–80.

32. Churchill, Reynolds and Miller, 1:252–56.
33. Kann, *Erzherzog Franz Ferdinand*, 223.
34. Williamson, *Austria-Hungary*, 151–54.
35. Franz Ferdinand to Berchtold, letter of 21 October 1913, in Kann, *Erzherzog Franz Ferdinand*, 233.
36. Conrad, 4:467–71; Kiszling, 268–69; Kann, *Erzherzog Franz Ferdinand*, 232.
37. Kiszling, 270.
38. Conrad, 3:406.
39. Conrad, 3:597.
40. Conrad, 3:670.
41. Fay, 2:224.
42. Kiszling, 266.
43. Conrad to Berchtold, telegram of 22 June 1914, cited in Crankshaw, 394.

THIRTEEN

The Fatal Invitation

1. Bestenreiner, 193–94.
2. Quoted in Asprey, 288–89.
3. Conrad, 3:436.
4. Quoted in Asprey, 289.
5. Conrad, 3:444.
6. Conrad, 3:445; Jeřábek, 75.
7. Conrad, 3:702.
8. Duke Max of Hohenberg in *Paris-Soir-Dimanche*, 4 July 1937.
9. Information from Professor Wladimir Aichelburg to authors.
10. Duke Max of Hohenberg in *Paris-Soir-Dimanche*, 4 July 1937.
11. Dedijer, 286.
12. Margutti, 136.
13. A. J. P. Taylor, *First World War*, 13.

14. Aronson, 100.

15. Dedijer, 203–4; 243; Albertini, 50.

16. Dedijer, 273–76.

17. Seton-Watson, *Sarajevo*, 109–10; Remak, 34; see Jeřábek, chapters 7 and 8.

18. Cassels, 144.

19. Jeřábek, 90.

20. Cassels, 144.

21. Dedijer, 286, 408–9; Remak, 29–30; Conrad, 3:444–45.

22. Cassels, 161.

23. Jeřábek, 75.

24. Smith, 153; Conrad, 3:475; Würthle, 179; Cassels, 144.

25. Mijatović, 219–20.

26. Seton-Watson, *Sarajevo*, 110.

27. Brook-Shepherd, *Victims*, 241; Remak, 116; Stojanović, 108.

28. Seton-Watson, *Sarajevo*, 109; Steed, 'Pact of Konopischt', 266; Palmer, 306–7; Margutti, 21; Dedijer, 247, 318, 410; Jászi, 125; West, 348; Remak, 116.

29. Sophie to Oktavia, Countess von Glauchau and Waldenburg, letter of 8 June 1910, page 2, in the Schloss Hinterglauchau archives.

30. See Bilinski to Potiorek, 3 July 1914, in Bittner, 8:289–391; Albertini, 2:111–15; Fay, 2:48–49; Remak, 117, 258; Conrad, 4:65–66.

31. Seton-Watson, *Sarajevo*, 107; E. Taylor, *Fall*, 8; Cassels, 160.

32. Seton-Watson, *Sarajevo*, 108.

33. Quoted in Chlumecky, *Erzherzog*, 363.

34. Cassels, 161; Seton-Watson, *Sarajevo*, 108; Dedijer, 409.

35. Marek, 430; Remak, 115–16.

36. Smith, 166; Dedijer, 410.

37. Cited in Dedijer, 411.

38. Seton-Watson, *Sarajevo*, 113.

39. Brook-Shepherd, *Victims*, 241; Remak, 116.

40. Cassels, 168.

41. Cited in Dedijer, 484

42. Quoted in Cassels, 161.

43. Cassels, 162; Polzer-Hoditz, 168; cited in Dedijer, 406–7.

44. Dedijer, 275.

45. *Srbobran*, Chicago, 3 December 1913.

46. Quoted in Höller, 226.

47. Note to Bilinski, 31 May 1914, no. 2213 from Berchtold, in Trivanović, 990.

48. Cited in Seton-Watson, *Sarajevo*, 106.

49. Cited in Dedijer, 406.

50. Czernin, 52–53.

51. Quoted in Sosnosky, *Erzherzog*, 196–97.

52. Nikitsch-Boulles, 210.

53. Eisenmenger, 264.

54. Brook-Shepherd, *Last Habsburg*, 26–27.

55. Palmer, 322; Sir Maurice de Bunsen to Lord Stamfordham, 26 April 1914, in RA PS/PSO/GV/CP609/6.

56. Palmer, 322.

57. Cited in Dedijer, 407.

58. Brook-Shepherd, *Victims*, 222.

59. Conrad, 3:700; Kiszling, 290; Corti and Sokol, 3:408; Morton, *Thunder at Twilight*, 227–28.

60. Brook-Shepherd, *Victims*, 222.

61. Conrad, 3:700.

62. Bestenreiner, 221.

63. Dugdale, 295; Eisenmenger, 264.

64. Duke Max of Hohenberg in *Paris-Soir-Dimanche*, 4 July 1937.

65. Nikitsch-Boulles, 210–11.

66. Eisenmenger, 264.

67. Duke Max of Hohenberg in *Paris-Soir-Dimanche*, 4 July 1937.

68. Dugdale, 295.

FOURTEEN

The Plot

1. On background see MacKenzie, *Apis*, 1–3; MacKenzie, *'Black Hand'*, 257.
2. Remak, 36.
3. Remak, 53.
4. MacKenzie, *Apis*, 125; Remak, 56.
5. Dedijer, 388–89.
6. Dedijer, 184–85, 283; Smith, 11; Cassels, 193; Albertini, 2:78–79; Remak, 54–55, 91–92; Magrini, 94–95; Owings, 46.
7. Remak, 59.
8. Dedijer, 28–30, 175, 192–93, 212; Remak, 60–62; Cassels, 145–46; Feurlicht, 70–71; Smith, 5–9, 36–37, 64–65; West, 426; *Sarajevski List*, no. 130, 29 June 1914.
9. Dedijer, 28–30, 175, 192–93, 212; Remak, 60–62; Cassels, 145–46; Feurlicht, 70–71; Smith, 5–9, 36–39, 63–65; West, 426; *Sarajevski List*, no. 130, 29 June 1914.
10. Dedijer, 447.
11. Fromkin, 119.
12. Owings, 56.
13. Fromkin, 119.
14. Remak, 64; Smith, 89; Dedijer, 175–78.
15. Owings, 56.
16. Dedijer, 175, 283–84, 289; Owings, 57, 65; Cassels, 193.
17. Remak, 67; Dedijer, 292–94; Cassels, 148; Smith, 91; MacKenzie, *Apis*, 136, 315.
18. Smith, 95.
19. Remak, 68–70; Dedijer, 290, 295–98; *Sarajevski List*, no. 130, 29 June 1914.
20. Remak, 79–90; Dedijer, 303–5.
21. Remak, 60–61, 90, 116; Dedijer, 175, 303–5, 318.
22. Remak, 93–97; Owings, 185–86; Albertini, 2:78–79.

23. See Fromkin, 129–31; Polzer-Hoditz, 163; Morsey, 488–89; Sulzberger, 381; Balfour, 344.

24. Williamson, *Austria-Hungary*, 125–47.

25. Cited in McMeekin, 48.

26. Albertini, 2:83–86; Remak, 57; E. Taylor, *Fall*, 197; Dedijer, 433; MacKenzie, *Apis*, 131; Gavrilović, 410–11; McMeekin, 47.

27. Gavrilović, 410–11.

28. Albertini, 2:83–86; McMeekin, 47.

29. Fromkin, 265.

30. Dedijer, 388–89; MacKenzie, *Apis*, 241–42.

31. Jovanović, 57–58; Albertini, 2:90.

32. Dedijer, 388–89, 502–3; Albertini, 2:90, 98, 100–9.

33. Remak, 71–72; Fromkin, 124–25.

34. Albertini, 2:99–105, 112–13; *New York Herald Tribune*, Paris edition, July 20, 1914; Dedijer, 395.

35. Kiszling, 288; Bestenreiner, 222; Albertini 2:102–3; Schmitt, 173; Bardolff, 181; *Neue Freie Presse*, 28 June 1924; *Neue Wiener Tagblatt*, 28 June 1924; Fay, 2:61–74, 2:152–66.

36. Remak, 77–78; Dedijer, 393–95; MacKenzie, *Apis*, 134; MacKenzie, *'Black Hand'*, 46.

37. Remak, 77–78, 110; Dedijer, 306–11, 393–95; MacKenzie, *Apis*, 134; MacKenzie, *'Black Hand'*, 46; Smith, 138–39; Albertini, 2:49.

FIFTEEN
'I'm Beginning to Fall in Love With Bosnia'

1. Pauli, 277; Brook-Shepherd, *Victims*, 228.

2. Czernin, 57; Funder, 498; Conrad, 3:700.

3. Brook-Shepherd, *Victims*, 233; Bestenreiner, 226.

4. Kiszling, 290–91; Nikitsch-Boulles, 209–10.

5. Morsey, 490–91.

6. Kiszling, 291; Nikitsch-Boulles, 212.

7. Hohenberg and Scholler, 28.

8. Sophie to Max, telegram of 25 June 1914, in Aichelburg, *Attentat*, 25.

9. Cassels, 163.

10. Franz Ferdinand to Little Sophie, telegram of 24 June 1914, in Aichelburg, *Attentat*, 18.

11. Kiszling, 291–93; Nikitsch-Boulles, 209–10; Conrad, 4:13; Morsey, 490–91; *Sarajevo Tagblatt*, June 26, 1914; *Sarajevski List*, no. 128, 26 June 1914.

12. *Sarajevski List*, no. 128, 26 June 1914.

13. Sophie to Max, telegram of 25 June 1914, in Aichelburg, *Attentat*, 25.

14. Kiszling, 291–93; Nikitsch-Boulles, 209–10; Conrad, 4:13; Morsey, 490–91; *Sarajevski List*, no. 128, 26 June 1914.

15. Holbach, 108–10; Munro, 26.

16. Remak, 39; Kiszling, 291; Nikitsch-Boulles, 209–10; Aichelburg, *Attentat*, 26–31; *Sarajevski List*, no. 128, 26 June 1914.

17. Franz Ferdinand to Little Sophie, telegram of 25 June 1914, in Aichelburg, *Attentat*, 24.

18. Holbach, 88, 96–97; Munro, 14–16.

19. Kiszling, 292; Morsey, 490–91.

20. Remak, 101.

21. Munro, 12.

22. *Sarajevski List*, no. 128, 26 June 1914; information from HSH Princess Anita of Hohenberg to authors.

23. *Sarajevski List*, no. 128, 26 June 1914; Nikitsch-Boulles, 209–10.

24. Fay, 2:51; Remak, 103.

25. Aichelburg, *Attentat*, 32.

26. Fay, 2:52; Remak, 103; Seton-Watson, *Sarajevo*, 113.

27. Dedijer, 10.

28. Kiszling, 291–93; Nikitsch-Boulles, 209–10; Conrad, 4:13; Morsey, 490–91; Albertini, 2:87.

29. Morsey, 490–91; Aichelburg, *Attentat*, 32; Kiszling, 291–93; Nikitsch-Boulles, 211–15; Remak, 106–7; Smith, 165; *Sarajevski List*, no. 128, 26 June 1914; *Sarajevski List*, no. 129, 28 June 1914.

30. *Sarajevski List*, no. 129, 28 June 1914.

31. Morsey, 490–91.
32. *Sarajevski List*, no. 130, 29 June 1914.
33. Remak, 111; Dedijer, 312–14.
34. Cited in Dedijer, 102.
35. Remak, 108.
36. Dedijer, 10–11.
37. Pauli, 281–82.
38. Remak, 108–9; cited in Dedijer, 10–11.
39. Nikitsch-Boulles, 213–15.
40. Nikitsch-Boulles, 215–16; Remak, 108–9; Morsey, 491; Bardolff, 182.

SIXTEEN
St Vitus's Day

1. Bestenreiner, 251.
2. Pauli, 152–53.
3. Bestenreiner, 252.
4. Dedijer, 9; Aichelburg, *Attentat*, 42.
5. Kiszling, 296–98; Dedijer, 11–12.
6. Dedijer, 11–12; Kiszling, 297–98; Remak, 114; Nikitsch-Boulles, 216–19; Chlumecky, *Erzherzog*, 363–64; Smith, 169. The number of cars in the motorcade has been variously given as four, five, and six. The surviving protocols accurately place the number at seven. See Aichelburg, *Attentat*, 42–43, 47.
7. Dedijer, 11–12; Kiszling, 297–98; Remak, 114; Nikitsch-Boulles, 216–19; Chlumecky, *Erzherzog*, 363–64; Aichelburg, *Attentat*, 42–43, 47; Smith, 169.
8. Brook-Shepherd, *Victims*, 244; Sosnosky, 'New Light', 207; Conrad, 4:65–66; Seton-Watson, *Sarajevo*, 112–14; Albertini, 2:111–15; *Sarajevski List*, no. 130, 29 June 1914.
9. Remak, 118; Dedijer, 313; Albertini, 2:111–15.
10. Feurlicht, 97.

11. Remak, 119.

12. Smith, 175.

13. Remak, 121–22; Dedijer, 12.

14. Dedijer, 12–13.

15. Chlumecky, *Erzherzog*, 363.

16. Remak, 122–23; Dedijer, 13.

17. Remak, 123–24; Dedijer, 12–13.

18. Dedijer, 319; Remak, 124–25.

19. Smith, 183.

20. Remak, 125; Albertini, 2:46–49; Sosnosky, *Erzherzog*, 215–22; Conrad, 4:19–20; Chlumecky, *Erzherzog*, 363–64; Morsey, 492–94.

21. Remak, 126–27.

22. Remak, 129; Kiszling, 298; Dedijer, 13; West, 331.

23. *Neue Freie Presse*, 29 June 1914.

24. Kiszling, 289; Dedijer, 14.

25. *Reichspost*, 29 June 1914; Dedijer, 13–14; Kiszling, 289.

26. Kiszling, 290; Holbach, 94; West, 332; Sosnosky, *Erzherzog*, 207; Nikitsch-Boulles, 215.

27. West, 332–33.

28. Sosnosky, *Erzherzog*, 207; Nikitsch-Boulles, 215.

29. Cited in Dedijer, 14.

30. Conrad, 4:40.

31. Remak, 132; Albertini, 2:36; Dedijer, 14–15; Kiszling, 199–200.

32. Chlumecky, *Erzherzog*, 363–64.

33. Conrad, 4:20–21.

34. Sosnosky, *Erzherzog*, 220; Kiszling, 199–200; Dedijer, 15; Albertini, 2:36.

35. Morsey, 496.

36. *Neue Freie Presse*, 29 June 1914.

37. Remak, 135; Dedijer, 15.

38. Dedijer, 15; Kiszling, 299–301.

39. Cited in Dedijer, 321.

40. Cited in Dedijer, 321.

41. *Sarajevski List*, no. 130, 29 June 1914; Morsey, 496.

42. Dedijer, 15, 346; Smith, 190–91.

43. Seton-Watson, *Sarajevo*, 103.

44. Remak, 138–39.

45. Jeřábek, 85.

46. Jeřábek, 85; Kiszling, 300; Sosnosky, *Erzherzog*, 219.

47. Kiszling, 300; Sosnosky, *Erzherzog*, 219.

48. Jeřábek, 85–86.

49. Sosnosky, *Erzherzog*, 219–20.

50. Information from HSH Princess Sophie of Hohenberg to authors.

51. Information from Nermina Letic to authors.

52. Kiszling, 301.

53. Morsey, 399; Aichelburg, *Attentat*, 60; Jeřábek, 86.

54. Morsey, 498; Aichelburg, *Attentat*, 60.

55. Bestenreiner, 251.

56. Dedijer, 16; Morsey, 399; Aichelburg, *Attentat*, 60.

57. Remak, 143–44; Brook-Shepherd, *Victims*, 2.

SEVENTEEN
'The Anguish Was Indescribable'

1. Brook-Shepherd, *Victims*, 256.

2. Information from Professor Wladimir Aichelburg to authors.

3. *L'Ouest-Éclair*, Rennes, France, 30 June 1914, no. 5670.

4. Sophie Nostitz-Ricneck in *Samstag*, 23 June 1984.

5. Brook-Shepherd, *Victims*, 256.

6. *Reichspost*, 2 July 1914.

7. *La Croix*, 4 July 1914, no. 9603.

8. Ferdinand Karl to Max, telegram of 29 June 1914, in Aichelburg, *Attentat*, 89.

9. Ludwig Salvator to Max, telegram of 29 June 1914, in Aichelburg, *Attentat*, 89.

10. Kiszling, 303.
11. Rumerskirch to Count Paar, telegram of 28 June 1914, in Aichelburg, *Attentat*, 63.
12. Margutti, 138–39.
13. Marie Valerie, diary, 28–29 June, 1914, in Corti and Sokol, 3:412–13.
14. Aichelburg, *Erzherzog Franz Ferdinand*, 42.
15. Marek, 437–38.
16. Bardolff, 183.
17. Brook-Shepherd, *Victims*, 255.
18. Margutti, 143.
19. Brook-Shepherd, *Last Habsburg*, 2–3.
20. Cited in Remak, 152.
21. Sir Edward Grey to Sir Maurice de Bunsen, telegram of 29 June 1914, cable no. 29072, item no. 14, in Gooch.
22. Sir Edward Grey to Count Mensdorff, 29 June 1914, item no. 15, in Gooch.
23. King George V, diary, 28 June 1914, in RA/GV/PRIV/GVD/.
24. Queen Mary to Augusta, Grand Duchess of Mecklenberg-Strelitz, letter of 2 July 1914, in RA/QM/PRIV/CC26/92.
25. Zweig, 237–39.
26. Dugdale, 290.
27. Quoted in Marek, 435.
28. Eisenmenger, 265.
29. Pauli, 11.
30. Polzer-Hoditz, 54.
31. Windischgraetz, 49; Albertini, 2:270–72; Remak, 152–53; McMeekin, 47; *The Times*, 30 June 1914.
32. *Novoye Vremya*, St Petersburg, 29 June 1914, no, 1273.
33. Both quoted in *Le Gaulois*, Paris, 30 June 1914, no. 13408.
34. McMeekin, 47–48; Crackanthorpe to Sir Edward Grey, 13 July 1914, no. 129, in Gooch.
35. Churchill, Reynolds, and Miller, 1:342.
36. Remak, 155–56; Appendix 9, *Austro-Hungarian Red Book*.

37. Akers-Douglas to Sir Edward Grey, telegram of 30 June 1914, cable no. 30386, item no. 30, in Gooch.
38. *Die Fackel*, 10 July 1914.
39. Prince Alphonse Clary to Daisy, Princess of Pless, letter of 29 June 1914, in Pless, *What I Left Unsaid*, 145–46.
40. Chlumecky, *Erzherzog*, 5.
41. Weissensteiner, 31.
42. Ludwig Salvator to Mrs Mary Stuart Boyd, letter of 3 July 1914, from the collection of Ian Shapiro.
43. Countess Elisabeth de Baillet-Latour to Queen Mary, letter of 30 June 1914, in RA/QM/PRIV/CC47/380.
44. Chlumecky, *Erzherzog*, 364; Churchill, Reynolds, and Miller, 1:260; Remak, 146 48.
45. Remak, 148.
46. Masic, 115–16; Smith, 194; Dedijer, 16; Meysels, 82.
47. Bankl, 145; Aichelburg, *Attentat*, 60; Masic, 117; Dedijer, 16.
48. Dedijer, 16; *Sarajevski List*, no. 132, 30 June 1914.
49. Masic, 118.
50. Smith, 278–79.
51. Information from Professor Wladimir Aichelburg to authors.
52. Bestenreiner, 252.
53. Dienes and Schneider, 34.
54. Aichelburg, *Attentat*, 72; Remak, 146–48, 166; Kiszling, 301–2; Albertini, 2:118–19; Chlumecky, *Erzherzog*, 364; *Sarajevski List*, no. 132, 30 June 1914.
55. Aichelburg, *Attentat*, 72, 76, 79; Kiszling, 301–2; Albertini, 2:118–19; Tattersall, 34; Remark, 167; Pauli, 291; Cassels, 182.
56. Aichelburg, *Attentat*, 72, 76, 79; Kiszling, 301–2; Albertini, 2:118–19; Tattersall, 34; Remark, 167; Pauli, 291–92; Cassels, 182.
57. Remak, 168.
58. Margutti, 140.
59. Information from HSH Princess Sophie of Hohenberg to authors.
60. Jászi, 125.

61. Meysels, 82.

62. Meysels, 82; Pauli, 291; Sosnosky, *Franz Ferdinand*, 226–27.

63. Margutti, 183.

64. Aichelburg, *Attentat*, 80; Remak, 176; Meysels, 86.

65. *L'Osservatore Romano*, Vatican City, 20 June 1914, no. 9600.

66. Remak, 151; Bestenreiner, 253; Akers-Douglas to Sir Edward Grey, telegram of 30 June 1914, cable no. 30386, item no. 30, in Gooch.

67. *L'Ouest-Éclair*, Rennes, France, 30 June 1914, no. 5670; *Le Gaulois*, June 30, 1914, no. 13408; *La Croix*, 5 July 1914, no. 9604.

68. Wilhelm II, 246; Sir E. Goschen to Sir Edward Grey, telegram of 28 June 1914, no. 2967, item no. 12, in Gooch; Sir Horace Rumbold to Sir Edward Grey, telegram of 8 July 1914, no. 30322, item no. 26, in Gooch; Weissensteiner, 37.

69. Kiszling, 304–5; Albertini, 2:118; Sir Maurice de Bunsen to Sir Edward Grey, telegram of 2 June 1914, no. 29388, item no. 18; Sir Maurice de Bunsen to Sir Edward Grey, 29 June 1914, in Gooch.

70. Brook-Shepherd, *Victims*, 259; Palmer, 322; cited in Dedijer, 407.

71. Sir Maurice de Bunsen to Lord Stamfordham, letter of 28 June 1914, in RA/PS/PSO/GV/C/P/609/7.

72. Sir Maurice de Bunsen to Sir Edward Grey, telegram of 4 July 1914, no. 30616, item no. 34, in Gooch.

73. Morton, *Thunder at Twilight*, 270.

74. Remak, 171–72; Wilhelm II, 246; Balfour, 343.

75. Remak, 172; Margutti, 141; Nikitsch-Boulles, 221.

76. Windischgraetz, 50.

77. Nikitsch-Boulles, 221; Remak, 172.

78. Brook-Shepherd, *Victims*, 263–64.

79. *Reichspost*, 5 July 1914.

EIGHTEEN
United in Death

1. *Reichspost*, 5 July 1914; Aichelburg, *Attentat*, 80; *Neuer Wiener Journal*, July 9, 1914.
2. Sir Maurice de Bunsen to Lord Stamfordham, 3 July 1914, in RA/PS/PSO/GV/C/ P/609/9.
3. Aichelburg, *Attentat*, 80–81; Remak, 169–70; undated letter from Lucy Fane Wingfield, 1914, in Artstetten Archives.
4. Aichelburg, *Attentat*, 80–81.
5. *The Times*, 4 July 1914.
6. Undated letter from Lucy Fane Wingfield, 1914, in Artstetten Archives.
7. Hammond, 185–87; *The Times*, 4 July 1914; Weissensteiner, 37; Kiszling, 303; Albertini, 2:118–19; Remak, 170; Aichelburg, *Attentat*, 81; undated letter from Lucy Fane Wingfield, 1914, in Artstetten Archives.
8. Seemann and Lunzer, 206, 89–92; Hammond, 185–86; Morton, *Nervous Splendor*, 262.
9. Aichelburg, *Attentat*, 80–81; Weissensteiner, 37; *The Times*, 4 July 1914.
10. Undated letter from Lucy Fane Wingfield, 1914, in Artstetten Archives.
11. Aichelburg, *Attentat*, 80–81; Weissensteiner, 37; *The Times*, 4 July 1914.
12. Radziwill, *Court*, 94; Radziwill, *Sovereigns*, 96; Ketterl, 128.
13. Remak, 170.
14. Kiszling, 303–4; Albertini, 2:118–19; Sir Maurice de Bunsen to Lord Stamfordham, 3 July 1914, in RA/PS/PSO/GV/C/P/609/9, 3 July 1914; *The Times*, 4 July 1914.
15. Sir Maurice de Bunsen to Lord Stamfordham, 3 July 1914, in RA/PS/PSO/GV/C/P/609/9.
16. *L'Ouest-Éclair*, Rennes, France, 6 July 1914, no. 5676.
17. *The Times*, 4 July 1914.
18. Sir Maurice de Bunsen to Lord Stamfordham, 3 July 1914, in RA/PS/PSO/GV/C/P/609/9.

19. *The Times*, 4 July 1914; Sir Maurice de Bunsen to Lord Stamford-ham, 3 July 1914, in RA/PS/PSO/GV/C/P/609/9.
20. Aichelburg, *Attentat*, 80–81; Remak, 171; Nikitsch-Boulles, 221.
21. Nikitsch-Boulles, 219–20.
22. Nemec, 189.
23. *Reichspost*, 4 July 1914; *Le Matin*, 4 July 1914, no. 11085; *La Croix*, 5 July 1914, no. 9604; *Journal des Debats*, Paris, 5 July 1914, no. 185.
24. Aichelburg, *Attentat*, 81–82.
25. Ketterl, 128.
26. Remak, 173.
27. Windischgraetz, 50.
28. Remak, 173.
29. Windischgraetz, 50; Nikitsch-Boulles, 220; Kiszling, 303–4.
30. Sir Maurice de Bunsen to Sir Edward Grey, 4 July 1914, no. 30616, item no. 34, in Gooch.
31. Margutti, 141.
32. Brook-Shepherd, *Victims*, 261.
33. *L'Ouest-Éclair*, 6 July 1914, no. 5676.
34. *Le Gaulois*, 6 July 1914, no. 13413.
35. Moore, 221.
36. Windischgraetz, 50.
37. Eisenmenger, 265.
38. Ketterl, 127.
39. Margutti, 139.
40. Sir Maurice de Bunsen to Sir Edward Grey, 5 July 1914, no. 30754, item no. 37, in Gooch.
41. Sir Maurice de Bunsen to Sir Edward Grey, 4 July 1914, no. 30616, item no. 34, in Gooch.
42. Sir Maurice de Bunsen to Lord Stamfordham, 3 July 1914, in RA/PS/PSO/GV/C/P/609/9.
43. *Le Matin*, 5 July 1914, no. 11086.
44. *Le Petit Parisien*, Paris, 5 July 1914, no. 13763.
45. *Wiener Zeitung*, 7 July 1914.

46. Nikitsch-Boulles, 221–22.

47. Remak, 178.

48. Remak, 178; Nikitsch-Boulles, 221–22; Kiszling, 305; Albertini, 2:119–20.

49. *Le Matin*, 5 July 1914, no. 11086.

50. Aichelburg, *Attentat*, 84; Nikitsch-Boulles, 221–25; Eisenmenger, 265–66; Kiszling, 305; Albertini, 2:119–20.

51. Aichelburg, *Attentat*, 84, 87; Nikitsch-Boulles, 222–24; Eisenmenger, 265–66; Kiszling, 305.

52. Information from Professor Wladimir Aichelburg to authors.

53. Aichelburg, *Attentat*, 85–87; Marek, 437; Eisenmenger, 266.

54. *Le Matin*, 5 July 1914, no. 11086.

55. Remak, 180.

56. Nikitsch-Boulles, 224; Bestenreiner, 263.

57. *Le Matin*, 5 July 1914, no. 11086.

58. Aichelburg, *Attentat*, 87; Nikitsch-Boulles, 225; Eisenmenger, 266; Brook-Shepherd, *Victims*, 269.

59. P. E. Fischer, *Ein Erinnerungsblatt*, 18; *Le Matin*, 5 July 1914, no. 11086; *La Croix*, 7 July 1914, no. 9605.

NINETEEN
Headlong Toward Oblivion

1. Remak, 190–201; Conrad, 4:82–85; Albertini, 2:174; Friedrich von Weisner, report, 13 July 1914, in Bittner, 8:10252, 10253.

2. No. 5 from Jovanović, Minister at Vienna, to Pašić, 30 June 1914, in *The Serbian Blue Book*.

3. Ritter von Storck, Secretary of Austrian Legation, to Count Berchtold, 30 June 1914, no. 2, in *Austro-Hungarian Red Book*.

4. No. 20 from Pašić to all Serbian Legations abroad, 14 July 1914, in *The Serbian Blue Book*.

5. Sir Maurice de Bunsen to Sir Edward Grey, 16 July 1914, no. 32282, item no. 50, in Gooch.

6. Mansergh, 219; Bittner, 8:9984.

7. Kautsky, 63; F. Fischer, 53–54; Tirpitz, 1:315–16; Clary-Aldringen, 158; Albertini, 2:135.

8. Kautsky, 109.

9. Crackanthorpe to Sir Edward Grey, Belgrade, telegram of 17 July 1914, no. 32459, item no. 53, in Gooch; Churchill, Reynolds and Miller, 1:355.

10. No. 30 from Pašić to all Serbian Missions abroad, 19 July 1914, in *The Serbian Blue Book*.

11. Bittner, 8:10395.

12. Gooch, 9:91.

13. Fromkin, 265.

14. No. 37 from Crown Prince Alexander of Serbia to Tsar Nicholas II, 24 July 1914, in *The Serbian Blue Book*.

15. Churchill, Reynolds and Miller, 1:416.

16. Fromkin, 186.

17. Fromkin, 265.

18. Churchill, Reynolds and Miller, 1:392–97; Albertini, 2:364–73; Ludwig, 203–17; Bittner, 8:10648.

19. No. 18, M. Dumaine, French Ambassador at Vienna, to M. Bienvenu-Martin, Acting Minister for Foreign Affairs, 22 July 1914, in *The French Yellow Book*.

20. Ashley, 278; F. Fischer, 67; no. 29, Count Berchtold to Count Mensdorff at London, 26 July 1914, in *Austro-Hungarian Red Book*.

21. McMeekin, 54–69; Albertini, 2:294.

22. Conrad, 4:162.

23. Dedijer, 337; Remak, 243.

24. Remak, 221.

25. Remak, 242; Dedijer, 345.

26. Remak, 243.

27. Dedijer, 346; Owings, 527–30.

28. Armstrong, 704.

29. Feucrlicht, 159–61.

30. Information from Professor Wladimir Aichelburg to authors; information from HSH Princess Sophie of Hohenberg to authors.

31. Dedijer, 245–46.

32. Countess Elisabeth Baillet-Latour to Queen Mary, letter of 30 June 1914, in RA/QM/PRIV/CC47/380.

33. Aichelburg, *Attentat*, 88; *Le Gaulois*, 5 July 1914, no. 13413.

34. Information from HSH Princess Sophie of Hohenberg to authors.

35. Margutti, 139.

36. Inventory of the possessions and assets of Sophie, Duchess of Hohenberg, conducted 15–18 July 1914, provided to the authors by Professor Wladimir Aichelburg; Hauser-Köchert, 274.

37. Aichelburg, *Attentat*, 91; Bestenreiner, 280–81; Aichelburg, *Erzherzog Franz Ferdinand*, 48.

38. Information from HSH Princess Anita of Hohenberg to authors.

39. Bestenreiner, 281.

40. See Brook-Shepherd, *Victims*, 231–32; Sosnosky, *Erzherzog*, 43–44.

41. Information from HSH Princess Sophie of Hohenberg to authors.

42. Aichelburg, *Attentat*, 91; Bestenreiner, 280–81; Aichelburg, *Erzherzog Franz Ferdinand*, 48; Praschl-Bichler, *So lebten*, 58–60.

43. Crankshaw, 411.

44. Brook-Shepherd, *Last Habsburg*, 213; E. Taylor, 352.

TWENTY

Ripples from Sarajevo

1. Morsey, 488; Bestenreiner, 282; Meysels, 102.

2. Information from HSH Princess Sophie of Hohenberg to authors; Meysels, 100.

3. Information from HSH Princess Sophie of Hohenberg to authors.

4. Meysels, 101.

5. Treaty of Saint-Germain-en-Laye, September 10, 1919, Part IX, Article 208, at http://www.austlii.edu.au/au/other/dfat/treaties/1920/3.html.

6. Information from HSH Princess Sophie of Hohenberg to authors.

7. Information from HSH Princess Sophie of Hohenberg to authors.

8. Information from HSH Princess Sophie of Hohenberg to authors; Bestenreiner, 282; Meysels, 102.

9. Information from HSH Princess Sophie of Hohenberg to authors.

10. Meysels, 108, 187.

11. Information from HSH Prince Albrecht of Hohenberg to authors.

12. Meysels, 108.

13. Information from HSH Prince Albrecht of Hohenberg to authors.

14. Meysels, 111–12.

15. Bestenreiner, 285.

16. Meysels, 108.

17. Information from Professor Wladimir Aichelburg to authors; Meysels, 188; *Le Figaro*, 24 January 1938, no. 24.

18. Information from Professor Wladimir Aichelburg to authors; Meysels, 188.

19. Meysels, 108.

20. Pauli, 304; Meysels, 108, 116–17; Bestenreiner, 286.

21. Information from HSH Princess Anita of Hohenberg to authors; Pauli, 304; Millard, 135–37.

22. Pauli, 304; *Le Figaro*, 24 January 1938, no. 24.

23. Meysels, 163–64.

24. Information from Professor Wladimir Aichelburg to authors; Meysels, 164–65.

25. Meysels, 176.

26. Millard, 150–52.

27. Meysels, 175, 189, 194.

28. Pauli, 304; Bestenreiner, 287; Meysels, 177–79.
29. Quoted in Meysels, 101.
30. Meysels, 176–78.
31. Millard, 154.
32. Information from Professor Wladimir Aichelburg to authors; Meysels, 169, 181–82.
33. Meysels, 180.
34. *L'Ouest-Éclair*, Rennes, France, 7 February 1940, no. 15793.
35. Meysels, 189.
36. Meysels, 181–82, 186–89, 194.
37. Meysels, 185.
38. Meysels, 189.
39. Meysels, 191–94.
40. Meysels, 195–96.
41. Meysels, 203.
42. Meysels, 201–3.
43. Information from HSH Princess Sophie of Hohenberg to authors.
44. Meysels, 212; Bestenreiner, 285.
45. Information from HSH Princess Sophie of Hohenberg to authors; Meysels, 208, 213, 220.
46. Information from HSH Prince Albrecht of Hohenberg to authors.
47. Information from HSH Princess Sophie of Hohenberg to authors.
48. Information from HSH Princess Anita of Hohenberg to authors.
49. Meysels, 218.
50. Meysels, 244.
51. Bestenreiner, 290–91.
52. Information from HSH Princess Sophie of Hohenberg to authors; Meysels, 245–46.
53. Information from HSH Princess Sophie of Hohenberg to authors.

EPILOGUE

1. Bory; information from Avdio Mirsad, Muzejski Sarajctisk, Sarajevo, to authors.
2. Information from Dr Ivan Udovicic, director of the Art Gallery of Bosnia and Herzegovina, to authors; Albertini, 2:47; Smith, 271; Aichelburg, *Attentat*, 87; DeVoss, 50.
3. Feuerlicht, 165.
4. Smith, 275.
5. De Voss, 45, 52.
6. Churchill, 54.
7. De Voss, 52.
8. De Voss, 45, 52.
9. Information from Avdio Mirsad, Muzejski Sarajctisk, Sarajevo, to authors.
10. Information from Dr Ivan Udovicic, director of the Art Gallery of Bosnia and Herzegovina, to authors; Albertini, 2:47; Smith, 271; De Voss, 50.
11. *Sarajevo Oslobodjenje*, 24 March 2006.
12. Feuerlicht, 162.
13. Information from Nermina Letic to authors.
14. Information from HSH Princess Anita of Hohenberg to authors.
15. Brožovsky, *Konopiště*, 25.
16. Brožovsky, *Konopiště Château*, 22–23.
17. Information from HSH Princess Sophie of Hohenberg to authors.
18. Information from HSH Princess Anita of Hohenberg to authors.
19. Information from HSH Princess Sophie of Hohenberg to authors.
20. Information from HSH Princess Sophie of Hohenberg to authors.
21. Information from HSH Princess Sophie of Hohenberg to authors.
22. Information from HSH Princess Sophie of Hohenberg to authors; *International Herald Tribune*, 19 February 2007; *New York Times*, 19 February 2007.
23. Information from HSH Princess Sophie of Hohenberg to authors.

24. Information from HSH Princess Sophie of Hohenberg to authors; *Prague Monitor,* 18 April 2011.
25. Information from HSH Princess Sophie of Hohenberg to authors.
26. Chlumecky, *Erzherzog,* 370; Dedijer, 115.
27. Thiériot, 88–89.
28. Dedijer, 397; Remak, 248; MacKenzie, *Apis,* 80; MacKenzie, *'Black Hand',* 259.
29. Albertini, 2:80–81.
30. Remak, 250, 256; MacKenzie, *'Black Hand',* 391.
31. Beutler, 65.
32. Information from Dr Christoph Hatschek, director of Vienna's Heeresgeschichtliches Museum/Militärhistorisches Institut, to authors; Aichelburg, *Attentat,* 92.
33. Smith, 281; BBC News report, 22 June 2004.
34. Aichelburg, *Attentat,* 92; Brook-Shepherd, *Victims,* 1; Smith, 169, 279.
35. Dedijer, 413.
36. Remak, 227.
37. Duke Max of Hohenberg in *Paris-Soir-Dimanche,* 4 July 1937.
38. See *Neue Freie Presse,* Vienna, 30 June 1914.
39. Jászi, 125.
40. Cited in Remak, 164.
41. Max Müller to Sir Edward Grey, 14 July 1914, item 33049, no. 70, in Gooch.
42. Remak, 257.
43. Bestenreiner, 251.
44. Jászi, 125.
45. Polzer-Hoditz, 165.
46. Steed, 'Pact of Konopischt', 266.
47. Steed, *Through Thirty Years,* 1:398–403.
48. See Seton-Watson, *Sarajevo,* 111; Seferović, 383.
49. Schiel, 449.
50. Smith, 71; Pauli, 262; West, 384; Remak, 165.
51. Pauli, 262–63.

52. West, 348.
53. West, 348.
54. Remak, 164.
55. Margutti, 308.
56. Remak, 164–65.
57. Information from HSH Princess Anita of Hohenberg to authors.
58. Information from HSH Princess Sophie of Hohenberg to authors.
59. Georg, 3rd Duke of Hohenberg, 293.
60. Information from HSH Princess Anita of Hohenberg to authors.
61. Sulzberger, 381.
62. Williamson, 'Influence', 434.
63. Information from HSH Princess Sophie of Hohenberg to authors.

BIBLIOGRAPHY

✤

ARCHIVAL SOURCES

Materials utilized in this book draw on both published and unpublished sources. Archives and abbreviations used within the notes are listed below.

Artstetten: Archives of the Archduke Franz Ferdinand Museum, Schloss Artstetten, Austria.

Nachlass: Collected papers of Archduke Franz Ferdinand, in the Haus-, Hof- und Staatsarchiv, Vienna.

RA: The Royal Archives, Windsor Castle.

Schloss Hinterglauchau: Archive containing letters written by Sophie, Duchess of Hohenberg to her sister Oktavia, Countess von Glauchau and Waldenburg, in the Castle Museum and Art Collection Hinterglauchau, Glauchau, Deposit Schönburg.

BOOKS

Aichelburg, Wladimir. *Archduke Franz Ferdinand and Artstetten Castle*. Vienna: Verlagsbüro Mag. Johann Lehner, 2000.

– – –. *Der Thronfolger und das Meer, k.u.k. Admiral Erzherzog Franz Ferdinand von Österreich-Este in zeitgenössischen Bilddokumenten*. Vienna: Neuer Wissenschaftlicher, 2001.

– – –. *Der Thronfolger und die Architektur, Erzherzog Franz Ferdinand von Österreich-Este als Bauherr*. Vienna: Neuer Wissenschaftlicher, 2003.

– – –. *Erzherzog Franz Ferdinand von Österreich-Este und Artstetten*. Vienna: Verlagsbüro Mag. Johann Lehner, 2000.

– – –. *Sarajevo: Das Attentat*. Vienna: Verlag Öesterreich, 1999.

Albertini, Luigi. *The Origins of the War of 1914*. Trans. and ed. by Isabella M. Massey. 3 vols. London: Oxford University Press, 1952–57.

Allmayer-Beck, Johann Christophe. *Ministerpräsident Baron Beck: Ein Staatsmann des alten Österreich*. Munich: Oldenburg, 1956.

Arco-Zinneberg, Ulrich, Graf von. *Erzherzog Franz Ferdinand, Von Mayerling bis Sarajevo*. Pöchlarn: Erzherzog Franz Ferdinand Museum, Artstetten, 1995.

– – –. *Meine Reise um die Erde: 100 Jahre Weltreise des Thronfolgers*. Pöchlarn: Erzherzog Franz Ferdinand Museum, Artstetten, 1993.

Aronson, Theo. *Crowns in Conflict*. London: John Murray, 1986.

Ashley, Percy. *Europe, from Waterloo to Sarajevo*. New York: Alfred A. Knopf, 1926.

Asprey, Robert. *The Panther's Feast*. London: Jonathan Cape, 1959.

Austro-Hungarian Red Book. Vienna: Ministerium des K. und K. Hauses und des Äussern, 1915.

Balfour, Michael. *The Kaiser and His Times.* New York: W. W. Norton, 1986.

Bankl, Hans. *Die kranken Habsburger.* Vienna: Verlag Kremayr & Scheriau, 1998.

Bardolff, Karl. *Soldat im altern Österreich: Erinnerungen aus meinem Leben.* Jena: E. Diederichs, 1938.

Beller, Steven. *Francis Joseph.* London: Longman, 1996.

Bestenreiner, Erika. *Franz Ferdinand und Sophie von Hohenberg: Verbotene Liebe am Kaiserhof.* Munich: Piper, 2004.

Beutler, Gigi. *The Imperial Vaults of the PP Capuchins in Vienna.* Vienna: Beutler-Heldenstern, 2007.

Bittner, Ludwig, ed. *Österreich-Ungarns Aussenpolitik von der Bosnischen Krise, 1908 bis zum Kreigsausbruch 1914.* Vienna: Österreichischer Bundesverlag, 1930.

Bled, Jean-Paul. *Francois-Ferdinand d'Autriche.* Paris: Editions Tallandier, 2012.

Bogle, James, and Joanna Bogle. *A Heart for Europe.* Leominster, Herefordshire, UK: Gracewing, 1990.

Bory, Eugena. *Spomen-Crkva Nadvojvode Franje Ferdinanda i Sofijn Dom u Sarajevu.* Privately printed, no date. Copy in Sarajevo City Archives.

Bourgoing, Jean de. *Briefe Kaiser Franz Josephs an Frau Katharina Schratt.* Vienna: Oldenbourg, 1949.

Brook-Shepherd, Gordon. *The Last Habsburg*. New York: Weybright and Talley, 1968.

− − −. *Uncrowned Emperor: The Life and Times of Otto von Habsburg*. London: Hambledon and London, 2003.

− − −. *Victims at Sarajevo: The Romance and Tragedy of Franz Ferdinand and Sophie*. London: Harvill, 1984.

Brožovsky, Miroslav. *Konopiště*. Prague: Central Bohemian Institute for the Preservation of Historic Monuments, 1999.

− − −. *Konopiště Château*. Prague: Central Bohemian Institute for the Preservation of Historic Monuments, 1995.

Buhman, Eugeniu. *Patru decenii in serviciul Casei Regale a Romaniei: Memorii, 1898–1940*. Bucharest: Sigma, 2006.

Bülow, Bernhard von. *Memoirs*. 4 vols. Boston: Little, Brown, 1931–32.

Cantacuzene, Julia. *My Life Here and There*. Boston: Scribner's, 1923.

Cassels, Lavender. *The Archduke and the Assassin*. New York: Stein and Day, 1985.

Cecil, Lamar. *Wilhelm II: Emperor and Exile*. Chapel Hill: University of North Carolina Press, 1996.

Chirol, Sir Valentine. *Serbia and the Serbs*. Oxford: Oxford University Press, 1914.

Chlumecky, Leopold von. *Erzherzog Franz Ferdinands Wirken und Wollen*. Berlin: Verlag für Kulturpolitik, 1929.

Chlumecky, Leopold von, et al. *Erzherzog Franz Ferdinand unser Thronfolger*. Vienna: Österreichischen Rundschau, 1913.

Churchill, Allen L., Francis J. Reynolds, and Francis Trevelyan Miller, eds. *The Story of the Great War,* vol. 1. New York: Collier, 1916.

Churchill, Winston. *The Unknown War.* New York: Charles Scribner's Sons, 1931.

Clary-Aldringen, Alfons. *A European Past.* London: Weidenfeld & Nicolson, 1978.

Conrad von Hötzendorf, Franz. *Aus meiner Dienstzeit, 1906–1918.* 5 vols. Vienna: Rikola Verlag, 1921–25.

Cormons, Ernst. *Schicksale und Schatten.* Salzburg: Müller Verlag, 1951.

Corti, Egon Caesar. *Elisabeth, Empress of Austria.* New Haven, CT: Yale University Press, 1936.

Corti, Egon Caesar, and Hans Sokol. *Der alte Kaiser.* Vienna: Syria Verlag, 1955.

Crankshaw, Edward. *The Fall of the House of Habsburg.* New York: Viking, 1963.

Czernin, Count Ottokar. *In the World War.* New York: Harper & Brothers, 1920.

Dedijer, Vladimir. *The Road to Sarajevo.* New York: Simon & Schuster, 1966.

de Waal, Edmund. *The Hare with Amber Eyes.* London: Vintage, 2011.

Dienes, Gerhard M., and Felix Schneider. *Erzherzog Franz Ferdinand von Österreich-Este.* Graz: Stadtmuseum, 2001.

Dugdale, Edgar. *Maurice de Bunsen, Diplomat and Friend*. London: John Murray, 1934.

Edwards, Tudor. *The Blue Danube: The Vienna of Franz Josef and Its Aftermath*. London: Robert Hale, 1973.

Eisenmenger, Victor. *Archduke Franz Ferdinand*. London: Selwyn & Blount, 1928.

Ernst, Otto, ed. *Franz Josef, as Revealed by His Letters*. Trans. by Agnes Blake. London: Methuen, 1927.

Fabiani, Rossella. *Miramar*. Trieste: Bruno Fachin Editore, 2000.

Fay, Sidney. *The Origins of the World War*. New York: Macmillan, 1929.

Feuerlicht, Roberta Strauss. *The Desperate Act: The Assassination of Franz Ferdinand at Sarajevo*. New York: McGraw-Hill, 1968.

Fischer, Fritz. *Germany's Aims in the First World War*. New York: W. W. Norton, 1967.

Fischer, P. Eduard. *Ein Erinnerungsblatt Von P. Eduard Fischer*. Vienna: Buchdruckerei Austria Franz Doll, 1914.

Fontenoy, Mme. La Marquise de. *Secret Memoirs of William II and Francis Joseph*. 2 vols. London: Hutchinson, 1900.

Franz Ferdinand, Archduke of Austria-Este. *Tagebuch meiner Reise um die Welt, 1892–1893*. 2 vols. Vienna: Hölder, 1895–96.

Fromkin, David. *Europe's Last Summer: Why the World Went to War in 1914*. London: William Heinemann, 2004.

Fugger, Princess Nora. *The Glory of the Habsburgs*. London: Harrap, 1932.

Funder, Friedrich. *Vom Gestern ins Heute*. Vienna: Herold Verlag, 1952.

Gainham, Sarah. *The Habsburg Twilight: Tales from Vienna*. London: Weidenfeld & Nicolson, 1979.

Galandauer, Jan, and J. Bruner-Dvořák. *František Ferdinand D'Este*. Brod: Fragment, 1994.

Gedye, G. E. R. *Heirs to the Habsburgs*. Bristol, UK: Arrowsmith, 1932.

Gerard, James W. *Face to Face with Kaiserism*. New York: George H. Doran, 1918.

Gooch, G. P., ed. *British Documents on the Origins of the War, 1898–1914*, vol. 11. London: His Majesty's Stationery Office, 1926.

Gribble, Francis. *The Life of the Emperor Francis Joseph*. London: Eveleigh Nash, 1914.

Hamann, Brigitte. *Hitler's Vienna: A Dictator's Apprenticeship*. Oxford: Oxford University Press, 1999.
– – –. *Kronprinz Rudolf: Ein Leben*. Cologne: Taschenbuch, 2006.
– – –. *'Majestät, ich warne Sie': Geheime und private Schriften*. Munich: Piper Verlag, 1979.
– – –, ed. *Meine liebe, gute Freundin: Die Briefe Kaiser Franz Josefs an Katharina Schratt*. Vienna: Ueberreuter, 1992.

Hamilton, Lord Frederic. *The Vanished Pomps of Yesterday*. New York: George H. Doran, 1921.

Hammond, Beate. *Habsburgs grösste Liebesgeschichte: Franz Ferdinand und Sophie*. Vienna: Ueberreuter, 2001.

Haslip, Joan. *The Lonely Empress*. London: Weidenfeld & Nicolson, 1965.

Hauser-Köchert, Irmgard. *Imperial Jewelers in Vienna*. Firenze: Spes, 1990.

Heiszler, Vilmos, Margit Szakács, and Károly Vörös. *Ein Photoalbum aus dem Haus Habsburg*. Vienna: Böhlau Verlag Gesellschaft, 1998.

Hohenberg, HSH Princess Anita of, and Christiane Scholler. *Wilkommen im Schloss: Anita Hohenberg über ihren Usgrossvater Thronfolger Erzherzog Franz Ferdinand von Österreich-Este*. Vienna: Buro Hamtil, 2011.

Holbach, Maude. *Bosnia and Herzegovina*. London: John Lane, 1910.

Höller, Gerd. *Franz Ferdinand von Österreich-Este*. Vienna: Ueberreuter, 1982.

Horthy, Admiral Miklós. *Memoirs*. London: Hutchinson, 1957.

Husslein-Arco, Agnes, ed. *The Belvedere Palace Chapel*. Vienna: Belvedere, 2010.

Husslein-Arco, Agnes, and Katharina Schoeller, eds. *Das Belvedere: Genese eines Museums*. Vienna: Belvedere, 2011.

Jászi, Oscar. *The Dissolution of the Habsburg Monarchy*. Chicago: University of Chicago Press, 1929.

Jeřábek, Rudolf. *Potiorek: General im Schatten von Sarajevo*. Vienna: Verlag Styria, 1991.

Johnston, William. *Vienna, Vienna: The Golden Age, 1815–1914*. New York: Clarkson N. Potter, 1980.

Kann, Robert A. *Erzherzog Franz Ferdinand Studien*. Vienna: Verlag für Geschichte und Politik, 1976.

Kautsky, Karl. *The Guilt of William Hohenzollern*. London: Skeffington, 1920.

Ketterl, Eugen. *The Emperor Francis Joseph I*. Boston: Stratford, no date.

Kiszling, Rudolf. *Erzherzog Franz Ferdinand von Österreich-Este*. Graz and Cologne: Hermann Böhlaus, 1953.

Krso, Aida, ed. *Sarajevo, 1878–1918*. Sarajevo: Muzej Sarajeva, 2008.

Kürenberg, Joachim von. *A Woman of Vienna: A Romantic Biography of Katharina Schratt*. London: Cassell, 1955.

Larisch, Countess Marie. *My Past*. London: Eveleigh Nash, 1913.

Leehner, R. *The Newest Plan and Guide of Vienna*. Vienna: Oldenbourg, 1911.

Legdr, Paul. *Austria-Hungary*. Chicago: H. W. Snow, 1910.

Leutrum, Countess Olga. *Court and Diplomacy in Austria and Germany*. London: Fisher Unwin, 1918.

Levetus, Sarah. *Imperial Vienna: An Account of Its History, Traditions and Arts*. London: John Lane, 1905.

Listowel, Judith. *A Habsburg Tragedy: Crown Prince Rudolf*. New York: Dorset Press, 1978.

Ludendorff, General Erich von. *Ludendorff's Own Story*. New York: Harper & Brothers, 1919.

Ludwig, Ernest. *Austria-Hungary and the War*. New York: J. S. Ogilvie, 1915.

Macartney, C. A. *The Habsburg Empire, 1790–1918*. New York: Macmillan, 1969.

MacKenzie, David. *Apis: The Congenial Conspirator*. Boulder, CO: East European Monographs, 1989.
– – –. *The 'Black Hand' on Trial: Salonika, 1917*. Boulder, CO: East European Monographs, 1995.

Magrini, Luciano. *Il dramma di Seraievo*. Milan: Athena, 1929.

Mahaffy, R. P. *Francis Joseph: His Life and Times*. London: Duckworth, 1908.

Mandache, Diana. *Dearest Missy*. Falkoping, Sweden: Rosvall Royal Books, 2011.

Mansergh, Nicholas. *The Coming of the First World War*. London: Longman, 1949.

Marek, George. *The Eagles Die: Franz Joseph, Elisabeth, and Their Austria*. New York: Harper & Row, 1974.

Margutti, Albert, Baron von. *The Emperor Francis Joseph and His Times*. London: Hutchinson, 1921.

Marie, Queen of Rumania. *The Story of My Life*. New York: Charles Scribner's Sons, 1934.

Masic, Izet. *First Hospitals in Bosnia and Herzegovina*. Sarajevo: Library of Biomedical Publications, 2001.

McMeekin, Sean. *The Russian Origins of the First World War*. Cambridge, MA: Belknap Press/Harvard University Press, 2011.

Mension-Rigau, Éric, ed. *L'ami du prince: Journal inédit d'Alfred de Gramont, 1892–1915*. Paris: Fayard, 2011.

Meysels, Lucian. *Die verhinderte Dynastie: Erzherzog Franz Ferdinand und das Haus Hohenberg*. Vienna: Molden Verlag, 2000.

Mihola, Rudolf. *Tajemství Konopiště*. Benesov: Nakladatelstvi Start, 2007.

Mijatović, Count Ghedomille. *The Memoirs of a Balkan Diplomatist*. London: Cassell, 1917.

Millard, Frank. *The Palace and the Bunker: Royal Resistance to Hitler*. Stroud, UK: History Press, 2012.

Miller, William H. *The First Great Ocean Liners in Photographs*. New York: Dover Publications, 1984.

Mirsad, Avdić. *Sarajevo 1878–1918 Guide*. Sarajevo: Museum of Sarajevo, no date.

Moore, George Greville. *Seven Years in Vienna, 1907–1914*. London: Constable, 1916.

Morton, Frederic. *A Nervous Splendor: Vienna, 1888–1889*. Boston: Little, Brown, 1979.
– – – . *Thunder at Twilight: Vienna, 1913–1914*. New York: Scribner's, 1989.

Müller-Guttenbrunn, Adam. *Franz Ferdinands Lebensroman*. Stuttgart: Verlag Robert Lutz, 1919.

Munro, Robert. *Rambles and Studies in Bosnia-Herzegovina*. Edinburgh: Blackwood and Sons, 1895.

Musil, Miloš, and Dana Hladiková. *Das staatlich Schloss Velké Březon.* Prague: Národni Památkový Ústav, 2008.

Nemec, Norbert. *Erzherzogin Maria Annunziata.* Vienna: Böhlau Verlag, 2010.

Nidda, Roland Krug von. *Der Weg nach Sarajevo.* Vienna: Amalthea, 1964.

Nikitsch-Boulles, Paul. *Vor dem Sturm.* Berlin: Verlag fur Kulturpolitik, 1925.

Nostitz-Rieneck, Georg, ed. *Briefe Kaiser Franz Josephs an Kaiserin Elisabeth, 1859–1898.* Vienna: Herold Verlag, 1966.

100 godina od aneksije. Sarajevo: Muzej Sarajeva, 2008.

Owings, Dolph. *The Sarajevo Trial.* Chapel Hill, NC: Documentary Publications, 1984.

Paget, Lady Walburga. *Scenes and Memories.* New York: Charles Scribner's Sons, 1912.

Paleologue, Maurice. *Three Critical Years.* New York: Robert Speller, 1957.

Palmer, Alan. *Twilight of the Habsburgs: The Life and Times of Emperor Francis Joseph.* New York: Atlantic Monthly Press, 1994.

Pauli, Hertha. *The Secret of Sarajevo.* London: Collins, 1966.

Platt, Owen. *The Royal Governor and the Duchess: The Duke and Duchess of Windsor in the Bahamas, 1940–1945.* New York: iUniverse, 2003.

Pless, Daisy, Princess of. *Daisy, Princess of Pless: By Herself.* New York: Dutton, 1929.

– – –. *From My Private Diary*. London: John Murray, 1931.

– – –. *What I Left Unsaid*. London: Cassell, 1936.

Polzer-Hoditz, Count Arthur. *The Emperor Karl*. London: Putnam, 1930.

Portland, William Cavendish-Bentinck, 6th Duke of. *Men, Women and Things*. London: Faber & Faber, 1938.

Pospiślová, M. *Ẑákupy*. Ćeská Lipa: District National Committee, no date.

Praschl-Bichler, Gabriele. *Das Familienalbum von Kaiser Franz Joseph und Elisabeth*. Vienna: Ueberreuter, 1995.

– – –. *Das Familienalbum von Kaiser Karl und Kaiserin Zita*. Vienna: Ueberreuter, 1996.

– – –. *Die Habsburger in Graz*. Graz: Leopold Stocker, 1998.

– – –. *Die Habsburger in Salzburg*. Graz: Leopold Stocker, 1999.

– – –. *So lebten die Habsburger*. Vienna: Pichler, 2000.

Radziwill, Princess Catherine. *Secrets of Dethroned Royalty*. New York: John Lane, 1920.

– – –. *Sovereigns and Statesmen of Europe*. New York: Funk & Wagnalls, 1916.

– – –. *The Austrian Court from Within*. New York: Frederick A. Stokes, 1917.

– – –. *The Royal Marriage Market of Europe*. New York: Funk & Wagnalls, 1915.

Remak, Joachim. *Sarajevo: The Story of a Political Murder*. New York: Criterion, 1959.

Röhl, John, ed. *1914: Delusion or Design?* London: Elek, 1973.

– – –. *Wilhelm II: The Kaiser's Personal Monarchy, 1888–1900*. Cambridge: Cambridge University Press, 2004.

Ruffer, Jonathan Garnier. *The Big Shots: Edwardian Shooting Parties*. Tisbury, UK: Debrett's Peerage, 2003.

Rumbold, Sir Horace. *Francis Joseph and His Times*. New York: Appleton, 1909.

Rutkowski, Ernst. 'Aus den Briefen des Thronfolgers Erzherzog Franz Ferdinand an die Grafin Marie von Thun und Hohenstein.' In *Mitteilungen des Osterreighischen Staatsarchivs*, pages 254–70. Vienna: Österreichischen Staatsarchivs, 2007.

Schiel, Irmgard. *Stephanie: Kronprinzessin im Schatten der Tragödie von Mayerling*. Munich: Piper, 1978.

Schierbrand, Wolf von. *Austria-Hungary: The Polyglot Empire*. New York: Frederick Stokes, 1917.

Seemann, Helfried, and Christian Lunzer. *Kronprinz Rudolf*. Vienna: Ueberreuter, 2006.

Seton-Watson, R. W. *Sarajevo: A Study in the Origins of the Great War*. London: Hutchinson, 1926.

Sieghart, Rudolf. *Die letzten Jahrzehnte einer Grossmacht*. Vienna: Ullstein Verlag, 1932.

Sitwell, Sacheverell, ed. *Great Palaces*. London: Weidenfeld & Nicolson, 1964.

Smith, David James. *One Morning in Sarajevo*. London: Weidenfeld & Nicolson, 2008.

Sosnosky, Theodor von. *Franz Ferdinand der Erzherzog Thronfolger*. Munich: Oldenbourg, 1929.

Steed, Henry Wickham. *The Hapsburg Monarchy*. London: Constable, 1919.
– – –. *Through Thirty Years*. London: Heinemann, 1924.

Stephanie, Princess of Belgium, Archduchess of Austria-Hungary. *I Was to Be Empress*. London: Nicholson & Watson, 1937.

Stojanović, Nikola. *La Serbie d'hier et de demain*. Paris: Berger-Levrault, 1917.

Strachan, Hew. *The First World War*. Oxford: Oxford University Press, 2001.

Sulzberger, C. L. *The Fall of Eagles*. New York: Crown, 1977.

Tate, E. Mowbray. *Transpacific Steam: The Story of Steam Navigation from the Pacific Coast of North America to the Far East and the Antipodes, 1867–1941*. Cranbury, NJ: Cornwall Books, 1986.

Tattersall, Kerry, ed. *Franz Ferdinand: The End of an Era*. Vienna: Austrian Mint, Schloss Artstetten, and Österreichs Haus-, Hof- und Staatsarchiv, 1999.

Taylor, A. J. P. *The First World War*. London: Penguin, 1963.

Taylor, Edmond. *The Fall of the Dynasties*. Garden City, NY: Doubleday, 1962.

Thiériot, Jean-Louis. *François-Ferdinand d'Autriche: De Mayerling à Sarajevo*. Paris: Éditions de Fallios, 2005.

Tirpitz, Grand Admiral Alfred von. *Memoirs*. New York: Dodd, Mead, 1919.

Unterreiner, Katrina. *The Hofburg*. Vienna: Pichler, 2009.

Unterreiner, Katrina, and Werner Grand. *Kaiserzeit vom Alltagsleben der Habsburger.* Vienna: Sutton Verlag, 2008.

Valiani, Leo. *The End of Austria-Hungary.* London: Secker & Warburg, 1973.

Van der Kiste, John. *Windsor and Habsburg: The British and Austrian Reigning Houses, 1848–1922.* Gloucester, UK: Alan Sutton, 1987.

Viktoria Luise, Princess of Prussia. *The Kaiser's Daughter.* New York: Prentice-Hall, 1977.

Vivian, Herbert. *Francis Joseph and His Court.* New York: John Lane, 1917.

Watson, E. T., ed. *King Edward VII as a Sportsman.* London: Longmans, Green, 1911.

Weindel, Henri de. *The Real Francis Joseph.* New York: Appleton, 1909.

Weissensteiner, Friedrich. *Franz Ferdinand: Der verhinderte Herrscher.* Vienna: Österreichischer Bundesverlag, 1984.

West, Rebecca. *Black Lamb and Grey Falcon.* New York: Penguin Books, 1994.

Wilhelm, Crown Prince of Germany. *Memoirs.* New York: Charles Scribner's Sons, 1922.

Wilhelm II. *The Kaiser's Memoirs.* New York: Harper, 1923.

Williamson, Samuel. *Austria-Hungary and the Origins of the First World War.* London: Macmillan, 1991.

Windischgraetz, Prince Ludwig. *My Memoirs.* New York: Houghton Mifflin, 1921.

Wölfling, Leopold. *My Life Story: From Archduke to Grocer.* New York: Dutton, 1931.

Würthle, Friedrich. *Die Spur führt nach Belgrad: Sarajevo 1914.* Vienna, Munich, and Zurich: Molden Verlag, 1975.

Zeran, Zdenek. *Konopiste: Der Rosengarten.* Prague: Sumperk, 1994.

Zweig, Stefan. *The World of Yesterday.* London: Pushkin, 2011.

PERIODICALS

Armstrong, Hamilton Fish. 'Confessions of the Assassin Whose Deed Led to the World War.' *Current History* 26, no. 5 (August 1927): 699–707.

Binion, Rudolph. 'From Mayerling to Sarajevo.' *Journal of Modern History* 47, no. 2 (June 1975): 280–316.

Chlumecky, Leopold von. 'Franz Ferdinands Aussenpolitik.' *Berliner Monatshefte* 12, no. 6 (June 1934): 455–66.

DeVoss, David. 'Searching for Gavrilo Princip.' *Smithsonian Magazine* 31, no. 5 (August 2000): 42–53.

Gavrilović, Stoyan. 'New Evidence on the Sarajevo Assassination.' *Journal of Modern History* 27, no. 4 (December 1955): 410–13.

Hohenberg, Georg, 3rd Duke of. 'Erzherzog Franz Ferdinand.' *Österreichische Monatsblätter für kulturelle Freiheit* no. 28 (June–July 1964): 291–95.

Jovanović, M. Ljuba. 'The Murder of Sarajevo.' *Journal of the British Institute of International Affairs* 4, no. 2 (March 1925): 57–69.

Kann, Robert A. 'Emperor William II and Archduke Francis Ferdinand in Their Correspondence.' *American Historical Review* 57, no. 2 (January 1952): 323–51.

May, Arthur J. 'The Archduke Francis Ferdinand in the United States.' *Journal of the Illinois State Historical Society* 39, no. 3 (September 1946): 333–44.

Meiss, Millard. 'Italian Primitives at Konopiště.' *Art Bulletin* 28, no. 1, (March 1946): 1–16.

Morsey, Andreas, Freiherr von. 'Konopischt und Sarajevo.' *Berliner Monatshefte* 12, no. 6 (June 1934): 486–99.

Reid, Peter H. 'The Decline and Fall of the Duke of Teschen.' *Royalty Digest* (July 1998): 6–11.

Schmitt, Bernadotte. 'July 1914: Thirty Years After.' *Journal of Modern History* 16, no. 3 (September 1944): 169–204.

Seferović, Anthony V. 'The Blame for the Sarajevo Murder Plot.' *Current History* 23, no. 3 (December 1924): 383–86.

Sellers, Edith. 'The Archduke Franz Ferdinand's Diary.' *Fortnightly Review* 94, no. 563 (November 1913): 828–43.

Seton-Watson, Hugh. 'The Archduke Franz Ferdinand.' *Contemporary Review* 19, no. 11 (August 1914): 288–303.

Sosnosky, Theodor von. 'New Light on Franz Ferdinand.' *Contemporary Review* 138, no. 6, (July–December, 1930): 58–66.

Steed, Henry Wickham. 'The Pact of Konopischt.' *Nineteenth Century and After* 65, no. 468 (February 1916): 253–73.

Trivanović, Vaso. 'Responsibility for the Sarajevo Assassination.' *Current History* 29, no. 6 (March 1929): 987–92.

Williamson, Samuel. 'Influence, Power and the Policy Process: The Case of Franz Ferdinand, 1906–1914.' *Historical Journal* 17, no. 2 (June 1974): 417–34.

Zeepvat, Charlotte. 'Three Months of the King.' *Royalty Digest* (May 2003): 319–23.

NEWSPAPERS

Chicago Tribune
Die Fackel, Vienna
Fremdenblatt, Vienna
The Guardian, London
Illustrated London News, London
International Herald Tribune, Paris
Journal des débats, Paris
La Croix, Paris
Le Figaro, Paris
Le Gaulois, Paris
Le Matin, Paris
Le Petit Parisien, Paris
Le Temps, Paris
L'Osservatore Romano, Vatican City
L'Ouest-Éclair, Rennes, France
Morning Herald, Sydney
Neue Freie Presse, Vienna
Neuer Wiener Journal, Vienna
Neues Wiener Tagblatt, Vienna

→ Bibliography ←

New York Herald Tribune
New York Herald Tribune, Paris edition
The New York Times
Novoe Vremya, St Petersburg
Paris-Soir-Dimanche
Prague Monitor
Prague Post
Reichspost, Vienna
Sarajevo Oslobodjenje
Sarajevo Tagblatt
Sarajevski List
Samstag, Vienna
Srbobran, Chicago
The Times, London
Wiener Zeitung, Vienna
Worksop Guardian, UK

LECTURE

'Archduke Franz Ferdinand and England.' Lecture delivered by Professor Francis Roy Bridge, London School of Economics and Political Science, 27 February 2012 (cited as Bridge lecture).

WEB SITES

Artstetten Castle Web site. http://www.schloss-artstetten.at/index.php ?lang=en.

Belvedere Palace and Museum Web site. http://www.belvedere.at/en /schloss-und-museum.

Brizi, Giovanna. 'The Religious Life of Emperor Karl: A Study of the Documents for the Beatification Process.' Rome: The Vatican, 1994, at http://emperorcharles.org/English/religiouslife.shtml.

'The Emperor's New Clothes: Joseph II's Break with Tradition.' *The World of the Habsburgs.* http://english.habsburger.net/module-en/des -kaisers-neue-kleider-2013-der-bruch-josephs-ii.-mit-den-tradi tionen.

The French Yellow Book, at http://wwi.lib.byu.edu/index.php/The_ French_Yellow_Book.

Heeresgeschichtliches Museum Web site. http://www.hgm.or.at/.

House Law of the Austrian Imperial Family, at http://www.heraldica .org/topics/royalty/hg1839.htm#1900.

Konopiště Castle Web site. http://www.zamek-konopiste.cz/en/.

The Russian Orange Book, at http://wwi.lib.byu.edu/index.php/The_ Russian_Orange_Book.

The Serbian Blue Book, at http://wwi.lib.byu.edu/index.php/The_Serbian_ Blue_Book.

Sophie von Hohenberg Web site. http://www.sophie-hohenberg-czech -rep.eu/.

Treaty of Saint-Germain-en-Laye, at http://www.austlii.edu.au/au /other/dfat/treaties/1920/3.html.

Velké Březno Web site. http://www.zamek-vbrezno.cz/.

INDEX

⁜

Accession Manifesto, 137

Act of German Confederation (1815), 35, 48

Aerenthal, Alois von, 155

Albert (Prince of England), 146

Albert I (King of Belgium), 88, 97

Albertini, Luigi, 182

Albrecht (Archduke of Austria), 18

Albrecht (Prince, grandson of Franz Ferdinand), 258

Albrecht of Württemberg, 119

Alexander (Crown Prince of Serbia), 156, 243

Alexander (King of Serbia), 64, 154, 175

Alexander II (Tsar of Russia), xxxi, 48, 89, 153

Alexandra (Queen of England), 124, 144

Alexandrovich, George, 28

Alois of Liechtenstein (Prince), 282

Alsace-Lorraine, 152

Andrassy, Julius, 286

Anita (Princess, great-granddaughter of Franz Ferdinand), 115, 141, 248, 280, 289
   on Chotek, Sophie, xxxiv
   on Chotek, Sophie, religious piety of, 106
   on Chotek, Sophie, serene nature of, 73, 78

Anna (Princess of Hohenberg), xxiii, 62

annexation, 155–56

anti-Semitism, 128

Appel, Michael von, 168, 198, 218

Archduke of Austria-Este title, 14

architectural preservation, 123–24

aristocratic tribute, 232, 236–37

army manoeuvres, 164–65, 192

art collection, 123–24

Artamanov, Viktor, 181–82

assassinations, 215
  of Alexander (King of Serbia) and
    Masin, 64, 154, 175
  by Black Hand organization, 165
  Čabrinović bombing attempt of,
    200–3
  conspiracy rumors about, 285–86
  details emerging of, 239–40
  of Franz Ferdinand and Chotek,
    Sophie, xxxii–xxxiii, 206–9
  Franz Josef not personally grieved
    about, 213–14, 231
  Karl receiving news of, 214
  Mary's comments on, 215
  nations responding to, 214–17, 223
  political, xxxi–xxxii
  Potiorek's responsibility in, 287–88
  Russian involvement in, 181
  Sarajevo plot of, 176–79
  Serbia celebrating, 240–41
  Serbian officials aiding plot for,
    182–83
  theories of Sarajevo, xxxiii–xxxiv,
    xxxv
Augusta Viktoria (Kaiserin of Germany)
  93
Austria, 154
  Dimitrijević hating, 175–76
  military intelligence of, 169–70
  provinces annexation proposals and,
    155–56
  Serbia and preventative war of,
    158–59, 162
  Serbia and ten demands from,
    242–43
  Serbia invasion rumors and, 175
  Serbia mobilizing army against, 244

Serbia propaganda against, 157–58
  stronger navy needed by, 25, 98
Austria-Hungary, 153, 156–57
Austrian Order of the Golden Fleece,
  36
Austro-Hungarian Empire, xxix, 38

Baillet-Latour, Elisabeth de, 124, 144,
  217–18, 247
Balkan provinces, 153–54
Balkan Wars, 159, 160–61, 177, 181
Bardolff, Karl von, xxv, 131, 166, 199,
  205, 213–14
  Bosnia visit and, 166–67, 173
  official dinner because of, 163
Battle of Königgrätz, 2
Bavarian Order of St Elisabeth, 149
Bayer, Eduard, 208
Beck, Max Vladimir von, xxv, 13,
  26, 54
Beethoven, Ludwig van, 37
Belvedere Palace, 45, 80, 87, 188
  beginning of year residence at,
    117–18
  children never allowed back to, 236
  moving to, 64–65
  renovation of, 65–66, 143
  winter social season at, 148–49
Benes, Edvard, 256, 269
Berchtold (Austrian Foreign Minister),
  170
Berlin visit, 93–94
Bilinski, Leon von, 168, 184, 288
Bismarck, (German Prince) Otto von,
  xxxii, 154
Black Hand organization, xxxiii
  assassination by, 165

Dimitrijević offering assistance from, 179–80
exposing ploy and, 183
Greater Serbia cause of, 157
role concealed of, 240
Young Bosnia Movement and, 178
Black Hand's Central Executive Committee, 184
Blankenberge, 120
Blumenskorso Flower Parade, 150
Boos-Waldeck (Austrian Count, owner of assassination vehicle), 199, 201
Bosnia, 154, 276
army maneuvers visit to, 164–65, 192
arriving in, 189–90
hostile environment of, 167
leaving for, 187–88
welcome demonstrated in, 190–91
Braunstein, Käthe, 105
Brook-Shepherd, Gordon, xxxv
Brosch, Alexander von Aarenau, xxv, 104, 129–30, 155, 217, 282
Brož, Jaroslav, 281
Buckingham Palace, 124
Budapest, 21–22
Bülow, Bernhard von, 92
Bunsen, Maurice de, 215, 224, 230, 233, 241
Vienna's British ambassador, 149, 214

Čabrinović, Nedeljko, xxvi, 177, 180, 191–93, 276
apology submitted by, 245
arrest of, 239–40
bombing assassination attempt of, 200–3
children writing letter to, 246

Cairo, Egypt, 28
Capuchin Crypt, 283–84
Carnot, Sadi, xxxi
Carol (King of Rumania), 88–90
Caspar, Mizzi, 16
Castello del Catajo, 15
Catholic faith, 13, 127–28
Cavendish-Bentinck, William, xxv, 125
Cecilie (Crown Princess of Germany), 93
Charles V (Habsburg Emperor), 2
Chelsea Flower Shows, 124, 125
children.
annual stipend provided to, 248
Belvedere Palace off limits to, 236
Čabrinović receiving letter from, 246
Chotek family background and, 37–38
Czech government taking income from, 257–58
Czechs declaring, Habsburgs, 255
as enigmas, 142
of Franz Ferdinand family, xxxiv, 107–10
Franz Josef's meetings with, 143, 247
Henriette providing comfort for, 248–49
Karl ensuring future of, 250
morganatic marriage influencing, 110
Schloss Konopischt and, 110, 249, 254–55, 257–58
See also Ernst; Maximilian 'Max'; Sophie
Chlumetz mansion, 121, 255
Chotek, Bohuslav (Count, Sophie's father), xxiii, 37–39, 44

Chotek, Karl Maria (Count, Sophie's
  grandfather), 37, 60–61
Chotek, Sophie (Franz Ferdinand's wife),
  xxiv
  Anita and religious piety of, 106
  Anita's comments on serene nature of,
    73, 78
  assassination of, xxxii–xxxiii, 206–9
  autopsy of, 218–19
  background and qualities of, 36–40
  calming husband's temper, 114
  domestic concerns of, 106–7
  as Duchess of Hohenberg, 94–95
  Eisenmenger recounts fears of, 173
  eternal resting place of, 237–38
  Ferdinand Karl and Otto ignoring,
    66
  financial upbringing of, 39
  Franz Ferdinand early romance with,
    42–44, 53–54
  Franz Ferdinand's love story with,
    xxvii–xxviii, xxix–xxx, 290–92
  Franz Ferdinand's marriage with,
    58–62, 78–80
  Franz Josef's relationship with, 66,
    78, 94, 149
  German imperial family embracing,
    93
  health and appearance of, 140–41
  House of Habsburg and treatment of,
    98
  independent life choices of, 40
  Isabella dismissing from duty, 45–46
  as Isabella's lady-in-waiting, 41–42
  King (George V) and Queen (Mary)
    of England's treatment of, 148
  military units presenting arms to,
    94–95
  morganatic union condemning,
    xxx–xxxi
  optimistic approach to life of, 115
  poisonous gossip about, 77–78
  pregnancy of, 73–76
  Princess Anita's comments on,
    xxxiv
  Princip shooting, 206–8
  Radetzky christened by, 86
  regulations excluding every privilege
    for, 68–72
  end of romance agreement of, 51
  Sarajevo visit of, 192–93
  serenity and grace of, 70–71, 85, 90
  shadowy nonexistence for, 56–57, 80
  simple dignity sought for, 72–74
  still born of, 119
  titles of, xvii–xviii
  Vienna society remained suspicious of,
    95–96
  wardrobe and religious life of, 105–6
  Windsor Castle visit of, 145–47
  See also Henriette; Oktavia; Wolfgang
Chotek family
  children and background of, 37–38
  end of, 281–82
  family tree of, xlii–xlv
  financial difficulties of, 39, 44
  marriage eligibility of, 48
Chotek, Wolfang (Sophie's brother) 50,
  60, 230
Christian of Schleswig-Holstein (Prince),
  145
Christina (Queen of Spain), 87
Churchill, Winston, 276
Ciganović, Milan, 179, 240, 282

Clary, Alphonse (Austrian Prince), 217
coat of arms, 228–29, 250
Collas (Count), 169
Conrad von Hötzendorf, Franz, xxv, 240, 287
  command relieved and restored of, 159
  Franz Ferdinand's animosity toward, 160, 161, 163–64
  military modernization idea of, 158
  policy of brigandage of, 159
  war urged by, 159, 161, 162
Count von Hohenberg. *See* Franz Ferdinand
court etiquette, 49–50
Čubrilović, Vaso, xxvi, 181, 240, 246
Čurčić, Fehim Effendi, 198–99, 202
Czechoslovakia
  children declared Habsburgs by, 255
  children losing income because of, 257–58
  illegal act of, 256
  independence declared by, 253–54
  retroactive linguistic manipulation of, 256–57
Czernin, Ottokar, 77, 103, 123
Czuber, Bertha, 237

Dachau concentration camp, 262–65
Dahn, Felix, 114
Daisy (Princess of Pless), 78
Dalmat (yacht), 189
Dedijer, Vladimir, xxxii, 178
Degenfeld, Ferdinand, 12
Die Vereinigten Staaten von Gröss-Österrich (Popovici, A.), 135

Dimitrijević, Dragutin 'Apis', xxvi, 154, 181–85
  Austria hated by, 175–76
  Black Hand assistance offered by, 179–80
  firing squad killing, 283
Dobneau, Dobner von, 237
Dolgorukaia, Catherine, 48
Doré, Robert, 106
Dual Monarchy, 133–35
Duchess of Hohenberg, 94–95
Duke of Hohenberg, xviii
Duke of Modena, 108, 109, 110
Dvorak, Frantisek, 104

ebenbürtig (equal for marriage), 35
Eckartsau hunting lodge, 122
education, 12–14
Edward VII (King of United Kingdom), 3, 87, 96–97, 122
Edward VIII (King of United Kingdom), xxx, 87, 96, 267
Egeregg, Heidler von, 28
Eisenmenger, Victor, xxv, 28–29, 43, 102, 104, 171
  assassination news comments of, 215
  Chotek, Sophie, fears recounted by, 173
  daughter delivered by, 73–74
  diagnosis by, 26–27
  as Franz Ferdinand friend, 119
Eitel Friedrich (Princess of Prussia), 93
Elisabeth (Archduchess of Austria), xxi, 66–67, 98, 282
Elisabeth (Empress, wife of Franz Joseph), 4–5

Elisabeth (Empress) (*cont.*)
  arranged marriage advice of, 35
  Franz Ferdinand appealing to, 22
  Franz Josef and murder of, 31–32
  tragedies faced by, 5
Elisabeth (Max's wife, Franz
    Ferdinand's daughter-in-law), 264
Elisabeth (Queen of Rumania), 89–90
Elisabeth (Rudolf's daughter, daughter-
    in-law to Franz Josef), 118
Empire of Federated States, 135
Empress of China (luxury liner), 24
equal status, for marriage, 36
Ernst (Franz Ferdinand's son), xxiii,
    xxxiv, 75–76, 103, 113–14, 141
  adult life of, 260–73
  children of, 278
  death of, 271
  in Nazi concentration camps,
    262–68
  parents death told to, 211–12
  paying respects allowed for, 231–32
  Vienna funeral not allowing, 230
  World War I rumors with, 152
Erzherzog Franz Ferdinand Unser Thronfolger
    (biography), 140
Este inheritance, 15, 109, 121, 255, 279
Eugen of Savoy (Prince), 64
Europe, 249

family crypt, 120, 279, 292
Family Statutes of 1839, 34–35
Ferdinand (Crown Prince of Rumania),
    89
Ferdinand (Tsar of Bulgaria), 96, 97
Ferdinand Karl (Archduke of Austria),
    xxi, 212

allowed to pay last respects, 237
archducal honors stripped from,
    83–84
Chotek, Sophie, ignored by, 66
with tuberculosis, 83, 282
violent scenes between brothers with,
    83
wedding not attended by, 59–60
Fiala, Elise, 105
Figl, Leopold, 264
firing squad, 283
First World War, rumours, 151–52
Fischer, Edmund, 188
Fischer, Ferdinand, 218
Flossenbürg concentration camp, 265
foreign royals, 86–87
Fourth Dimension Ball, 8
Franz (Max's son), xxiii
Franz Ferdinand (Archduke of
    Austria-Este), xxxiii
  accidentally discharged gun and,
    147–48
  Archduke of Austria-Este title of, 14
  as art collector and architect, 123–24
  artwork of, 104
  assassination of, xxxii–xxxiii, 206–9
  autopsy of, 218–19
  bidding farewell to life, 188
  Brosch's character sketch of, 129–30
  Cairo visit of, 28
  charm lacking in, 16, 77
  Chotek, Sophie, early romance with,
    42–44, 53–54
  Chotek, Sophie, love story with,
    xxvii–xxviii, xxix–xxx, 290–92
  Chotek, Sophie, marriage and,
    58–62, 78–80

Conrad's animosity from, 160, 161,
    163–64
as demanding but kind to servants,
    106–7
display of emotion by, 42
education of, 12–14
Elisabeth appealed to by, 22
eternal resting place of, 237–38
financial dealings of, 109–10, 247–48
Franz Josef's relationship with,
    19–20, 30–31, 131–33
Great War planned by, 254
health of, 31
honorary promotions of, 15
hope and fear evoked by, 32–33
hunting, love of, 121–22
illegitimate children rumors and,
    17, 259–60
as introverted and aloof, 11–12,
    15–16, 32
Isabella complaint about conduct of,
    47–48
Karl and fears of, 171
language talents lacking in, 13
letter to uncle by, 54–55
Maria Theresa and expression of
    happiness by, 115
marriage support sought by, 54
marriage terms agreed to by, 56–57
Mary and visit of, 145, 147
missed wedding and visit with, 143–44
myths surrounding, xxxii–xxxiii
opinions about, xxix, 19
political changes contemplated by,
    134–38
political modernization ideas of, xxix
potential brides for, 33–34

Princip shooting, 206–8
privilege and duty of, 9
provinces annexation agreement of,
    155–56
Sarajevo trip of, 164–65, 172–73
Schloss Blühnbach purchased by,
    122–23
siblings and childhood of, 10–11
state funeral denied for, 231
temperament of, 104
trifling defect in family tree comment
    of, 49
trusted friends of, 119
tuberculosis diagnosis of, 26–28, 43,
    140
violating oath never considered by,
    76
voyage around world of, 22–25
wife's treatment angering, 71–72
Wilhelm II relationship with, 91–92
Windsor Castle visit of, 145–47
See also Habsburg dynasty
Franz Ferdinand family
    annual routine of, 117–18
    children of, xxxiv, 107–10
    Chlumetz mansion and, 121
    commemorations of, 283–84
    dinner time of, 111–13
    evenings of, 113–14
    George V of England private visit
        with, 144–45
    happy marriage and, 114–15
    horrors endured by children of,
        xxxiv
    invented scandals against, 142
    loving family life of, xxxi
    malicious gossip about, 76–77

Franz Ferdinand family (*continued*)
  property battles of, 280–81
  Schloss Konopischt sanctuary for,
    101–3
  as strictly personal matter, 141–42
Franz Ferdinand Museum, 278–79
Franz I of Austria (Emperor), 35
Franz Josef I (Emperor of Austria), xxi,
    xxxiii, 157
  annual stipend provided by, 248
  assassination not personally grieving,
    213–14, 231
  children's meetings with, 143, 247
  Chotek, Sophie, relationship with,
    66, 78, 94, 149
  conservative ways of, 132
  death of, 250
  Elizabeth killed and, 31–32
  family relations and, 5
  Franz Ferdinand's relationship with,
    19–20, 30–31, 131–33
  impending disaster in court of, 6–7
  isolation and prejudices of, 3–4
  marriage terms to be set by, 55–56
  Montenuovo publicly defended by,
    234
  morganatic marriage disapproval of,
    47–49, 57, 62
  morganatic marriage to be allowed by,
    56
  new style awarded by, 80
  renunciation of succession rights and,
    57–58
  Rumerskirch telegram to, 212–13
  Sarajevo visit of, 167–68
  serious illness of, 171–72
  unsuccessful attempt killing, 175

  wedding punishment from, 59–60
  wife's venereal disease from, 5
Franz V of Modena (Duke), 14
Friedrich (Archduke of Austria),
    xxi, 41
Fromkin, David, 178, 243–44
Fugger, Nora, 30, 35, 133
funeral of Franz Ferdinand
  Franz Ferdinand denied state, 231
  Karl and shared arrangements for,
    222
  Montenuovo denying military honors
    for, 227–28, 232
  morganatic marriage and, 224–25
  no foreign representatives invited to,
    223–25
  public resentments about, 232–34
  at Schloss Artstetten, 236–38
  train journey to Vienna for,
    220–22
  transporting bodies to Artstetten and,
    234–35
  in Vienna, 222–25, 227–31
  viewing period and public sympathy
    at, 229–30

Garfield, US president James, xxxi
Georg (Max's son, Franz Ferdinand's
    grandson), xxiii, 133, 269, 289
George V (King of United Kingdom),
    4, 96, 124, 144–45, 215, 230
Gerard, James W., 152
Gerde, Edmund, 169, 180, 199, 205
German imperial family, 93
golden pheasants, 151
Goluchowski, Agenor, 30–31, 58
Göring, Hermann, 263, 264

gossip
    Elisabeth spreading scurrilous,
        66–67
    malicious, 76–77
    morganatic marriage, 52–54
    poisonous, 77–78
Grabež, Trifko, xxvi, 177, 180, 202,
        205, 276
    arrest of, 240
    death of, 246
    guilt admitted by, 245
Gräf & Stift Bois de Boulogne touring
        car, 199
Grand Cross of the Elisabeth Order,
        149
Great Britain, 25, 146–48
Grey, Edward, 214, 243
Grüscha, Anton, 58
Gudenus, Ernst, 273

Habsburg dynasty, 156
    brink of disaster for, 250
    Budapest nationalism against, 21–22
    Charles V as Emperor of, 2
    conservative education in, 12
    conspiracy theories and, 286–87
    death to, 170
    Empire of Federated States and, 135
    fall of, 253
    family tree of, xl–xli
    Hungarian nationals and, 90–91
    marriage eligibility and, 48
    morganatic marriage and, 52–54
    properties nationalized of, 253
    sovereignty and, 134
    in Vienna, 1–2
Habsburg Family Statutes, 54, 56

Hahn, Kurt, 259–60
Hahn, Marie, 17
Harrach, Franz, 199, 205, 207–8, 284
Hartwig, Nicholas de, 181, 216
Haushofmeister (master of household),
        106
heart disease, 141
Helene of Orleans (Princess), 33–34
Henckel-Donnersmark (Austrian Count),
        122
Henriette (Sophie's sister), xxiv, 211,
        230, 231
    children's comfort provided by,
        248–49
    children's safety worries of, 254–55
Herzegovina, 154
Hesshaimer, Ludwig, 208
Hikisch, Dean Wilhelm, 61
Hildebrandt, Johann Lukas von, 64
Himmler, Heinrich, 267
Hitler, Adolf, 128, 261
Hitler Youth, 266
Hofburg Palace, 69–70
Hofdame (lady-in-waiting), 40
Hohenberg, Anita von (Princess), xxxiv
Hohenberg, Count von. *See* Franz
        Ferdinand
Hohenberg family, xlii–xlv, 266
Hohenstein, Jaroslav Thun und
        (Austrian Count and Prince), xxiv,
        30, 39, 42, 248, 254
Hohenzollern (yacht), 150
Hohenzollern, Josephine, 59
Holy Alliance of 1815, 136
Holy Roman Emperors, 2
honeymoon, 62, 64
Hong Kong, 24

honorary promotions, 15
Horthy, Admiral Miklós, 23
House of Habsburg, 83–84, 98, 290
House of Hohenberg, 250
Hradschin Castle, 9, 37
Hungarian Life Guards, 228
Hungarian nationals, 90–91, 134–35
Hungary, 127–28, 136
hunting trips, 121–22, 146–48

Ihre Hoheit (Your Highness), 94
Ilić, Danilo, xxvi, 176, 180, 240, 246
Ilidže, dining in, 193–94
illegitimate children rumours, 17,
    259–60
Imperial Appanage Department, 132
imperial ball, 7–8
imperial court, 79–81
Imperial Court Ball, 97
Imperial House, 66
Imperial Russian Cavalry, 86–87
imperial succession, 14
imperial throne, 50
imperial yacht (*Lacroma*), 118
Isabella (Archduchess of Austria), xxii,
    40, 99, 149
    Chotek, Sophie, dismissed by,
        45–46
    Chotek, Sophie, lady-in-waiting for,
        41–42
    condemnation from, 52
    daughter's marriage sought by,
        44–45
    Franz Ferdinand conduct complaint
        by, 47–48
    unforgiving nature of, 67
Izwolsky, Alexander, 156

Janaczek, Franz, xxv, 106, 188, 266,
    282
Jaroslav (Count and Prince of Thun),
    xxiv, 30, 39, 42, 248, 254, 281
Jonke, Heinrich, 260
Jonke, Mary, 17
Jovanović, Jovan, 184
Jovanović, Ljuba, 183
Jovanović, Misko, 180
Jungwirth, Alois, 104
Jüptner, Johan, 102

Kabiljo, Elias, 190, 191
Kaiserin Elisabeth (cruiser), 22
Kaltenbrunner, Ernst, 267
Karageorgevich dynasty, 154
Karl (Archduke of Austria), xxii, 53, 75,
    108, 236
    assassination news reaching, 214
    as Emperor, xviii, 250–51
    Franz Ferdinand's fears expressed to,
        171
    Montenuovo dismissed by, 250
    shared funeral arrangements argued
        by, 222
    Zita marrying, 99–100
Karl Ludwig (Franz Ferdinand's father),
    xxii, 9–10, 19–20, 27
    conservative religious instruction and,
        12–13
    Maria Theresa third wife of, 11
    typhoid, 29
Kaunic, Pavao, 218–19
Kennedy, John F., xxxiii
Ketterl, Eugen, 80, 107, 233
Kingdom of Serbia, 153
Kirchner, Alexander, 104

Klopp, Onno, 12

Koerber, Ernst von, 54

Komitádjis (would-be terrorists), 176

Konak, 277, 284

Koppay, Joseph, 104

Kugler, Mila, 21

Lacroma (imperial yacht), 118

lady-in-waiting (*Hofdame*), 40, 41

Lancaster Tower, 145

language, 13

Larisch (Austrian Countess), 173

Lateiner Bridge, 276–77

League of Catholic Schools, 127

Leo XIII (Pope), 53

Leopold Ferdinand (Archduke and
    cousin of Franz Ferdinand a.k.a.
    Leopold Wölfling), 23–24, 84

Leopold II (King of Belgium), 6

Life Guard Archers, 228–29

Lobkowicz Hall, 112, 151

Lohner-Porsche, 111

Lónyay, Elmer (Austrian Count), 53

Lord High Chamberlain
    (*Obersthofmeister*), 106

Loritz, Hans, 263

Löwenstein-Wertheim-Rosenberg, Alois,
    61

Loyka, Leopold, 199–202, 207, 282

Ludendorff, Gen. Erich von, 285

Lueger, Karl, 128

Luise, Viktoria (Crown Princess of
    Prussia), 92

Magyar extremism, 128

malicious gossip, 76–77

Malobabić, Rade, 176, 185

Mannlicher rifle, 121

Margarethe (Franz Ferdinand's sister),
    xxii, 10, 33, 59–60, 81

Margutti, Albert von, 34, 77, 134, 164,
    221, 233, 288

Maria Annunciata (Archduchess of
    Austria), xxii, 10, 61–62, 98, 282

Maria Christina (Archduchess of
    Austria), xxii, 41, 45, 47–48

Maria Josepha (sister-in-law to Franz
    Ferdinand), 81–82

Maria Theresa (Archduchess of Austria),
    xxii, xxvii, 2, 27, 230

  death of, 282

  family influence of, 11

  Franz Ferdinand expressing
      happiness to, 115

  hunting lodge built by, 122

  Karl Ludwig third wife, 11

  Marie Antoinette daughter of, 65

  shared funeral arrangements argued
      by, 222

  stepson support from, 51–52

  wedding letter to, 63

  wedding location offered by, 59–60

  Wilhelm II approached on Max's
      behalf by, 249–50

Marie (Crown Princess of Rumania), 90

Marie Antoinette (Queen of France), 65

Marie Henriette (Queen of Belgium),
    38

Marie Louise (Archduchess of Austria),
    49

Marie Thun-Hohenstein (Countess),
    30, 34

Marie Valerie (Emperor Franz Josef's
    daughter), 50, 54, 149, 213

Marie Valerie (*cont.*)
marriage, 48, 58–62
  Chotek, Sophie, role in, 78–80
  equal status for, 36
  Family Statutes of 1839 obeyed for,
    34–35
  Franz Ferdinand agreeing to terms for,
    56–57
  Franz Ferdinand seeking support for,
    54
  Franz Ferdinand's happy, 114–15
  Franz Josef to set terms of, 55–56
  Isabella seeking daughter's, 44–45
  scepticism fading about, 84
  Stephanie and Rudolf's failed, 38–39
  vows exchanged for, 61
marriage (*ebenbürtig*), 35
Marschall, Gottfried, 12, 51
Mary (Queen of England), 217–18, 230,
  247
  assassination comments of, 215
  Chotek, Sophie, invitation and, 96,
    124–25
  Franz Ferdinand visit with, 145, 147
Masaryk, Charlotte, 257
Masaryk, Tomáš, 256, 280
Masin, Draga, 64, 154, 175
masquerade ball, 43
master of household (*Haushofmeister*),
  106
Maximilian 'Max' (Franz Ferdinand's
  son), xxiv, xxxiv, 75, 103, 113–14,
  141
  adult life of, 260–73
  children of, 260, 278
  death of, 272
  Duke of Hohenberg title of, xviii

Maria Theresa efforts on behalf of,
  249–50
  in Nazi concentration camps, 262–65
  parents death told to, 211–12
  paying respects allowed for, 231–32
  Vienna funeral not allowing, 230
  wife and sons of, xxxvi, 133, 264,
    269, 289
  World War I rumors with, 152
Mayer, Laurenz, 75
McKinley, US president William, xxxii
Mehmedbašić, Muhamed, xxvi, 176,
  180, 200, 239, 283
Mellich (Franz Ferdinand's personal
  barber), 102
Mensdorff, Albert von, 124, 144, 145,
  148, 214
Merenberg, Sophie von, 48
Merizzi, Erich von, 196, 199, 201, 204
Mihacevii, Brother, 209
Mikhailovich, Michael, 48
Milan (King), 154
Military Chancery, 217
  as alternative political center, 131
  Dual Monarchy and, 133–35
  military and political advice from,
    128–29
  St Vitus's Day date and, 166–67
Military History Museum, 284
military intelligence, of Austria, 169–70
military modernization, 158
military units, presenting arms, 94–95
Mirsad, Avdio, 277
Miserere, 228
mistress of the robes (*Obersthofmeisterin*),
  40
Mocker, Josef, 101

monetary values, xviii–xix
Montenegro, 239
Montenuovo, Prince Alfred de
(Emperor Franz Josef's
chamberlain), xxv, 118, 148, 172
administrative pettiness of, 221
brutal conduct of, 29–30
court etiquette adherence of, 49–50
death of, 282
Franz Josef publicly defending, 234
funeral military honours denied by,
227–28, 232
Karl dismissing, 250
petty hatred of, 72
regulations excluding every privilege
by, 68–72
vindictiveness of, 50–51, 67–69,
85–86, 234
morganatic marriage, 47–49
children influenced by, 110
continued difficulties from, 143–46,
149–50
court etiquette and, 49–50
death and, 229
dignity of throne lowered by, 64
foreign royals and, 86–87
Franz Josef to allow, 56
Franz Josef's disapproval of, 47–49,
57, 62
Habsburg dynasty gossip and, 52–54
Hungary recognizing, 136
imperial throne and, 50
Montenuovo's regulations
influencing, 68–72
Queen Elisabeth's sympathy for,
89–90
renunciation of succession rights in,

56–58, 75–76, 137–38, 197, 256
royal couple suffering from, 73–74
of Stephanie, 53
Vienna funeral and, 224–25
Morsey, Andreas von, 104, 151, 189,
193, 206–7, 278
Mössner, Karl, 110
motorcade route, 199–200
musical tastes, 113

Napoleon, 2, 49
Nazi concentration camps, 262–68, 292
Neipperg, Adam, 49
Neumayer, Josef, 234
New York, 25
Nicholas II (Tsar of Russia), xxviii, xxx,
23, 243
forging relationship with, 136
Imperial Russian Cavalry and,
86–87
Vienna visit of, 30
Nicholas of Montenegro (King), 215
Nikitsch-Boulles, Paul, 79, 103–4, 115,
173, 188
Emperor's lack of emotion and, 231
Sarajevo trip comments of, 171
North America, 24–25
Nostitz-Rieneck, Erwein (Austrian
Count), 254
Nostitz-Rieneck, Friedrich (Austrian
Count), 258–59, 267

Obersthofmeister (Lord High Chamberlain),
29, 106
Obersthofmeisterin (mistress of the robes),
40
Obrenović dynasty of Serbia, 154

Odbrana, Narodna, 156, 240

Oktavia (Duchess of Hohenberg and Sophie's sister), xxiv, 73, 95, 105

Old Town Hall, 277

Order of the Golden Fleece, 261, 272

Order of the Star Cross, 94, 149

Otto (Archduke of Austria), xxii, 10, 12, 52, 277, 291

   Chotek, Sophie, ignored by, 66

   death of, 82

   as flamboyantly hedonistic, 16

   Habsburg mantle inherited by, 258

   life of debauchery of, 81–82

   as possible heir to throne, 30–31

   wedding not attended by, 59–60

Ottoman Empire, xxxii, 97, 153, 156, 159, 160

Paar, Eduard, 78, 213

Pact of Konopischt, 152, 254, 256

Palairet, Michael, 261

Pašić, Nikola, 157, 183–84, 240–43

Pavlova, Anna (dancer), 124

Peter I (King of Serbia), 154

Pfeffer, Leo, 239, 286

Piffl (Cardinal), 231

Pius X (Pope), 223

Pius XII (Pope), 264

Plochl, Anna, 48

policy of brigandage, 159

political assassinations, xxxi–xxxii

political changes, 134–38

political modernization, xxix

Polzer-Hoditz, Arthur, 286

Popović, Cvjetko, xxvi, 181, 240, 246

Popović, Rada, 179

Popovici, Aurel, 90, 135

Potiorek, Oskar, xxv, 158, 164, 184, 201

   archduke visit insistence of, 165–66

   assassination responsibility and, 287–88

   bad decisions of, 170

   concerns dismissed by, 194–96, 204–5

   security precedent ignored by, 168–69

Prague dance, 42

pregnancy, of Chotek, Sophie, 73–76

Prince of Wales, 146

Princip, Gavrilo, xxvi, xxvii, 180, 191, 193, 201

   arrest of, 239–40

   Franz Ferdinand shot by, 206–8

   hailed as martyr, 216, 276

   imprisonment and death of, 246

   not a criminal statement of, 245

   tuberculosis of, 177, 246

property battles, 280–81

Protestant outcry, 127–28

public opinion, 80

public resentments of the pair's funeral service, 232–34

public sympathy of the pair's funeral service, 229–30

Puntigam, Anton, 193, 209, 246, 284

Queen Victoria's Diamond Jubilee, 31

Radetzky (dreadnought), 86

Rainer (Austrian Archduke), 52–53

Ramberg, August, 104

Redl, Alfred, 160

Redlich, Josef, 215

religion, 12–13, 51, 105–6

Remak, Joachim, 225

renunciation, of succession rights,
      56–58, 75–76, 137–38, 197, 256

Robinson, Louise, 82

romantic indiscretions, 83–84

Roosevelt, US president Theodore, 97

Rose Garden, 110

Rose Salon, 111–12

Rosegger, Peter, 114

royal court visit, 88–89

Royal Horticultural Society, 124, 125

Rudolf (Emperor Franz Josef's son),
      xxiii, 21, 118
   as self-absorbed and melancholy, 6–7
   Stephanie's failed marriage with,
      38–39
   suicide of, 18
   warnings from, 17–18

Rumania, 216, 224

Rumerskirch (Austrian Baron), 189,
      199, 202, 204–5
   household issues and, 106
   telegraph to Franz Josef by, 212–13
   warning on wording by, 193

Russia, 181, 243–44, 268–69

Sachsenhausen concentration camp, 266

St Moritz, 117

St Peter's Graveyard, 123

St Vitus's Day, xxxii, 166–67, 184,
      286

Salvator, Hubert (Austrian Archduke),
      272

Salvator, Leopold, 165

Salvator, Ludwig, 212, 217

Sarajevo, xxvii, 276
   assassination plot in, 176–79

Chotek, Sophie, visit to, 192–93

Franz Ferdinand attempts to cancel
      trip to, 172–73

Franz Ferdinand's trip to, 164–65

Franz Josef's visit to, 167–68

frenetic pace of, 190

impromptu visit to, 191

motorcade route in, 199–200

not friendly territory of, 165–66

police in charge of security in,
      168–69, 195

route change discussed for, 205

St Vitus's Day and, 166–67

theories of assassination in,
      xxxiii–xxxiv, xxxv

threats involving trip to, 195–96

threats reported about visit to, 169–70

training pulling into, 198

violence erupting in, 218

Saxon court, 39

Schaffgotsch, Friedrich, 267

Schloss Ambras, 123

Schloss Artstetten, 119
   bodies to be interred at, 222
   bodies transported to, 234–35
   family crypt beneath, 120, 279, 292
   funeral at, 236–38
   as museum and residence, 278–79
   Nazi's seizing, 266

Schloss Blühnbach, 122–23

Schloss Konopischt, 45, 73, 75
   children and, 110, 249, 254–55,
      257–58
   as family sanctuary, 101–3
   honeymoon at, 62, 64
   leisure time at, 111
   as major attraction, 279–80

Schloss Konopischt (*cont.*)
park open to public at, 187
royal visitors to, 150–51
subject to seizure of, 255
Schloss Reichstadt, 59–60
Schneiberg, Gustav, 199
Schönbrunn Palace, 149, 172
Schönerer, Georg von, 127
Schratt, Katharina (actress, Emperor
Franz Josef's mistress), 5, 50, 59
security, insufficient, 168–69, 195
Serb nationalists, 167, 194
Serbia, 153
archduke's visit disturbing, 184
assassination celebrated in, 240–41
Austria and mobilized army of, 244
Austria and propaganda of, 157–58
Austria-Hungary perpetual ferment
with, 156–57
Austrian invasion rumors and, 175
Austria's preventative war against,
158–59, 162
Austria's ten demands of, 242–43
Black Hand organization fight for, 157
conciliation and defiance of, 240
Greater Serbia, 154–55
officials aiding plot for assassination
and, 182–83
Russia's interests in, 243–44
Serene Highness (*Durchlaucht*), 80
Seven Weeks War, 2
shah of Persia, 69
Simpson, Wallis, xxx, 87
Sophie (Franz Ferdinand's daughter),
xxiv, xxxiv, 73–74, 103–4, 113, 141
See also Chotek, Sophie (Franz
Ferdinand's wife)

adult life of, 258–59, 269–73
children of, 259, 269–70, 278
death of, 273
parents death told to, 211–12
paying respects allowed for, 231–32
Vienna funeral disallowed to, 230
Sophie (Emperor Franz Josef's mother), 4
Sophie (Austrian Princess), 279–80,
289, 292
Sophie of Greece (Crown Princess), 93
Stackler, Heinrich, 221
Stadler, Josef, 209, 220, 286
Stankowsky, Otto, 108, 211–12
Steed, Henry Wickham, 87, 152, 254,
286–87
Stephanie (Crown Princess of Austria),
xxiii, xxxiii, 6, 287
friendliness of, 66
morganatic marriage of, 53
Rudolf's failed marriage with,
38–39
Sunarić, Josip, 169, 194

Taj Mahal, 23
Tankosić, Vojislav, 176, 179, 185, 240,
283
Tchirsky, (German) Count von, 288
tennis, 111
terrorists, 157, 176, 178
Tersztyansky, Karl von, 162
Three Emperors' League, 136
Thun, Franz von, 54
Thun, Jaroslav (Count and Prince),
xxiv, 30, 39, 42, 248, 254, 281
Tirpitz, Admiral Alfred von, 151
Tisza, István, 215, 285–86
Treaty of Berlin, 153, 156

Treaty of London, 160–61

Treaty of Saint-Germain-en-Laye, 255–56, 280

Trieste castle (Miramar), 118, 150

trifling defect in family tree, 49

Triple Alliance, 135–36

tuberculosis

Ferdinand Karl and death from, 83, 282

Franz Ferdinand diagnosed with, 26–28, 43, 140

of Princip, 177, 246

typhoid, 29

Valic, Ludmila, 219

Vechkovsky, Alexander, 182

venereal disease, 5, 100

Vercellana, Rosa, 48

Vetsera, Mary, 18

Victims at Sarajevo (Brook-Shepherd), xxxv

Victor Emmanuel II (King of Italy), 48, 78

Victoria (Queen of England), 87, 89

Victoria Eugenie (Princess of Battenburg), 87

Victoria Palace Theater, 124

Vienna

Berlin visit embittering, 93–94

Bunsen, British ambassador in, 149, 214

Chotek, Sophie, suspicions of, 95–96

discontent and melancholy erupting in, 8

funeral in, 222–25, 227–31

funeral trains journey to, 220–22

Habsburg dynasty of, 1–2

newly weds moving to, 64–65

Nicholas II visit to, 30

social distinctions in, 39

viewing period, funeral, 229–30

Viktor, Ludwig, 5

Viribus Unitis (dreadnought), 98, 150, 188–89

Vladimir of Russia (Grand Duchess), 34, 145

Vladimir of Russia (Grand Duke), 88

voyage around the world, 22–25

Vulović, Ljubomir, 183

Wallace Collection, 124, 144

Wallenburg, Lanjus von, 107, 189, 199, 201, 209, 286

Wchinitz, Wilhelmina Kinsky von, 37

Welbeck Abbey, 125, 144, 147

West, Rebecca, xxxi, xxxii, 121, 288

Wilhelm (Crown Prince of Germany), 158

Wilhelm II (Kaiser of Germany), xxxv, 87, 96, 141, 187, 212

abdication of, 251

advice from, 241

Franz Ferdinand's relationship with, 91–92

Great War supposedly planned by, 254

Maria Theresa's letter to, 249–50

Franz Ferdinand meeting with, 150–51

missed wedding and visit with, 143–44

war averted by, 161

Williamson, Samuel, 291

Wilson, US president Woodrow, 214, 230

Wimpffen, Simon (Austrian Countess), 40

Windischgraetz, Ludwig (Austrian Prince), 224, 233

Windsor Castle, 145–47

winter social season, 148–49

Wolfgang, Karl, 209, 218

Wood, George, 260

Wood, Marie-Therese, 260, 267–68

Woved, Caroline, 73

Wurmbrand, Leo, 27

Wuthenau, Karl von, 44

Young Bosnia Movement, 178

Young Bosnia Museum, 276

Young Turk Rebellion, 154–55, 159

Your Highness (*Ihre Hoheit*), 94

Yugoslavia, 276

Žerajić, Bogdan, 165, 193

Ziehrer, Karl, 95

Zita (Archduchess and Empress of Austria), xxiii, 99–100, 137, 172, 214

Zivković, Peter, 283

Zweig, Stefan, 77, 215